IN SEARCH OF PHILOSOPHIC UNDERSTANDING

Professor Edwin A. Burtt was born in Groton, Massachusetts, in 1892. He graduated from Yale University in 1915 and received the B.D. and S.T.M. degrees from Union Theological Seminary. Dr. Burtt was awarded a Ph.D. degree from Columbia University and is also the recipient of an honorary degree from the University of Chicago. He has held professorships at the Universities of Chicago, Harvard, Stanford, Hawaii, and most recently at Cornell, where he was Susan Linn Sage Professor of Philosophy. Dr. Burtt served as President of the eastern division of the American Philosophical Association in 1963–64. He has written several other books and has been a frequent contributor to philosophical journals.

In Search
of Philosophic
Understanding

Edwin A. Burtt

HACKETT PUBLISHING COMPANY
Indianapolis • Cambridge

Library of Congress Card No.:80-82748

ISBN 0–915144–12–3
ISBN 0–915144–11–5 (pbk)

For further information, please address
Hackett Publishing Company, Inc.
Box 55573, Indianapolis, Indiana 46205

*In the long run truth wins the race with falsehood
and error—and it wins because it is truth.*

Contents

a systematic linguistic theory; Positive appraisal; Critical appraisal; The promise and the limitations of this philosophy

Foreword to the Reader

I put into your hands a book that has been in the making a long time; and I hope you may find it a worthy companion in your search for philosophic understanding.

Each of us is already a philosopher, in his own way; nonetheless this search is full of adventure. One who embarks on it reaches out beyond his present horizon, both in breadth and in depth, seeking insights that are continuous with the best we now know and prize, but are not limited by it.

Since I want the book to be good company in your search, it offers no philosophical system. Indeed, I find that in my own case I increasingly take it for granted that searching is endless; no system will satisfy for long, and no answers will be found that could not be improved upon. So instead of proposing conclusions my main aim is to raise questions that cannot be ignored by a seeker for truth, to put them in the most promising form I can, to open vistas ahead by probing in various directions and sketching fertile possibilities, and to entice you to roam farther in whatever way you judge likely to be rewarding. Yet I know that if one is to roam farther with any confidence he needs some findings, which can provide a base at each stage for the search beyond. So I want also to share the findings that now provide that base for me. None of them is wholly satisfactory, but to fill this constructive role it does not need to be. I think of what I offer here as a reconnoitering survey of a vast and tangled domain—for you and others to use in exploring that domain better.

The most provocative note in the findings I want to share is the conviction that philosophy must come fully to terms with the psychoanalytic conception of the human mind. In view of the solid confirmation and spreading influence of this conception the crucial fact can no longer be ignored that behind anyone's way of thinking there are not only motivations other than the desire for truth, which we vaguely knew already, but also unconscious motivations—or at least, those that are such till they are lifted to conscious awareness. Here and there a philosopher has begun to recognize this crucial fact; thus far, however, it seems to be taken into account only when he has in mind some other thinker or thinkers than himself. The evident reluctance to make wider use of this recognition betokens, I believe, a perceptive realization that it would be unpardonably arrogant to make wider use of it merely in this self-righteous fashion. But when the presence of such motivations in one's own philosophizing as well as in that of others is fully acknowledged, there is no arrogance, and I am sure that the acknowledgment can lead to confident progress. How it can do so the following pages try to show.

The time is ripe for this search. In the arena of debate among academic philosophers a hesitant pause is noticeable; champions of all the rival schools seem no longer to be sure of the paths they have recently followed, and are wondering where the line of dependable advance now lies. They will find here an essay in the philosophy of philosophy, which—since we have not yet mastered the art of wise philosophizing—fills as important a function as the philosophy of science, or of morals, or of religion, or of art. These pages offer some guideposts which I hope will prove dependable. In the arena of thought at large, the notion long prevailing in many quarters that philosophy is dead now appears to have been somewhat hasty; it may apply only to the kind of philosophy whose death should cause no tears. There is a growing expectation of a philosophical rebirth, in a form appropriate to the challenge of the present epoch—a form that will reveal how, in the midst of proliferating knowledge in every field, unifying wisdom need not be lost. May this response to that expectation, as you develop it in your own fashion, bear fruit.

And there is a special need today, which perhaps only a reborn philosophy can wisely meet. One of the most salutary discoveries and at the same time one of the most malignant diseases of our century goes by the name of "moral relativism." So far as such a view indicates an expanded awareness of the great variety of moral values that have somewhere and some time been accepted, and of the degree of success commitment to each set has won, it has brought an illuminating perspective; so far as it has led to the idea that one pattern of cultural life is as good as another, and that intelligent discrimination between values can fill no positive role, it is one of the saddest superstitions that have found currency among educated people. You will find that an underlying aim in the second half of this book is to open a path from moral relativism beyond moral nihilism, guided by the vision of a truly ultimate value—a value that is universal while making full room for variety, all-encompassing and yet dynamic, free from dogmatic pretensions and thus ever open to revision.

As you read, I hope you will find yourself moving from whatever basic presuppositions you have been taking for granted to others. May this happen, however, not because you feel coerced by any demonstration—indeed, is any coercive demonstration possible at the level we intend to probe?—but because you find that the new presuppositions are more relevant and enlightening than the ones you had accepted before. And they will surely not be identical with mine. If you should forget that I am not offering a philosophical system you will probably exclaim here and there, in some exasperation: "Tell us more clearly what you mean!" My reply is that if you have come across a sheer contradiction or if the elusiveness that offends is confusing instead of suggestive, the defect certainly needs to be remedied and maybe you will help remedy it. But in other respects the statement in question means whatever any honest seeker for understanding finds it to mean as he puts it to use in his further search. This is not, of course, to promise approval for all the conclusions such a seeker may reach. Would there be any virtue in two or more thinkers coming to understand in just the same way? *Are* they thinkers if that is what happens?

I want now to say a few particular things about this book, which may avert possible misinterpretations.

For one, the themes dealt with are such that, although the course of thought has a natural beginning and end and there is an underlying evolution of the whole, any earlier stage needs the later ones for its full understanding. Hence the evolution exhibits a spiral instead of a unilinear movement; all the major themes have to recur from time to time, either in a primary or a secondary role. I trust therefore that you will be ready in almost every chapter for a significant development of topics other than those forming the main subject of that chapter.

For another, in this venture I cannot avoid trenching on many areas in which I am very ignorant, and in each of them I doubtless say some things that experts will be sure should be said differently. My scholarly conscience is troubled on this account, and I would never have entered these areas if I were not convinced that there can be a valuable function for this kind of error. The reason for that conviction is that every thinker, whether he fully realizes it or not, has an overall orientation which guides the way he selects and interprets his facts. This orientation is never as wise as it might be; it magnifies unduly some facts while it blinds him to others. The only way for him (and through him the world at large) to advance toward a wiser orientation is to put into words as best he can the one he now holds, counting on other thinkers to help correct it by their specialized knowledge. My appeal to the experts, as I do this with my own orientation, is that if the focal ideas seem to carry any promise they will pardon the detailed missteps and show in each case what correction is needed. There may even be an advantage in my ignorance. Awareness of it discourages me from assuming that this essay can accomplish more than to glimpse possible insights, put them in communicable form, and reveal something of what they involve. Even where an important insight is sound, I am sure that many distinctions need to be made that I have not made, and that happier illustrations can often be found than the ones I have picked. In this connection, I realize that many of my assertions are not couched in the modest language that should be used; this is because it proved awkward to add in every instance the appropriate qualification.

The third hint is a natural consequence of these two. I have sought to give the essay sufficient unity so that it can serve as a foil against which readers can test their own evolving philosophy, while leaving enough loose joints so that any part that proves unacceptable can be laid aside without prejudice to the rest.

For a fourth and last hint, in the passages where I expound what other thinkers have said there is no pretense of giving an adequate presentation of their philosophy. I hope that I say nothing misleading about their position, but my purpose is simply to use certain features of their thought that are especially relevant to an important stage in our search.

Readers who have no special interest in contemporary developments among academic philosophers in the Anglo-Saxon countries may skip

Chapter III without losing the main thread. In view of the large element of pioneering in this enterprise, I trust it will not appear presumptuous if I add here a list of pages in the book whose importance might easily be missed. On each of them an idea is expressed which is essential to understanding the course of thought as a whole. The pages I have in mind are: 113 f., 119 f., 135, 181 f., 209 f., 214–217, 225, 226 ff., 271, 297 f. I am aware that those who are pioneers in their own fields may feel that when I reconnoiter those fields my suggestions lead in an unwise direction, or even mean a retrogression; in some cases that feeling will prove to be right.

When I come to acknowledgments of valued help, I am baffled. In a sense this book was in preparation as soon as I began to reflect on topics of broad human concern. How can appreciation to the universe at large be properly expressed? Everything that has entered my experience and every idea that met a need in my evolving philosophy plays some part in what is here presented. However, I am especially thankful to friends, colleagues, and students at the universities I have served; interaction with them over the years has naturally had a strong influence on my way of thinking.

For three particular debts I want to express deep gratitude. As the book made its way from earlier drafts toward the final one, several friends whose judgment I greatly prize generously took time out from important work to read chapters (or groups of chapters) in which I felt sure they would have a special interest. They gave me overall appraisals that have been encouraging, and critical suggestions that have saved me from serious blunders. These kindly helpers include Archibald MacLeish, Reinhold Niebuhr, Sidney Hook, the late Aldous Huxley, Brand Blanshard, Arnold Toynbee, and my Cornell colleague Hans Bethe. It goes without saying that they are not responsible for any defects that remain; very likely none of them would approve everything the book now says. Another debt is to the editorial staff of The New American Library, and in particular to Mr. Thomas J. Davis III and Mr. E. L. Doctorow. The former, with sympathetic understanding, saw the typescript through the final stage of sprucing it up for the press. The latter, who was with The New American Library during the preceding stage of editorial criticism, aided me very much in avoiding unfortunate foibles and in working out a needed reorganization of the first half of the book. My gratitude also goes to the secretaries who with cheerful patience have typed draft after draft—especially to Mrs. Mary C. Grimes, Mrs. Doreen M. Wallace, Mrs. Dora H. Beach, and Mrs. Charlotte Morrissey.

I cannot express what I owe to the one who for many years has shared everything with me, including each of the main ideas here developed.

E. A. Burtt

Ithaca, N.Y.
June, 1965

IN SEARCH OF PHILOSOPHIC UNDERSTANDING

1

Is philosophy needed?

A philosopher is a strange man. He draws distinctions where nobody else sees any need of them and is puzzled by problems that are problems to none of his fellows. When, for example, he is concerned with moral issues he is not satisfied with finding out how to do the right thing; he must also wonder whether doing the right thing is the same as doing the best thing. When he turns to questions about knowledge he not only wants to know the things that other people do; he also wants to know how to tell when he has knowledge and when he hasn't.

What is he really good for?

This question can of course be put to the philosopher himself, and he will reply: "Philosophy is one of the greatest liberators of man. It saves him from folly, prejudice, and confusion; it guides him into a richer and more stable world. Without philosophy, man's life and thought are in bondage to dark forces from which, with it, he can become free. But to achieve this liberation it must at times appear picayune, at times even fanciful, to those who are not philosophers."

Is there truth in this bold claim, or does it merely reveal the philosopher's skill at self-justification?

There is only one way to find out, and that is for each of us to undertake our own search for philosophic understanding. This is the adventure I propose to the reader. It will not be as novel as it may sound, for all of us philosophize in our own fashion, even though the professional philosopher may appear so strange. The road that leads toward this understanding will not be easy, however; we must be prepared for rough traveling from time to time.

I

Let us step at once onto the philosopher's peculiar terrain so that we may become more familiar with it. We will not be limited to that terrain, but obviously nothing can be called philosophy whose theater of activity shows no continuity with it. Hence we shall begin with a sweeping survey of what Western philosophers have been doing since their enterprise took its distinctive form two and a half millennia ago.

After the Greek thinkers were through with their early gropings and philosophy had settled down to a continuous development it became— and remained till late medieval times—basically a theory of *being;* during modern times it has been mainly a quest for *method.* The first of these ideas is very odd, and even the second raises puzzling questions. How did they come to fill such a central role?

We can begin to understand if we try to see with the eyes of those pioneering Greek philosophers. The universe lay before them; to inquire directly into its structure seemed natural and appropriate. As they did this the concept of "being" soon offered itself as the focal philosophical concept. Even before Plato and Aristotle gave the idea a more sophisticated meaning it had begun to fill a function similar to that which it was to fill for many centuries.

Everything in the world obviously *is*—i.e., it somehow shares in being. The key question is then: What is it to *be?* From the point of view thus expressed, there would be no need to separate what we now call science from metaphysical philosophy. Why should particular forms of being be investigated apart from study of the universal nature of being that each must exemplify? And what could be more worthy of a philosopher than to probe the pervasive fabric of this vast totality within which everything is—to lay bare the grand pattern of being through which the varied events that other sciences study piecemeal hang together in an inclusive whole? With this aim many philosophers philosophized for eighteen hundred years. During that long period they were expected to achieve, and could achieve, what has now become quite impossible—namely, an expert grasp of the entire body of knowledge in every field.

But by the late medieval period a worrisome problem had arisen and could not be ignored. Different schools of philosophy championed different systems of being; even Aristotle had failed to gain permanent and undisputed possession of the master's seat. Prospective philosophers began to wonder how a metaphysical edifice should be erected in order to succeed in its aim. Hence the next step in the logic of philosophical evolution was as natural as the first, and it marked the radical change that was to occur in modern times. It was evident that earlier philosophers had been taking for granted something that should not be taken for granted. How could this mistake be corrected?

Again the answer seemed obvious. When different minds reach different results about the same problem it must be that not all are following the right path—and that perhaps none has yet followed it. The new primary question, which now displaces the inquiry into being as the central philosophic quest, becomes: What is the right method for reaching truth?

Accordingly, the great philosophers for many generations focused their energies on this question. Bacon and Descartes, Leibniz and Locke, Hume and Kant—the answers offered by these men vary widely, but all agree in making the search for method, and for the conditions necessary to the gaining of knowledge, their main concern. Indeed, there has been no basic change from their day to ours. Each of the competing schools of philosophic thought early in the present century championed its own solution of this problem, and the major achievement of the new schools arising in recent decades—logical empiricism, existentialism, linguistic analysis—is the method that each has proposed for gaining the truth that philosophy seeks.

This intensive concentration on method enabled the philosophers to make a momentous contribution to the history of thought; but they were still faced with the same difficulty that had baffled their predecessors in the quest for a convincing metaphysic. They were successful in the search for a sound method; however, when it was found, it became the method of science. The sciences could now separate from philosophy; they had the conceptual tools with which they could pursue their independent and victorious career. The difficulty was that philosophers continued to disagree on everything except the method of science.

Indeed, in this setting the difficulty has become even more fundamental, at least from the point of view of thinkers in other fields. The question can hardly help arising: Does philosophy now have any role at all? Earlier, its right to exist was never seriously challenged; today, however, the kind of inquiry that is clearly justified seems to be exemplified by these doughty youngsters, the sciences—no longer by her from whose fertile womb they were born. To possess a method is to have a way of deciding what questions may sensibly be raised, and how to progress toward definite answers. Scientists obviously have such a way; do philosophers? Philosophy—so many in every modern generation suspect—was a legitimate enterprise only while men had not yet learned how to ask questions or look for acceptable answers; once this naïve innocence is outgrown, what, if any, constructive role can she fill?

But this contemporary doubt assumes, as the ancients did, that philosophy's task is the same as that of science and should be judged by the same criterion. Our survey of its evolution has encouraged such an assumption; we have thus far confined ourselves within the narrow bounds of philosophical history, where this notion long prevailed as a matter of course. Let us now view the question in the wider perspective of philosophy's relation to other fields of human thought.

A very instructive conclusion emerges. In this wider perspective it becomes evident that philosophers have from time to time provided a new orientation, or, if you will, a prophetic vision, in the light of which some forward-looking tendencies of their epoch could hopefully unfold. Look again at the rise of modern science; this fruitful achievement could not have taken place without the visions of the two Bacons, of Bruno, of Galileo, of Descartes—visions sufficiently articulated so that those who shared their hopes could observe the world around them in the new framework thus provided, and see something important that had not been clearly seen before. Other illustrations also come to mind. Think of the Stoic philosophy in its relation to the history of Roman jurisprudence and the varied role through the centuries of the concept of "natural law"; think of the political theories of Locke, Montesquieu, and Rousseau in relation to the evolution of Western democratic institutions; think of the philosophy of Marx and Engels in relation to the present development of the Communist political and economic structures with their challenge to the rest of the world.

Moreover, in this broader setting one perceives that the greatest among these geniuses achieved something still more significant: they bequeathed a permanent addition to man's understanding of himself and his world. Much of Aristotle is now a basic part of what the educated man calls common sense, and much of Plato is reflected in the same man's aspiration to reach beyond common sense. It is apparent then, from this larger historical viewpoint, that philosophy has made a vital contribution to man's intellectual progress and has guided his growth in every phase of life. The question, therefore, of philosophy's value today obviously requires further consideration. If its role is not now preempted by science, what may that role be?

II

In order to pursue our quest for philosophic understanding I propose to introduce a concept that I find fertile and illuminating—the concept of "presupposition." It will be more thoroughly analyzed in Chapters V and VI; at present I will rely on whatever meaning the reader may associate with the word and on the illustrations soon to be given. My reason for choosing it is that it is now a frequently employed concept in philosophical discussion and, as currently used, its meaning is very close to the one I wish to give it. Indeed, it has penetrated other areas besides philosophy; one finds it appearing in political, historical, literary, and scientific essays. I believe it will have a still more significant use in the future.

Let us briefly clarify this concept in its relation to the survey that we have already begun. Any theory of being, or of method, or of anything else, inevitably rests on certain presuppositions, which for a time are taken by many, or perhaps even all, philosophers to be justified. Subsequently, however, history shows that these presuppositions are not in fact as indubitable as they seemed to be, and when their inadequacy is recognized, philosophy advances in a new direction that leaves behind some of the errors of previous presuppositions and leads to constructive results that had not previously been possible. We shall try to grasp the essential pattern of this corrective process as it is revealed through the centuries.

Turn again to the ancient preoccupation of philosophers—the task of building a metaphysical system. Under the circumstances in which Aristotle found himself two thousand years ago there was ample warrant for elaborating a general theory of being as he did. It seemed to be the promising step to take. Knowledge was expanding; a unifying framework was needed; and the framework he provided was natural and enlightening. As a result of his work, some of the paths that thought had earlier followed became no longer respectable, and some of the categories of being that he articulated have since played an indispensable part in Western thinking. Most obvious among these are the categories of substance and potentiality, along with those involved in his logic.

This much achieved, philosophers came to realize that some of the hopes that had inspired this grand metaphysical enterprise had met with disappointment. Gradually, further attempts of this kind were abandoned, or at least postponed, in favor of the quest for a dependable method. To describe this process in terms of our chosen concept, certain basic presuppositions of the investigation of being—such as, that being in general can become the object of demonstrative science, and that the world of nature in its changes can be mastered by the methods of geometry and the Aristotelian syllogism —were revealed as mistaken. Moreover, as a result of the concentration on method, a few principles of sound inductive inquiry became firmly established; from that time on they have commanded respect from every seeker for truth in the realm of observable fact.

As this second quest developed, the same process was repeated. Philosophers came to doubt certain presuppositions about the nature of knowledge and the ideal of truth. As a result, all philosophers now realize that knowledge is not the simple affair it had previously been taken to be. A more exacting standard of what constitutes knowledge has emerged, and a clearer understanding of the conditions required for attaining it under different circumstances has been gained. Much the same has happened with respect to the theory of truth. For many centuries a widely accepted definition of truth was that it consists in the correspondence of an assertion with the fact to which it refers. Few today would be satisfied with this definition, for "correspondence" is no longer a self-explanatory idea. It is true that the Latin word often used (*adaequatio*) is more precise than the English "correspondence": it implies that the thing known and the knowing mind "become equal to" each other. But to modern thinkers this kind of equality is not self-explanatory either. Furthermore, certain distinctions have now become current that had not been fully recognized before—for example, the distinctions between necessary and contingent truth, and between truth as confirmable by scientific techniques and truth that can only be won in other ways.

It appears then that philosophical evolution is in its own fashion self-correcting, and that genuine progress in the long run takes place through the correction of inadequacies, oversights, and missteps in previously accepted presuppositions and their replacement by presuppositions that interpret man's enlarging experience with keener insight. To be sure, this radically reconstructive role is not the only one that philosophy fills. Many philosophers perform needed functions that lie on the border between this prophetic task and other areas of thought and experience—such as mathematics, art, religion, history, and the empirical sciences. But their distinctive contribution always reflects the more comprehensive setting that is directly revealed in this fundamental role.

And when we turn from the past toward the future, the major question is whether we can master this process of revising presuppositions in such a way that it may go forward with greater boldness and assurance, freed from all needless obstructions.

2

From common sense to basic presuppositions

We embark on our exploration by looking at man's common-sense knowledge in the form it takes at any given time, and at its instructive relation to science and philosophy. There are three truths about it that are important to keep in mind.

First, the world that everyone finds himself living in when his mental powers awaken is the world as common sense perceives and interprets it. He enters the larger universe that opens before him by reaching out from that world.

Second, no one is willing to stay in the world of common sense. One may think he is willing to—this is the natural belief of the man in the street who is not conscious of playing any part in the gradual revision of common sense. But it is impossible to remain in it. It has many virtues, but its vices are too serious. Its ideas are vague, loose-jointed, and ambiguous—even contradictory; also they are often found not to square with the realities they claim to describe. Moreover, there is another defect: Common sense lacks a universal perspective; its world is always the world of a limited society with its limited cultural heritage.

Third, in its own fashion, common sense provides the goal of sincere inquiry as well as its starting point. We instinctively feel that Walt Whitman must somehow be right when he says in his "Song of Myself":

Only what proves itself to every man and woman is so,
Only what nobody denies is so

and that a keen thinker can properly claim no esoteric grasp of reality but, at best, the virtue affirmed of the sage by Mencius: "The sages only apprehended ahead of us what our minds mutually approve." Unless the truth glimpsed by an intellectual pioneer is confirmed in the growing experience of all men, it is less than truth. The mind of the common man provides the ultimate court before which true knowledge and insight are gradually distinguished from false. This court is not, of course, the mind of the common man as it spontaneously views its world, but rather as it is capable of becoming through the wise leadership of the sage.

Now while each of these three characteristics teaches a very significant lesson, it is the second on which we need to concentrate for the present. We want to find out how the revision of common sense in the direction of a wiser common sense is accomplished, and what role changing presuppositions play in the process. To perform this task has been the essential function of science and philosophy. How have they met their challenging responsibility? By what methods have thinkers learned to distinguish between an idea that deceitfully promises to lead in this direction and one that reliably does so?

To answer, we must go back to the origin of these two enterprises and watch them evolve into their present form. This process has not taken place in the same way everywhere in the world; we shall here be tracing the pattern revealed in the history of our own heritage.

II

Thus far Western thought has hit upon three main methods in the quest for a trustworthy way of correcting common sense. These appeared in a definite order. Surveying them in that order we may call them the ways of intuitionism, rationalism, and empiricism. To be sure, the first of these was not consciously thought of as filling this role; only when we look back on it in the light of the others does it appear as a method of intellectual progress. However, to regard it as such helps to illumine the whole history of methods employed by seekers for truth.

Taking intuitionism then as a distinctive way of revising common-sense beliefs, let us imagine ourselves in the age of the Hebrew prophets and the early Greek poets and tragedians who vividly illustrate it. During the same age farmers and artisans were slowly accumulating scraps of what would now be called technical lore, but no leader of civilized thought at that time seems to have recognized the importance of this process. The manner in which these bits of knowledge were acquired did not attract attention. But the intellectual elite—the shamans, seers, and prophets—did notice something else: the crucial and mysterious moment when a new idea, conveying a persuasive answer to some urgent perplexity, is born. Interpreted by the religious concepts which as yet were the only ones available for the purpose, these intuitions were naturally taken as revelations of the divine —oracles, inspired seizures—each carrying its voucher of authenticity on its face. Knowledge, thus interpreted, is an aggregate of such intuitions, bound together by no rational order; any two of them might jar with each other. The criterion for determining their truth was in effect just the potent "compellingness" of each idea as it came.

It was this lack of coherence that proved in the long run intolerable. Intuitions did conflict with each other, and yet the method of intuition supplied no principle by which to resolve the conflicts. Ideas appearing in this way were ultimately incomparable, and when two of them were in opposition one had to be arbitrarily abandoned in favor of the other.

The discovery of mathematics—and reflection on its method—was the main factor in opening a hopeful vista in this situation. A second essential phase of knowledge-getting became the focus of attention —the process of deductive inference, with the systematic consistency of thought which it made possible. In its own field mathematics brought these scattered intuitions into logical connection with each other; certain groups of them were seen to be so bound together that when some were accepted, they inflexibly dictated acceptance or rejection of many others. One might intuit a way of squaring the circle, or of making the diagonal of a square commensurate with its side, but when the axioms of Euclidean geometry are also intuited, and are too illuminating to be abandoned, an inescapable series of steps proves that the former intuitions are deceptive. Thus a reliable base for rational demonstration is established. As Aristotle remarks in the *Metaphysics,* "Into the subtleties of the mythologists it is not worth our while to inquire seriously; those, however, who use the language of proof we must cross-examine." And they can be cross-examined, for intuitions are now adopted and articulated in such a way that their meaning is the same to every tutored mind and their implications are systematically traceable.

Moreover, mathematical axioms revealed another magnificent virtue. They had the power to anticipate dependably a wider range of factual experience than any other intuitions that had captivated men's minds; all quantitative relations that might be found in it were brought under intelligent mastery. This virtue offered more than adequate compensation for the otherwise pallid and unexciting character of these ideas, so the mathematical sciences were eagerly pursued, and a method derived from them was developed and applied to the advancement of knowledge everywhere. The ideal of knowledge as coherently organizable and demonstratively certain came to dominate Western thought, especially when the basic lesson of mathematics was confirmed by the logical syllogism of Aristotle. This formal pattern revealed the way in which the mind must proceed from any subject-predicate premises to a conclusion if the inference is to be valid. Through the genius of the Greeks in mathematics and logic our forebears discovered the significant function of discursive reason.

As a result of the profound influence of this idea, the concepts by which men had clarified the way of intuition were now either abandoned, or transformed so that they could fit into this new approach and harmonize with its demands. "Theory," for example, which originally meant a revealed vision or an intuitive beholding of truth, came to mean contemplation of things as bound together in an organized pattern. We may best refer to this revolutionary orientation, which once adopted is so easily taken for granted, by the word "rationalism."

The way of rationalism, once its virtues were sufficiently understood, became a definitive achievement. It represented an advance over the earlier conception of knowledge that has never been lost. Knowledge was now viewed as a system of truths bound together by strands of logic. No longer to be taken or left on the authority of a seer or the compulsion of some vivid idea, every piece of it was capable of demonstration. One could trace its necessary relations to a set of ultimate principles, which, when clearly grasped, appeared self-evidently true.

So far as concerns the status of those principles, the viewpoint of intuitionism remained in control, and what seemed still valid in its presuppositions was thus preserved. Their character as intuitions was obvious, yet they were intuitions of a special kind. They were not barren, but astonishingly fertile; a wide range of other important truths was inferable from them. They were thus rational insights on which a vast structure of knowledge could be firmly built. Mere "inspired visions," unable to find a place in such a logical order, were no longer quite respectable—save in such fields as religion and art, where rationalism was long impotent to gain a secure foothold. Yet even there intuitionism of the earlier vintage, at least, was forced into a losing struggle. The way of systematic demonstration, once successful anywhere, seemed clearly the way that ought to be successful everywhere. Reason, in its power to apprehend deductive form and self-evident axioms, is a single faculty, and once it has found itself it claims universal authority. So this at least was the confident assumption of the philosophers, who soon appeared on the scene. Their task was to extend the rationalistic method to *all* subjects, and to show that no range of human experience lay beyond the power of logical demonstration to master it. In this, under the lead of Plato and Aristotle, Descartes and Spinoza, Kant and Hegel, they were surprisingly successful. Plato, indeed, was never an unqualified rationalist; he was sure that there are ultimate mysteries to which reason can lead us, and which are not inharmonious with its demands, but which can only be grasped by superrational insight and expressed in poetic myth. Aristotle, replacing these myths by the bold extension of this or that rational framework and thus weaving a comprehensive system in which God, morality, political organization, and art were all assigned their places, was the rationalist par excellence among the Greeks.

Orientation won its victory. Propositions incapable of domestication in the system of truths established by its method no longer seemed to exemplify the proper ideal of knowledge. They were stray ideas, expressing some individual's or group's opinion; they might be true but their truth had not been proved.

However, the realm that could be conquered in this intriguing fashion was limited. As men searched its horizons they gradually found themselves in the presence of something opaque—something they could not master merely by the method of rationalism. In the presence of that disturbing, irrational interloper which could not be conjured away, the neat deductions of this method revealed the same crucial defect that had marred the earlier way of isolated intuitions. Just as those intuitions could not be compared on any common base—so that in case of conflict a reasonable decision might be made—in the same way the tidy systems of the rationalist, when used to explain the observable facts of nature, sometimes led to diverse explanations, between which only an arbitrary choice could be made. How was this defect to be overcome?

Thinkers gradually learned that the only reliable way to settle such conflicts between two or more explanations, equally justified by their axiomatic foundation and their rigorous logic, was to concentrate on the observable facts—not casually, but with persistent patience, so as to devise a method capable of coping with their distinctive challenge. When Galileo realized that the truth about falling bodies could not be unambiguously anticipated by deductions from accepted rational principles he turned to meticulous observation. When, a few centuries later, non-Euclidean geometries were conceived, it could no longer be taken for granted that the spatial structure of the physical world must be Euclidean; whether it is or is not had to be decided by appeal to facts of perception. So arose in the Western world the novel conception of knowledge and method that goes by the name "empiricism." Certain features of this method had already appeared in ancient times and were to be found in such thinkers as Hippocrates and Archimedes. Now, however, the empirical sciences assumed a dominant role and provided in their own fashion a respectable method of reconstructing common sense.

How was this new orientation achieved? Investigators turned to systematic observation and experiment as the ultimate court of appeal, guided by canons that were laboriously clarified through a process of trial and error, while retaining the rationalistic method so far as it was still pertinent. The outcome was a sound procedure for choosing between different explanations of any set of facts—the most reliable procedure available at any given time, and capable of indefinite improvement as its results are noted and the lessons they teach are learned.

Intuitions—even the axiomatic principles—were now demoted from the status they had retained under rationalism. Their pretensions to self-evidence could no longer be allowed; those testable by observation are but "hypotheses," or candidates for knowledge, whose right to this title depends on their power to gain verification. The forms of deductive inference, in their bearing on the acquisition of knowledge, were also reinterpreted. No longer demonstrations of truth, to be accepted solely on the warrant of their logical validity, they became a network of reliable highways by which thought could pass from a conceived hypothesis to propositions that must be true if it is true but are subject to observation as a general hypothesis is not. Galileo could not verify directly a general law of falling bodies—e.g., that the velocity increases proportionately with the time of the fall—but he could verify by careful experiment what this law implied about the motion of a particular body allowed to fall in a particular way.

It is difficult today to realize how hard it was for this orientation to gain acceptance. The inspiring hope of eager minds was on the side of rationalism; with some thinkers it is so still. The realm of observed facts is messy and confusing. It would be much more congenial to our intellectual prepossessions to dispense with any detailed appeal to it. There was a strong temptation to continue to assume that logical consistency somehow controls the world of sense-perception—that facts must behave just as our rational explanations of them would require. But all such hopes and prepossessions have been dashed beyond repair. The problems that the sciences seek to solve could not be solved by the rationalistic method. We want our understanding of facts to serve the end of fuller anticipation and control of future facts as they unfold through time, and nature recognizes no obligation to accommodate us in the way they unfold; she disappoints as well as fulfills anticipations based on systems of knowledge already established. When this sobering truth was sufficiently realized the new orientation had to be accepted. Hence, the time when knowledge could consist of axiomatic principles, together with the conclusions reached by rational demonstration from them, is past. It is now the sum total, at any given time, of verified hypotheses whose claim to truth is relative rather than absolute, since new facts of observation may at any time compel their revision. Knowledge thus becomes a living and growing affair, not merely in the minor sense in which a deductive pattern grows—through adding further inferences from its premises—but in the much more radical sense in which the premises themselves are always being improved through man's progress in mastering the infinitely complex world disclosed to sense-perception. It becomes clear that, in Francis Bacon's words, "nature can only be mastered by being obeyed."

The success of the way of empiricism has likewise proved definitive. Once established, its drastic reconstruction of the presuppositions of rationalism has been retained. A system of propositions unable to square itself with the relevant observable facts is no longer quite respectable. Within the various branches of science, during the often lengthy periods when their underlying presuppositions are unassailed by doubt, empiricism has continued to prove adequate. It has thus given the educated man a new perspective on the world in which he lives and thinks. In the era of intuitionism his world was what custom and habit had traditionally taken for granted, modified slowly by novel ideas that appealed to this or that keen mind and were gradually accepted by others. In the era of rationalistic confidence his world was the system of principles generally regarded as self-evident, along with the inferences about the cosmos that could logically be drawn from them. Now, in the era of empiricism, his world is the arena of facts of observation, organized in more or less comprehensive theories and continually expanding through new discoveries. It is in that world that you and I live today, and it is slowly becoming accepted by all civilized men.

In the setting of this historical development the essential function of what we call the scientific enterprise becomes clear. The disciplined application of man's cognitive powers in mathematics and the empirical sciences corrects common sense by methods that can be understood by all and systematically employed by anyone trained in them.

III

However, the search for truth does not and cannot limit itself to the areas in which these sciences reign. Because of this, the way of empiricism suffers in its own fashion from the same defect as its predecessors. When we contemplate the problem thus arising we see more clearly what sort of thing a basic philosophical presupposition is.

Facts of observation do not always speak an unambiguous message with a clear voice. When they do so speak—when all thinkers agree on their occurrence and proper interpretation—one can appeal to them with confidence to settle any relevant question. And most facts in most situations do fill this role successfully. But there are times when inquirers are forced to realize that the questions: What is and what is not a fact? Which facts are and which are not relevant to a given problem? are questions whose answers are not simple and obvious. The answer depends on the criteria taken for granted by whoever happens to be observing the facts involved.

An event that is one kind of fact in terms of certain presuppositions may become a very different fact—indeed, it may lose its factual character entirely—in terms of a different set of presuppositions. Can a miracle be a fact? Yes, says the devout Catholic, because his theistic faith renders such an interpretation of certain events legitimate. No, say most non-Catholics today, since their presuppositions about nature allow no event to be thus interpreted. Yet both Catholic and non-Catholic might agree that the empirical method is the proper method of science. This agreement thus assures cooperative progress within the framework established by the current scientific criterion of fact, but it provides no guidance when the question is raised about possible limitations of that framework. As Whitehead has remarked in his *Adventures of Ideas:* "A great deal of confused philosophical thought has its origin in obliviousness to the fact that the relevance of factual evidence is dictated by theory. For you cannot test a theory by evidence which that theory dismisses as irrelevant." [1]

In this setting we face again the inescapable question about the presuppositions that dominate thought at any given time. The slightest acquaintance with intellectual history teaches that what people confidently take to be fact varies enormously from age to age and culture to culture. To the modern Westerner ghosts are not facts in the external world, but they were so to most Europeans during a long period and they are today to millions of people in many countries. Look at the experience of primitive man—remembering that a millennium or two ago our own ancestors belonged in that category. F. B. Jevons is quite right when he says in his *Introduction to the History of Religion:* "For savages now existing the incidents of which fairy tales are made up, and . . . which seem to us most extravagant and supernatural, are matters of ordinary if not everyday occurrence. The transformation of men into beasts and vice versa is not only believed to take place, but is actually witnessed by savages, and in the case of witches has been proved in many an English court of law." [2]

Today our sophistication tempts us to assume that such beliefs are sheer superstitions which educated men have now outgrown. Perhaps with these particular beliefs that is so. But the problem thus thrust upon us cannot be evaded in this easy fashion. During the last century many developments have insistently reminded us that it cannot; we shall briefly note three of them.

One is exemplified in the continuing hot debate among champions of opposing social theories. The same facts may be radically different when seen from the perspective of two different economic or political systems —such as Marxism and the way of "free enterprise"—and similar situations appear in other areas of social thought. In his Foreword to a survey of the diverse theories of learning advocated by several highly respected psychologists, Professor A. T. Poffenberger confesses: "Each theory appeared to exist within its closed system and to defy direct comparison

and the pooling of data. Concepts, techniques, apparatus, units of measurement, and definitions of terms were peculiar to a given theory and could
not safely be lifted out of their own frame of reference." [3] Unlike the natural scientists, thinkers in this region have no criterion of fact that is universally accepted.

The discoveries of anthropology provide another example: they show
that what is taken to be a fact, and how it is described and explained, are
relative to traditional cultural habits and to the linguistic structure in
which they have found expression. Snow is just snow to the south European; to the Eskimo it is an exceedingly complex affair, revealing manifold
distinctions that he never forgets.

For a third example, survey the historical changes that have taken place
in natural science itself. What can be discovered as fact depends on the
instruments of observation and the methods of measurement available;
ponder the astounding difference between the world of facts taken for
granted by scientists before the invention of the telescope and the micro-
scope, and the world of facts in which present-day scientists live!

Moreover, not only are better instruments and methods constantly de-
vised, but scientists will also now and again adopt a new set of concepts in
terms of which their observations are expressed. When we recall the remark of a contemporary of Copernicus—"What a fool! Couldn't he use his
eyes?"—we realize that like other great scientists Copernicus used his mind
so effectively in interpreting what people see with their eyes that the very
framework of accepted belief was transformed, and our eyes today see the
astronomical world quite differently from the way it was seen in his day.
Indeed, in virtue of the acceleration of scientific progress, there may be an
even more radical change in what will be observed as fact by people four
hundred years hence. The scientist easily forgets this relativity as long as
the criterion he has been taking for granted continues to work successfully.
When it fails to do so and leads him to an impasse—as happened to
Einstein when he faced the question, How do we tell when two events
occur simultaneously?—he has to stop his experimental work in the area
involved until a criterion that can give him reliable guidance is forthcom-
ing. Condillac was evidently expressing the simple-minded but mistaken
empiricism of the eighteenth century when he taught, in effect, that our
presuppositions add nothing to our experience of objects, and that therefore the truths of nature will stand out clearly to all who are not perversely
blind to them. How strange, to such a confident empiricist, would seem

Faraday's simple request to his friend Tyndall, who was about to show him a novel experiment: "Tell me what I am to look for!"

In the presence of such a radical relativity, where is any absolute fact to be found? Viewed in this setting, what we call a fact becomes a problem rather than a self-vouching entity—a source of further questions rather than a conclusive answer to all questions that might be raised about it. When we talk about facts we are talking about what people in our social milieu now take as facts; they were not always so taken in the past nor will they necessarily be so taken in the future.

I V

If we ask who has the responsibility to explore the region into which these inescapable reminders lead us, the answer toward which our whole course of thought points is: the philosopher. In entering this region we have passed from common sense and science to philosophy; when a scientist enters it—as he sometimes needs to—he becomes a philosopher. The alternative criteria that have been seriously championed in the history of thought appear most obviously in the various sets of basic presuppositions that distinguish one philosopher from another, and especially one philosophical school from another. In their presence we realize that the presuppositions of concern to philosophy vary considerably in importance; the ones we have now uncovered are quite fundamental.

For example, the realist of fifty years ago had a criterion of fact which enabled him to claim factual status for the simple elements reached by logical analysis of an observed object, although those elements could not themselves be observed. His main opponent at that time—the idealist —had a criterion which required him to deny that those elements were facts, while he claimed that status for certain inclusive wholes which the realist was unable to discover. The pragmatist, in his turn, had a criterion different from both of these: he was ready to recognize as fact whatever proved to have practical significance in man's ongoing experience, but refused to recognize as such anything that did not. And so it goes with each philosophical school.

The philosopher would seem then to be operating in the daring and difficult area that lies beyond the distinction between fact and fiction. The world-views he champions reflect diverse presuppositions as to where the line may best be drawn between the real and the unreal; he accepts the task of helping to decide what entities future generations will regard as dependably real. Moreover, when this role is fully appreciated, precisely the same situation appears in the case of our criteria of rational form. We want to draw valid inferences about the facts that at any given time are accepted as such, and to arrive at systematic explanations of them. Our heritage from the age of rationalism gives us tested help in doing this. But by what logical axioms should we be guided? Different philosophical schools have proposed different answers to this question also, and different periods in the history of thought have been dominated by different answers.

Take an outstanding example. For many centuries it was taken for granted by almost every Western philosopher that the correct logical axioms are embodied in the three so-called laws of thought, which appeared to be universal and necessary. These laws have been variously formulated; I shall attempt a formulation in harmony with the linguistic approach to logical problems that is now in fashion:

1. Law of Identity: A verbal expression means what it means, and not anything else.
2. Law of Contradiction: Of two mutually contradictory statements only one can be true.
3. Law of Excluded Middle: Of two mutually contradictory statements one must be true.

Notice carefully the intrinsic interconnection of these laws. The word "contradictory" appears in the second and third, and it is implied in the first. That is, to respect the law of identity is to employ a word or phrase in such a way that one use of it is not inconsistent with another. Notice also that the implication of the first two laws is negative: it may be summarized in the maxim "One must not contradict oneself." The third law, however, gives warrant for positive action; it implies the maxim "One may confidently affirm whatever the avoidance of contradiction permits him to affirm."

To illustrate these implications, take the statement "Telling a lie is sometimes right." The first law warns us that we would contradict ourselves if we were to assume that in one use of "lie" or "right" the word might mean something different from what it means in another use; a constant meaning must be adhered to. The second law assures us that of the two statements, "Telling a lie is sometimes right" and "Telling a lie is always wrong," one must be false; both cannot be true. The third law affirms that if (for whatever reason) we are certain that "telling a lie is sometimes right" is false, then we can be certain that "telling a lie is always wrong" is true. We may then ask: Do these apparently innocent axioms harbor any dubious presuppositions?

Consider first the negative maxim "One must not contradict oneself." Conscientious thinkers usually accept this assertion without hesitation. And it must obviously be obeyed in any system of purely formal reasoning such as logic or mathematics; if A is B it cannot in the same context be not-B. And elsewhere, too, it rarely serves any wise purpose to make a statement and then, in the same context, to assert the opposite.

But observe that it is quite crucial in explaining this maxim to include the phrase "in the same context." And when this limitation on its valid ity is pondered, it becomes evident that no one ever stays within the same context very long. As living minds we are always growing, and the context that affects the meaning of what we say is always changing. When building a formal system the context is under our control; absence of contradiction can be secured by adopting and respecting an explicit definition of the concepts involved. But how about the concepts employed in statements through which we communicate a novel experience? Here meanings change, and without advance warning. A word that was serviceable in one context is naturally used and often proves promising in another, but when employed there, its implications will not be exactly the same as before. Moreover, from time to time we find that our whole framework of presuppositions has been left behind and yet many old words are still used. When this irrepressible exuberance of thought is recognized, is it not clear that no living mind can always obey the laws of identity and of contradiction? Indeed, the freer and more creative that mind is, the more often it will be likely to violate them. The alternative would be to remain imprisoned by earlier definitions, regardless of how distorting or cramped they become in the new situation in which the words must be used.

However, a valid maxim underlies the command to avoid contradiction and to respect the law of identity. Perhaps it could be phrased thus: "A thinker should not acquiesce in contradiction or in ambiguity, torpidly rejecting all responsibility to resolve the one and to draw clear distinctions in the other." To contradict oneself or lose identity of meaning is no sin; the sin is to evade the opportunity thus created to advance from inconsistency or confusion toward truth. So long as either of these illogicalities is present and nothing has been done about it something is amiss; but progress toward true understanding is achieved whenever contradiction is overcome or ambiguity cleared up. To remain contentedly in inconsistency or confusion, as though a truth-seeking mind could do so permanently, is to sin against reason.

However, this maxim leaves open two alternatives. Granted that one should not acquiesce in contradiction, shall we escape it at once, lest our mental skirts become unclean, or shall we be willing to live with it for a while, taking whatever time may be needed to overcome it wisely? This is a crucial issue; and here is where the law of excluded middle can teach an instructive lesson. In learning that lesson we will square ourselves with the claims of the positive maxim that it implies, i.e., "One may affirm whatever the avoidance of contradiction permits him to affirm." Is this a sound maxim?

Aristotle believed, when he gave the West its first articulated system of logic, that this law is just as absolute as the law of non-contradiction and that it can be applied everywhere (except, perhaps, in propositions about a future event). In our time, however, many thinkers have rejected its claim to absoluteness. In a formal system with only two "truth-values" it will still be valid, but logical theories have now appeared that are not limited to the two traditional values "true" and "false." For example, a given proposition may be "indeterminate" with respect to its truth. In this case the falsehood of one proposition cannot establish the truth of another. If not-p is false, we do not thereby know that p is true; it may be indeterminate. The importance of recognizing such a third alternative lies in the fact that by doing so we can be judiciously patient about avoiding contradiction. When sure that a certain proposition is unacceptable we need not commit ourselves at once to its opposite. The concept of indeterminacy gives us room to explore further any considerations that might be relevant before we decide.

What could this "indeterminate" alternative mean outside of a formal system? Modern thinkers have become aware that a proposition may be indeterminate for various reasons. It may be so because it lacks sense; we may be trying to talk about a subject-term in predicates that are sensible only in another realm of discourse. If the assertion that "love is fragrant" is false, does this imply that "love is not fragrant" is true? Or are these assertions neither true nor false, because "fragrant" is an inappropriate predicate here? Again, a proposition may be indeterminate not because it is senseless but because evidence by which to decide its truth or falsehood is now lacking. Also, a statement may be even more radically indeterminate —not just because further evidence is needed but because the current criteria that guide us in seeking acceptable evidence are proving insecure, and are likely to be replaced by different criteria. At a certain period in the history of chemistry, for example, all statements about "phlogiston" became indeterminate; investigations were taking a turn that rendered this concept no longer serviceable. If we are to reason wisely, all these possibilities must be kept in mind.

More or less drastic changes take place, then, in the accepted criteria of logical form as well as in the dominant criteria of fact. Looking at what has happened with the law of excluded middle, we naturally face the possibility of similar changes in the formal axioms now generally accepted by logicians. And the problems posed by such changes clearly constitute a philosophical responsibility.

Just as it has been the task of philosophers to propose revisions of the prevailing criteria of fact when man's quest for truth appears to require it, so it is their task to revise the prevailing criteria of logical form when insight reveals an inadequacy in the presuppositions underlying those criteria. It will soon appear that there are also basic criteria of value, which from time to time need philosophical revision in the same way; indeed, it may be that our criteria of fact and of form ultimately depend on them.

Enough, for the time being, of the past history of science and philosophy. There are before us many living philosophical movements challenging the attention of thoughtful men; a few of them exert wide influence and are specially worth thorough understanding. The particular form now taken by these significant movements will doubtless have its day, but each exemplifies an approach to all philosophical problems that is surely more than transitory. We shall try to master their basic presuppositions, as these are shown in the criteria by which they deal with questions of logic, with the selection and interpretation of facts, and with other issues of philosophical concern. In each case, after exploring the movement in its own terms, we shall give it the most constructive appraisal we can—asking how it might fulfill its promise more completely than it already has and at what points the limits set by its present presuppositions need to be left behind.

3

*The philosophical analysis
of ordinary language*

I

One of the most important processes in human life—perhaps the most important—is the sharing of experience through communication. Hence, a decision to deal with the whole realm of philosophical problems in the setting of a fuller understanding of language is especially hopeful, for to provide the medium of such sharing is the basic function of language.

This general approach to philosophy can be followed, however, in more than one direction. The particular direction exemplified by the viewpoint we now seek to master reveals at many points the background in recent British philosophy out of which it has developed. Born in this historical setting, it is a branch of the movement known as "analytic philosophy," which first took definite form around the turn of the century and is today the most influential movement among academic philosophers in the Anglo-Saxon world.

Analytic philosophy is a way of thinking that emphasizes the logical dissection of concepts and statements to reveal their precise meaning, and tries to draw all the distinctions required if this process is to be carried out with scrupulous thoroughness. Why is such meticulous discrimination important? Because no thinker has ever been able to deal with any serious issue without careful analysis; to be concerned with a problem is by that token to wish one's understanding of it to be clear, accurate, and systematic. In the absence of such discrimination one inevitably falls into obscurity, confusion, and loose-jointedness.

Take a recent analysis of the central principles of Gandhi's ethics.* The content here is quite different from the themes with which analytic philosophers are usually occupied, hence it provides a good example of the universal pertinence of this procedure. The author lays those principles bare, one by one, indicating which are logically primary and demonstrating how the others are related to the primary axioms and to each other. As a result one sees more clearly than in Gandhi's own writings—or in those of his followers—what the essential structure of his ethical philosophy is. One knows what he is committed to if he adopts it and can therefore better judge which features of it he should adopt. Nothing of substance is changed by this analytic "axiomatization" if it is accurately done; its virtue lies in clarifying the meaning already there. (Of course it is no substitute for Gandhi's own ethical statements, for his purpose includes much more than a logical exposition of his basic ideas.)

Analytic philosophy therefore fills an essential role. It does for our responsible thinking in general what mathematics does for the sciences; it secures clarity, precision, and rigor in whatever we choose to think about. The viewpoint we are now to explore combines then in its own way the virtues of conscientious analysis with those of an approach to all philosophical problems through the systematic study of language.

A brief survey of its background in earlier analytic philosophy is necessary. In the opening decades of this century the analysts constituted a branch of the philosophical school known as realism, whose basic tenet was that the external world exists independent of mind, and hence that, when the latter becomes acquainted with an object, it simply apprehends the character already possessed by that object. The most prominent rival

---

* Arne Naess, "A Systematization of Gandhian Ethics of Conflict Resolution," in *Conflict Resolution*, Vol. II, No. 2 (June, 1958). I am passing no judgment, of course, on whether the analysis is accurate.

school was idealism, which denied this independence and held that the world owes to mind the character apprehended in it.

The problem that strongly attracted the attention of most of the analytic realists—among whom were Bertrand Russell, C. D. Broad, Samuel Alexander, and John Laird—was the relation between philosophy and science; and their central conviction was that philosophy must itself become scientific on a realistic foundation if its results are to command respect, but that it has certain distinctive tasks beyond those which scientists perform. So far as concerns the detailed work of the latter in describing and explaining the world, philosophy has no role. It accepts without question the results reached. But by employing the analytic method it can fill the important function of clarifying and organizing the logical principles that science needs to use. Also, by investigating what these principles imply about the ultimate structure of the world as thus explained, it can build a sound metaphysic. In the discussion that follows I am thinking especially of Russell's interpretation of analytic realism as presented in his writings during the second decade of this century. None of the others above mentioned would agree in every important respect with his position.

In the course of a few decades the realists were succeeded on the center of the philosophical stage by the positivists, and they in turn have been succeeded by the philosophers of ordinary language. Each of these three schools exemplifies in its own fashion the analytic orientation: all aim at revealing the logical principles that accurate thinking must respect and at showing by their analyses how philosophical errors need to be corrected. But they vary in their convictions as to how this function is properly performed. Each of them has its own distinctive presuppositions that constitute its answer to such important questions as: What analyses are worth undertaking? What conditions must be met by an acceptable analysis?

The positivists took over the theory of logic handed on by the realists, except for a different interpretation of the nature of logical form. That theory had diverged from earlier tradition by developing a new and more general theory of relations; before it appeared, a special emphasis had been given to the grammatical relation between subject and predicate. The most important departure of the positivists from the presuppositions of the realists was an uncompromising rejection of metaphysics. The realists had believed it possible to replace the speculative cosmologies of an earlier day by a scientific metaphysic, but to the positivists this enterprise appeared illegitimate. They adopted a theory called the "verification principle," the essential significance of which is best stated negatively: Unless one can specify a procedure by which a given assertion is testable, so that either it or the contradictory assertion can be confirmed by adequate evidence, the assertion not only has no right to claim truth—it has no sense. On this basis, only hypotheses capable of being investigated by the methods of science have sense; the doctrines of metaphysics are senseless, since no procedure is available by which one system can be verified and all systems that conflict with it disproved.

This left as the constructive task of philosophy simply the clarification, by logical analysis, of the concepts and statements employed by science. When a positivist says something that is not a part of such analysis he does so to reveal the confusions into which those who have not respected the rules of meaningful use of language have unfortunately fallen. Ludwig Wittgenstein in his first major work expresses this orientation succinctly by saying, "Whatever can be said can be said clearly (i.e., in the purified language of science)." And "whereof one cannot speak, thereof one must be silent." [1]

The basic presuppositions held in common by this school and by the philosophers of ordinary language—as well as the crucial difference between them—can best be introduced by turning to the two major books written by that rare philosophical genius just mentioned: the *Tractatus Logico-Philosophicus* (whose English translation first appeared in 1922), and the *Philosophical Investigations* published in 1953. The former inspired the rise of logical positivism and the latter set forth the distinctive ideas characteristic of this third school in its original form. Both these books proceed on the conviction that philosophy's business is not to offer a comprehensive theory of the universe; its proper concern is with such questions as how words mean what they mean and what we need to do in order to use them correctly. The author is sure that this is a vitally important concern, because one can easily be misled by seductive analogies into assuming that one's meaning is clear when it is not. If a thinker succumbs to such seductions, serious consequences arise. He is trapped in certain mistakes that could otherwise be avoided. As Wittgenstein remarks in the second of these books, "An unsuitable type of expression is a sure means of remaining in a state of confusion. It as it were bars the way out." [2] The remedy is to uncover the source of the confusion and reorganize our linguistic habits so as to guard against temptation by these analogies. This is the true function of philosophy.

But there is a fundamental difference between the two books as to the nature of the confusion and where a reliable cure is to be found. In the *Tractatus* the solution the author proposes consists in laying bare the skeleton of the ideal language through which the structure of any fact that we might talk about can be accurately revealed. In this language alone, which is the proper language of science, can one intelligibly speak, and when one violates its logical syntax the only possible outcome is nonsense. In the *Investigations* this solution is renounced. So far as concerns the words in which philosophical questions are stated, the way men naturally express themselves in the varied circumstances of life is the right way and does not need to be improved. What is needed is simply a perceptive grasp of these current uses, and Wittgenstein's main aim is to show how such a grasp can be gained.

I I

"Ordinary language is correct language."
This was the early slogan of those who followed Wittgenstein in this novel direction.* But like most brief slogans it can be, and has been, misconstrued. A more cautious formulation would be: The ordinary use of linguistic expressions is a unique resource for revealing their correct use.

To see how a serious thinker might be led to adopt such a maxim, let us neglect for a moment the historical origin of the ordinary language school and try to grasp in our own fashion the persuasive appeal that the maxim can have.

Suppose that we put ourselves in the place of a philosopher who, having acquired some mastery of the history of his subject, finds himself puzzled about the diverse theories that his predecessors have proclaimed and the apparent impossibility of demonstrating the truth of any of them. He has, perhaps, concocted his own theory, but now sees that it is inadequate. He is on the verge of giving up philosophy, as a hopeless tissue of presumptuous claims and unanswerable questions. Then something occurs that gives him a new clue. His special interest, for example, might have centered on problems about human knowledge, and he has become familiar with the theories of knowledge propounded by philosophers in the past. It is evident that each of these theories offers its own definition of the word "know"

* See Norman Malcolm, "Moore and Ordinary Language," in *The Philosophy of G. E. Moore,* ed. by Paul Schilpp (Evanston and Chicago: Northwestern Univ. Press, 1942), pp. 357, 362. He has since expressed some regret at having offered this formulation, because of the misinterpretations to which it led.

and contends that this definition has caught once for all the true meaning —any other definition that might be adopted is false. The new clue appears when our philosopher turns away from the artificial setting of philosophical controversy and mixes with people who are uncorrupted by such academic sophistication. He observes that they frequently employ the word "know" as they talk with one another and that their uses of it are unexpectedly varied. Some of these are clearly analogous to the use of the word by scientists when explaining their discoveries (which he has perhaps taken for granted as its standard use); but some carry a quite different meaning and yet seem to communicate successfully. Among these latter he notices, let us say, the following: "I have known him a long time"; "I've never done that but I'm sure I know how"; "To know Thee is life eternal"; "Well, what do you know!"

He reflects on these interesting uses, comparing them with philosophical theories about the meaning of "know." Suddenly the new idea dawns. The philosophers have gotten nowhere (except to fall into confusion and error) because they have failed to realize that in the case of such words successful understanding and communication do not depend on the ideal definitions they have been seeking; the meaning is simply what comes to light in the way the words are used, with special reference to the manifold distinctions that are revealed and the subtle nuances that appear in varied circumstances. In their eagerness to find a single and final essence of knowledge philosophers have missed many of these distinctions; but careful attention to them leads to clear understanding of what it is to know, and resolves the puzzles that have been generated by the philosophical search having gone astray. Not that departures from familiar uses are necessarily wrong, but the departures characteristic of philosophical theories are obviously wrong—they ignore these well-established uses and put in their place some queer use whose main virtue is that it fits the requirements of a speculative system.

Thus the axiom that ordinary language is correct language comes to this: The true meaning of any philosophically significant word or phrase is disclosed by looking at the ways we now habitually use it in talking about any situation in which it is naturally employed. There is no possibility of distinguishing profitably between meaning and use, and when in our philosophizing any such difference is assumed, we inevitably fall into error. It is both presumptuous and a distortion of our role to suppose that we can discover the sole proper definition of this or that fundamental concept, which will be superior to the network of meanings revealed in the ways in which it is used. The scientist must sometimes propose new uses of words; his task is to correct false ideas about the world by true ones, and in doing this he may need more accurate definitions of current words. But this is not the philosopher's business. He does not add to our information; his role is to deal with the concepts that all of us acquire in the course of our common experience, and he frees them from confusion by reminding us of the meanings with which we are already familiar. His skill can be employed in devising methods by which the logical texture of these established uses will shine through the tangles into which thinkers have fallen.

This interpretation of the axiom will become still clearer if we observe how the ordinary language philosopher, when guided simply by his basic presuppositions, answers objections that other philosophers are likely to raise.* "How," they will ask, "can you justify the idea that ordinary language is all right?" The rejoinder is: "Let's examine the way we use the word 'justification' in various circumstances, and when this is done we will see how it is properly used and that there is no place for the kind of justification you are looking for." Or the plea may be: "Don't we often need to correct customary ways of talking by our experience of the things talked about?" The reply is: "But consider how the word 'experience' is used, and if we do so we will see how any problem involving experience is resolved and that no such appeal from language to something beyond language can accomplish anything." Finally, the baffled philosopher will demand: "But surely reality is the ultimate court of appeal, not words about it. Aren't we responsible to make our statements agree with reality?" To which the answer will be: "All right, how is the word 'reality' used, when we leave aside philosophical speculations and notice the way it functions in ordinary parlance? Do you suppose that by some sequestered armchair maneuver you can invent a meaning for it that improves on the fertile and living meanings it has already acquired?" In short, each of these answers boils down to two contentions. The weaker one is: How arrogant for a philosopher to think that he can reform ordinary language! It exhibits richer resources, more securely grounded, than any he could possibly possess. The stronger one is: He cannot step out of ordinary language even if he wishes to.

* Wittgenstein himself suggests these answers, especially in the case of "justification." See *Philosophical Investigations* (New York: The Macmillan Company, 1953), I, 97, 134, 482–486. But the procedure implied in these cases is more vividly revealed in his treatment of other words, such as "game," "red," "pain," "intend," or "language" itself.

J. L. Austin expresses the weaker contention persuasively when he says: "Our common stock of words embodies all the distinctions men have found worth drawing, and the connections they have found worth marking, in the life-time of many generations." These words, he says in his well-known paper entitled "A Plea for Excuses," "are likely to be more numerous, more sound since they have stood up to the long test of the survival of the fittest, and more subtle . . . than any that you or I are likely to think up in our armchairs of an afternoon." [3] Stuart Hampshire succinctly expresses the stronger one in his contribution to *Contemporary British Philosophy* (Third Series): "We cannot step outside the language which we use, and judge it from some ulterior and superior vantage-point." [4] And if a skeptical philosopher asks why we cannot, the reply is something like this: A person who uses words is not, by his individual fiat, in control of their meanings. What they mean is determined by the "form of life" which he shares with other members of his society and in which the language he uses has evolved; their essential role is to be a medium of communication from one person to another within the setting of that form of life. If someone insists on calling "hot" what everybody around him calls "sour," he not only finds that communication breaks down, but also that he cannot even carry through this departure so far as his own thinking is concerned. Thinking occurs within a linguistic framework that is social; whenever we use a given word in such and such circumstances we are assuming the whole "grammar" of that word in its ordinary employment and cannot escape doing so. Speaking a language is like playing a game. If one chooses to play a given game one's moves must conform to the established rules that make it the kind of game it is. Moreover, we even perceive things in accordance with our current ways of talking about them, and our very habits of perception would be thrown into confusion by a rebellious departure from those ways.

III

But the champions of this viewpoint do their analytic work with some fundamental concepts that have not yet been explained. Let us join them in investigating the grammar of a philosophically important word, such as "know," "true," "real," "good." How does one go about ferreting out this grammar, in view of the often baffling multiplicity of established uses that may turn up?

It will certainly help if we look first for uses of the word that were learned when we acquired the language of which it is a part, or that we would pick when trying to teach it to someone not yet familiar with that language. In the case of the word "know" such uses would presumably include: "I know Mr. Herman"; "I know how to skate"; "I know there are two apples in the fruit bowl." No one has any real question about the propriety of these uses or their power to communicate the intended meaning. It is necessary, however, to raise a further question: In what kind of situation does any such use fill its role with obvious success? For example, under what circumstances is the last of these three meanings revealed with crystal clarity? The answer would be: In the situation where a person who had wished to find out what was in the fruit bowl has investigated the matter, as a result of which he says, "I know there are two apples in it." This is an example of what the ordinary language philosopher calls a "paradigm" use—that is, one that provides a dependable standard against which more doubtful uses of "know" in this sense can be appraised.

All these inquiries contribute toward and culminate in an "elucidation of the logic" of the uses that are being investigated, and a formulation of the "rules" revealed by an accurate description of this or that use under such and such circumstances. What conception of logic and of rules is present here, and how does it differ from conceptions that have prevailed in the past? This question will have to be answered at some length.

Traditionally, logic has been concerned with two kinds of sentences: those making assertions about some fact or facts, and those stating rules according to which two or more such assertions can be combined in a valid inference. The latter sentences articulate logical form. Everyone is familiar with the form of the Aristotelian syllogism: If this object is an A and all A's are B's, then this object is a B. In practice, to articulate form is to exhibit the meaning of the connectives by which one assertion is logically related to others ("if . . . then," "not," "and," "or") and of the quantifiers that affect these logical relations ("all," "no," "some," "most," etc.).

Wittgenstein took this conception for granted in his early *Tractatus*, although he gave it a novel interpretation. When he reacted against the position taken in this book he swung to the opposite extreme in his view of logic as he did in many other matters. Two aspects of his later thought reflect this extreme. For one, he came to the conclusion that there are innumerable kinds of sentences, which can be combined in many ways, and that each of these combinations has its own logic—that is, the set of conditions under which it successfully communicates. Since these linguistic uses are innumerable it is impossible to build a complete theory of logic. What can be done, and what he was concerned to do, is to bring to light a number of instructive uses that philosophers have especially failed to notice. For the other, since a comprehensive logical theory is unattainable, the important thing is not to articulate a set of rules—many of which would be vague and their range of application uncertain—but to develop expertness in quickly perceiving whatever logical feature needs to be grasped if confusion is to be avoided.

Wittgenstein hoped to inculcate a skill, or art, that others would be able to use in carrying on his work of correcting and forestalling philosophical errors. But few of the ordinary language philosophers could master this flexible art, nor were they ready to reject the possibility of systematic logical theory. Instead, they developed a new and interesting notion of logic, which differs from the traditional notion in just the way we would expect; it is a theory of the structure of ordinary language, aiming to reveal the conditions essential to the avoidance of confusion and to the correct use of whatever words are employed.

First, while agreeing with Wittgenstein that there are innumerable kinds of uses, they see no reason why the kinds that are of special significance should not be identified and their distinctive structural features analyzed. They find several such kinds in addition to those given a place in traditional logic. The outcome of this inquiry is that a number of "types" of sentences are now generally recognized; chief among them are interrogative sentences, exclamatory sentences, imperative sentences, grading or evaluative sentences, performatory sentences, and ascriptive sentences. In most cases the characteristic function of each type will be sufficiently clear from the adjectives used.

Second, many of them explicitly embark on the quest to detect and state the rules governing the use of this or that sentence under such and such circumstances, confident that this can be done successfully. We shall examine an instance that involves no philosophical concepts and therefore provides a very simple illustration. Close attention to a few details is necessary, however. Two sets of rules are proposed, one to describe the logic of the sentence "Please open the door" and the other of the sentence "Put the dishes away," in the circumstances of their natural use.*

I. Asking H (the hearer) to open the door.
   1. There shall be a certain door in the vicinity, which is singled out by something in the context.

* This illustration was suggested by Professor W. P. Alston.

2. This door shall not be open at present.
3. It shall be possible for H to open the door.
4. S (the speaker) shall have an interest in getting this door opened.

II. Telling H to put the dishes away.
   1. There shall be some dishes in the vicinity, which are singled out by something in the context.
   2. These dishes shall not be put away at present.
   3. It shall be possible for H to put these dishes away.
   4. It shall be in accordance with S's will that H put these dishes away.
   5. S shall be in a position of authority relative to H.

Notice that rules 3 and 4 in the case of both sentences are identical or nearly so except that the objects referred to are different. Why is this? Consider rule 4 first. The near-identity is evidently due to the fact that even though the first sentence belongs to the type that would be called "requests" and the second to the type that would be called "commands," these types have much in common and that similarity is reflected in this rule. The difference is that the one entreats while the other is an order, but the two kinds could easily be combined under a more general type which we might call "directive" sentences. With this in mind, examine the role of rule 5 in the logical analysis of "Put the dishes away." Its function is to indicate that this sentence implies a situation in which to command is proper; it brings out one of the features that distinguish the setting of an order from that of a request. Now consider rule 3. Here (except for the different objects involved) there is complete identity, and when we ask why, it becomes apparent that this rule has an even wider scope than the generalized rule 4. It would apply not only to these two types but also to performatory sentences and to those expressing a moral duty—in fact, to any sentence that expects some action on the part of the hearer. Perhaps we could stretch the meaning of the adjective "prescriptive" so that it would cover the very general class of sentences thus identified. The similarities that appear in rules 3 and 4, and the distinctive features in rule 5, thus reveal one of the functions of a set of rules of use—namely, to indicate the type under which the sentence whose logic is being described falls.

When we turn to rules 1 and 2 it is obvious that their function is different; they too have phrases in common but their function is to emphasize the unique features of the situation in which each of these sentences is used. They assert that "Please open the door" and "Put the dishes away" communicate intelligibly when and only when the particular facts described in those rules are present.

Why now is the quest for a correct formulation of these rules regarded as an enterprise in logic? Because, in carrying out such an analysis, the ordinary language philosopher is guided by the basic logical principles of implication and non-contradiction. However—and this point is crucial —instead of assuming that these principles are absolute, as in traditional theories of logic, he construes them as relative to the situation in which a given sentence is used. Let us see how this is so and what it involves.

If we reflect on the relation between "Please open the door" and rules 1 and 2 under it, we note that the request does not absolutely imply those rules; there would be no formal contradiction between asking someone to open the door and the statement that there is no door in the vicinity or that the door is already open. But in the situation of its natural use the request does imply those rules; there would be a kind of contradiction if it were made and the facts they describe did not obtain. That is, in such a case communication would fail; anyone hearing the sentence spoken would be at a loss to know how to interpret it. The phrase "self-defeating" is often employed to describe this relative "contradiction" between "Please open the door" and "The only door in the vicinity is already open." The latter statement denies a condition normally required for the former to be intelligible.

This difference between formal and situational contradiction is fundamental for the philosophy we are now examining. "That person is a mother of three sons, but she is not a woman" are two statements that contradict each other absolutely; we can imagine no case in which they could be rationally combined. But exceptional circumstances can easily be imagined in which the combination in the paragraph above would become intelligible. It might be that the door is behind the back of the person making the request, and that since he last looked at it someone has quietly opened it. In such a case, when a description of the exceptional circumstance has been given, the unintelligibility otherwise haunting the combination disappears.

This then is what it means to elucidate the logic of the use of a given sentence.* It is properly called an enterprise in logic because it systematically employs the traditional logical principles in reaching whatever rules are formulated. But it is a logic of use, because it probes their function in

* The reader interested in becoming more familiar with this conception of logic will find in P. Nowell-Smith's *Ethics* (Oxford: Basil Blackwell & Mott, Ltd., 1957) Chaps. V, VI, and VII, an illuminating exposition of the logic of use in general and of basic moral concepts in particular.

the varied circumstances of their ordinary employment. Their meaning in purely formal reasoning becomes a special case within this wider field —the case that is present when the differences between one set of circumstances and another are not taken into account.

IV

Thus far an important fact about the ordinary language philosophy has been neglected, namely that it has been going through a significant evolution, which is not yet complete. More than one trend in this evolution can of course be detected. I shall describe what seems to me the most instructive trend; the outstanding change revealed in it bears directly on these notions of logic and of rules.

In the early years, the champions of this philosophy emphasized the correction of specific confusions into which other thinkers had fallen through their failure to respect ordinary language. But before long a more positive emphasis became evident, and it took a form that pointed toward the development of a general philosophical theory—though of course a theory of a distinctive kind. One can readily anticipate the nature of this new emphasis if he keeps in mind the revised conception of logic described above, and the growing concern to classify types of use and to formulate the rules that govern a given type. The clue to an understanding of this development is the fact that these types naturally fall into a hierarchy, some being relatively specific and others more general—each including several specific types. This means that the rules that can be formulated also fall into a hierarchy. Some apply to this or that sentence in its quite specific meaning. Others apply to a limited type of sentence, such as the requests or commands mentioned on page 34. Still others apply to a more inclusive type, such as "directive" sentences. If our comment on the relation between these three types is justified, such rules would formulate conditions of intelligibility that hold good for both requests and commands. But the quest for general conditions of the intelligible use of language would not need to stop here; where lies the upper limit of the hierarchy? Would something important be achieved by such a quest that is not at once evident?

It turns out that the quest makes fruitful contact, in an illuminating way, with the work of philosophers as it has been pursued in the past. The possibility emerges of reconstructing whole branches of philosophy, so that they take a form harmonious with the ordinary language orientation. Ethics, epistemology, and philosophy of law, for instance, would seem to differ from each other in the fact that each deals with sentences belonging to a certain broad type. Indeed, rules might be discovered that apply to all types of sentence without exception and would thus give meaning to the traditional concept of universal categories. At any rate, the trend we are now exploring aims precisely at this kind of reconstruction.

Its pioneer is J. L. Austin, who ever since 1940 has contributed papers leading in this direction. He has been concerned not only to detect the fine nuances that are revealed in the ordinary uses of significant words—and the light they can throw on philosophical problems—but also to organize in a new and instructive fashion the hints they provide. One might describe him as a philosophical surveyor of language, whose task is to draw a map on which both the important uses already recognized and others needed to supplement them can be located. In carrying out this task he points the way toward a systematic theory of certain types of use. Much of his work seems to aim at a thorough treatment of "performatory" uses in this fashion, and as a result large areas of moral and legal philosophy appear in a new and fruitful perspective.

The most decisive step to date in this direction, so far as I am aware, is taken by three books published late in the 1950's. Their characteristic feature is that they not only deal with whole branches of philosophy rather than with more limited problems, but that they attempt an analysis of the entire structure of ordinary language. They seek to discover rules that apply universally—rules that must be obeyed in any use of any linguistic expression under any circumstances if that expression is to communicate intelligibly. The first of these was Stephen Toulmin's *The Uses of Argument,* which appeared in 1958; the other two, both published in 1959, are Stuart Hampshire's *Thought and Action* and P. F. Strawson's *Individuals: An Essay in Descriptive Metaphysics.*

Toulmin approaches this task by proposing a reconstruction of logical theory—at least, of the large part of it that is concerned with the structure of inference from a set of premises to a conclusion. Since inference is involved in all reasoning, whatever its subject matter, every type of sentence that can function as a premise or conclusion falls within the area of his concern. In carrying out this reconstruction he distinguishes between those aspects of inference that are "field-invariant" and those that are "field-dependent"—the former remaining unchanged whatever the subject reasoned about, the latter varying with it. He proposes a suggestive model for the field-invariant aspects, namely: Conclusion C is warranted (W) by data D with degree of assurance Q when the warrant is appropriately backed (B), unless exceptional conditions R obtain.*

Clearly, if any such proposal is sound, it will describe the universal structure of ordinary language as it functions in inference. Hampshire's *Thought and Action* and Strawson's *Individuals* attempt to analyze this structure without being confined to that function; their aim is to lay bare the requisite conditions of any use of ordinary language. The former does this very briefly, as an introduction to a study of the linguistic categories of ethics, while the latter does it as an essential part of the quest for a metaphysical theory of the nature of individual entities as they enter the domain of speech.

The work of these men thus reveals a promising direction in which this movement is evolving. They are building an original kind of philosophical system; they are offering the world an organized theory about the varied uses of language in the light of which whole branches of philosophy, including metaphysics, are reconstructed in a novel way. It would be surprising if this trend does not develop further and take forms that cannot at present be anticipated.

v

Let us now, as an essential part of our search for philosophic understanding, appraise the presuppositions of the ordinary language philosophy, exhibiting as clearly as we can their points of strength and of weakness. There will be no pretense that a critic can stand outside such a living movement and pronounce judgment on it from the vantage-point of a superior set of presuppositions. Our aim is rather to share its positive insight as fully as possible and try to see where, if anywhere, its limitations become too cramping.

In the initial half of the appraisal we shall seek to bring out its important historical contribution, which in many branches of thought—ethics, logic, theory of knowledge, legal philosophy—is quite impressive. My suggestion is that this constructive achievement is mainly due to three presuppositions.

First, the ordinary language philosopher is evidently convinced that

* The meaning of these concepts is shown by an illustration: Presumably (Q) Harry is a British subject (C) because he was born in Bermuda (D), since anyone born in Bermuda will be a British subject (W, B) unless his parents were aliens or he has become naturalized in another country (R). (See Stephen Toulmin, *The Uses of Argument* [London: Cambridge Univ. Press, 1958], pp. 97–107.)

when one decides to philosophize he must begin where he is rather than somewhere else. It is very tempting to abandon where one is and look around for a shortcut to some starting-point that appears more hopeful. Religious thinkers, for example, are eager to begin with God—or at least to get to Him as soon as possible—since in their eyes everything else depends on Him; the empiricists wish to begin with the data of sense perception, since those data alone can validate truths about the experienced world; the logico-mathematical thinkers are anxious to begin with the abstract entities that form their chosen realm, since they are sure that only in such terms can anything be precisely explained.

Yet, how are we supposed to get from where we are to a more reasonable starting point, and how do we tell which among these tidier realms is the right one to choose? Each philosophy gives its answer, but the answer is obviously determined by its own presuppositions which every opposing philosophy rejects. So, no safe or universally acceptable shortcut turns up; we must begin right where we are. What does that imply?

The ordinary language philosophy gives an enlightening answer. Whatever else may be the case when we begin to philosophize, all of us share in the "form of life" of our society and employ in talking with each other the resources of the language it has evolved. When this is realized, it becomes clear that the varied lessons that have been so fully and steadily confirmed through its experience that they are now funded in these ways of speaking cannot be ignored.

Second, the champion of this viewpoint is sure that by turning thoughtfully to these lessons we do become aware of many assumptions underlying philosophical departures from ordinary use, which few would accept if they realized what was involved.

Take an interesting example from Bertrand Russell (summarized in *My Philosophical Development,* New York: Simon & Schuster, Inc., 1959). He has insisted that if certain well-established facts about visual perception are taken into account, it follows that when we look at an object what we really see is not the external object but an image located in our own brains. The decisive fact which leads him to this surprising conclusion is that it takes time for light to travel from the object to the retina of the eye, and for an impulse from the latter to reach the visual center in the brain; if, therefore, what we see is the external object, we must see it an instant before this transmission is complete. The unexpressed assumption is that "seeing" cannot spread over a stretch of time but must be instantaneous.

At first sight this assumption may be quite persuasive. Yet, if we commit ourselves to it, we are also committed to holding that what we see is always contained in a tiny point of space in the brain, since if we were to see something at any distance from this point the seeing could not be instantaneous. A choice must therefore be made between this assumption and another, which expresses a long-established belief about perceiving an object. But when the consequences of each choice are weighed, would anyone seriously hesitate? If Russell's position is adopted, our visual acquaintance with everything beyond our brains must be pronounced illusory. Moreover —and here appears the distinctive role of the appeal to ordinary language in such a situation—it would seem clear that when we talk about seeing an object we *mean* a relation of our organ of vision to the surface of the object some distance away, not the observation of an entirely different and very minute area inside our heads. Are we ready to abandon this conception of what seeing is? If not, whatever scientific knowledge is gained about the process of perceiving must be reconciled with this conception, and any assumption we might have adopted that stands in the way must be revised. Why not think of seeing as a temporal process, at least till some serious difficulty turns up? This is not to say that the appropriate solution of such a conflict is necessarily of this sort; what the appeal to ordinary language provides is a reminder, which in many cases will be decisive.

Third, the ordinary language philosopher is sure that when one's reflection turns in this fashion from philosophical systems to ordinary modes of speech one becomes aware of the great variety of ways in which a given word is used, and realizes, as he probably had not done before, that this diversity is neither irrelevant nor trivial but highly instructive. Why would these variations ever have appeared in the language of a living culture if they were not needed? The seductive belief that there is only one correct meaning for any philosophically significant word, which the right theory can seize and fix for all time, now appears very naïve—a naïveté illustrated by the manifold meanings of "know," which its ordinary uses quickly reveal.

But full acceptance of this diversity of uses has another important virtue: It enables us to correct an aberration that is very congenial to philosophical minds—namely, the wholesale "reductionism" into which many have fallen. Whether it is the reduction of a moral concept to a psychological one— e.g., of "good" to "pleasant"—or of the theoretical ideal of "truth" to the practical one of "usefulness," or of an inductive problem to a deductive one, this passion for construing one thing as though by our determined fiat it could be transformed into another has been a major bane of philosophy. Reductionism is the perversion of a salutary principle—namely, that it is worthwhile to seek unity in diversity and to render the complex simple. Wherever this can be done without violence to the significant differences between things, well and good. But if such differences are denied or obscured, a fundamental responsibility of thought has been betrayed. When philosophers clearly recognize the diverse circumstances in which words gain their meaning it becomes apparent that one type of linguistic utterance cannot be reduced to another logical type on pain of hopeless distortion.

Look for instance at the hoary problem of freedom and determinism. The champions of ordinary language encourage us to break away from the straitjacket of traditional debates and the encrusted concepts with which they have been carried on—such as "free will," "fate," "chance," "necessity,"—and to turn instead to the familiar expressions "You can do so-and-so," "I may be able to," "He could have acted thus if . . . ," and "It couldn't be helped." When we examine what these expressions communicate in the everyday situations in which people use them, not only do all the familiar philosophical solutions appear too simple, but we are freed from the grip of monolithic theories like naturalism, emotivism, and behaviorism (in its original form, at least), which have aggressively attempted to reduce moral realities to something else. It becomes obvious that ethical words have distinctively ethical meanings, and that there is every justification for continuing to respect those meanings.

To sum up this positive appraisal: The ordinary language philosophy calls us away from the oversimplified speculations of the past and the present, with their extravagances and often pretentious claims, to the manifold dependable lessons of experience that have been so fully confirmed over the years that they are now solidly established in the ways of speaking taken for granted by members of a successful "form of life" in their day-by-day communication with each other.

VI

The second and more adventurous half of our appraisal will aim to discover the major weaknesses and limitations in this philosophy, and to see as clearly as possible in what direction they should be corrected. We shall try to glimpse how its orientation could be wisely revised so that its distinctive genius would be more completely fulfilled.

A fundamental question gives us a promising point of departure. Consider again the maxim: Ordinary language is correct language. A natural implication, however the maxim be interpreted, is that it is always proper to adhere to ordinary uses, but that any departure from them calls for explicit and sufficient justification. If, for example, one extends the meaning of a word to cover a wider field than it has covered in the past, he is responsible to explain the extension; if he gives it a metaphorical meaning, the relation between the metaphorical and the literal meaning must be made clear. Is this demand warranted?

Suppose we answer: "Quite so, but whenever anyone communicates by language to another person, he is thereby doing all that is needed in this regard. In any given case, of course, his words may fail to communicate, and if so he has not done what is needed. But usually they succeed; and it is evident that success is possible even when he departs rather widely from current uses of the words spoken. Is not this success, in general, sufficient to justify his way of using them?"

In short, our question is this: Does not the ultimate criterion of the proper use of a word lie in its ability to achieve successful communication, not in its having already become current coin? Since the intrinsic purpose of language is to share experience, any way of using words that does convey to the hearer what the speaker wished to convey would appear by that fact to be a legitimate use; whereas any mode of speech that cannot do so is in that situation unjustifiable. I do not mean that successful communication is always or in every respect immune to criticism. The point is simply that it often fills a constructive role even when it diverges from established uses. This would seem to be the criterion implicitly assumed in daily life, and it also appears to be taken for granted in the more technical discussions of specialized groups such as scientists or philosophers. If such a conclusion is sound, it follows that, in general, we do not first find out what the rules governing language are and then decide by their aid what can be successfully communicated. The reverse sequence is the primary one: we set ourselves to communicate, hoping for success, and if the hope is justified, the rules of language must make a place for whatever way of speaking has thus succeeded. Indeed, the ordinary language philosophers do not mean to deny this truth.

What then can be successfully communicated? Perhaps the more revealing question is, What cannot be? Any phase of experience, and any attitude toward it that a person might naturally feel can be communicated—I can express to others a description, a command, a promise, an evaluation, or any of the subdivisions within each of these types. With regard to descriptions, for example, I can convey information about this or that fact, and also general truths about a whole class of facts. I can even share with others—though this is more difficult—a novel criterion of fact, in the light of which all objects and events will be interpreted differently than they had been before.

When these possibilities are realized, is it not apparent that the basic problem for linguistic philosophy is this: What are the conditions of effective communication, in the varied situations in which people seek to share experience? Ordinary uses, with their virtues and limitations, will best be understood in this setting. It is easy to anticipate some of the intriguing sub-problems that would appear. One of them would concern the relation between verbal and nonverbal communication. Another would arise from the fact that often a vital function of language is to entice the hearer to put himself in the speaker's place—to achieve sufficient rapport with him so that his words may become a medium of successful sharing when they are not already such. Sometimes this achievement is relatively simple; sometimes it means that the hearer must enter a new world. When one contemplates this role of language one is aware that speaking or writing can be a profoundly creative process. Indeed, a great artist or a great prophet might be defined as a person capable through his genius of awakening in others the perception of a richer universe; he does not allow them to live any longer in the cramped world that they inhabited before. Can the great philosopher in his own way do this, too?

Such a shift of emphasis from the "rules of ordinary use" to the conditions of successful communication is far-reaching. When one realizes that communication can be original and creative as well as respectful of current uses, many significant consequences for philosophy follow.

In the first place, a far more dynamic quality in language than is apt to be clearly glimpsed without such a shift becomes evident. Language is in constant change, and each of us participates in this process. We try new uses, some of which are adopted by others and thus soon become current media of communication. One might even defend the view that mere repetition of an established use is the exceptional rather than the normal case; usually a speaker is adding his bit to the steady transformation of language. If then a philosopher with his eye on established idioms tells us that "we cannot step outside the language which we use," we might well answer: "This is precisely what we are doing much of the time." Customary modes of speech are being replaced by somewhat different ones that, perhaps in as-yet-unnoticed corners, are coming to the fore. Clearly, then, the analogy between language and a game, stressed by Wittgenstein and many of his followers, is seriously misleading. Spontaneous innovation in language occurs frequently and (if perceptively done) is accepted as quite proper. Spontaneous innovation in a game with its established rules is unfair; it threatens to ruin the game and is thus unacceptable to those who wish to keep on playing it.

If such is the case, language can only be adequately understood in this dynamic dimension. What is most important is not the aggregate of uses already established but the trends of change that might be discerned. We need to analyze language in terms that enable us, so far as possible, to anticipate where these trends are leading. And a vital corollary is that in any given situation novel uses may be more instructive with regard to future linguistic behavior than customary modes of speech.

But in the second place, when this dynamic character of language is recognized, even the phrase "anticipate the trends of change" will not quite suffice. Reflect on the fact that linguistic uses change for the better and they also change for the worse. A new way of speaking is sometimes a happier way than the one it replaces. It may take account of a larger area of human experience; it may draw its materials together in more stable and consistent fashion; it may be more fertile in its capacity for continued growth. On the other hand, it can lead to greater confusion—not just temporarily, which may be unavoidable—but for a long time. Consider, for example, Wittgenstein's statement in the *Investigations* that "a machine cannot think." The performance of present-day computers is inducing many people to say that such machines *do* think, and this way of speaking may become widely accepted. Such an outcome would be unfortunate, for it encourages the lamentable idea that human minds are nothing more than complicated machines. Can we then avoid asking, when we analyze language, in what direction *should* present uses change, if the change is to be a wise one?

This challenge is especially obvious with the words philosophers worry about. For example, not many centuries ago it was acceptable to say, "I saw a spirit on yonder ridge"; and at present, in parts of the world where a prescientific explanation of eclipses still reigns, it is acceptable to say, "I know that Rahu swallowed the moon yesterday." Today, to sophisticated Westerners, such uses of the words "see" and "know" are not permissible. And the change is surely a good one; more adequate criteria for identifying and describing facts of observation have been gained. This process has not ceased. It is reasonably certain that the accepted use of all philosophical words a hundred years hence will have been noticeably transformed, wisely or unwisely, from their accepted uses today. Can a philosopher, aware of this fact, avoid trying to tell which alternatives to current idioms will guide the course of change along fruitful lines? So far as in him lies, will he not "substitute conscious direction for unconscious drift?"[5]

In philosophical parlance, is it possible to separate a "descriptive" analysis of language from a "normative" analysis? The champions of ordinary language urge us to engage in the former, while carefully avoiding all taint of the latter. But will not every philosopher want the part he plays in the living intercommunication between persons and groups to contribute toward an outcome in which language fills its role as effectively as it might? He cannot help serving either this end or a less salutary one. Indeed, when we view in this light what the ordinary language philosophers are doing, is it not obvious that in their own fashion they share this revisionary aim? They are not just describing given linguistic uses; they are also revising our habits of speech in the direction of the ideal goals that seem to them worth realizing. All of them seek to introduce greater clarity into those habits and to make available richer resources, through detecting important distinctions; were this not the case their labor would be superfluous. And the system-builders are seeking a coherent organization of linguistic uses, realizing thus the further virtues that wise theory can foster.

Over and above these general considerations, there are two quite specific reasons why a philosopher can hardly fill his function without proposing changes in established uses.

One is that current uses, being multifarious and logically undisciplined, often have contradictory implications for the problems with which he is concerned; he cannot offer any solution to them without violating some established idioms. Take the problem of the relation between mind and body. Current modes of speaking include familiar ones that imply the independence of mind (or soul) from the body; people refer to the former as "inhabiting" the latter, and feel no incongruity when it is said of a person that his body is sickly but his mind is not sick. They also, however, include phrases that imply an intimate interdependence of mind and body: "Her eyes were full of sadness"; "his chest heaved with rage." Here we are talking about mental feelings that are also physical; there is no hint that the mind as a separate entity is making the eyes or the chest an instrument for its expression. Such a situation reveals the fact that the ordinary uses of today embody philosophical theories from the past, disclosing their persistent conflicts as well as whatever agreements have been reached. One must propose changes in some of these uses if one is to be a responsible philosopher.

The other reason is that the pace of world events constantly reveals situations in which concepts fundamental to their understanding and guidance desperately call for reinterpretation—and the analytic talent of philosophers is needed in achieving a wise reinterpretation. For example, the concept of "free enterprise" in economics once had a fairly clear and consistent meaning; now much confusion surrounds it. Yet few wish to abandon it entirely; how should it be reinterpreted in order to become a realistic and effective instrument in our economic thinking? Or take such concepts as "the right of peoples to self-determination" and "noninterference in the internal affairs of other nations." In abstract form everyone accepts these principles as sound. But it is increasingly clear that there are severe limits to their feasible application—in fact, today, no nation can help interfering in the internal affairs of others. The problem challenging the political philosopher is how to construe these concepts in such a way that they will serve as wise guides in meeting the delicate and dangerous situations that have to be dealt with by their aid. In all these cases an appeal to ordinary uses would be ironic, but a philosopher who combines analytic skill with perceptive understanding of the human issues at stake can make a unique and vital contribution.

Let us then engage boldly in this revisionary task, alert for promising linguistic uses that have not hitherto been learned or taught, but which, when people have come to realize their advantages, will supplement or replace the uses at present taken for granted. Shall we allow the danger of falling into speculative extravagances keep us from performing one of the greatest tasks that the philosopher can perform—the task of anticipating and creating happier ways of speaking than those now current?

One thing is clear: Not only have all philosophers essayed this pioneering role at some points, but a few of the geniuses of history have filled it with astonishing skill. They have proposed novel uses of language through which a more adequate understanding of some significant area of experience could be expressed and effectively communicated. Aristotle is the outstanding example in Western philosophy. As we noted in Chapter I, he proposed sufficiently fertile uses of a dozen or more key words so that subsequent European thought for eighteen hundred years followed his proposals in its thinking about the world—indeed, the generally accepted scientific picture of the universe throughout that period was framed in his axioms and categories. Augustine and Thomas Aquinas achieved something analogous in the field of religious philosophy. Descartes is the thinker who has filled this role most successfully during the last four hundred years. When one forgets the perennially intriguing problems arising from his metaphysical dualism or his theology and concentrates on the radical departure from earlier tradition that impressed his contemporaries, one feels the same amazement at his anticipatory power that Aristotle's achievement arouses. He conceived the world of nature as a mathematical structure exhibiting a uniform mechanical order throughout, thus encouraging exact formulation of the quantitative laws and correlations that might be discovered. The social as well as the physical sciences would not have become what they are today without their heritage from him; its importance escapes us only because it is taken so completely for granted.

The outstanding example in our day is Wittgenstein himself. When one turns from his teaching about ordinary language to his practice as a pioneering philosopher it becomes obvious that he departed rather drastically from established ways of speaking—and some of the extraordinary uses he introduced have already become current coin in philosophical discussion.

In certain cases the words themselves are new; notice the tendency among philosophers to talk about a significant step in an argument as a "move," thus reflecting the Wittgensteinian view of language as a game. Other key terms are "family of meanings" and "paradigm." The distinctive flavor of the emphasis on ordinary speech is revealed in several idioms that have become popular; instead of the quasi-technical "analyze," philosophers now often "unpack" a concept, and instead of "clarifying" a confused area of thought, they now "tidy it up." In other cases traditional words are retained while their meanings are transformed. Consider the crucial words "logic," "rule," and even "philosophy" itself. Thinkers who were trained in an earlier era did not learn to use these words in the novel senses they have now acquired, largely through Wittgenstein's influence. The idea that logic is concerned with the grammar of discourse in all the varied situations in which it is employed would have appeared a quite incredible idea till the linguistic philosophers of today made it a plausible one. Similarly with the other two words. In earlier days it would have seemed very strange to call "philosophy" an analysis of ordinary language to discover the "rules governing its use." The champions of this philosophy can hardly commit themselves to a position that would make it inexplicable and illegitimate for such a work as Wittgenstein's *Investigations* to appear on the speculative stage and to communicate its ideas successfully.

Pondering these striking historical instances, we must try to solve two puzzles that the ordinary language orientation may make more puzzling than they really are.

One of them poses the question: How is it possible for a new philosophical insight to be communicated? It will be expressed in non-technical words, and the thinkers committed to this orientation assume that hearers or readers will simply take those words in their accustomed meaning. How then can any novel idea ever be shared with other people? Yet nothing is more certain than that this kind of communication does take place. How does it? How did Wittgenstein himself accomplish it?

The answer is not difficult if we forget a priori quandaries and look at what happened. In his case, the new idea that he wanted to convey was couched in arresting phrases; it was given homely illustration from all sorts of human situations; it was clarified by being used in treating various philosophical problems. Others responded to it; they found the insight promising and the method fruitful. They began to think in the concepts it provides; they gradually revealed its significant differences from the philosophies that preceded it; they applied it to many areas of human thought and especially to the traditional branches of philosophy. The fact that it involved a drastic departure from the established uses of several key words did not prevent them from coming to understand it in this way and making it their own. In the light of such an example it is clear that language can awaken in the reader or hearer an experience similar to that of the writer or speaker, however novel that experience may be. Of course there is no advance guarantee that any such daring venture will succeed. But the history of philosophy shows that it sometimes does succeed; a great genius meets no insuperable difficulty in communicating a new insight to those who come after him.

The other puzzle arises from a famous remark of Wittgenstein when responding to the question: "In what state does the philosopher who has been freed from his errors by turning to ordinary language find himself?" His answer was, in effect: "He is left just where he was before; nothing has changed." * This is a very astonishing answer. But many of his followers adopted a similar position, to the extent of maintaining that when philosophy has done its work things are left as they were, the only difference being that confusion has been replaced by clear understanding. One is reminded of a dictum occasionally asserted by others, namely that the

* See G. J. Warnock, *English Philosophy Since 1900* (London: Oxford Univ. Press, 1958), pp. 86 ff.

wise philosopher simply says what everybody already knows. This is a bit like contending that nothing really is changed when a baby is born except that he is now outside the cramping prison of the womb instead of inside it.

In any case, when we look at Wittgenstein's own example, an illuminating addition to these statements can be made. It is one thing to say what everybody already consciously knows and fully understands—and if this is the case it is superfluous to say it; it is quite another thing to say what everyone will gradually realize to be so *when you have said it clearly and persuasively,* and when under its guidance the new universe in which the hearer will then live has been experienced. It is in this sense that the great philosopher says what everybody knows. Such a thinker does not just answer questions that have been asked in the past; he changes people's minds, including their ways of asking and answering all questions. They find themselves living in a new dimension of reality.

To summarize the central truth which the philosopher intrigued by the appeal to established idioms may forget: The ordinary use of a given word or phrase becomes incorrect rather than correct, if by employing some non-ordinary use a speaker can lead others to a more adequate mastery of what he is talking about than adherence to the ordinary use would assure. Such a departure will not mislead if it is happily attuned to the hearers' growing experience. In the case of words that are philosophically important, his challenge is to envision the richest role that they might fill—including their pioneering possibilities as well as their proven power to communicate lessons learned in the past.

If these conclusions are persuasive, the debate between the champions of an ideal reconstruction of language and the defenders of ordinary language is easily settled. Each side has been under a deceptive illusion. The actual criterion of both, clearly revealed in their practice, is a wise balance between the ordinary and a more ideal use of the words by which we communicate. And is not the necessity of such a balance now obvious? Without due respect for actual uses, as one finds them currently employed, any proposal of an altered use will have little chance of being accepted—and if accepted, may cause misunderstanding in case it conflicts too sharply with the uses to which people are accustomed. Without sensitivity to more ideal possibilities, there would be no point in making any proposal at all; one would be content to leave present uses as they are, with all their ambiguities and inconsistencies, expressing whatever degree of enlightment or stupidity they may. Let each thinker therefore, aware of this twofold need, put into words as best he can whatever he is eager to share with others, recognizing his dependence on the resources of language as they now exist but never allowing himself to be bound by them.

VII

One is tempted to ask how far this outcome can be accepted by the ordinary language philosophy without forsaking presuppositions that are essential to it. But to raise such a question would imply that the philosophy under appraisal can be tied down to a fixed set of presuppositions and that we, standing off in Olympian detachment, can pronounce which of them are sound and which are mistaken. This is hardly the role of a seeker for philosophic understanding. Instead, let us extend this inquiry and continue to search both for further promising roles that the method of appeal to ordinary language might fill, and for conclusions that put the most severe strain on its presuppositions as they have thus far been revealed. Each reader will judge for himself where the horizon of this philosophy must be left behind, and will develop his own insight as to how it might best advance toward a fuller realization of its constructive possibilities. Surely the promise of an approach to philosophy through the study of language is far from exhausted.

A hopeful guiding question to raise is this: Why is it that linguistic uses already well established need continually to be improved?

Two considerations are worth reflecting on as we look for an answer. One is that, prima facie at least, ordinary language is always the language of a particular and limited culture, whereas the concern of philosophers has been and surely will continue to be with issues that are universally human —the problems of man as man. Therefore, in order to express this concern, we have to transcend the limitations of ordinary language as from time to time they come to light. The other is that we cannot abolish the distinction between experience and reality on the one hand, and how we have come to talk about experience and reality on the other; this distinction seems to be quite indispensable in philosophy as elsewhere. Thus, established uses of language need to be corrected by our growing experience of reality.

As an illustration that reveals the challenge of both these considerations, take the concept of logical necessity—the necessity exhibited in the structure of any valid inference. Philosophers have perennially meant by this phrase a reality which is a priori and therefore independent of all empirical facts, including the variations of linguistic habit between one society and another. They have thus taken for granted that logical necessity is a universal norm, standing above the customary uses of "necessity" and its synonyms in any particular tongue, and providing a criterion for judging them. But the ordinary language philosophers are naturally tempted to suppose that the phrase means what it does because it has acquired its established use in whatever tongue happens to be employed. What the logician knows when he knows the necessary laws of logic—so Norman Malcolm affirmed in the early days of the movement—is simply such facts as that people use interchangeably the statement "This is larger than that," and the statement "That is smaller than this." * Such an affirmation appears to assume not only that no normative reality transcending all languages is involved, but also that our established uses of "larger" and "smaller" in contemporary English are all we need to appeal to. Other phrases expressing logical necessity would be dealt with in the same way, such as: "This surface is red all over and hence it cannot be green all over"; or "This object is a member of class A, all of whose members are in class B, and therefore this object is in class B."

But this is not quite what the champion of ordinary uses intends to maintain; he is aware that we do distinguish between necessities (if they may be called such) that rest merely on the conventions of this or that language and the necessities that hold for human reason as such. In Chinese any idea capable of being expressed must be such that it can be grounded on one or more of the two hundred and fourteen Chinese radicals, but this is hardly a necessity of human thought at large.

How do the ordinary language philosophers believe that this distinction can be made, and the limitations set by varying linguistic conventions overcome? One way—and it has been adopted by some—is to plead as follows: (1) We are dealing with concepts, not merely with words, and a concept is intrinsically universal; (2) When we look around we do find conceptual uses that are not limited to any particular tongue. Much of the language employed by people is a universal medium of communication, shared by all cultures. If one were to object: "But your method obviously identifies each concept with a set of words as used in some particular language, and this shows what sort of thing you think a concept is," they will reply: "These words can be translated into other languages; what we have in mind as a concept is the meaning thus shown to be common to various tongues."

* See his paper "Are Necessary Propositions Merely Verbal?" in *Mind,* Vol. 49 (April, 1940), especially pp. 197 f., 199 f.

All right. But a crucial question emerges here. What concepts *can* plausibly claim to be universal—to be capable of precise translation from one language to another—and what needs to be done in the case of words that at present can make no such claim?

We find that in some realms, e.g., that of the exact sciences, this claim appears to be justified. Mathematics is a universal language, capable of translation or of transplantation without loss from one tongue to another. Hence in the areas progressively mastered by exact science the limitations of this or that particular language are left behind; there can arise an international society using a medium of communication that meets its needs so far as this special sphere of interest is concerned. When we think of ordinary uses in that medium, the presupposition that we are dealing with universal concepts seems to be sound.

However, in the realm with which philosophy is concerned, it has been a conviction of the ordinary language school that the words which need to be clarified are in a different case. Their meaning is revealed in their everyday uses by people with no technical sophistication. And it is evident that these meanings are in many cases incapable, at least as yet, of being accurately translated from one tongue to another. They have no precise equivalents; it seems therefore that when they are employed no universal concept is present. The most obvious illustrations are found in the words that lie at the heart of the ideological conflicts dividing the world. "Freedom," "democracy," "individual rights," have meanings in the Western languages and also in the languages of the Communist world, but the two meanings in each case are quite different. When we turn to issues involving the ways of thinking of the Occident and the Orient, it appears that this is equally true of many words that arouse no ideological fervor. These words cannot be precisely translated. Universal concepts seem thus to be absent from the area dominated by these contrasts; such concepts are yet to be discovered or brought into being.

In the presence of this challenge the ordinary language philosopher of course rejects the quite brazen linguistic imperialism that would tempt him to say: "The meaning of the concepts involved in these issues is wholly determined by established uses in my own language. Hence if those who speak other languages have different ideas, they are wrong; so far as their words embody such differences they are meaningless." But the temptation to a less obvious imperialism is not so easy to reject, especially when the meaning of logical and metaphysical words, which thinkers have long taken for granted as underlying all sound reasoning, is involved. Here it is natural to assume that a careful analysis carried out in the medium and with the resources of one's own language can disclose the essential structure of all language—that no detailed examination of the structural differences revealed in other tongues is needed. Strawson and Hampshire seem to adopt this position. Strawson recognizes that there are such disparities between one language and another, but his whole argument reflects the assumption that an analysis in English can uncover the necessary conditions of communication by anyone about anything.* Hampshire's conviction is similar.†

Is this assumption justified? Can a philosopher hold it when he has mastered languages with a radically different syntax from his own? The grammar of the Chinese language has no copula and does not even recognize subject and predicate terms as Westerners understand them; the needs of communication are met in a different way. The "universal" pattern that would be discovered by examining it will therefore diverge considerably from the pattern reached by analysis of a Western language, with the long-developed theories of philosophical logic embodied in it.

How then should the task of locating or creating truly universal concepts be carried out? We shall return to this problem later in another setting; here a brief sketch of a proposed solution must do. The philosopher who adopts it will simply open his mind, as best he can, to the distinctive modes of thinking and talking in other cultures, hampered by no rigid assumptions. He will seek to discover through such an exploration what the logical fabric of this or that alien language actually is. As he proceeds with this task he will gradually learn where its structure diverges from that of his own tongue and where it is the same. He will thus be gaining insight into the universal basis of human thought, and also distinguishing more clearly the varying conventional patterns that have here and there developed on that basis. Such insight is of course never final or complete. But by this route progress is possible toward an understanding, by philosophers from each culture, of how the universe has come to be structured in all cultures. Today, with rapidly increasing interaction between peoples all over the world, and with the resources of the growing science of comparative linguistics, there is an unparalleled opportunity to accelerate this progress.

* P. F. Strawson, *Individuals: An Essay in Descriptive Metaphysics* (New York: The Humanities Press, 1960). Note especially pp. 148–151.

† Stuart Hampshire, *Thought and Action* (New York: The Viking Press 1960), especially pp. 9, 11–18, 39 f., 54–58, 66–68. Hampshire's main difference with Strawson is that he is not committed to the acceptance of any changeless linguistic structure; he holds that the basic categories as well as others have a history.

An intriguing future opens before the ordinary language philosophy when its method is viewed in this wider setting. The challenge appears in two forms, each of which holds enticing possibilities. For one, it is not necessary to confine ourselves to the lessons that can be learned by appealing to ordinary uses in our own tongue, which inevitably reflect a limited cultural form of life. Since every linguistic medium has its illuminating parallels and contrasts, why not seek the light that might be thrown on philosophical problems by ordinary idioms everywhere, in any language—especially the idioms that have developed in languages with a very different structure from our own? For the other, it is also unnecessary to confine the philosophical theories of linguistic uses, now hopefully developing, to the arena of uses in a single language. It is obviously possible—though immensely difficult—to work our way toward a theory that would be all-inclusive as well as systematic. The vision opens before us of a conceptual scheme that would make a place for the significant lessons the structures of all tongues might teach.

At this point the second consideration, which has been waiting in abeyance, confronts us. We said that thinkers need to distinguish between reality and the way they have thus far come to talk about it. For reality is not so obliging that it will meet us on our present terms or else leave us alone. This is in fact the ultimate reason why current uses in any language always need to be improved. So far as we are alive and alert, we are continually learning more about reality than we knew before and are revising our ways of talking accordingly. How do we tell which revisions are wise and which are not? The criterion is always our widening experience, as it suggests and compels revisions of established idioms to render them more adequate to whatever reality is involved.

But a difficult problem must be faced. How does the appeal to this criterion work, in the ranges of experience that are of special concern to philosophers? In everyday situations and in scientific inquiry we all know how it works. However, when the widening experience is such as to render plausible a revised meaning for some philosophical concept, we have to consider what the appeal to it requires and in what form the relevant reality appears. When facing this problem it is important to avoid assuming that by "reality" some static metaphysical structure must be meant.

At present we shall content ourselves with an answer that merely extends our appraisal of the ordinary language philosophy; in Chapter IX a fuller answer will be attempted. The champion of that viewpoint is tempted to assume that since his present presuppositions about such concepts express a long-evolved cultural orientation, no enlarged acquaintance with reality is needed. But if he succumbs to this temptation he will remain imprisoned in those presuppositions and will fail to share the insight that a challenge from some other thinker to revise them might bring. The prime task of philosophic understanding is to catch any such insight and, if it has been awkwardly expressed, to give it a happier articulation. It may turn out to be inconsequential; but there is a chance that without it our growing comprehension of the universe would be the poorer.

The following illustration should be peculiarly suitable to clarify this answer because it involves the meaning of the concept "reality" itself.

Among the startling statements which have been made by those who probe beneath the surface of things is one that affirms that "time is unreal." In due course this assertion fell into the hands of G. E. Moore, who translated it into the assumed equivalent, "there are no temporal events." The blithe simplicity of this translation may captivate us. Let us see, however, if it does not have a fatal defect. The persistently challenging position which has over the centuries been articulated in this assertion is that of the mystic; but Moore's translation gives not the least hint of what the mystic is trying to say when he denies the reality of time.* He means that the entire temporal realm is in an important sense unreal, because to one who has entered the mystic experience it acquires a different total form in virtue of which everything about it, including its temporal aspect, is changed. If he is philosophically competent, he will spell out what he means by clarifying his concept of reality and expounding in detail his view of events that occur in time. For a criticism of his assertion to be relevant it must express an appreciative understanding of such a perspective on the temporal world.

To be sure, the mystic is rightly challenged to answer any questions that a non-mystic philosopher confronted by this perspective is moved to ask, and he will do so as best he can. But it would be unrealistic to expect all who have gained such a vision to be expert at articulating the insight that it involves. The philosopher who wants to understand may have to help in that achievement, and his guiding maxim will be: Search out and master with sensitivity the distinctive experience that lies behind this way of speaking and is provocatively interpreted by it! If the speaker's attempt to communicate it is clumsy, find a way to express it better, and to bring it

---

* It is true that the thinkers Moore primarily had in mind were not the mystics but the neo-Hegelian idealists of the late nineteenth century. These philosophers believed they could show (on their own presuppositions, of course) that the concept of time is self-contradictory.

into coherent relation with other instructive experiences. The pertinence of this maxim is especially obvious in the present case because the mystic vision is not as esoteric as it sometimes seems. Many people without metaphysical sophistication have vivid moments in which the claims of time as we usually view it fade away, and they sometimes sense that these moments are illuminating rather than deceptive. An insight that transcends that view of time may contain truth; this possibility is confirmed by the fact that one's power to deal wisely with temporal vicissitudes may be strengthened rather than weakened by it. Westerners often think of mystics as withdrawn from the world; but this is not the case with all. When describing the mystic in *The Two Sources of Morality and Religion,* Bergson remarks: "There is an exceptional, deeprooted mental healthiness which is readily recognizable. It is expressed in the bent for action, the faculty of adapting and readapting oneself to circumstances, in firmness combined with suppleness, in the prophetic discernment of what is possible and what is not, . . . in a word, supreme good sense." [6] In the light of these considerations, is it not clear that a translation of "Time is unreal" into nonsense is a serious mistranslation? The experience that lies behind this assertion deserves to be understood.

Reality thus contains much more than our current ways of talking about it have grasped, and through openness to new possibilities—in the large as well as in the small—those ways can be steadily improved. It is doubtless true that significant improvements in the large come rarely; few in any generation become successful philosophical pioneers. Nonetheless, the distinctive role of philosophy can hardly be understood without recognizing the essential function of the pioneer, and realizing that others may not fall as far short of that function as one is apt to think.

4

Existentialism

What is it to be an "existentialist"? When a thinker thinks "existentially," how is he thinking?

One quandary can be disposed of quickly. It arises from lack of agreement as to how narrow or broad a meaning should be given this term in dealing with the current philosophical scene. Some think of existentialism as the philosophy of Jean-Paul Sartre (In his pre-Marxian period) and his followers; some extend the term to include several other continental philosophers, among whom Martin Heidegger, Karl Jaspers, and Gabriel Marcel are the best known. Others give the word a still wider scope, embracing all thinkers since Kierkegaard who have been deeply influenced by him. It is in this last and broadest sense that "existentialism" and its cognate terms will be used in this chapter.

The existentialists have ready a capsule answer to our question: A philosopher thinks existentially when he has accepted Sartre's famous maxim "Existence precedes essence" and has made it the basis of his philosophy. Heidegger, it is true, has rejected this maxim, but if it is carefully construed it does express in succinct form the core of the existentialist position.

What does the maxim mean? In the long history of philosophy such a dictum would have been construed in various ways. The medieval nominalist might have said it; he would have meant that particular objects, e.g., animals, are in the nature of the case prior to the universal concept "animal," which is simply their common name. The modern empiricist might have said it; he would have meant that perceived facts are prior to the general laws that explain them. When the existentialist says it, however, he means something more and different. He is thinking of *man's* essence and existence. And he is saying that when a person tries to concentrate on the universal essence of man instead of on the living and poignant existence directly exemplified in himself, he is turning away from human reality instead of growing toward a sound understanding of it. By this route one will inevitably find man's essence in his faculty of reason, and will employ merely rational thinking in the endeavor to understand it.

A man, however, is a full person, not just a cognitive mind, and it requires all the resources of a full person to understand him. To win these resources one must face the fact of one's own existence, with its emotional involvements and its fateful possibilities of weal and woe. Everyone has been thrown into the turbulent current of life, and whether he is aware of it or not this predicament is the determinative factor in all that he does—including his apparently rational thinking. Until one recognizes, in this setting, that existence precedes essence, one cannot hope to understand man or the deeper realities of human experience.

I

For a long period the background of the existential point of view lay almost entirely in the area of religious thought. Western theology, ever since the time of Augustine at least, has been profoundly influenced by the existential orientation, but philosophers—with few exceptions—followed a separate course until, under the challenge of Kierkegaard and his successors, they were forced to take the existential way of thinking into account.

Indeed, the course they followed during the two hundred years after the birth of modern philosophy—i.e., from the first half of the seventeenth to the first half of the nineteenth century—revealed increasing confidence in the power of reason to answer by its own resources all the questions that philosophers are moved to raise. The new methods of mathematical rationalism and empirical induction then being developed proved so successful that thinkers were captivated by their promise; and when their limitations gradually became clear, the transcendental rationalism of Kant and his successors seemed to provide the key to philosophic understanding. This long epoch of intellectual assurance reached its peak in Hegel (1770–1831), who was convinced that reason can attain absolute truth and rightfully assign to everything in the universe its ultimate place, and who thus stands out as the philosophical rationalist par excellence of the modern West.

After Hegel came the turning point. The thinker who initiated the radical reaction that occurred was Sören Kierkegaard, whose provocative writings have been the fountainhead of both philosophical and theological existentialism during the century since his day. In his early twenties Kierkegaard became an enthusiastic devotee of Hegel. And when, a few years later, he decisively broke with that aggressive champion of reason, the break was at one central point only; the rest of his predecessor's framework he retained and skillfully adapted to his own ends. He held firmly to Hegel's guiding aim and to the basic concepts of his system, but he resolutely rebelled against its pervasive rationalism.

Let us make full use of this clue. The essential continuity between the two thinkers lies in the fact that the dominant concern of both is with man's capacity to leave behind the limitations of his present experience and to grow toward the realization of truth in its wholeness. For both, this growth is a "dialectical" process involving certain distinguishable "stages" and "moments"; it aims at a "synthesis" in which the steps that have led to it are not lost but are preserved in their authentic meaning. Moreover, for both, insight is communicated to others by progressively transforming their experience; the thinker who has gained a higher illumination leads the common man, step by step, from where he now is to the final truth, which he will then realize as the ultimate truth for himself.

The crucial difference between the two philosophers is that for Hegel this growth is a rational process, revealing a logical necessity throughout; for Kierkegaard it is an existential deepening, which involves the reconstruction of one's entire self, including one's ways of reasoning along with everything else. Hence Hegel's dialectic is "abstract" while Kierkegaard's is "concrete"; Hegel's "moments" are logically determined steps in the dialectic while Kierkegaard's are moments of "decision" by one's growing personality as a whole; Hegel's synthesis is a systematic self-disclosure of the Absolute while Kierkegaard's is the intuitive realization that can only take place in the mind and heart of each individual. We must pause briefly over each of these vital contrasts.

Nothing is clearer to a perceptive student of Hegel than that he wished his dialectic to be a dialectic of man's living experience, and he firmly believed that he had made it so. But Kierkegaard was sure that this belief was mistaken. To him, it seemed clear that Hegel's root error is the presupposition that human existence can be contained in a logical concept. When one falls into this error, life is reduced to a sheer abstraction and its concrete reality has slipped away. As Kierkegaard often expressed it, reality is essentially "ethical reality"—that is, it is a living process that decides how far this or that person succeeds in realizing his moral selfhood. When the nature of existence is understood in this setting, it "constitutes the highest interest of the existing individual, and his interest in his existence constitutes his reality. What reality is cannot be expressed in the language of abstraction." [1] In short, through the fateful actuality of existing one becomes, or fails to become, one's true self, and nothing was clearer to Kierkegaard than that the surest way to fail in this crucial task is to flee from the inexorable challenge into the realm of logical abstractions. That way lies, not life for the soul, but death.

At first sight this interest might seem to be an intolerably self-centered concern, at which a philosopher with a social conscience ought to be appalled. But Kierkegaard's response to such a reproach must be clearly grasped. It is precisely because one has become aware of a deep-seated self-centeredness sundering him from God and his fellows, which his rational faculty has been sedulously concealing, that this decisive interest in his own ethical reality grips him. The self thus enslaved must find salvation. And Kierkegaard insists again and again that if one rejects the transcendent claim of this interest, one does not thereby become free from bondage; instead, one's sinful egoism and incapacity for love are buried in the dark recesses of the soul, where liberation becomes more difficult.

For Kierkegaard, the "moments" in this dialectic are not steps in a self-unfolding logic as they were for Hegel; they are moment-ous crises, in each of which an existing individual makes his decisions. If he passes from the "esthetic" stage, where he is the prey of external enticements to immediate enjoyment, to the "ethical" stage of responsible freedom, it is not because of any logical necessity but because, in awareness of the inescapable stakes, he actively decides for the latter way of life instead of the former. Likewise with his passage from the ethical stage to that of religion, which is the last of the major stages of existential realization that Kierkegaard recognizes.

These decisions express a commitment of one's whole personality, and each of them transforms one's entire experience.

At such revealing points as these then, Kierkegaard kept the shell of the Hegelian system while revolutionizing its substance. And the radical reorientation is displayed as strikingly in his style as in his conclusions. When he faced his task as an author he saw that the existential approach to philosophy requires a novel mode of communication with the reader. Most people have not learned what real happiness is, nor are they aware that it can only be achieved by the route of existential realization. They fear to take the decisive step that would lead them to it, lest they lose the transitory happiness they now have and the illusory security it brings. Kierkegaard's problem was: How shall I write so that my readers cannot escape the challenge to take this step—so that their whole existence will be transformed in the direction of authentic selfhood?

The solution, to use his own words, was that communication must be "indirect." Since his prime purpose was not to give a reader intellectual instruction but to arouse him to shake off his lethargy and venture beyond his present horizon, the predicament in choosing and arranging words was how to attract him— but to do it "without deception, to attract the higher but repel the lower in a man." [2] And Kierkegaard was sure that two things are essential to this kind of communication. For one, he must accept others as and where they now are, and lead them with the keenest vision he can achieve as far toward existential realization as they are able to go. For the other, this is only possible when their freedom and their "individual subjectivity" are fully respected; he must communicate an uncoerced awareness that he understands them better in the deepest dimension of their existence than they have thus far understood themselves. Only under such genial persuasion will they muster the courage to turn from the relative ends they have thus far been pursuing, place in jeopardy their present mode of existence, and undergo an inward rebirth with whatever it may involve— the courage, in short, to take the leap from the fragmented selves they now are to the new and unified selves they can become.

What was Kierkegaard's significant contribution, as he wrote the books that came fast and furiously from his pen? Viewed in historical perspective, it was twofold: (1) a set of keen analyses in the area of depth psychology, which became indispensable to later philosophical existentialism; and (2) a restatement of Christian theology, which became an inspiring and fertile source of later theological existentialism.

The first of these has been thus described by his outstanding interpreter among American philosophers: "The intellectual significance of the Kierkegaardian literature . . . consists in [its] mapping out the sphere of the inner life, the subjective life of the emotions, with constant reference to the ideal." [3] And indeed this mapping of the inner life is rich in detail and profound insight. The key to the map lies in the conviction that life is basically a process of choosing and deciding, and that underlying all other choices is the choice of self. No one can escape deciding explicitly or implicitly the question, What person shall I be? Kierkegaard was well aware that most people are not conscious of making any such solemn decision. Nonetheless, everyone does make it, and the tragedy in cases where it is done without consciousness is that the decision will be the result of chance; the high potentialities of selfhood that might have been realized will not be realized. It was Kierkegaard's further conviction that this process constitutes the only setting in which the quest for philosophical truth can hopefully be pursued, for one's entire universe takes its form in accordance with the nature of whatever self one is choosing to be. Thus the model of a statement significant for philosophy is not to be found in science—as the analytic thinker tends to assume—but rather in statements through which the choice of self is expressed, with its commitment to a supreme value and a final destiny.

When these convictions are adopted, every branch of philosophy is radically transformed. In epistemology, for instance, "knowledge" can no longer serve as the central concept. Because of the influence of science, Western thinkers usually mean by "knowledge" a clear grasp of the actual state of affairs in this or that region of experience, which gives reliable guidance to action. But the existential viewpoint requires a more inclusive concept, within which such an achievement fills its important but limited function. The most appropriate word for expressing this concept is "realization." By it is meant the conscious quest of a person for wholeness, revealing various degrees of cognitive clarity, of emotional stability, and of effective control of action, according to the stage that his progress has reached. The subject that "knows" is participating in this quest, and the nature and significance of his knowledge cannot be unaffected by it.

But Kierkegaard's second contribution is equally significant, and it points in the direction of present-day theological existentialism. True, much of his insight, even in the case of religion, is essentially independent of the sectarian framework within which it is usually presented. However, his probing of man's spiritual potentialities and the way to their fulfillment did lead him to the specifically Christian commitment that pervades his theology; in his case the two contributions were existentially bound together. He was sure that the greatest among the ancients, namely Socrates, for whom he felt a deep reverence, achieved the stage of "immanent" religion; but there is a higher stage of "transcendent" religion, which can only be realized through suffering. This realization appeared to Kierkegaard attainable in Christianity alone. In the experience of truly "becoming a Christian" one finds one's self, but at the cost of a harrowing ordeal in the depths of the soul.

For two-thirds of a century Kierkegaard was almost forgotten, but during that period several bold ideas appeared whose influence on contemporary existentialism has been very significant. Three great thinkers reinforced, each in his own way, a major aspect of its orientation. All of them, in fact, strengthened its crucial insistence that human reason is not independent, as it claims to be, but is under the sway of emotional and volitional forces. First, there was the explosive challenge of Nietzsche's philosophy—now often described as a form of existentialism—uncovering as it did, with devastating sarcasm, some of the rationalizations of previous philosophers and drawing the conclusion that what these thinkers announce as a quest for objective truth is a more or less disguised will-to-power. Then there was the disconcerting historical analysis of Marx, reducing men's ways of thinking in general and their social theories in particular to protective supports of the economic interests they have come to share. There were also the cumulative revelations of modern anthropology, showing persuasively that how people reason about their world reflects the values that shape the culture to which they belong. These revelations were generalized in the so-called "sociology of knowledge," with its doctrine that all theories about man inevitably reflect interests other than the concern for truth—interests whose distorting influence can only be overcome by an impartial awareness of their presence. Finally, and most important of all, there was the revolutionary psychology of Freud, supplying a wealth of detailed confirmation for a basic postulate in all these doctrines—namely, that some of the forces determining men's beliefs are operating below the level of the conscious mind. And Freud developed his own method for lifting these forces into the light of clear perception so that a unified personality with full self-understanding can be achieved. The intimate relation between psychotherapy and the existential orientation is attested by the fact that when psychoanalysts seek the best way in which to integrate their findings with other phases of human experience they naturally fall into the language of existentialism. Carl Rogers, for example, describes the profound readjustment that results from successful psychotherapy by the phrase "existential living." [4]

Today all these and other historical forces* have converged, and it is not surprising that existentialism has become a vigorous and spreading movement. So far as philosophy is concerned, Heidegger, Jaspers, Sartre, Marcel, and others have dealt with its traditional problems in an existential perspective, and younger disciples are expanding their work. Outside the universities, in France and to a lesser degree elsewhere, the field of literature is expressing an existential orientation, and earlier writers like Dostoyevsky are being posthumously annexed. The distinctive feature of what is vaguely called "modern" art is that its underlying philosophy is existential: it does not hesitate to portray human emotion in all its grief, its joy, its fury, and its untamed fantasies. As regards religion and theology, the whole Protestant world is being radically transformed under the guidance of existential presuppositions, while prominent efforts are made to restate the foundations of Jewish and Catholic theology in a way that reflects the existential approach.

II

No detailed exposition of even the best-known existentialists is required for our purpose. But before turning to a critical and constructive appraisal of their position we do need to understand more fully the unique characteristics of their way of thinking, characteristics that sharply demarcate it from other Western philosophies.

Indeed, existentialism is not only intellectually unacceptable to opposing schools; it confounds and disturbs them. With each other, they can argue on some common ground; with the existentialist, no common ground seems available. We may think here especially of the analytic philosophers, who are on the whole more disturbed than others by the existentialist's drastic departures from what they have confidently taken for granted. They feel nothing less than that the existential way of thinking corrupts philosophy—that by its very nature it exhibits a hopeless aberration from standards essential to all rational thought.

The existentialist, however, refuses to admit that he has given himself

---

* At the turn of the century, there also appeared the aggressive pragmatism of William James in America and Ferdinand Schiller in England, maintaining that truth is nothing but a set of human beliefs that successfully work; and that belief, in moral and religious matters at least, is the product of our "passional" nature quite as much as of our need to respect intellectual standards.

over to slipshod and irresponsible thinking; there are, he insists, important realities that cannot be caught in the analyst's net and he must honestly face them. "If you can appreciate what we are about," he will add, "you will see that we even prize systematic analysis as much as any philosopher does. But our analyses are *existential* analyses—that is, their character is what it is because its presuppositions are existential and must be understood as such. Only if you judge them in terms of other presuppositions will you find them loose and illogical."

So the existentialist is not embarrassed by the analytic thinker's dismayed condemnation. In fact, from his standpoint it is the analyst who ought to be embarrassed, because the existentialist is sure that *he* is dealing with philosophical problems in a more inclusive perspective—a perspective which allows for everything that other philosophers are concerned about but gives it its truthful place in a larger whole. And the distinctive nature of what he calls an existential analysis arises from the pervasive presence of that larger whole.

Let us examine three especially provocative presuppositions reflected in these existentialist convictions. Can we so interpret them that they will become intelligible to non-existential philosophers?

The first of these is concisely expressed in Kierkegaard's oft-quoted assertion that "truth is subjectivity." In the eyes of other schools of philosophy, to accept this doctrine is to abandon truth completely, for whatever else may be said about it, it is necessarily objective. But what the existentialist means by this shocking assertion is that the realm of objective truth falls within the dynamic totality of subjective truth, not vice versa. He does not deny objective truth, nor does he impugn its value. Within limited areas, such as mathematics and the exact sciences, the ideal of objectivity is valid and can be closely approximated. But as one approaches the region where man's deeper values are at stake and his choice of self is involved, such objectivity becomes impossible and undesirable. Here one's thinking is completely existential; here truth must be individually realized. And this truth includes all other truths, such as those with which science and common sense are concerned, for it is inevitable that at each stage of progress toward a person's authentic self the objective order acquires a different meaning and takes on a different relation to the rest of his experience. His very conception of impartial truth does not remain the same; it cannot help reflecting whatever stage of deepening insight he has reached. Existential truth is then the most inclusive truth that can be attained.

A second important presupposition is that when a thinker deals with realities that are not caught by his present logical net, the prime concern must be that nothing be excluded, no matter what seeming inconsistencies may be needed to describe it. A human self, for example, proves to be a very complicated and paradoxical affair; perhaps we cannot avoid saying that each person is a single self and is also a plurality of more or less conflicting selves, even though that will not be a satisfactory final solution.

This disquieting challenge confronts us most forcefully in a phenomenon which philosophers have found easy to ignore but to which novelists and dramatists have by no means been blind. Several existentialist philosophers have realized that the perplexing region it opens up must be explored; Sartre in particular has devoted a lengthy and difficult chapter to it—the chapter on "Bad Faith" in his *Being and Nothingness*.

I refer to the phenomenon of self-deception, which can hardly be described without apparent contradiction, for when it happens a person is blinding himself to consequences that he knows are likely to happen. But there can be no doubt of its occurrence. Watch a woman in dalliance with a man whom she knows she must reject, and knowing also that what she is now doing will make the rejection harder. She hides this undeniable fact from herself in order that the enticing pursuit may continue. How does such self-deception take place? A philosopher is tempted to insist that the deceiving self and the deceived self cannot be identical, but it is very difficult to carry this explanation through successfully. Were it correct, there would be nothing that could naturally be described as *self*-deception. Moreover, when such instances are carefully observed, it seems obvious that in some sense the deceiving and the deceived self *are* the same. A woman is here making herself ignorant of something that the same woman knows.

I am far from claiming an adequate grasp of this puzzling phenomenon. However, we must try to draw the distinctions needed for an acceptable explanation, and something like the following picture might provide them: In each of us there are many emotionally potent urges which may dominate thought and action. They often conflict with each other. But besides these there is a more or less effective striving toward a coherent unity of these clashing parts. This is the mature self in process of becoming, but if it has not yet won a position of stable control it too may be in conflict with any of the lesser selves that have not accepted defeat. They are not in complete mastery, but whenever in the turbulent jockeying of our mental life one of them gains the upper hand, all clear vision of consequences which otherwise would stand out sharply fades away. What that dominant urge wants to see is seen, and what it does not want to see is brushed aside—although awareness of it is not entirely lost. One thus deceives himself; seduced by the prospect of an appealing good that can only be pursued by refusing to see the consequences, he willfully turns his mind from them.

In the case of a philosopher the temptation to self-deception takes a special form, very hard to resist. This is to refuse to acknowledge the continued presence within him of selves that do not conform to the standards of his logical self, and their distorting influence on his ways of thinking. His image of himself is the image of a wholly rational mind—or at least of a mind able to become wholly rational at a moment's notice. Hence these irrational but potent pieces of himself are a serious threat to his self-esteem; the ever-appealing way to meet the threat is to deny their presence, obvious though it is.

A third presupposition concerns the aim of an existentialist author when he writes a philosophical essay. If, as Kierkegaard realized, every person is in the process of choosing between one self and another, each choice either leading or failing to lead toward true integrity, an author cannot help being aware of the influence he is exerting on this process in his readers. This means that his quest for fuller understanding will be part of and subordinate to his desire to transform the reader's experience. In existentialist parlance, his aim will not be simply to clarify the ultimate choice that everyone is making but to entice each reader to make the wiser choice—to leave behind the inauthentic mode of existence that now holds him captive and to realize the authentic self that he might be.

At this, the non-existential philosopher is horrified. He will exclaim: "But this is to degrade philosophy into propaganda, to make it a technique for converting one's readers instead of a pursuit of impartial truth." To which the existentialist will reply: "Unless the reader awakens from his lethargy, from absorption in the routine patterns of his divided self to the determined search for true selfhood, he cannot enter the realm where significant philosophical truth is discovered. Whatever is said to him will either have the effect of leaving him where he is, in bondage to his present limitations, or will galvanize him to break from them and enter into the experience that provides the matrix for clear understanding. Is it not obvious that only the latter effect can fulfill the role of philosophy? My primary task is then to awaken each reader to live in the dynamic universe that his quest for full selfhood will open before him." F. C. Copleston is quite right in saying that "a rough definition of existentialism . . . might be that existentialism is the descriptive analysis of man as free self-transcending subject, a descriptive analysis which is itself designed to promote authentic choice." [5] Or as H. J. Blackham trenchantly remarks in *Six Existentialist Thinkers,* "the main business of this philosophy is not to answer the questions which are raised but to drive home the questions themselves until they engage the whole man and are made personal, urgent, and anguished. . . . In this sense, existentialism goes back to the beginning of philosophy and appeals to all men to awaken from their dogmatic slumbers and discover what it means to become a human being." [6]

How about this plea? To convert is surely an evil exercise of persuasive power, in philosophy as elsewhere, if it is simply conversion to the pet doctrines of the one who seeks to convert. But what if it is conversion toward that unified self in which the one converted will find his free and unfettered fulfillment? Ideally, at least, this is the kind of conversion that the existentialist intends. When he addresses other philosophers he hopes that his words may exert this kind of influence. The heart of his challenge might be thus expressed: Realize, now, that your future self may be different from your present self so far as concerns the ultimate presuppositions that constitute your philosophic mind; advance then toward that future self, in alert awareness of this process of living growth and of the momentous choice you are making!

III

An appraisal of existentialism in the widest perspective we can achieve is now in order, and we embark on it in the same mood as in our appraisal of the ordinary language philosophy. Just as in assessing the promise of that movement we assumed no vantage-point outside its presuppositions from which to launch our criticism, so with the present way of thinking. We shall share its distinctive insight as fully as we can, and our basic questions will be: What form must an appraisal take if it is to reveal the illumination existentialism can bring to philosophy and to human experience? Can we glimpse some regions in which its distinctive genius could find greater fulfillment than has been achieved thus far? Where, if anywhere, do we need to go beyond the horizon set by its presuppositions?

The answer to the first question is of course that the appraisal itself must be an existential appraisal; otherwise it would be assuming a perspective alien to the philosophy appraised and would render impossible any answer to the other questions. This is an extraordinarily difficult task. It means that we must seek to grasp the innate dialectic of existential growth—that is, the natural sequence of stages through which one passes when he accepts

the existential orientation and deepens his experience under its guidance—
and to give it the clearest and most systematic articulation we can.

The perplexing difficulty in such an enterprise is twofold. On the one
hand, since the sequential pattern is existential, its structure is not rigid:
the succession of stages will naturally vary for different individuals, different periods, and different cultural backgrounds. In this regard our aim will
be to detect the pattern that holds in general for the Western world of our
day and will, when described, gradually be verified by its thinkers. On the
other hand, an even more sobering difficulty arises from the fact that since
the dialectic is existential, the validity of any proposed description of its
course cannot be tested by viewing it from the outside, but only by living
through it. For if the existential orientation is sound, the sequence of stages
only becomes visible by living through them; otherwise a thinker will simply see everything as it is structured by the presuppositions of the stage he
now occupies. On both these accounts any proposed interpretation of the
dialectic must be tentative and exploratory, making no claims of any kind.

I shall try merely to clarify the starting point of the dialectic and three
major stages that evolve from it. The first of these will be reflected on in
company with Heidegger, and we may describe it as the stage of facing the
void and renouncing all our demands on the universe. The second will be
pondered in company with Sartre; it might be portrayed as the realization
of purposeful freedom undeterred by the manifold forms of human vice.
The third we shall enter with Christian existentialism, and we may view it
as the stage of rising through the starkness of evil to new life in love and
hope. In each case our aim will be to show why the challenge of that stage
cannot be escaped, and how it is incomplete without the stages that succeed
it.

Fortunately the starting point is fairly clear, at least if we confine ourselves to the existentialism of the present century. That point is located by
asking where, from its perspective, man's existential predicament shows
itself most plainly. As a person deepens his awareness of the situation he
inescapably confronts as a living and conscious individual, what is it that
threatens to make his existence meaningless and thus becomes the persistent focus of his anxious concern?

The answer, in intellectual terms, is man's recognition of his finitude in a
universe in which he is conscious of the infinite. In emotional terms it is
the dread of death, acutely felt because he can anticipate the endless time
that stretches beyond death. This anxiety does not arise in those who have
an unquestioning faith in the Santa Claus concept of God, as a being who

gives them kindly protection during life and encourages the hope of still more satisfying gifts after death. But when that comforting faith weakens or disappears, as is increasingly the case with modern men, a harrowing fear of the annihilation that death appears to betoken inevitably takes its place.

Heidegger is the existential philosopher who has pioneered in facing death and all that it involves. Moved by traditional philosophical puzzles, he is absorbed in the ancient problem of the nature of Being, but he deals with it in the setting of this existential concern. He is sure that man can only apprehend Being truly as he passes from inauthentic to authentic selfhood—from the state in which he is lost among the mass of his fellows, blinding himself to the nature of his plight, to a state in which he clearly understands what the future will bring, fully accepts it, and lives in the light of that undeceived acceptance. Now whatever else the future may or may not promise him, it promises certain death; everyone is living to die. The core of authentic selfhood consists therefore in calmly recognizing this fact and becoming at home, even now, with the nothingness that looms starkly ahead. Only when a person lives through this poignant experience is he able to grasp the otherwise obscure nature of Being and to fulfill his true vocation.

Is Heidegger right?

Many a non-existential philosopher has, as he thinks, fortified himself against the approaching end of his existence and finds it hard to appreciate the existential perspective at this point. It seems to him clear that a man ought to be able, through his command of reason, to accept the inevitability of death without pining. This attitude is well expressed by George Boas in a philosophical symposium on existentialism. He vigorously chides the existentialist for being so distressed about death:

> If human beings were the only things in the universe which went out of existence, then one might legitimately ask why this was so. But since we all know the mechanism of conception, and something of the development of the mind, a philosopher might accept with some equanimity his kinship with the general order of existence. . . . It may be discouraging to have a universe which so incompletely fulfills our desires, but it is surely no cause for despair, anguish, or even nausea.[7]

The existentialist's reply to this exhortation is that a man may intellectually accept death without having achieved real adjustment to it; he may have pushed down to the unconscious level of his mind the anxious feelings it arouses. It may be that the philosopher who trusts reason is mistaken in assuming that because it is unreasonable to demand that one live forever, this demand can easily be laid aside. And it is important to realize that the word "death" should not be taken quite literally here, although the certainty of one's own death does reveal in vivid form what the existentialist means. His crucial point emerges more precisely when we speak of the threat of "emptiness." One may find himself facing this emptiness and discover that he has failed to come to terms with it, not through anxiety about his own annihilation but through the sudden death of a beloved person on whose presence he has come to depend. If he cannot quickly transfer his attachment to another, he may feel such an unbearable void that life cannot go on. Or he may confront it at the time of retirement from an active career; this drastic change can make him acutely aware that the routine responsibilities of daily work had given the needed substance to his life, and that in their absence he is emotionally lost. A very large number of men die of some innocent ailment a year or two after they have retired; instead of the freer activity and unqualified enjoyment that had been expected they have found unendurable emptiness.

These experiences illustrate the many situations that give clear meaning to what the existentialist bids us recognize, and all of them point to this conclusion: The mere fact that a person's surface mind has accepted his coming fate is no indication that on a deeper level he has made peace with the reality of death and the yawning emptiness that it symbolizes in vivid and ultimate form. He may have done so, and if this is the case he is fortunate. But unless he has learned the lessons to which the existentialist is calling our attention, the chances are many to one that he has not. When these lessons are mastered, in the setting of man's persistent searching in all ages and climes, they clarify concepts that are otherwise puzzling. The confrontation of emptiness provides the clue to what the Buddhist means by his acceptance of the "void" and his entrance into "nirvana" (which means literally "nothingness" or "extinction"), as well as to the meaning of the medieval mystic's "dark night" through which the soul must pass.*

The void in general and death in particular cannot be taken casually by a being with power of unlimited awareness. Indeed, a merely superficial acknowledgment that they are inevitable may betoken a strenuous need,

---

* It also shows the philosopher how to deal with Heidegger's famous analyses of "nothing," which will mean nothing unless he takes them in this orientation. In the living experience Heidegger has in mind, this concept is far more than a logical or metaphysical abstraction; it means the forlorn emptiness that none who face death without comforting expectations can escape. See especially his *Was Ist Metaphysik?* (Frankfurt am Main, 1943).

which cannot succeed, to dodge their emotional impact. Death does pose the ultimate challenge to man. When it comes, will we still be attached to the things that it inevitably brings to an end? Or will we, by fully accepting the fact that our present ego must perish, have taken the first step toward another and wiser solution? It is easy to assume that this step has been taken when the arduous realization required has not yet been gained.

What *does* happen when one confronts death and emptiness in this realistic fashion? Some, as we know, turn away from the void and cram what remains of life with exciting pleasures and compulsive activities, blinding themselves to all but the immediate consequences. But this is to meet the situation by denying our human power of awareness instead of giving it full expression. What is the first stage that a person would enter when he resolutely faces the issue and makes the latter choice?

IV

The existentialist in whose company we can best seek an answer to this question is Jean-Paul Sartre, who achieved astonishing skill at revealing the abysses of human emotion that open before one when he accepts the emptiness of death and the apparent senselessness of life. Sartre realized clearly that the medium of literature is as necessary as that of the systematic philosophical essay to communicate the truths thus discovered. They are the truths that cannot be escaped when one looks at life and the world through the eyes of a realistic artist, and they call for expression in the medium he naturally employs.

With the publication in 1960 of the first volume of his *Critique of Dialectical Reason,* it became evident that Sartre's philosophy has undergone a profound transformation; he can no longer be regarded as an existentialist in the same sense as in his earlier years.* He has committed himself fully to a Marxist interpretation of social history, and his existentialism now fills its role within that Marxian framework. From his own viewpoint it may well be that there is more continuity between this later position and his earlier writings than most readers will find, although a decisive turning point in his thinking did apparently come in the year 1952.† It is not yet clear what differences this shift of orientation will

---

* See Hazel E. Barnes's translation of the introductory essay in this volume under the title *Search for a Method* (New York: Alfred A. Knopf, Inc., 1963).

† See his essay on Merleau-Ponty in *Situations,* tr. by Benita Eisler (New York: George Braziller, 1965), especially pp. 285–291.

involve for the details of his teaching about freedom and responsibility with which we are concerned; his whole approach to all such problems seems now to be quite different.

In his earlier writings Sartre dealt with these problems in terms of the experience of an individual confronting the surrounding world of things and other people. He evidently believed it possible to solve them in an independent existentialist perspective. Now, committed to a Marxian orientation, his main concern is with the course of social history; he wants to show how existentialism can save Marxism from falling into a dialectic of abstractions that have lost contact with the concrete, living realities of man's experience. He is sure that this philosophical role is indispensable in the current historical epoch, when human life is still dominated by an economics of scarcity—which only Marxism adequately interprets—and when Marxist thinkers are tempted into explaining everything that happens simply in terms of the major forces Marxism puts at their disposal. In this historical situation freedom is largely illusory rather than real, and the ways in which individuals express such freedom as is open to them largely escape a sound philosophical interpretation. Only when the epoch of scarcity and all that goes with it have been left behind, will it be possible to imagine what a truly free life for man would be like and to develop an authentic philosophy of freedom.

Hence the following discussion deals with Sartre's pre-Marxian position, when existentialism as he then conceived it expressed his general philosophical orientation. My interpretation of that position lays as much weight as it seems plausible to lay on the ideas expressed in his famous lecture on existentialism before the Club Maintenant in 1946.* For our purpose that position is important because it represents a vital stage in the existential dialectic, one that much of modern experience and thought is clearly passing through.

According to this "early" Sartre, a twofold realization naturally comes when a thinker, freed from the unrealistic yearning that the universe be kindlier than it is, faces the impermanence of all things and accepts life as inevitably advancing toward death and dissolution. First, he will be able to accept all that life reveals, including the somber evils that are easy to ignore or gloss over when viewed through the eyes of a sentimental faith. All

* More than one English translation is available: see *Existentialism*, tr. by Bernard Frechtman (New York: Philosophical Library, Inc., 1947), or *Existentialism and Humanism*, tr. by Philip Mairet (London: Methuen & Co., Ltd., 1948). That position is most fully developed in his *Being and Nothingness*, tr. by Hazel E. Barnes (New York: Philosophical Library, Inc., 1956).

the tragic, hateful, and revolting realities, especially those for which man himself is responsible, can be confronted in their full force. Now one might expect that unshrinking recognition of these demonic realities would lead to moral paralysis, but Sartre discovered that it does not need to, and here is the second half of the realization. He found that it can lead instead to a freedom and strength that had been impossible before. Our aim will be to take advantage of his help in mastering this dual realization in the form that challenges many Western thinkers today. We shall watch for insights that are implicit in his thought as well as for those explicitly stated.

A brief pause over the first half of the realization will be enough.

Sartre's primary conviction is that one can penetrate to bedrock in the existential quest only when he is fully aware of the worst that men are capable of. What is that worst? Any reader of Sartre's novels and plays is quickly given a pretty fair sample. Men can be wild, villainous, and sadistically cruel; they maim, torture, and slaughter other men. They display the ugliest, slimiest, and most loathsome behavior; no imaginable obscenity is beyond the possibilities. They are capable of a dreary dullness, a submissive torpor, or a senseless vacillation of mind that is often more discouraging to any optimism about man than these notorious vices. Moreover—and this is perhaps the most hopeless depravity of all—a person who is obviously in bondage to these hateful or repulsive traits may delude himself into a pompous assurance that he is compassionately devoted to the good of all people, as does the "Self-Taught Man" in Sartre's *Nausea*.

But awareness of these dark abysses need not plunge us into numb despair or callous self-centeredness. Sartre is equally emphatic about the other half of the realization. Though life may well appear brutal and nauseating, to face its absurdity in full awareness is a decisive step toward the acknowledgment of freedom and the acceptance of responsibility. Whatever each of us is, he has made himself to be by his own choice. When he recognizes this fact, clearly and unflinchingly, the process of free self-making will continue, but now on the stable foundation won by renouncing all self-deception. And with such recognition there is intrinsically bound up an awareness of his responsibility for other men who are endowed with the same freedom.

This side of Sartre's philosophy calls for fuller explanation, and the explanation leads us to his ultimate presuppositions as an existentialist.

Freedom, to him, is both an ontological and a moral datum in man's experience. Ontologically, Sartre finds two kinds of entities in the universe: those whose nature is to be "in-themselves" and those whose nature is to be "for-themselves." The former, illustrated by physical objects, have a massive solidity and are self-sufficient; they exist absolutely. The latter, illustrated by conscious beings such as men, enjoy no such absoluteness. In fact they have no positive character at all, unless a capacity for choice and action be such a character. Awareness, which is their distinctive mode of existence, is simply a translucent revelation of whatever "in-itself" is the object of awareness. Existing thus, they have no substance, no enduring essence, no part in any causal sequence. This means among other things that each of them is unqualifiedly free. Although at any given moment he exists under certain circumstances instead of others, those circumstances are what they are because of his own choice, and he can always make a different future if he so decides.

Freedom is likewise a moral datum. As an active being each individual faces an inescapable dilemma, and there are only two alternatives. One is the weak and futile alternative of passing the buck; he can blame the evils that he suffers or perpetrates on some external fate. But to follow this route is to reject all responsibility and to deny his freedom—to adopt the role of puppet. This is just what many men do, for absolute freedom is very disquieting; they long to rest on some authority or to conform to some rule. But there is no God and no moral law; all are "condemned to be free." Hence one must realize that if he becomes a puppet this is what he has chosen. The other alternative is resolutely to affirm his freedom and assume his responsibility. In this case he must affirm all the consequences that are bound up with freedom. He will acknowledge responsibility for whatever he is and will accept responsibility for others too, despite the anguish that is unavoidable in doing so. He does this because, when he realizes that by every act he makes himself what he is going to become, he also realizes that every act is an example to others. When he chooses one act instead of another he is thereby revealing his image of man as man ought to be, for he cannot avoid (except by a fraudulent double-dealing) the thought: "What if everyone acted that way?" Hence he knows that no act can be really good for him unless it is good for all.

This forthright ethical note in Sartre's philosophy leads to a robust humanism by which, he believes, we can rise above the threat of meaninglessness that haunts man. Renouncing all wishful self-deception, we can fulfill our true manhood. We see that our task is to give meaning to life by our own free and responsible action and to create a human community that accords to every person the independence and dignity truly belonging to him. For to express one's integrity through freedom requires not only that one respect the freedom of other men; he must also commit himself to ending the injustices that obstruct their freedom and stand in the way of their self-realization. We achieve authentic selfhood in society, not in isolation, and we can often join our efforts with those of others to bring about changes that all responsible men approve—changes that will serve the greater freedom of mankind as a whole.

But Sartre has not taken us quite as far by this vigorous assertion of freedom and responsibility as he may appear to; it is important to see just where he stops in this direction and why he could not go farther. There is a less sociable note in his conception of freedom, which reflects the long evolution of that conception in the West, with its emphasis on freedom *from* whatever blocks the satisfaction of an individual's natural desires and aspirations. This emphasis accords with Sartre's notion of absolute freedom and the way it inevitably finds expression. Recall that the ontological meaning of freedom rests on the radical difference between the "for-itself," which is free because it has no positive character, and the "in-itself," which is intrinsically self-sufficient. Both the ontological and the moral meaning converge in Sartre's doctrine that man, as being for-himself, is not passive but has a capacity for active effort. He strives to overcome his lack of self-sufficiency. He expresses his freedom by aggressively seeking to master the in-themselves around him, aiming thus to achieve the absoluteness they enjoy while still retaining the for-itselfness that belongs to his nature as a conscious being. The goal he is thus trying to reach is symbolized by the Christian concept of God, who is conscious and therefore exists for-Himself but also possesses the absolute independence of an entity that exists in-itself. The quest is foredoomed to failure, but man is nonetheless driven to pursue it.

What does this aspect of Sartre's view of freedom imply about man's relation to his fellows?

While each person must respect the freedom of others and join with them toward common goals, the urge to express his own freedom and to achieve such self-sufficiency as he can, makes the relation one of essential rivalry. In the presence of other people his freedom is always freedom from and over them, never (without qualification) freedom with them. "The relation between [human] consciousness is not essentially a *'mitsein';* it is conflict." [8] This is the case because another person's freedom is inevitably a threat to his own. Just as I seek to appropriate objects around me and make them into the kind of world I choose, so do others. Just as I observe other people from the outside and thus turn them into objects, so I am aware that they are turning me into an object. Just as I try to master their wills so that they will serve my desires, so I attribute the same attempt to them. Sartre undauntedly interprets the experience of love in such a way as to fit it into this picture of mutual rivalry;* even a gift, he holds in one passage, may really be a subtle form of appropriation rather than the benefaction it appears to be.

At this point his present Marxian orientation may well involve a significant difference. The above picture of man in relation to his fellows is qualified to the extent that he now recognizes men as capable of forming "groups-in-fusion," in which a real togetherness and sense of fraternity are achieved.† He evidently hopes that in the future this experience will be far more significant than it can be today. At present these groups usually arise only in the presence of a common danger, and the sense of fraternity is easily lost when that danger has passed. Thus, so far as our epoch is concerned, the earlier picture seems to be still valid, except that a persistent striving for a better future must be recognized. In this epoch, a person's basic attitude in the presence of others cannot help but be one of aggressive demandingness or suspicious self-protection. He is concerned to secure his own freedom against theirs and to guard himself against any threat.

What shall we say about this picture? Much in human experience supports it; but something vital is surely omitted in a concept of freedom that involves this futile quest for self-sufficiency. Can love transcend the attempt to possess and control others, becoming a true gift of self? It is Gabriel Marcel's genius as an existentialist to envision an ideal of freedom through which this emotional isolation and anxious rivalry are overcome; this ideal reveals with simple clarity a quite different value in man's relation to his fellows that can be realized without waiting for any large-scale social transformation. According to Marcel, man finds his fulfillment, even now, not in individual self-sufficiency but in giving himself freely—becoming "available" to every other man with whom he is present—and thus expressing a sense of union with them which is his true being. Marcel is sure that freedom and personal integrity are not weakened by this response to others; rather they achieve their fullest expression through it. He thus recovers, and places at the center of his interpretation of man, the compassionate love for all his fellows which according to our religious pioneers constitutes man's moral perfection and without which wholeness of selfhood

* *Being and Nothingness, op. cit.,* pp. 364–379, 413–430.
† *Cf.* in his *Critique de la raison dialectique,* Vol. I (Paris: Gallimard, 1960), the discussion of "le groupe" that begins on p. 381.

cannot be won. And it is a happy circumstance that he develops this view in non-theological terminology drawn from experiences of daily life. Two people may, he points out, be physically in each other's presence but emotionally apart. If that is not the case it is because one of them at least has broken down the wall and opened himself to the other. When this happens without reservation, the awareness of each other's presence is transformed. Whatever protectiveness and urge to dominate have lurked in it are overcome; competitive conflict is replaced by sharing in mutual respect.

In this creative experience Marcel finds the clue to a deeper existential understanding than Sartre seems to have envisioned. The dark passions of which man is capable are not denied; the person who gives himself fully acknowledges them and discovers in doing so that the positive emotions of love, hope, fidelity, and joy are not crushed but rather awakened into full expression. The moral significance of this insight is obvious, but Marcel holds that it has profound philosophical and psychological importance too. The experience thus described fills an essential role, he is sure, in man's quest to know himself and other selves as full persons. What can be known by an objective psychology has its vital value, yet it is severely limited; the man thus known is a truncated man. But when two people are available to each other and realize unobstructed communion this limit is transcended; knowledge of self and of the other person in his wholeness becomes possible.

> In treating another as an object open to public inquiry I can build up a precise and objective knowledge of him in which he is like myself and all others. In my communion with him as "thou" I do not add to this kind of knowledge; what I know is not his common human nature but his personal existence, his presence in whatever he gives himself to and his presence with me. . . . It is his presence or absence, his power to give or to withhold himself, that I experience, and this is his personal being which cannot be known objectively. In so far as I am open to him, present with him (that is, treat him as "thou"), I help him to be free, to give himself and to be present.[9]

V

Is Marcel introducing us to a further stage of existential realization?

We shall explore the experience that opens up when one follows him. If he is right, one who enters that experience has accepted a world in which any imaginable wickedness can appear, but he has found in that world a freer and more hopeful relation to his fellows and a serener relation to ultimate reality than Sartre could discover. He sees that world as part of a greater whole in which the otherwise appalling evil is overcome by good. Marcel intimates that our key to understanding here is the experience of love. Everyone knows that the morose description of love in Sartre's early work is true of much that goes by this name, but no one into whose life the blessing of real love has come will fail to sense a yawning gulf between the two emotions referred to by the same word. Gandhi once said that when true love is present in a single person it can neutralize the hate of millions. His meaning was that it is the very nature of love to accept a world in which all the forces of hate are at work and, just by being itself, to transform that world.

Many existentialists have probed this or that corner of the realm into which this insight leads, but we shall turn to those who exemplify the theological strain in Kierkegaard—of whom the best known abroad are Karl Barth, Nikolai Berdyaev, and Emil Brunner, and in America Paul Tillich and Reinhold Niebuhr. We do not need, however, to expound the thought of any of these men or to appraise the interpretation of religious doctrine that they offer. What is needed is to go back to the sources in early Christian experience of the insight that underlies all theological interpretation during subsequent centuries. These thinkers speak about that experience in an ancient language; the truths they proclaim are couched in teachings about sin, repentance, grace, and forgiveness. Because of this traditional garb it is easy for modern men to misunderstand the concepts in which these teachings are expressed. It is especially easy to confuse the existential insight we now seek to grasp with earlier religious ideas—in particular, with the comforting idea that the man of faith will providentially be protected from all evil here and hereafter. Moreover, the truths that have been kept alive through the centuries by Christian theologians have hardened into sectarian dogmas by which we must not allow ourselves to be imprisoned.

Let us enter this realm and search for the essential source by returning to Sartre's conception of God. Its serious defect is that it takes account of only a part of what Christian insight offers to existential understanding. That part, to be sure, has been emphasized in traditional Catholic and Protestant theology. It derives from what is common to the conception of God in Greek philosophy on the one hand, and the Jewish prophets and Synoptic Gospels on the other. The God thus portrayed is unqualifiedly self-sufficient; He combines the absoluteness of an ultimate metaphysical cause with the absoluteness of an unlimited monarch. Nothing can derogate from His perfection, whatever happens to or in the world He has created. Nature and man are wholly dependent on Him; He is wholly independent of them.

But there is another part, in which what is most distinctive in Christian experience comes to the fore. It implies a quite different conception of God, one that reveals the hopeful possibilities in man that Marcel delights to portray. The Biblical source of this conception is the Gospel of John, which teaches in its Christian form the insight caught by all religious pioneers when they broke down the wall erected by our fearful and anxious selves and began to explore what happens when a person opens himself in full responsiveness to other persons and to what is ultimate in reality.

If we are to grasp the heart of this insight, the vices of life thrust before us by the realists and cynics must first be faced in all their horror. But it will be best to leave aside the absurd and disgusting evils emphasized by Sartre and to reflect on the evil referred to by the word "tragedy." The experience of tragedy can be most enlightening at the point we have now reached. When this word is used either in common life or in tragic literature, not loosely but with precise meaning, one has in mind an unavoidable catastrophe that overwhelms a victim who least deserves such a fate. Not only is death confronted, but death under conditions which bring an extreme threat of meaninglessness and despair; the universe is behaving in a way that seems unutterably wrong. And yet, Christian experience has found that in tragedy there are the seeds of a richer illumination and a deeper realization than appear in any other experience; when they germinate, the hardy humanism of Sartre can be fully appreciated, and when they flower the path that leads beyond it lies open.

There are two ways in which such a dire catastrophe can be met. One is to succumb to the irresistible force in prostrate paralysis. This way is devoid of constructive value; it is the way of sheer defeat. The other is to play the part, with whatever strength and insight one can, of the tragic hero. This role does have constructive value, but to understand the dialectic of existential realization we must distinguish two kinds of tragic hero, which I shall call the secular and the religious.

The tragic hero of literature—Hamlet, for example—illustrates the former. He meets the destructive force that is bearing him down by defying it to the bitter end; he is overwhelmed, but not till he has revealed the greatness of which man is capable in the presence of ineluctible fate. The ennobling value of his heroism is shown by the fact that a spectator watching such a tragedy on the stage is purged and uplifted instead of thrown into gloom; for he has seen the unconquerable spirit of man, which can still be expressed even if all that he has stood for goes down to ruin. This heroism is clearly in tune with Sartre's moral philosophy; there is the common conviction that when man faces overwhelming evil it is only by conquering the impulse to weak submission that he can realize his dignity and freedom. And such a display of invincible fortitude may inspire others to act heroically when a similar fate becomes their lot.

But however moving this valiant defiance may be, its promise for man's existential fulfillment is limited. It lacks something, for which we must now look in the religious tragic hero. The clue to what is lacking appears when we observe the incongruous assertion of self-sufficiency in the presence of doom that seems to be essential to the secular hero's defiance. Though it expresses a sense of dignity that must not be lost, this posture betrays a limiting preoccupation with self instead of a releasing identification with something greater than self. Can the lack be overcome by a different response to tragedy? Vanzetti, condemned to death four decades ago, with his friend Sacco, for a crime they did not commit, is quoted as saying:

> If it had not been for these things, I might have live out my life talking at street corners to scorning men. I might have die, unmarked, unknown, a failure. Now we are not a failure. This is our career and our triumph. Never in our full life could we hope to do such work for tolerance, for justice, for man's understanding of man as now we do by accident. Our words—our lives—our pains—nothing! The taking of our lives—the lives of a good shoemaker and a poor fish peddler—all! That last moment belongs to us—that agony is our triumph.[10]

What did he mean? Somehow in that awful experience he found it possible to leave behind the mood of intrepid self-sufficiency as well as that of helpless despair. He transcended the sheer unconquerable defiance of the secular tragic hero. By accepting an unjust death for himself, in compassionate concern for justice to others, he realized a positive and hopeful meaning in the ordeal that had fallen to his lot; and through that realization, what would otherwise have been a futile agony became a redeeming triumph. Vanzetti gives us here an illuminating glimpse of how man is capable of a transforming and fulfilling identification that lies beyond the horizon of the existential stage above described.

By meeting his fate in this way he exemplified the religious tragic hero.*
But to grasp this further stage in its clearest form we must turn back to the
outstanding spiritual pioneers of the Western world—Jeremiah, Socrates,
and Jesus of Nazareth. And the last of these provides the most dramatic
illustration of the tragic hero in the sense we are now considering.

When Jesus saw that if he were to continue his mission in Judea the
outcome would be death on the cross, he was strongly tempted to leave
that region and carry on his work elsewhere. But he resisted the temptation.
That would be the way of escape: it would mean abandoning his own
people as beyond redemption; he would be forsaking the many who responded hopefully but weakly, and who needed his comfort and counsel.
He decided that, come what may, he would not fail them; he would share
with them to the end whatever light and love he had to give. He had been
moved by the story of Jeremiah, who six hundred years earlier had acted
likewise, and by the teaching of Second Isaiah, who had caught a profound
insight into what such unstinted devotion could mean for the overcoming
of evil. This decision made, the spiritual rebirth that had been the prime
feature of his experience since the time of his baptism quickened toward
its completion. Fear for himself was wholly overshadowed by concern to
prepare his disciples for the trials and tribulations that he foresaw would
befall them after his death. At the Last Supper, as John describes the scene,
his heart overflowed in love for them. Forgetful of the approaching hour
of his own suffering, he realized the understanding, the tenderness, and the
inner peace and joy that such utter self-forgetfulness can bring. The words
in which his message culminated were these: "I have told you all this so
that you might have the happiness that I have had, and that your happiness
might become complete." †

The existential contrast between the experience of the secular and that
of the religious tragic hero emerges clearly when we compare the picture
of Jesus and his disciples at the Last Supper with the picture of Ibbieta and
his companions in Sartre's book *The Wall.*

* The records seem to show, however, that he did not wholly free himself from
the defiant attitude of the secular tragic hero.

† John 15:11. (Smith and Goodspeed translation, Univ. of Chicago Press,
1935). John was apparently the only one of the disciples who could respond to
what happened on this occasion with more than uncomprehending devotion. As he
looked back upon it many years later, after his own existential realization had
been achieved under its guidance, he could interpret it as none of the other gospel
writers was able to. It is no accident that John gives one-fifth of his gospel to an
adoring and illuminating portrayal of the Last Supper, which the other gospels
are content to describe in a few verses.

The latter scene occurs during the Spanish Civil War. Ibbieta and the others are prisoners of the Falangists; they spend the night in a cold cell, not knowing how many or which of them are to face a firing squad at dawn. Ibbieta tells the story; the natural reactions of men in such a dire extremity are vividly displayed. Most revealing, however, is the picture he gives of himself. His fear in the presence of imminent death and his lack of ultimate faith strip him of all capacity for self-transcending emotion. He is unable to rise above the primitive concern for his own fate; he cannot bring strength and comfort to those with him who are soon to be shot, nor can he understand compassionately the situation of his guards as they fill their assigned role. All he can do is to become and "stay hard"—that is, he can meet his own ordeal unflinchingly through the sense of self-respect that comes to the fore in his soul. He can exemplify the secular tragic hero. Jesus, by contrast, was able to rise above his own unjust fate in tender thoughtfulness for his disciples, and for all men as they meet both the cheering and the desolating experiences of life. In that self-transcending outflow, and the revelation that it brought of hitherto unglimpsed potentialities in man, the tragic evil that lay ahead was overcome in a greater good.

But such an experience would have been impossible had he not been sustained by a new insight into the nature of the Divine, reaching beyond all insights previously gained. The Synoptic Gospels, in their conception of God and His relation to man, belong with the prophetic writings of the Old Testament. God, besides being the creator of all things, is for them essentially the moral governor of the universe and the good Father in relation to men as His children. John's insight was that this conception is far from adequate; rather, what Jesus had disclosed at the Last Supper is the clue to the true nature of God. And Jesus himself must have caught the essence of that vision, although its verbal expression, with him, probably remained in the form of parable and practical counsel. God is really a redeeming power, radiating everywhere in the universe and through all time the transforming love and sustaining hope that Jesus radiated in the limited temporal and geographical setting of his career. When this new insight was fully developed in the form of Christian doctrine it was no longer enough to think of Jesus as the promised Messiah. He must be the incarnation in human form of the infinite spirit of God, who has chosen to share the limitations and sufferings of men in order to awaken in them a responsive union with His boundless love. The celestial majesty and absolute self-sufficiency that were essential in the earlier idea of God are now implicitly renounced; God becomes one with man in order that man may become one with God.

To put this insight into language unencumbered by the perplexing associations of ancient dogma, Jesus exemplified a new ideal of fulfillment and integrity for man.

But this ideal rests on a broader foundation than the simple experience of meeting tragedy with such devotion and insight as Jesus revealed; that experience vividly expresses, illumines, and liberates a creative energy that has never been absent from human life. Throughout history love has shown itself in many restricted forms—the self-forgetful tenderness of mothers, the faithful affection of wives and husbands, the unswerving loyalty of friends, the sacrificing zeal of patriots—and had it not been ever renewed in these forms, showing itself time and again stronger than any contrary force, the human race would have perished long ago. In John's vision, love is freed from all restrictions; it becomes an unqualified openness to and compassionate concern for all persons without limit. In its restricted forms love for one person often spells hate toward another. This new insight brings the realization that if love fails to embrace all men it is not quite love in its full meaning. In the Johannine conception of God this insight takes dramatic and appealing form. But in its essence that form is not unique. The Eastern world was gaining the same insight at the same time in the Buddhist ideal of the Bodhisattva, who renounces his own right to enter nirvana in order to share the woes of others, and thus gives himself for the sake of the ultimate salvation of all.

Why then is the religious existentialist sure that the vision just described, and the realization to which it leads, mark a further stage beyond the stage we explored in Sartre's company?

First, love and expanding awareness intrinsically belong together. Hate, fear, greed, bitterness, and other dark emotions blind those whom they dominate. In their grip men see only the consequences projected by these mad emotions on their objects; all other consequences, no matter how likely and important, are blotted from their sight. Love, by contrast, can see all the results to which any act or chain of events may lead; by its very nature it seeks the best fulfillment for every person affected, and this requires the most realistic and prophetic awareness attainable.

Second, it is the nature of love to awaken love in others. Once it is present anywhere its redeeming power is at work everywhere; it transforms the destructive passions, born of man's frustrated self-seeking, into energies that are wholly creative. Not that it does so at once, nor that it succeeds in every situation. The process is slow and its achievements often invisible. Evil and suffering do not disappear—in fact, they may take more appalling forms than before, and in our day we are grimly aware of this peril. But if an orgy of nuclear devastation should come, such a catastrophe would prove more vividly than ever where the path of true existential realization lies, and would reveal to all survivors the suicidal ruin that is the doom of those who forsake that path. In any case, whatever may befall, love is always absorbed, not in the dire occurrence of evil but in the creation of good in the midst of evil.

The central insight of religious existentialism is that the search for authentic selfhood is a search for love, and that this search provides the inclusive setting in which all experience and every way of thinking can be wisely understood. As a child, man's consuming need is to be loved, so that he can find his way from anxiety, frustration, and anger in the presence of the harsh realities that surround him to an acceptance of his adult role in the universe. As this acceptance is firmly established, his aspiration is to love as he had longed to be loved, but with the deeper understanding that maturity brings. Growing in power to express this aspiration, he knows that he is pulling his weight in the human adventure—and more than his weight, for love does not calculate any *quid pro quo*.

A person can fulfill this adult role because he has experienced in himself the child's need, and also the disappointment, pain, and resentment that in a world not made for him are inevitably involved. To pass from one role to the other, in unobstructed awareness, is to realize that the untamed tangles of emotion, and the urge to deceive oneself about them, are not present merely in a person's feared and hated enemies—as it is tempting to assume; their roots are also in him. Through this humbling realization he acknowledges his share of responsibility for the evil these wild forces produce; if the convulsive hate of others should happen to sweep him down to destruction, he accepts the punishment as never wholly unjust. He feels his oneness with all who sin and all who suffer, and knows the liberation from puerile demandingness that this sense of oneness brings. Fulfilling in this way his adult power to love, he also perceives the truth of the Christian insight that he is loved as well as loving. For what could be a clearer proof that he is the object of Divine love than to find himself becoming a medium of its expression to others?

The heart of this whole existential realization is stated very simply by George Fox, at the time when his youthful struggles were resolved and his searching became a finding: "I saw that there was an ocean of darkness and death; but an infinite ocean of light and love flowed over the ocean of darkness. In that I saw the infinite love of God." [11]

In this setting the vicissitudes of Christian theology through the centuries can readily be understood. The challenge of John's vision to Christians was: Become one with the God in whom this creative power is perfectly embodied! Leave behind everything in your present self that blocks the way, and everything in traditional notions of Him that fails to square with the insight that has been won; build a theology that will illumine and guide the quest for that life-bringing union! But before men and women can realize their capacity for mature and sensitive compassion they need, like children in the enfoldment of family affection, a long period in which they feel themselves the objects of a warm and accepting love. How else could they believe in its reality, and be moved to identify with it? Hence what actually happened in Christian history was the emergence of a compromise with earlier tradition. The continued yearning to be cherished and protected made it necessary to retain the kindly Father of the late Old Testament, who holds the whole world in His omnipotent hands and providentially cares for each of His children; this picture of God was combined, in an unstable association, with the new picture in John. All the difficulties of the problem of evil that have haunted Christian thought arise from the need to keep together these two concepts of the Divine. When the former concept is presupposed, it seems that evil ought not to exist—at least not in forms that foster disbelief and despair. When the latter concept prevails, this problem does not arise. One accepts reality with all its evils and, demanding no security for himself, plays his part in the slow process of overcoming these evils with good.

VI

We now ask if this stage of existential realization is the last stage that can be clearly glimpsed, or if the dialectic leads beyond it.

Here is the same challenge that we met when seeking to complete our appraisal of the ordinary language philosophy. Let us meet it in the same way, trying to catch the clearest possible vision of an existentialism in which the promise of its approach to philosophic understanding would be completely realized. I shall outline the possibilities that seem most hopeful to me, trusting that each reader will use them as aids in developing his own insight as to how existentialism might further fulfill its genius and where, if anywhere, its distinctive orientation should be left behind.

This arduous quest might lead in several directions. For example, we might engage in a critical examination of the distrust of reason which has haunted existentialism ever since the time of Kierkegaard. The main lesson that would almost surely emerge is that it is one thing to be aware that reason has limits; it is another to treat it as an enemy of truth. However, all but two paths will have to be neglected. In following those paths, my aim will be to clarify an existentialism that on the one hand would be *universal* and on the other unqualifiedly *dynamic*.

In general terms, to realize universality in the existential perspective would mean that one's search for understanding has left behind all partisan obstructions and sectarian dogmas and is aiming at the truth that a man who is seeking wholeness might realize simply as man. These encumbrances are of more than one kind; today the most obvious block to universality is an aggressive ideological commitment. The Marxist cannot see the values in free enterprise, which the course of history will be unwilling to surrender; the anti-Marxist cannot see the values that a socialist organization of society makes possible. Also, religious dogmatism is still very pervasive, and it plays a vital part in these ideological conflicts; consider then the obstruction posed by religious sectarianism and why a universal existentialism would need to overcome it.

Its characteristic form is familiar. Christian existentialists through the centuries have almost unanimously maintained the traditional claim of their religion to exclusive truth. And when we place ourselves in the environment of early Christianity this conviction that only through Christ can men be saved is quite understandable. It did not express any animosity toward the religions of the East; it was a natural expression of the fact that spiritual rebirth was experienced by Christians through their whole-souled commitment to Christ, and in no other way. The religious cults with which they were acquainted lacked something that seemed vital to this rebirth; and they were unaware of the way in which a similar spiritual renewal can and does take place in other religions.

But this urge to claim exclusive truth tends to persist even when such awareness can no longer be avoided. A typical example is Brunner's little book *Faith, Hope and Love*, which affirms that "only if we are at peace with God can we have real peace in ourselves and with our fellow men. And peace with God we can have only through His forgiveness, through His taking away the burden of our past in the Cross of Christ." [12] Such an assertion would be quite consistent if one's way of deciding whether or not a person is forgiven and wins real peace is wholly non-experiential—if, for example, the question is simply: Is his name written in the Book of Life, which will be brought down from heaven at the Last Judgment? But Brunner does not quite mean this, nor do the other Christian existentialists. If the sound way to decide the question requires us to ask: Does his life reveal the fruits of the spirit, so that by them we know he has realized union with the Divine?—then the saints who have found redemption through the other religions stand before us in their spiritual radiance. They too have passed from death to life; they too have become, as clearly as Christian saints, co-creators of life in others. In the presence of this experiential fact one can appreciate why Gandhi was moved to say, in sorrow, that the Christian claim to exclusive religious truth is "perhaps the greatest impediment to the world's progress toward peace." [13] For it betokens a rigid clinging to limited and local sources of religous insight, which conflicts with an openhearted responsiveness in respect and equality to the experience of earnest seekers in the non-Christian world. In their eyes it cannot fail to appear as a self-righteous assumption of spiritual preeminence, which fosters divisiveness and conflict instead of unity in love and mutual understanding.

Such a dogmatic claim is especially incongruous in an age when, under the inspiring influence of the Hindu leader just quoted, the Christian religion is undergoing a more significant transformation than has occurred for many centuries. Guided by his teaching, and his example of nonviolent resistance to the evils entrenched in social institutions, many Christians today are experiencing a revitalization of their faith, rendering it a more effective power for both individual and social renewal than it had previously been. By sharing his conviction that love is not only the supreme ideal in individual relations but can also become a force for the conquest of social injustices of every kind, they are giving their faith a revised interpretation which in time will affect their basic theology. Gandhi's name is increasingly placed beside that of Christ by those who are devoting themselves in this conviction to the cause of ending such dire evils as racial segregation and the nuclear arms race. Through his influence, Christianity in the future will be different from Christianity in the past—clearer in spiritual understanding and bolder in political action.

Today this claim to the exclusive possession of saving truth is less prominent among religious existentialists than it has been in the past. A more generous attitude is often evident in Protestant existentialism, and is not lacking among Catholic thinkers. But there is still a stumbling block in the strong feeling that religious faith intrinsically involves "commitment" to a particular religion; this is easily construed as implying an assurance of its superiority over others. It is hard to see that a spiritual state, in which a deepening realization of the truth in one's inherited religion can be united in complete harmony with a deepening realization of the truth in others, is possible.

Karl Jaspers is the existential philosopher who has taken the lead in championing a fully nonsectarian orientation. He explicitly conceives existentialism as universal—embracing the entire panorama of man's search for the true and the good, with special emphasis on the insights that have come from religious philosophies in the East and the cultural values they express. He is sure that every serious thinker today, wherever he lives, must recognize that "a world unfolds before us for which European history is but a provincial affair, democracy a rare and rather unsuccessful experiment in political techniques, and Christianity a comparatively recent arrival among religions. We of the West . . . must play a much more modest part henceforth. . . . India and China must be accepted as equal partners at first, perhaps as superior before long. The values we have dismissed as aberrations from our standards now claim . . . the same right as our own." [14]

By following this path toward universality we are daring to glimpse an era when the earnest adherents of every religion will freely learn from each other's experience and when the resources of all faiths will be brought together in a single perspective—including the resources that have not yet taken any traditionally religious form. What a challenge to the theologians of the future—to apply their talents to the task of organizing these resources within a single conceptual framework that will do justice to the spiritual lessons that might be learned from each!

Turn now to the second path. What would it mean to realize a fully dynamic existentialism?

There is an obstacle that might remain even when the universality just described has in essence been attained. If a confining wall is erected by dogmatic loyalty to the sectarian claims of an ideology or religion, is not such a wall also present wherever there is a failure to achieve complete openness to the future—that is, unqualified readiness to reach beyond the truth already won to the larger truth that lies ahead? Some existentialists, especially among the non-theological group, have acknowledged that every truth thus far attained is partial and that openness to fuller insight is therefore always needed; Heidegger has even maintained that the self-correcting process involved in the quest for philosophic understanding will never come to an end. But the implications of this acknowledgment are more drastic than has been generally realized. Most important is its implication for the status of one's own presuppositions. An existential philosopher readily perceives the forces that entice other thinkers to regard their present presuppositions as assured dogmas, but he finds it hard to recognize that the foundations of his own way of thinking are not absolute and will almost surely need revision. When he writes a book he may try, as non-existential philosophers have usually done, to convert the reader to his own orientation, forgetting the vital insight of Kierkegaard that the true aim of an existentialist is not to convert others but to encourage them to embark on the quest for their own self-realization. He is strongly tempted to assume that when the particular existential factors to which he calls attention are clearly understood, a philosophy has taken form which can more adequately fill the same role that a philosophical system has been supposed to fill in the past.

To fulfill its genius must not existentialism leave behind all such assumptions, and become dynamic without reservation? Can a thinker achieve authentic selfhood without a deepening awareness of his own presuppositions, in their weaknesses as well as their virtues?

Unbounded possibilities of discovery and creation would seem to lie before this way of philosophizing when its champions not only share the aspirations of every people, race, and religion, but have also overcome all bondage to their present presuppositions. The search for true selfhood calls for unending growth in an infinitely evolving universe, and this means openness to change at the deepest levels of thought and insight. A philosopher committed to a pre-existential perspective is likely to be living in a very limited universe, namely, the aggregate of objects which people in his cultural milieu at present take for granted. When he adopts the existential orientation he realizes how limited that universe is; he knows that one who inhabits it is capable of participating in a vaster process, at each stage of which his surrounding cosmos is more or less radically transformed. But he may still assume that his present interpretation of that process is adequate, in need of no improvement. When the vision of a universal and fully dynamic existentialism has been gained, will this expanding realization have reached its culmination? Will existentialism have then become identical with philosophy itself, in its quest to comprehend the sweep of man's unfolding experience at full tide?

5

Philosophical presuppositions and motivations

The two ways of thinking just surveyed by no means exhaust the living philosophies that might be profitably mastered and appraised in similar fashion. And one other living philosophy can be so instructive that we must pause briefly to see how the method employed in the preceding chapters would be exemplified with it. Our aim has been to expound each philosophy in terms that reveal the grave limitations haunting it, but also—and more especially—in terms that bring out clearly its promising possibilities and enable us to glimpse how they might win their most significant fulfillment.

I

This instructive philosophy is Marxism, which provides today the theoretical foundation on which half the world is building its framework of thought and by which it is guiding social action.

IN SEARCH OF PHILOSOPHIC UNDERSTANDING : 94

Marxism is a difficult philosophy to discuss with scrupulous and sympathetic impartiality. One reason for this lies in its radically dynamic character. It has been passing through rapid changes, some of which are quite fundamental. Also, as it spreads among people of different cultures and social conditions, it has taken noticeably and sometimes strikingly different forms. Hence it is harder to pin Marxism down to any neat set of presuppositions than any other current philosophy. The best way to meet this aspect of the difficulty in a brief appraisal is to define it as consisting of certain central ideas in Marx and Engels, along with certain revisions and additions in Lenin, which together are now generally accepted as composing the Marxist orientation.

A deeper reason for the difficulty lies in the fact that its own way of stating its basic position more easily reveals—to those who do not respond with ready assent—its serious weaknesses than its great virtues. On this account one needs to restate that position in somewhat different terms if he is to bring out its constructive possibilities. The achievement of a consistent and durable theoretical formulation is not the main concern of Marxists.

The core of Marxism, as its champions present it, runs something like this: Everything in the universe is changing; there are no static realities. But there are laws of change which can be scientifically grasped, and when they are grasped, those who understand them are able to guide the changes toward humanly desirable ends. The fundamental laws are dialectical—that is, they reveal that the universe is a ceaseless process of the generation, interplay, and resolution of antagonisms between opposing forces. This set of ideas constitutes the doctrine of "dialectical materialism."

But the Marxist's serious interest is limited to the application of this doctrine to the social evolution of man, and the outcome of that application he calls "historical materialism." Like everything else, man and society are in constant change, and the same dialectical laws are evident here. The ultimate forces that determine the course of social change are the forces at work in the production of the goods by which men live. The antagonisms generated in this phase of the universal process are antagonisms between economic classes—and specifically between the class that at any given time occupies the ruling position and the others who have to submit to its domination. This antagonism, once generated, gradually becomes sharper; a new class consolidates itself out of those who were previously exploited; in due time it wins the victory over its rival and establishes a new economic order in which *it* holds the dominant position. At each stage in this struggle between classes a "superstructure" of ideas and practices arises from the process—in politics, law, religion, morals, philosophy. These take a form that favors and justifies the position of the then ruling class. The ideas seem to those who hold them to be self-evidently true, but they are really a disguised reflection of the underlying productive forces and relations, and inevitably change as the latter change.

From the vantage-point of man's present situation, the Marxist sees four major stages in this historical evolution. Feudalism dominated social life for a long period and still does in some areas. In Western Europe it was overthrown by capitalism, through whose establishment the middle class rose to economic and political power. The third stage is socialism, which is brought into being by a revolution of the proletariat, led by enlightened intellectuals. This revolution has already occurred in the Communist countries; it waits to occur in the rest of the world. The essential duties of a socialist government thus achieving political power are these: to end the exploitations under which the masses have suffered, by guaranteeing security of employment, equality for women, educational opportunity and health insurance for everyone; to transform those whose organizing talents are needed into servants of society as a whole; to assert the coercive control required to guard against counter-revolution; and to realize as rapidly as possible the conditions under which the fourth state—that of the Communist classless society, can be dependably achieved.

In this evolutionary panorama the Marxist sees a unique advantage and an exhilarating role for himself as compared with other thinkers who are still under the illusions of a non-Marxist orientation. Just as man in general —through knowledge of the laws governing physical nature—can make it serve human ends, so he— through his knowledge of the science of society and his ability to see through the deceptions in other people's thinking— can play an active part in making the course of history serve the end of an ideal society. He can anticipate future phases of the dialectical process and can give himself with complete assurance to the task of building the happier world that is to come. He has a moving vision for which he is ready to sacrifice all—the vision of a new form of social life in which freedom from every injustice will have been won and each person can grow to the full stature of his human capacities.

However, when one contemplates this Marxist vision of a goal of history that is both inevitable and good, and the tremendous effort it has inspired to change the world in the direction of that goal, he cannot help wondering whether we need, for full understanding, another way of articulating this philosophy than the way its proponents provide. Perhaps Marxism itself has not escaped the unconscious process, exemplified in other philosophies, of disguising its ideas. It may be that the most important forces reflected in it are somewhat different from those that it is disposed to emphasize. Let us try to uncover these forces—not with the aim of displaying the deceptive disguises that thus appear, but simply so that we can see the fuller picture. And we want to see it, partly to bring out clearly the weaknesses haunting this philosophy, but even more to open up positive possibilities that are left rather obscure in its own preferred statement of its position.

Is not the Marxist animated by a fervent passion to create a great social good, and to do so by destroying root and branch the monstrous evil that he sees standing in the way? Gripped by this passion, he launches a crusade whose aim is to remake the world, bringing liberation to the masses of men from the exploitations of the past and from the insecurity, degradation, and crushing poverty that they involve. He says to himself, and to others whom he seeks to convert: "That liberation must come, and it will come; let us give ourselves to the task of achieving it. Look around, and we will see—as others dominated by their blind class interests cannot see—a vast sequence of changes going on, which show that it can come and is inevitably coming. Forces are at work, intrinsic to the exploitative situation itself, which point toward the goal and reveal the route by which it will be realized. Understanding that process, we can devote ourselves to the task with full conviction and assurance."

In short, it is in this impassioned perspective that he views the scene before him, projecting the forces that thus stand out over the whole course of social evolution. He interprets the entire history of man so as to fit the requirements of this confident projection. Just as the pious Christian thinker through a long period gave himself to the task of carrying out the Divine Will for man and unhesitatingly construed the whole temporal process as the progressive fulfillment of that Will, so the devout Marxist views history as the inevitable progress of humanity from the cruel injustices of the past toward the ideal society of the future. He is the contemporary heir of Western religion in its prophetic commitment to the realization of the Kingdom of Heaven on earth.

When one sees Marxism as a set of presuppositions generated in large measure by this zealous motivation, both its grave weaknesses and its constructive promise come vividly into view.

One obvious weakness is the encouragement it gives to millenarian expectations. Through a radical social change, the Marxist believes, a society can arise in which people are animated by an entirely different cluster of motivations than before. After the proletarian revolution has taken place, he is sure that no problems comparable to those of exploitative capitalism can arise; there will be no urge for power on the part of the rulers nor any unsocial desires among the liberated workers. Hence when such evils inevitably appear, he is driven either to deny them or to explain them in terms that obscure their persistent and perilous reality.

Equally obvious is the weakness of a blithe and dogmatic self-righteousness. This is by no means peculiar to Marxism but it is especially central in its orientation. The Marxist is keenly aware of the self-deceptions and unconscious rationalizations of the defenders of capitalism, but he finds it almost impossible to recognize his own. He sees himself as not subject to the disguises that delude other men. In this fanatical assurance he can be quite ruthless in sacrificing others as well as himself to the Communist cause; he knows what is good for them better than they know themselves. Thus he rejects the Golden Rule, and follows without scruple the maxim that the end justifies the means. The divisive effect of this self-righteousness, when communism takes root in several countries not dependent on each other, is already evident, and it may be catastrophic if not corrected. Each leader with sufficient power at his command assumes that his interpretation of Marxism is the only right one and ought to be authoritative everywhere; he may even condemn the stubborn heretics more bitterly than the capitalist infidels.

A third weakness is directly caused by the intensity of the Marxist's social passion. His basic conceptual framework is closely bound by his ardent emotion to the provocative challenge of a particular historical situation; everything in the vast tide of social evolution is made to fit that framework. Although this challenge today is surely a momentous one, the framework provides too narrow an interpretative structure to serve as a universal key to historical understanding. A more serious tension arises than was the case with Christian theology, as that framework is confronted by the kaleidoscopic and rapidly changing facts of social life; when applied to them it quickly proves to be a distorting simplification.

But if these weaknesses were left behind and the Marxian philosophy restated so as no longer to imply them, it could become a very illuminating philosophic orientation. Freed from such handicaps, its constructive core would by no means be lost, but rather could stand out more clearly than it does now. And I suggest that this core would be a view of human history that sees its dynamic panorama as essentially a gradual progress from the unjust evils of the past and present toward the freely cooperative world community of the future—a progress guided by growing knowledge expressed in increasingly effective social action. Were this framework to replace the present impartial one, Marxism would embody a creative insight whose promise is rich and appealing. We shall dwell briefly on four presuppositions through which the essence of that insight might be set forth.

1. There is a dialectic of history, which works through dynamic social forces as well as through the forces in the individual recognized by existentialism. It is a dialectical movement because it inevitably involves conflict as well as collaboration, conflict being a necessary generator of the tension whose resolution spells progress.

2. The laws according to which these forces operate can be understood by the human mind, which thus puts itself in a position to direct them toward desirable ends. Indeed, understanding and action are not separable, as most theories of knowledge have assumed. On the one hand, man begins life by acting, and in the course of acting he acquires the knowledge by which he can act more efficiently. On the other hand, the pursuit of knowledge itself involves experimental action, and the test of true knowledge is that it guides achievement of the ends for the sake of which it was gained. The philosopher as well as the scientist not only interprets the world; in doing so he changes the world.

The understanding thus gained is always capable of being improved, not only in details of policy but also in the ultimate philosophical principles. Hence there is always more to learn from growing experience, from other Marxists, and from opponents of Marxism.

3. In the interplay of forces, which constitutes the dialectical process, economic forces play a special role so long as man has to live in a scarcity economy. In this situation, constant striving for the means to live and the means to exert effective power inevitably focuses on the production and distribution of essential goods. The economic relations thus arising profoundly influence all other phases of culture, including the moral, political, and social ideals that at any given time prevail. These ideals cannot be adequately understood when isolated from their economic base. But they also always influence the economic relations; the interaction is in both directions.

Although this situation has characterized human life thus far, it does not need to do so forever. By a rapid and persistent expansion of industry and scientific agriculture, the scarcity economy can be replaced by an economy of abundance in which human life will be freed from the oppressive natural and social conditions of the past, and a different and better society than any possible hitherto can be brought into being.

4. The ideal goal toward which this historical process is moving, and which we can help realize by intelligent action, is a brotherhood of man in which class distinctions will have disappeared and all persons will recognize by attitude and conduct that they are members one of another. By bold changes in our social institutions important anticipations of this brotherhood can be realized even now—economic security can be assured for all, equality between the sexes, races, and vocational groups can be fully practiced, and the educational process can foster the habit of thinking in terms of "we" and "our" instead of "I" and "mine." As the necessary conditions are progressively established, a new society will appear, in which the talents of each person can find expression far more freely than in the past —a society that will assure him everything he needs for his fulfillment and will benefit in every possible way by the contribution he can make.

It is vital to remember that the means to be chosen in pursuing this goal must be in essential harmony with that goal, otherwise what is actually achieved will be a different goal. Hence, wherever possible, nonviolent must replace violent revolution as the main instrument of social change.

II

Consider the three philosophies we have surveyed—the ordinary language viewpoint, existentialism, and Marxism.

Our quest for understanding requires that we bring them within a single perspective, without losing the distinctive genius that each displays. This is most difficult, for their basic presuppositions are radically different—so different that the universe of each seems at first sight completely alien to the universe of either of the others. But there is a virtue in this striking difference. If in such a situation we can advance toward an impartial understanding, that achievement should reveal how philosophers, whatever their particular convictions, have performed their adventurous role in the evolution of thought; and it ought also to throw light on how that role might be performed with maximum wisdom and assurance.

Whether or not there has been progress in the history of philosophy, there is certainly change—and change not merely in the details of doctrine but in the ultimate presuppositions underlying the orientation of any philosophical school as it arises, exerts whatever influence it does, and then passes away. Here is an assured fact with which to begin our present task. How can this continuous process be clearly and hopefully understood?

One of its essential aspects has already come to light; it may be called the formal or structural aspect. When we view any segment of the process in the course of which one philosophical school is succeeded by another, and put into words the presuppositions that can be detected, we always find that certain presuppositions are preserved through the change while others are abandoned and replaced by different ones. Such a pattern of continuity and difference is clearly revealed by a formal comparison of the earlier and later sets of presuppositions.

This aspect appears prominently in the history of analytic philosophy, as we traced it from the early realists through positivism to the philosophy of ordinary language. Several important presuppositions remained unchanged through this whole period. One is the conviction that the major task of philosophy is the analysis of propositions or statements to discover what they mean. Another is the assumption that the purpose behind this analysis is to replace confusing or misleading statements by ones that are clear and communicate successfully. A third is the insistence that any such analysis is a "logical" achievement. All of these schools held that their analyses are valid independently of any appeal to the observable facts to which the statements analyzed refer; and this makes them logical analyses. A fourth is the acceptance of a thoroughgoing pluralism in their view of the world and of statements about it; all reject the idea that it is the duty of philosophy to erect a monistic system.* As for the presuppositions that were abandoned and replaced in the course of this succession of schools, several of these were mentioned in Chapter III.

The same aspect can also be identified in the history of existentialism. In the case of certain major concepts a common meaning is apparently presupposed by all its influential representatives; among these the concepts of "realization," "authentic selfhood," and "existence" itself might be listed. Other important concepts undergo a significant change as we pass from one existentialist to another; such a difference has been noted in the meaning of the concepts "freedom" and "love." It would not be difficult to find

* There is a difference, however, in their interpretation of this pluralism. In general, the realists and positivists believed that the world consists of simple or "atomic" facts, none of which depends for its existence on the others. Such a belief is not essential to the ordinary language philosophy; its pluralism is shown in the idea that the ordinary uses of words vary according to circumstances, and that what is true about the use of an expression in a certain situation may be false or nonsensical when applied to its use in another.

illustrations both of continuity and change in any temporal segment of philosophical evolution that might be picked; they would turn up in an exposition of Marxism if its development through the past century were traced in detail.

But in the interest of constructive philosophic understanding this may be the least important aspect of the process constantly going on. Were it the only one that could be identified and understood, the history of philosophy might easily seem to be nothing more than a succession of transitory fads. As each school appears on the scene it continues to exemplify certain virtues in previous ways of thinking while avoiding certain blunders that it sees in them; beyond this, it simply treats in its own novel fashion the problems with which philosophers are always concerned. And no fashion lasts very long. Some disquieting consequences can hardly fail to catch our attention when we watch this rapid transition from one set of basic presuppositions to another.

For example, consider the fact that during the decade of the nineteen-thirties scores of essays appeared in German, British, and American philosophical journals (likewise in books, such as the first edition of A. J. Ayer's *Language, Truth and Logic*), whose basic argument presupposed the soundness of the verifiability theory of meaning championed by the positivists—a theory now, so far as concerns its aggressive claims, almost universally given up. Some of the demonstrations offered in these essays did not involve this theory; in their case its abandonment did not necessarily invalidate them and a few have made an enduring contribution. But the many analyses that did involve it have lost their relevance and today appear mistaken.

Is any way of philosophizing possible that would, in some significant measure, avoid this sad waste of effort? If so, can we identify the aspect of philosophical change that provides the key to our understanding and realization of this possibility?

A suggestion that would make this question superfluous is sure to be offered, but it will not do. Was each of these transitions required by the acquisition of important knowledge that had not been available before? If that is so, then philosophers were simply adjusting themselves by the change to a definite scientific advance. In the history of philosophy this has occasionally been the case. Kant's theory of space and time, for instance, rested at certain points on the assumption that Euclidean geometry is unqualifiedly true of physical space; when mathematical science found that it had to abandon that assumption these features of his teaching had to go with it. But usually this is not the case. So far as concerns the scientific truths involved, thinkers knew before the transition took place as much as they did afterward. And when it is a change in the basic presuppositions that constitute a criterion of fact or form, this suggestion is obviously irrelevant.

Existentialism gives its confident answer to the question. Its champions are convinced that there is an essential aspect in this process which provides the key we are looking for and which, when recognized and understood, can become an instrument of philosophical progress. At first sight it might seem that to acknowledge such an aspect would mean to give up the search for any key and to reject all possibility of progress. For existentialism insists that emotional motivations play a part in any thinker's passage from one set of presuppositions to another; and that this is inevitable because he is philosophizing as a full person, not as a mere intellect. And if the above interpretation of Marxism is sound, it confirms this insistence in an instructive way. Marxism explicitly holds that the thinking of its opponents is determined by an unconscious emotional commitment to their class interests, and it implicitly reveals its own emotional commitment to the cause of ending exploitation and realizing the ideal community.

Is this a universal aspect of philosophical change? If it is, how can constructive possibilities be found in it?

III

This challenge is especially searching in the case of the analytic philosophers. They find it easy to ignore the aspect in question and to assume that, so far as emotional motivation presents any problem, a philosopher can overcome through his power of reason whatever influence it has been exerting. If that assumption proves to be mistaken, and if we can see the source of the mistake, we may thereby have found the key to an understanding of the dynamics of philosophical change and to the constructive insight we are hoping for.

Survey again the three analytic schools that rapidly succeeded each other during the last half-century. As each of them arose and gradually won an influential position it has exhibited an interesting temporal pattern. This pattern is probably exhibited, in some form, by every philosophical movement; hence to recognize it places us, so far as concerns the factors it reveals, in an impartial perspective on the history of philosophy. Every movement seems to pass through certain stages in a definite order, and in the case of the analytic schools each stage has required roughly the same amount of time—a decade—for its completion. There are three such stages; thus approximately thirty years have been needed in their case between the first emergence of a new school and the time when it attained its maturity.

In order to explain this peculiar evolutionary pattern, these stages must be described and illustrated.

In the first stage the champions of a new philosophy, confident of its soundness, toss out bold assertions of the position they have adopted without realizing its limitations or embarrassments. Their opponents quickly pounce on these weaknesses and offer challenging criticisms; however, the champions pay little attention to criticism at this stage because they are sure that any inadequacies must be merely apparent. A good illustration is provided by the positivist theory noted above. At first, in the mid nineteen-twenties, its basic doctrine was unhesitatingly stated by the leaders of the Vienna Circle in essentially this form: The meaning of a proposition consists in the experiences by which it can be verified or disproved. Critics soon pounced on the crucial phrase at the end of this slogan; certain natural ways of construing it, they pointed out, would make the doctrine quite unacceptable. Is any proposition verifiable, in strict accuracy, except one describing a presently observable fact? For if time is needed for the verification, how be sure that during that time no change has taken place in the fact? If this is the case, far too many propositions that seriously concern thinkers become meaningless. For a while the positivists almost ignored such criticisms, convinced that their fundamental position ought to be self-evident to any reasonable philosopher.

In the second stage the proponents of the new viewpoint begin to be troubled by these criticisms, but believe that any difficulties can be met by drawing a few distinctions. They are now disposed to admit that if the words used were to mean what opponents have taken them to mean, the difficulties are real; but they maintain that with these distinctions all objections are answered. In the second decade of positivism its leaders felt it necessary to give a systematic reply to the objections that had been raised, and opponents found themselves regaled with a list of unexpected distinctions. Positivists gradually realized that to clarify their position they must distinguish between "direct verifiability" and "verifiability in principle," between verifiability in the present and verifiability in the future through techniques not now available, and finally between "empirical" and "logical" verifiability. Indeed, this list is not complete; several other distinctions were suggested also.

In the third stage, champions of the new way of thinking are forced by continued criticism to face the question of whether these distinctions and reinterpretations are consistent with what they had asserted in the beginning, and to reformulate that original doctrine so as to reconcile it with them. Only when this stage has been worked through does the essence of their viewpoint achieve stable clarity, and only then can the arena of discussion become reasonably free from the confusion of rash claims on the one side and facile misinterpretations on the other. In the case of positivism, toward the end of the second decade antagonists began to ask whether the distinctions that had now been drawn did not contradict what had thus far seemed essential to the new philosophy. This was a serious challenge with some of those distinctions, especially that between empirical and logical verifiability. If the positivists had found themselves compelled to rest their case on the latter, it would have been hard to maintain that anything was left of their original appeal to experience; in that case they would have adopted the conception of meaning characteristic of an a priori rationalism.* Any proposition would be logically verifiable if it did not contradict itself.

However, as the discussion progressed through the third stage toward the point where the essence of the positivist position would be clear and its significant contribution to a sound theory of meaning could be distilled, it became known that Wittgenstein, who had been a powerful influence behind the movement, had shifted to the viewpoint of the ordinary language philosophy, and writings in which that viewpoint was involved began to attract attention among the philosophers participating in this controversy. As a result, positivism was soon jostled off the center of the stage in Britain and America; and the remaining problems have been discussed in the setting of the philosophy that took its place.

These stages, of course, are not sharply separated from each other. While some champions of the new position continue to write essays characteristic of a given stage others will be anticipating the stage that follows it.

Why are thirty years or so required for a new philosophical school to arise, reach maturity, and give way to its successor? It seems rather strange that as much time as this is needed.† Why cannot philosophers jump at

* This issue was explicitly discussed in connection with certain formulations of the positivist position proposed by Carnap, Neurath, and others.

† The reader will find it instructive to analyze similarly the pragmatic theory

once to the end of the third stage as soon as the central idea of a novel way of thinking has been stated?

A twofold answer to this question has been partially anticipated. In the first place, the formal factors involved in the emergence of a new philosophy take time to work themselves out. At the beginning its central idea is thin and still in the rough; it has to be enriched and more precisely defined. Alternative interpretations and variant emphases are possible; choice must be made between them. And in order that a choice can be made, the implications of different interpretations must be made explicit and their bearing on the major problems with which philosophers wrestle revealed. We can hardly imagine any situation in which these processes would not take time.

But no fixed period is required for this formal elucidation; it can work itself out more slowly or more quickly. Why does it proceed as slowly as it has? Here we need the second part of the answer. Powerful emotional forces are operating also—specifically, the force mentioned at the conclusion of the preceding chapter, namely a fervent attachment to our basic presuppositions, so that we strenuously resist any pressure to modify them. When a new viewpoint first emerges on the stage its proponents are zealously committed to their pioneering presuppositions, while those who attack it cling zealously to their accustomed ones. Each side sees the other through its own spectacles, and on both sides there is blithe assurance that these spectacles are the only ones through which to see anything aright. So long as philosophers are moved by such an attachment it may take a good deal of controversy to loosen them sufficiently so that fruitful communication becomes possible, and a new philosophy brought to the point where it can be impartially assessed.

It may well be that such a motivation is present in all philosophers, of whatever school. Indeed, do they not share it with their fellowmen at large? Look at the widespread longing of people for security, and the vigorous demand that it must be possible to achieve it through their present ideas, their familiar habits, their established institutions. To reform these is an arduous business; a call to do so is felt as a worrisome threat. The conservative feels this in the case of all current ideas and institutions, while the liberal feels it in the case of those that have not attracted his critical attention. Our strong attachment to the basic presuppositions we now hold

---

of truth that developed around the turn of the century (especially in James), and the ordinary language philosophy since 1940. Each exhibits the same stages and approximately the same tempo in its evolution. The last-named is now (1965) in the third stage.

is the natural expression, in that ultimate cognitive situation, of such a longing and demand.

An unusually frank revelation of this emotion and the accompanying assurance of the rightness of one's convictions is found in a famous passage that antedates the rise of analytic philosophy. F. H. Bradley, after summarizing his main doctrines about Absolute Reality, goes on to say:

> With regard to the main character of the Absolute our position is briefly this. We hold that our conclusion is certain, and that to doubt it logically is impossible. There is no other view, there is no other idea beyond the view here put forward. It is impossible rationally even to entertain the question of another possibility. Outside our main result there is nothing except the wholly unmeaning, or else something which on scrutiny is seen really not to fall outside. Thus the supposed other will, in short, turn out to be actually the same; or it will contain elements included within our view of the Absolute, but elements dislocated and so distorted into erroneous appearance. And the dislocation itself will find a place within the limits of our system.
>
> Our result, in brief, cannot be doubted, since it contains all possibilities. Show us an idea, we can proclaim, which seems hostile to our scheme, and we will show you an element which really is contained within it. And we will demonstrate your idea to be a self-contradictory piece of our system, an internal fragment which only through sheer blindness can fancy itself outside. We will prove that its independence and isolation are nothing in the world but a failure to perceive more than one aspect of its own nature.
>
> And the shocked appeal to our modesty and our weakness will not trouble us . . .[1]

In the paragraphs that follow Bradley explains why such an appeal will not trouble him. He reviews patiently the results of his "demonstrations," all the while appearing unaware of the fact that except to thinkers committed to the same presuppositions these proofs are not a whit more cogent than those that can be and have been urged in behalf of quite different philosophies.

Similar examples of this attachment and assurance, though less belligerently expressed, can be found in Russell, Wittgenstein, and other recent philosophers.* Moreover, we find that such an attachment can be strengthened by an experience which, it might be thought, would weaken it. Look

* See Russell's *Scientific Method in Philosophy* (New York: Oxford Univ. Press, 1914), p. 54; Wittgenstein's *Tractatus, op cit.,* p. 29.

again at the rapid shifts in the present century from one set of presuppositions to another. Not only have British and American philosophers
watched two instances of this kind of revolution in their lifetime; many
of them have also participated in at least one of those shifts themselves.
Some who began their career as realists became positivists after a few
years, and a larger number who began as positivists became ordinary language philosophers.

One might suppose that after a philosopher has undergone such a transformation he would hold his present presuppositions with less confidence
than he felt about those he has now renounced, and would be open to further change. But precisely the opposite outcome can appear instead. He
may feel humiliated at having had to renounce a position that he had publicly championed. To be humiliated in this fashion again would be more
than he could bear; so he may cling to the position he has now adopted
even more resolutely than he did to the one he has left behind.* The state
of mind possessing him, if put into words, would be this: "It took me some
time in my stupid wanderings to discover the true way, but at last I've
found it."

When we contemplate this powerful and widespread motivation, two
further possibilities are naturally suggested. Does each philosophy also
reflect motives that help explain why its distinctive convictions were
adopted? Moreover, this zealous attachment to one's present presuppositions obviously does not affect the content of those presuppositions; it simply strengthens their hold on those who have adopted them. If there are
motives that explain why a particular set of presuppositions were adopted
in preference to others, they may make a difference to the very content of
those presuppositions and hence to the essential nature of the philosophy
thus arising.

Let us see if we have already become acquainted with an interesting
illustration of these possibilities.

In Chapter II, while surveying the function of philosophy in revising
our criteria of logical form, we traced the historical vicissitudes of the three

---

* Philosophers have often blinded themselves to the occurrence of a shift in
their thinking, especially if it happens after they have published a system to the
world. They feel ashamed to have changed their minds. Kant is an excellent example. He had claimed in the first edition of his *Critique of Pure Reason* a
definitive solution of the problems there discussed. But by the time the second
edition appeared, six years later, he had modified his position on several major
points. He was unable to acknowledge this shift frankly, and his efforts to dis-
semble it add confusion to a philosophy already very difficult to master.

"laws of thought" and especially of the law of excluded middle. Those who accepted the axiom embodied in this law believed that the possible answers to any question could be organized in a neat disjunctive system, so that whenever they were sure that all answers but one are false they would know that the remaining answer is true. Throughout much of Western history this law appeared valid to almost all philosophers, but in modern times it has by many been rejected.

What motive led to its adoption and its preservation during that lengthy period?

A very plausible answer is: an impatient demand for prompt and definite solutions to all problems that have to be confronted. Our longing for certainty and the painfulness of any state of doubt or suspense readily engender such a feeling. When it dominates our minds the law of excluded middle exerts a powerful appeal; thinkers are eager to have available a disjunctive system whose alternatives are mutually exclusive and, taken together, exhaustive, so that to accept one is to reject another and to reject one is to accept another. A neat method is thus at hand by which every question can be decided quickly, and it is easy to assume that puzzled or frustrated waiting for the right answer is rarely necessary.

Friedrich Waismann has discussed the influence of this motive on the presuppositions about logical form that prevailed for many centuries. "Aristotelian logic," he says, "is the logic that meets our desire for decisiveness better than other types . . . which do not include the law of excluded middle." [2] Moreover, when we view the history of thought in the light of this impatience it is easy to understand why many thinkers have not only assumed that an exhaustive list of answers to any question must be possible, but have also been seduced into oversimplifying complex issues so that there are only two alternatives. When a difficult problem has been browbeaten in this fashion it is merely necessary to reject one possible answer in order confidently to adopt the other; a quick decision becomes easier than ever.

The kind of situation that reveals most vividly the driving force of this emotion and its relation to the law of excluded middle appears in the tense international conflict that we are familiar with as the Cold War.

Faced by the complicated issues that confront the world, the extremist on both sides of the iron curtain impatiently reduces them to a single issue and recognizes only two mutually exclusive alternatives, no matter what serious considerations are ignored by doing so. He confidently divides the world into angels and demons—that is, those who stand with him and those who do not. If he is a dogmatic Communist he is ready to pronounce all at home or abroad who do not accept the present party line, agents of capitalism. If he is a dogmatic anti-Communist he will not recognize differences in the Communist world; since none of its leaders stand on his side, all alike seem to be diabolical enemies. In either case his passionate need is to apply the law of excluded middle and to commit himself without delay to a simple solution. The moderate, by contrast, is open to more than two alternatives, aware of the danger in simple solutions and of the vital importance of considering all possibilities.

Among recent philosophical schools, positivism is an excellent example of this ardent oversimplification. Its champions insisted that any verbal expression must either be meaningful or not, with no third possibility admitted, and that in the former case the meaning must be one or the other of two definite kinds—a formal tautology or an empirically verifiable statement.

It is very important to notice that this impatience for a simple and quick solution affects the very content of the philosophical position adopted under its influence. The doctrines of positivism just mentioned were integral to its philosophical viewpoint, and the conviction that the law of excluded middle is unqualifiedly valid was integral to the theory of logic long held by most philosophers. In such cases a change of motive would inevitably bring a change in the basic presuppositions adopted.

What has happened to bring this motive under increasing distrust in modern times? It would seem that if philosophers today were as incorrigibly impatient as many of their predecessors, insisting on deciding each question at once on whatever grounds are already available, the law of excluded middle would still be accepted as unquestionably valid. The answer then would naturally be. Our gradual realization that impatience can seriously handicap the pursuit of knowledge and that the law of excluded middle must therefore be cut down to size. The law is of course valid whenever exhaustive and mutually exclusive alternatives are stipulated in a formal system of logic. Its validity may also be assumed in practical situations where a decision must be prompt if it is to be of any value. But thinkers have been learning through woeful experience that in most other situations this impatience obstructs our quest for truth instead of serving it. Oversimplification is a serious danger, for significant possibilities may be left out; and eagerness for a quick decision will make us unable to see alternatives that might prove important.

Scientists in their laboratories and men of affairs around their conference tables have long since refused to be bound by the law of excluded middle. Their natural impatience, their wish for a quick answer, is kept under control. He would obviously be a bad scientist who, in the presence of two hypotheses or theories each purporting to explain a certain group of facts but irreconcilable with the other, insisted on deciding at once which of them to accept. A company whose executives were unable to tolerate indecision while they explored all promising possibilities would soon succumb in the stress of competition to other concerns whose leaders were not so impatient. Happily for the company's prospects, those who surround the conference table are aware that if a wise common decision is to be reached none can allow himself to be irretrievably committed to any proposal that he might initially favor, nor to assume any fixed set of alternatives. In the atmosphere of this openmindedness, a policy that approves itself to all participants can be distilled, and very likely it will differ in important respects from any of the policies originally proposed.

Modern thinkers more and more realize that on any weighty question there is likely to be a range of relevant considerations that have not yet been adequately explored, and that when they are explored the grounds for decision already available may appear insufficient and the alternatives that seemed to be exhaustive beforehand may no longer seem so. The emotional demand for a quick solution must not be allowed to dominate our minds but must be mastered instead.

IV

An intriguing but very perplexing region has opened up. A serious challenge confronts us—the challenge posed by these emotional motivations and their influence on philosophical thinking. The traditional assumption has been that the psychology of philosophers is entirely irrelevant to the quest for truth—that a philosophical position can be judged without attending to its motivating sources. There is no doubt that it can be formally analyzed without doing this; and if we had never become aware of any influence of emotional forces on our thinking, that kind of analysis would have to suffice. But it is clear not only that there is such an influence, but also that an appeal to it may explain why a particular presupposition has been adopted and why it is later replaced by another. It would be very arrogant, of course, to appeal to these forces if we did not recognize their presence in our own thinking as fully as in the thinking of others.

The heart of the perplexity in which this challenge involves us can itself

be described in precise philosophical terms. It is that of the relation between the cognitive adequacy of a basic presupposition and the motivating
cause of its adoption. Neither, we see, can be neglected by a seeker for
understanding. Now it is obvious that the two are not in intrinsic harmony; were that the case, all basic presuppositions, adopted by anyone at
any time, would be true. On the other hand, they cannot be intrinsically
divorced from each other. Were that the case, we would be condemned to
perpetual falsehood in our ultimate convictions. How, then, do psychological causation and truth come harmoniously together when these convictions are concerned?

The temptation to escape such a challenge is very strong.

But the crucial fact is that in all action and all thought some motive is
being expressed, and that every motive has an emotional dimension. Indeed, emotion seems to be the driving energy behind whatever we do;
without it our minds as well as our bodies would be completely torpid. It
may be that man's fundamental problem throughout his whole history has
been that of conquering and redirecting his emotions through expanding
awareness of their influence on him. So we must look around this region
carefully, making sure that all sides of the difficult quandary are recognized
and that whatever hopeful clues are available will not be missed.

Every use of language is, among other things, an expression of feeling. It
may be that originally animals made cries just to express their feelings. In
man's case these cries developed into speech, as they took a form capable of
filling the role of communication in all the varied situations in which communication is needed. But the original function of expressing feeling has
not been lost; how could it be?—in that case nothing would be said. Indeed, philosophers are now coming to realize this ubiquitous role of motivation. The ordinary language thinkers talk about our being "inclined" to
say so-and-so in a given set of circumstances, and any such inclination must
express some motive. R. M. Hare has even invented a technical term for
referring to a presupposition in its full emotional setting; he calls it a
"blik." *

Nonetheless, philosophers are still strongly swayed by the appeal: "Keep
your emotions out of your reasoning! Only thus can objective conclusions
be reached." They find it hard to see how, otherwise, they can fulfill their
intellectual responsibilities. The humorous feature of this situation is that
one may readily observe that the thinking of colleagues who disagree with

* See *New Essays in Philosophical Theology*, ed. by A. Flew and A. MacIntyre
(London: Student Christian Movement Press, 1955), pp. 99 f.

him is subtly (or not so subtly) affected by emotions of which they are not fully aware, even while he rejects any hint that his own commitment to truth might be similarly sullied. Hence philosophical debate often proceeds under a tacit log-rolling agreement: "Will you be kind enough not to mention the emotional surd that you see in my thinking, and I will be discreet about the emotional surd that is obvious in yours."

Nor is it enough today simply to recognize this pervasive role of motivation, in one's own philosophizing as in that of others. In our century a salient event has occurred, which on one side renders our difficult problem even more difficult while on the other it provides the clue to a constructive solution.

This event is the rise of psychoanalytic psychology to a position where its profound significance for all areas of thought is becoming evident and is being taken more and more seriously. The psychoanalytic orientation is meant in the broad sense of that phrase, not in the sense of any particular theory such as the Freudian. The vital contribution it makes is indicated by a phrase that naturally cropped up a moment ago—we spoke of "emotions of which they are not fully aware." The discoveries reached through this orientation show clearly that in every person's mind there are unconscious as well as conscious emotions, and that until these are brought into awareness they affect whatever he does in ways of which he is ignorant and are therefore beyond his rational control. The implications of this fact are drastic indeed; the most drastic for a philosopher is that these unconscious motivations inevitably influence his reasoning about philosophical problems.

Moreover, this implication takes an especially radical form, which our recent illustrations have anticipated. Not only do these motivations supply the driving energy behind his thinking, but we also realize that they may affect the very content of his ultimate beliefs. In the heyday of positivism, presumably none of its champions was conscious of any influence of an emotional demand for excessive simplification; in the period dominated by Aristotelian logic, no one was conscious of any connection between the impatient yearning for quick solutions and the place occupied in that logic by the law of excluded middle. But from the vantage-point of our day it is hard to deny those motivations a significant role. In the pre-psychoanalytic era it was plausible to assume that even though some motivation may influence a philosopher's adoption of this or that ultimate belief, its content is fully subject to his conscious control. Under this assumption a basic presupposition could be regarded as a purely cognitive entity, capable of being dealt with as such. Marxism is especially illuminating at this point. The Marxist is quite sure that his passionate concern does not determine the substance of his presuppositions, even while he is equally sure that his opponents think the way they do because of their class-conditioned motivations. In the psychoanalytic era every thinker must ask, in his own case as in that of others, whether an ultimate presupposition is not in essence an emotionally buttressed and molded conviction that, while it dominates a person's thinking, is but half-conscious at best; only when he suspects that it is inadequate and begins to envision alternatives is it likely to be clearly recognized.

The decisive consequence of this realization is that where such a presupposition is concerned the existentialists are right; our conscious intellect, however sincerely truth-seeking, cannot alone fill the role that philosophers have expected it to fill.

This sobering fact emerges in sharp focus when we think again of the maxim "Keep your emotions out of your reasoning." When one adopts this maxim his hope is to split off the cognitive function of his mind from the rest and, for the time being, to identify himself with it. What happens when a conscientious thinker makes this heroic attempt? Does he succeed? Yes, in part. He succeeds all too easily in the splitting, and his conscious mind rises above the play of irrelevant feelings; but he does not succeed in becoming a pure and dispassionate intellect. The springs of emotion are still there; without them he would be sunk in lethargy. Has he not forgotten that a resolution of this kind can be effective only in areas where we are already aware of alternative possibilities—and of the illicit support that a seductive bias may be giving to one of them against the others? It is impotent with the presuppositions forming the core of our thinking at any given time, of which we are not yet clearly aware. As long as those presuppositions are partially hidden by the unconscious emotions that led to their adoption, we cannot think *about* them for the simple reason that we think *with* them.

Ponder well an instructive analogy from the history of science. For a long period many inquirers concentrated on the surface qualities of objects in their directly observable relations. Science as they conceived it had to explain everything in terms of the hot and the cold, the dry and the moist, the regular and the accidental, the state of being in motion and the state of being at rest; they did not realize how systematic knowledge of the atom, the cell, or the electron could improve our understanding of the surface qualities and especially of the laws governing the way they change. The provocative possibility now confronts us that to be satisfied with awareness of conscious feelings in their relation to our philosophical thinking is to limit our quest for ultimate understanding in the same fashion. If the psychoanalytic orientation is sound, a philosophy cannot help expressing the philosopher's whole personality, including his unconscious emotions. As long as they are not lifted to awareness his reason cannot deal with them, nor can it decide what basic presuppositions he will accept; the decision has been made by his pre-rational self.

But there is also a positive and hopeful promise in this analogy. What is now beneath the surface does not need to remain so, and the psychoanalytic conception of the human mind shows how this expanded awareness of the forces within ourselves can be gained. When thinkers master the art of probing beneath the surface, bringing previously hidden presuppositions and their motivations to full consciousness, they may be taking as forward-looking a step for philosophy as the corresponding step was for science. Then those forces become subject to intelligent guidance. Like the scientist, every responsible philosopher seeks the truth. Only in the area of these deep-lying factors in their dynamic relation to his cognitive activities has he allowed this search to be blocked. His long reluctance to probe in that area is easily understandable. But no progress toward truth is ever made by evading truth. With the dawn of the psychoanalytic approach to the dynamics of mind, he must enter that area and try to comprehend what goes on there. As the existentialists have realized, a crucial part of the philosophic quest—indeed the foundation of every other part—is the quest for truth about oneself. The resources now available enable us to return in a new and fruitful perspective to the Socratic maxim that has only haltingly influenced philosophy in the past: Know thyself!

Reflect thoughtfully on each of the crucial steps that have brought us to the point we have now reached:

1. Every act, including the act of adopting a basic presupposition, is the effect of some motive.
2. That motive may influence the content of a presupposition as well as cause its adoption.
3. Unconscious as well as conscious motives are operating in this fashion; and until they are lifted to conscious awareness their operation cannot be rationally controlled.
4. Some of these unconscious motives may conflict with our primary concern for truth; but when that fact is realized, the way is open to replace them by motives that do not thus conflict.

V

The philosophical orientation to which this course of thought leads is revolutionary—especially in the momentous cognitive role it gives to emotional motivation, and particularly to unconscious motivation. We will be wise to find out by an independent check whether that orientation rests on as secure a base as it seems to.

Happily there is a way of doing this that is interesting and instructive on its own account. A philosopher not yet fully persuaded might say: "If motivation does fill the role just described, it should be possible to verify its presence in all phases of human thought, and not merely in the special situations that have been discussed. A thorough analysis of man's quest for knowledge in general ought to lead to the same important conclusions. Does it do so?"

Let us see if this justifiable challenge can be met, and if the trenchant insights that have taken form are confirmed. The simplest way to do this is to reflect carefully on our daily experience of objects and events, so as to bring out clearly the factors to which all perception and all interpretation of the world around us are relative. If emotional motivation does play the crucial part that the above analysis appears to reveal, its presence should stand out sharply through an examination of these factors.

Centuries ago Aristotle remarked that everything known is known "after the mode of the knower." He thus recognized the inevitable and pervasive relativity of knowledge.* What then is "the mode of the knower" when we spell it out in sufficient detail? It is our good fortune that much material bearing on this question is available from studies in the psychology of perception and related fields. We shall select a few of the simplest considerations that seem to teach the fundamental principles that need to be recognized.

Examine first the main factors that can be detected in our perception of an object or event. It is obvious at once that whenever we perceive anything, what is perceived is determined not only by the object but also by such factors as the distance and spatial perspective from which the perceiver is viewing it. Whatever presents itself in our field of vision— table, tree, hill, cloud—appears as it does, with the particular size and shape that it shows, because it is relative to these factors. A round penny for example is ordinarily perceived from such an angle as to look elliptical.

* Aristotle did not, however, recognize all the relativities that will now be discussed.

Next, what is seen is affected by the condition of the intervening medium between perceiver and object. What one sees in clear air as contrasted with what is seen through a mist—its color, apparent distance, distinctness of outline, and many other features—is relative to this factor. Further, what is perceived varies with the state of the observer's sense organs. We perceive in objects only the colors and sounds that correlate with the range of vibrations to which we can respond. If one is color-blind or suffers from any similar limitation, he does not perceive all that other people can perceive. What is seen also varies, of course, with whatever instruments may be employed—spectacles, microscopes, rulers, amplifiers, etc.—to supplement or correct the senses that nature gave us. Further still, what we perceive depends on the condition of the nervous system, especially the brain. When this organ fails to function as it should, various abnormalities of perception arise.

But these do not exhaust the factors that we need to have in mind. An object is perceived in such a way that it fits into the standard habits that perceivers in general, or perceivers in our cultural milieu, have formed. An instance of the former is the fact that we apprehend an object as remaining the same through successive perceptions of it despite the minor changes that might be noticed if we were alert to them. My present perception of a shrub outside my window is not identical with my perception of it a few moments ago, but I apprehend it as the same shrub. An instance of the latter is the fact that we perceive everything in terms of some available word in the language of our culture, with all the metaphysical and social theories that it implies. Westerners usually perceive a male sibling as simply a brother; the Chinese perceive an elder or a younger brother, in each case with the special privileges and duties traditionally involved in the relationship.

Finally, and most important, what is perceived is relative to the interests of the perceiver, which express varying degrees of emotional force. The lessons that can be learned by examining this factor are exceedingly illuminating. Nietzsche was not exaggerating when he asserted that "even in the 'simplest' processes of sensation the emotions dominate." [3] Consider three distinguishable ways in which this factor of motivating interest is revealed.

In the first place, an object is often perceived incorrectly because of the power of some interest. If one watches himself he will find that cases of wishful perception occur rather frequently, just as cases of wishful thinking do. A few months ago, shortly before income tax returns were due, I was walking along a business street of my city. My attention was suddenly attracted by a sign above a store door, which I read as "We cut taxes." The sign actually said: "We cut tags."

In the second place, even when no outright error occurs, we perceive the structure of an object under the influence of a controlling interest; in the parts that catch our attention and in their relations to each other we select from an indefinite number of alternatives. In each case the object assumes a different character as a result. Consider what is seen by a farmer, an artist, and a real estate dealer when viewing the same meadow from the same spot by the roadside.

In the third place, again with no outright error, the relations perceived between what we are looking at and its environment constitute an interested selection from various alternatives. A couple of simple illustrations are provided by the following figures.* What confronts us is a pattern of lines, curving and straight, but we imaginatively supplement those lines and perceive them as part of the object thus constructed. In each of these cases two different objects can be constructed, and the vital role of interest appears in the fact that our perception immediately responds to whatever interest dominates. In the one case, if we think of a duck we will perceive a duck's head; if we think of a rabbit we will perceive a rabbit's head. In the other case, if we look for a white flower that is what we will see; if we wish to see a Maltese cross that is easily possible.

Hardly an hour passes in the experience of any person without his exemplifying this factor in one of these last two ways.

Perception then is no mere passive reception of what an object tells us, but an *interaction* between perceiver and object, in which each plays an essential part. And among the factors that play a crucial part on the side of the perceiver is his controlling interest.

But another half of the story remains to be told. If we consider the way in which a person describes or explains what is perceived, the problem posed by this relativity arises again. When it is faced in that form, how does the above account need to be enlarged?

Our first clue is that in these activities one is always selecting and emphasizing some *connection*—either between the parts of an observed object

* The gestalt psychologists have experimented with many figures of this kind.

or between it and other objects. This is what "describing" or "explaining" involves. So the next questions will naturally be: What forces are at work in this selecting and emphasizing; what are the laws according to which they operate; and what connections are we thus equipped to notice?

The answer has traditionally been provided by the so-called laws of association; and among the laws recognized for many centuries are those of similarity and contiguity. From the perception of any object our minds naturally pass to the idea of something that is like it or has been experienced in close conjunction with it. But these laws are not the only ones. In the course of time other factors that influence this process have been detected, and two of them are especially important. One is the factor of frequency. When the same connection has been experienced several times it readily comes to mind when one of the objects thus connected is experienced again; each of the instances reinforces the association. The other is the factor just emphasized in the case of perception—namely, our controlling interest or emotion.* An object readily, and often very vividly, suggests some desired end which we might realize through its aid, or some entity which we fear lurks in or behind it.

A second clue appears when we examine more fully how these principles of association work. And the most instructive lesson is that *the factor of motivating interest plays an ultimate role in relation to all the other factors.* It operates as an active principle of selection among the various ideas that are suggested under their influence. Our minds fasten, among these alternatives, on one that we especially like, or dread, or hope for, or are anxious about. Take the factor of similarity. Anything entering our experience is similar in some respects to an indefinite number of other things; the similarity we actually emphasize in any given case is largely determined by our dominant interest. Likewise with contiguity. Whatever we perceive is contiguous in space or time with many other things; our selection among them is an interested selection. And interest powerfully reinforces in its own way the factor of frequency. That factor seems to be at work independently; habits of expectation are built up through repeated experience of a given connection between two objects or events. But of the many regularities thus soliciting our attention we primarily notice those that are important to our interests. We are especially alert, for example, to the regular tempo-

* Edward L. Thorndike recognizes the importance of this factor by adding to the laws of similarity and contiguity the law of effect. See his *Educational Psychology* (New York: Teachers College, 1913), Vol. I, p. 172; Vol. II, pp. 22 ff.

ral connections between events, because they provide the basis for a causal explanation, which is always valuable.

It is crucial not to miss the bearing of these forces and principles on our scientific thinking. It is tempting to regard any scientific explanation as constituting part of nature's order, because it is a verified hypothesis or a theory confirmed by extensive evidence. But before it can be verified, a hypothesis must occur to someone as a possible explanation. And the laws of association reveal the conditions under which a hypothesis about the connection of one event with another can thus occur. Hence a scientific truth may be described as the most adequately verified, to date, of the explanations that have occurred to human minds under the influence of these conditions.

The ultimate role of motivating interest among these principles of association teaches some very illuminating lessons.

For example, it obviously explains the fact that a person strongly tends to perceive, in an object to which his attention turns, what he wishes or fears to perceive instead of what is really there. Because of the ultimate role of interest and emotion, one's expectation is determined by them except so far as their influence has become modified by other factors; and one perceives what he expects to perceive except so far as his mind is open to other possibilities.

This maxim has drastic implications. It means that if an expectation completely dominates the mind, with no doubt present and no alternative recognized as possible, a perception is necessarily controlled by it—nothing else can be perceived. But ample evidence confirms this conclusion; think of persons under the sway of a psychosis. One can perceive something different only when his expectation is tentative rather than absolute, and thus leaves room for other possibilities. In the light of this truth we can understand the well-authenticated cases from primitive life where an individual has dropped dead on discovering that he had unknowingly violated a taboo whose inexorable penalty was death. His fearful expectation was so powerful that he had to perceive himself dying.* The best present-day

* A living authority can often create such a vivid emotional expectation that facts have to be perceived accordingly. Wovoka "ordered the Dakota pilgrims to kill a buffalo on their way home, to cut off the head, tail, and four feet, and to leave them; he declared that the buffalo would come to life again. He also told them to call upon him if they were fatigued when travelling home, and he would shorten their trip. In evident good faith the delegates reported that the words of Wovoka had been fulfilled on their journey; they had killed a buffalo and it was

example is found in an impassioned defender of a political ideology. The committed Marxist can only see the course of events everywhere in terms of the Marxian "laws" of history, no matter how implausible the resulting description may be; while the fearful anti-Communist can only see every unfortunate event as the product of Communist machination.

In the presence of such facts as these, it is not hard to understand why man has only slowly learned how to distinguish ways of perceiving that offer trustworthy guidance in his subsequent experience from those that mainly reflect a strong emotional motivation, and why, in interpreting what is perceived, even conscientious thinkers tend to cling to presuppositions supported by intense feelings long after they should have been abandoned. A group of psychiatrists state the essential truth when they say that a major obstacle to achieving objectivity in our thinking is the "need of all human beings to organize their perceptions to fit into preexistent conscious and unconscious expectations, needs, and wishes, and to reject, minimize, or 'fail to see' things that would upset their basic views about the nature of reality." [4]

But there is strong historical evidence for the encouraging conclusion that over the years man has advanced from a situation in which each wish or fear or established habit easily dominates his perception and interpretation of objects toward one in which this control is sufficiently modified by the lessons of experience so that only the motives that do not conflict with reality determine these processes. If this is so, his mind has been gradually gaining in openness and flexibility as he faces a world not made for him and in constant change. With an increasing range of his experience he is able to welcome alternative possibilities; no emotionally supported preference among them irresistibly masters him in advance.

VI

A basic question is inescapably raised by these relativities. Is objectivity in our description and explanation of the world possible, or are we condemned to an incurable skepticism?

Almost all thinkers today are sure that the objectivity we seek can be achieved. For example, Whitehead, after remarking that "observational discrimination is not dictated by the impartial facts. It selects and discards,

---

restored to life; they had prayed to Wovoka when tired of a night 'and in the morning we found ourselves at a great distance from where we stopped.' " (Robert H. Lowie, *Primitive Religion* [London: George Routledge & Sons, 1925], p. 255).

and what it retains is rearranged in a subjective order of prominence," goes on to say: "We have to rescue the facts as they are from the facts as they appear." [5] Yes, but when we are aware of all that is involved in the relativity of knowledge, how is this accomplished? How can the subjective order in our perception and interpretation of facts be replaced, except by one that is equally subjective in the sense of being likewise conditioned by variable human interests? What *is* objectivity, when understood in full recognition of the ubiquity of these forces?

One need not forget, in stressing the unavoidable relativities, that there is always a reality that is being perceived and interpreted. Will turning to it help us here? The situation in which the presence of a real object comes home most clearly is that in which, our underlying presuppositions and the interest they reflect being taken for granted, we are choosing between different instruments for observing or measuring that object. The instrument chosen makes a difference in what is observed; conversely—and this is now the crucial point—when the choice has been made, the result is determined by the object. The length of a stick will vary according to the kind of ruler used, but once the ruler is chosen the length is dictated by the stick.

The familar concept of "size" provides a good illustration of the essential principles involved when the presence of a real object is taken into account along with the inevitable relativities. Our presupposition that any physical object must have some size is relative to our interest in measuring it and comparing it quantitatively with other objects. Without such an interest we would have no idea of size, but any entity that can be dealt with in terms of that interest will have size. Further, that it has this or that particular size is relative to the measure selected; using a yardstick will give one result, a meter rod another. But when the measure has been chosen, the size is determined by the object.

Since this principle appears to apply universally, the presence of the object remains evident when changes other than a change from one measuring instrument to another take place on the side of the observer. Its presence remains evident when he falls under the sway of some particular wish or fear. For the world confronting us does not conveniently change so that the expectation generated by such a feeling will always be confirmed. If our observation or interpretation is to square with reality, we must be prepared for any expectation to be corrected in the course of our dealings with that world.

Nonetheless, the threat of subjectivism has not been escaped. Whenever the influence of some particular interest or emotion is thus recognized and corrected, the process of correction itself reflects the influence of another interest—hopefully, one more dependable in our quest for truth, but still an interest. Thus observation and interpretation are always motivated observation and interpretation. Though the object is there, whatever we say about it is said by us, not by the object. Our knowledge and insight are gained through a process of interaction which is constantly affected by factors on both sides. A humanistic relativism would seem to be unavoidable; what we take anything to be reflects deep-seated motivational forces in ourselves.

A generation ago, when the insistent challenge of these facts was frankly faced, many philosophers with an empirical and realistic bias adopted a theory called "objective relativism." * We shall appropriate the phrase and see what can be learned from this theory. One who champions it has abandoned the attempt to interpret any object as though it could be identified with the entity directly perceived when we look at it; he recognizes that these relativities render such an interpretation untenable. But since the relativities can be discovered, and the effect of each of them on our perception of the object can be determined, he sees a plausible solution of the problem they pose. Why not identify the real object with what is perceived when this task has been carried out, and the object thus placed in the full setting of the various factors that condition our experience of it? We can, he hopes, overcome all subjectivism in this way.

To illustrate his proposal: Although a stick is perceived as straight under the conditions that usually obtain, we cannot say that it is really straight without qualification, because when partly immersed in water it is perceived as bent. How describe its reality then? Simply by taking the relativities explicitly into account. We shall say that it is a straight stick when observed in air, but also (and just as really) a bent stick when seen with one end in water. So the objective relativist recommends that we adopt the following axiom: Whatever characteristic is revealed by an object under any specified conditions of observation is a real characteristic of it under those conditions. Hence we can know its true nature despite these relativities; they themselves become a part of our objective knowledge.

It is natural, in describing the point of view espoused in this theory, to take a word that is familiar in a certain limited setting and extend it to a

---

* I believe Professor A. E. Murphy first introduced this phrase. See his "Objective Relativism in Dewey and Whitehead," *Philosophical Review,* Vol. XXXVI, No. 2 (March, 1927), pp. 121 ff.

much wider setting. This is the word "perspective." People are accustomed to use this word in the narrow area of spatio-temporal perspectivity, and some extension of it beyond that area is not infrequent. But these are special cases of a quite general principle. There are many other factors that affect the appearance of an object, such as the ones discussed above. When they vary, it varies accordingly. Why not, then, extend the concept of perspective to include all the conditions to which our observation (and likewise interpretation) of an object is relative? In that case any object will be conceived as inevitably refracted—not only through space according to the laws of spatial perspective, but also through all these other conditions according to the laws governing their influence on how it appears. All that is needed in order to operate with this concept would seem to be a full description of the factors that affect the way it is perceived under varying circumstances, and the laws of their behavior.

An enticing idea! Can it be carried through successfully? What we find when this program is followed out is that in the case of some factors, such as the intervening medium and the physiological organs involved in perception, the relevant laws are already known fairly well; in the case of others our ignorance is considerable but science can confidently progress in discovering their laws; in the case of one factor, a unique and baffling difficulty is met. This factor consists of the underlying interests that control our interpretation of objects by determining the very criteria of fact and of valid explanation that we employ. How so? Why can we not allow for them and their distinctive effect just as we do for the others?

In the case of the factors whose influence everyone quickly comes to understand, all of us detect without undue effort the difference they make in a perception, and know how to allow for it. Everyone has mastered the laws of spatial perspective and readily learns how to allow for such factors as color-blindness. With somewhat more effort we can detect the influence of particular and transitory interests in ourselves and others, at least if they appear frequently and we have noticed how they affect the way an object is perceived or explained. If it is these interests that we have in mind Ellwood is on firm ground when, after saying that "it is only as we eliminate the personal equation that science becomes possible," he adds: "In this sense the desires, wishes, interests, beliefs, and ideas of individuals in society can be studied as objectively as any other social phenomenon." [6]

The conclusion is that in the areas affected by these relativities, where one can distinguish between what he individually perceives and what another person under such and such different conditions would perceive, his observation can achieve objectivity. But in the case of what we have been calling the "dominant interest" of an individual or a group, a quite different situation confronts us. By this phrase is meant the motive (simple or complex) that at any given time pervades all the mental processes, including perceiving and interpreting, of an individual or a society. It has been referred to as the "determining tendency" by some recent psychologists. Such a motive is normally unconscious till it is lifted to explicit awareness. We have described it as the factor *with* which the individual or society observes and thinks—so completely and confidently that it is very difficult to break free enough from its control to think *of* it.

Why then, in summary, is neither our empiricism nor our realism able to help when such an all-pervasive interest is involved?

The empirical orientation tempts us to say: "If it is true that anyone's mental operations reflect the influence of some motive, this circumstance itself is a fact discoverable by empirical method—by a verified finding that such a relation between the motive and the outcome of those operations exists." But empirical method can only be applied to motives that we are already able to view from the outside, so that we can tell at once when they are there and can notice how they are related to other factors in our experience. With the underlying interests that form the core of our minds, one cannot distinguish on demand between the motivating concern and the observation that might verify some statement about it. The former is so embedded in the latter that no line between them can be drawn until one has achieved an explicit awareness of the motive and of the difference it has been making in his experience. Before then it inevitably operates as a subconscious criterion of fact rather than as a fact that can be observed as such.

The realistic orientation tempts us to say: "But there is always a real object that is being observed or explained. Does it not compel a thinker, as soon as he honestly seeks the truth about it, to become aware of whatever effects in his mind are due to varying motives, so that his observing and explaining will no longer be determined by them but only by the object?" The answer, however, seems equally clear. Yes, the process of becoming aware of these effects constantly goes on. But a distinction must be drawn between the way it goes on with the motives that are specific enough to be capable of clashing with observed fact, and the way it takes place with the interests that are so omnipresent that they determine the criteria by which we decide what is and what is not a fact. In the case of the former the conflict soon becomes obvious to a normal person; he will realize that wishes are not horses and so beggars cannot ride. The latter, however, cannot be detected and thus corrected in the same way. In their case there is no conflict between the interest and any observable entity, because what any entity is taken to be depends on the interest. If such an underlying interest diverges from the concerns that would control an ideal truth-seeker, the fact as it is perceived and described will reflect that divergence. A conflict is still likely, to be sure, but it is a conflict with the inclusive reality gradually revealed in the process of periodically revising our criteria of fact—not with any fact itself.*

To return now to the question that led us into these puzzling difficulties —does this mean that there is no such thing as objective knowledge? No; what man has achieved in his quest for truth has been achieved. What then *is* objectivity, and how is it possible?

The objective relativist, we recall, expects to discover the laws obeyed by the various factors to which our perception and interpretation of an object are relative, so that any given perspective can be translated into terms of what would be perceived from any other perspective. Now when this is successfully accomplished, as it often is, what actually happens? The supposition long prevailing in many quarters—that when we thus correct errors in previous judgments about an object all activity in our minds is eliminated, so that the object tells its own story to a purely passive recipient— has lost all plausibility. Activity is intensified rather than eliminated, and if it were eliminated no story would be told at all. What a mastery of the laws of perspective seems to achieve is that we conquer our variable and shifting individual wishes, expectations, and fears about the object, so that we can describe it in dependable, socially shared terms. We thus "objectify" a cognitive situation which otherwise would remain the prey of undependable subjective forces.

How is it possible for such translations to be made? Perhaps all that can be said at this juncture is that a human being has the power to place himself in the position of other perceivers, so that he can tell how the object looks to those who view it from a different vantage-point and under other conditions. To observe it thus is analogous, in perception, to the achievement of fairmindedness in controversy—one transcends his previous self so that he sees in the "given" facts not what his personal biases would dictate but what an unbiased witness would see.

This translation into sociable terms can be accomplished most easily when the differences that need to be allowed for have been frequently

* This conflict is discussed in the following chapter.

experienced by everyone. The laws of spatial perspective are so well understood that people know how the shape of a coin would appear even from a position they have never occupied. It is hardest where emotionally potent interests are playing their role; in the presence of the differences they cause one cannot jump at once out of himself into the perspective of another person. One can only move step by step in that direction, through sensitivity to what that person is perceiving and clearer awareness of the forces that obstruct one's power to share the experience of others. But progress in this direction is constantly going on; to live successfully in a social medium and to become adjusted to a wider network of human relations inexorably requires it.

The outcome of our inquiry into the relativity of knowledge then is that when man's cognitive enterprise is thoroughly examined, it reveals all the forces that existentialism, Marxism, and psychoanalysis have insisted on. They bear on human thinking in general and on philosophical reasoning in particular in essentially the way that these contemporary movements emphasize. Among other things, the strong attachment of thinkers to their present presuppositions is easy to appreciate. The pervasive intensity of the interests expressed in that conceptual framework prevents one from seeing beyond the horizon it sets, except feebly and haltingly; whatever one sees is seen with those interests and inside that framework. No wonder that G. J. Warnock is led to remark, at the end of his perceptive essay on *English Philosophy Since 1900*, on "the difficulty of becoming aware at any given time of the deepest, most unquestioned presuppositions of the day," and to suggest that it may be "the course of prudence to await with due humility the verdict of history."[7] That difficulty is indeed very real and humility is surely appropriate. But now that we realize the forces at work in the adoption, preservation, and revision of those presuppositions, why wait? Has the time not come to uncover them, and to probe their function in relation to the deep-seated interests they reveal? Can we not, by meeting this challenge boldly, play a part in shaping the verdict of history?

Let us therefore search wherever truth seems to lead, expanding our awareness as best we can in every direction, including the direction of our hidden motivations. Three centuries ago Spinoza discovered that through knowledge of one's emotions, reason and feeling can win a stable union that they were impotent to win before. Had he realized the powerful role of unconscious emotion he would belong to the twentieth century as well as the seventeenth.

And we must never forget, in our realistic sense of the perplexities facing us, that there is a hopeful promise in this enterprise. Through our ultimate concern for truth, about our underlying motivations as about everything else, progress is surely possible. The contribution you and I can make toward it may be slight, but others will join in the venture and will improve on whatever we achieve. It may be that a generation of philosophers in the not too distant future will say: "What a tragically impoverishing mistake it was to try to shut out from philosophic awareness—as we did for so long—the stupendous currents of emotional energy flowing in each of us, inevitably present in all our thinking and especially in our basic presuppositions! We saw in them only a sinister threat to our pursuit of truth, so we desperately avoided looking at them; we did not see that they can and must become its effective servant. In the past, philosophy could progress rationally only within the framework of some set of presuppositions, expressing whatever motives were dominant. When a transition from one set to another occurred it appeared to be a nonrational accident— a sheer leap from the cognitive framework previously taken for granted to a different one. Now, through expanding awareness of our motivations, we have learned how to include these periodic revolutions in a wider philosophical perspective, and thus to make each of them a constructive step toward the larger truth that lies ahead."

6

The dynamics of philosophical progress

I

The main conceptual tools that we are using in this enterprise need to be sharpened and set in order. Two concepts are evidently quite fundamental: those of presupposition, and of the motivations revealed in the adoption, maintenance, and replacement of presuppositions. Several distinctions need to be drawn in each case, and the significant relations between them form a rather intricate pattern.

Presuppositions of varying degrees of philosophical importance have already been discussed. It is obvious that this word has a unique meaning; although it has something in common with such familiar terms as axiom, or postulate, or principle, or suppressed premise, it is not identical with any of them. A formal definition would have little value and will not be offered,* but everything hitherto said indicates that when we are looking

---

* P. F. Strawson defines a presupposition, in effect, thus: A statement that asserts

for a presupposition we are looking for a belief which in some sense underlies an utterance that has attracted our attention. What sort of "underlying"
this is will best be revealed by proceeding with our present analysis.

Look at a couple of simple illustrations. For one:

> I eat my peas with honey;
> I've done so all my life.
> It's true they do taste funny,
> But they don't roll off the knife.

This little rhyme obviously presupposes that one naturally eats peas (and
doubtless other solid foods) with a knife. For the other:

> "Every evening I drink at least five cups of coffee."
> "Man, doesn't it keep you awake?"
> "It helps."

Here two opposing presuppositions are revealed, one held by the first
speaker and the other by the second. The reader will find it good practice
to formulate them—and likewise the presupposition that the two speakers
hold in common.

What distinctions are needed in which to raise and answer any philosophical problem about presuppositions? *

One distinction would seem to be indispensable. We shall call it the
distinction between "ultimate" and "non-ultimate" presuppositions. By the
former is meant presuppositions that are taken (by a certain individual or
group at a given time) as beyond doubt; by the latter, presuppositions that
are recognized as subject to doubt. For example, in any particular use of his
measuring tape a surveyor presupposes that the tape is accurate. But he
knows that it may have stretched through long use and needs to be checked
from time to time against a more dependable measure. That it is accurate is
therefore a non-ultimate presupposition. Whereas a scientist, when carrying out an experiment, presupposes that the event he is studying occurs

---

p presupposes q if q must be true for p to be capable of either truth or falsehood.
(*An Introduction to Logical Theory* [New York: John Wiley & Sons, Inc.; London: Methuen & Co., Inc., 1952], p. 175.) The main difficulty with this definition is that other forms of utterance besides assertions have presuppositions.

* All philosophers who have come to realize the importance and promise of
this concept are deeply indebted to R. G. Collingwood, and especially to his
Essay on Metaphysics (New York: Oxford Univ. Press, 1940). His primary
distinction is between "relative" and "absolute" presuppositions; see pp. 20–31.
If the course of thought in the present book is sound, no absolute presuppositions
in his sense can be admitted.

under certain causal conditions which can be discovered. He does not regard this presupposition as questionable and hence, so far as his thinking is concerned, it is an ultimate one. Our course of thought has emphasized the lesson that presuppositions which have been assumed to be ultimate may turn out to be non-ultimate instead; even a long-held and highly respected conviction may, under stress of further experience or critical reflection, prove to need revision. The principle that every event has a definite cause has functioned as an ultimate presupposition through most of man's intellectual history, but serious questions are now being raised as to its right to fill this role.

It will also be convenient to use the phrase "basic presupposition" from time to time; that phrase will mean any presupposition, ultimate or non-ultimate, that proves of special philosophical importance. Those that we are concerned with will usually be ultimate (for many thinkers) as well as basic.

Let us turn now to the motives expressed in our presuppositions, and draw some vital distinctions about them.

A philosopher who ventures on this topic today finds himself in a special difficulty. Not only are psychologists and sociologists rapidly accumulating more knowledge about motivation, as it is revealed in the interaction of people with each other and with the world around them; they also differ about the concepts and methods that can be appropriately used in studying this area, and new ones are being proposed. Also, schools of philosophers like the existentialists and the defenders of ordinary language are deeply involved in these issues, and are championing more or less novel ways of analyzing them. In this area all is in flux, and it is not yet apparent what "conceptual harness" (a favorite phrase of Gilbert Ryle) for dealing with it will win general approval when these debates have run their course.

In such a situation it would seem wisest to adopt a few concepts that have come to be widely employed, and which, despite some vagueness and ambiguity, can be given the needed meaning. We shall trust that these concepts will be readily translatable into more adequate ones when the latter have emerged in generally accepted form. "Motivation" itself, like "presupposition," will be given no formal definition; it will gain clarity as we use it.

Wherever a motive is at work there is revealed, in its active aspect, what is called "desire," and in its affective aspect what is called "feeling." "Desire" has many partial synonyms, each with a nuance of its own, such as "wish," "want," "longing," "aspiration." As for feeling, whatever other features it may have by which we distinguish between feelings of different kinds—e.g., warmth, disappointment, loneliness—there is always a positive or a negative tone; it is something that we like and wish to maintain, or something we dislike and wish to replace by a different feeling. On this account it involves "valuation"; we either value the present feeling sufficiently to want to preserve it, or we disvalue it, at least in comparison with some alternative that is more attractive. The very important word "interest" is generally a synonym for positive valuation, in both its active and affective aspects.

The word "emotion," which we have already emphasized, is sometimes simply a synonym for feeling; more often it means an especially intense feeling, which absorbs the mind and exerts a potent force. Happily, in the present context this ambiguity need give no concern. Our basic presuppositions, especially those functioning as ultimate, constitute the core of our very selves, hence the feelings involved in their adoption, preservation, and abandonment are intense ones. Any that at first are not intense come to be so if they prove able in the course of time to dominate our thinking. We can therefore freely speak of "emotion" as well as of "feeling" when referring to them. "Need" is also a word that cannot be avoided; it usually means a desire (with its accompanying emotion) that is rendered urgent by the realities of the situation in which it is felt.

Consider now the subjective and objective implications of these words. They are clearly involved in the analyses that will be needed, for desire, feeling, value, and interest do not exist *in vacuo;* they always focus on some object, event, or idea. Over the years a characteristic way of using the words in this aspect of their meaning, which we can accept, has developed. People think of a feeling or an emotion as a psychological force identifiable as such without reference to the object or idea involved; this is the way such words as "curiosity," "zest," "anxiety," etc., are frequently used. "Value" is assumed to be a quality of some object or goal, although it is generally recognized as implying a valuing subject. "Interest" is regarded as a psychological factor, implying a subject, but in most cases it is described in terms of its object or goal—we speak of an interest in music or in the success of a certain enterprise.

With the aid of this battery of concepts the necessary distinctions about motivation, in its relation to our cognitive pursuits in general and our presuppositions in particular, can be drawn.

First, there is the important distinction between motives that in a given thinker at a given time are so strong that their control over his thinking is complete, and those that are less blind or compulsive, being affected in some measure by awareness of their welcome or unwelcome consequences. Whatever presuppositions one holds under the sway of the former will naturally be held as ultimate; one will feel no need to question them. When under the sway of the latter he will realize that his presuppositions are not superior to doubt; since his mind is not tightly imprisoned by them, it will be open to the possibility of alternative motives and presuppositions.

This distinction is vividly illustrated in two familiar situations. One is the period frequently evident in the history of a society when certain motives are so widely shared that they dominate the intellectual scene without serious competition. In such a case the presuppositional framework that articulates them continues to appear reasonable, however serious its defects. Ambiguities are ignored, critics appear so completely out of step that they are neglected instead of answered, inconsistencies are tolerated since alternatives then at hand to the beliefs that involve them seem quite fantastic, and no one with intellectual influence has eyes for the considerations that would, if examined, disclose its inadequacies. The other is the situation marked by vigorous controversy between champions of opposing ideologies. Here both sets of motives are likely to be of the blinder kind, and to each side the position of its opponent seems completely irrational. The essential reason for the ominous peril of the fierce international conflicts today is that in the minds of extreme partisans in both East and West the motives underlying their presuppositions are of this kind. Whether civilization destroys itself or not may well depend on how rapidly the world can succeed in passing from the threat of domination by these motives to a state in which the motives alert to likely consequences are in firm control.

A second distinction is equally basic, but in a quite different way. It is needed to provide a foundation for solving the crucial problem of how assured progress toward truth is possible under the constant play of our motivations. This is the distinction between motives that hamper our quest for reliable understanding, and those that support it.

Reflect on a few random instances of the former. There is fear of novelty in a world constantly revealing novelty; there is admiring identification with some persuasive speaker when such a speaker may be wrong instead of right; there is anger toward whatever frustrates our desires, obstructing impartial judgment; there is the longing for an ostrich-like protection in a very perilous universe. Prime instances of the latter are the urge to uncover facts that have previously been hidden (which is what we mean by "curiosity"), the passion for precision, the yen to discover regularity in apparent disorder, the urge toward a dependable systematization of ideas, the wish to share the experience of others, and the need to accord with reality. Within limits, these motives aid our search for truth; only under special conditions do they fail to do so. Indeed, the need to accord with reality would seem to be a dependable guide without any qualification. Did we lack such motives as these, or were they unable to grow in strength, progress toward understanding the world in general and gaining philosophic wisdom in particular would be impossible. The pursuit of sound knowledge in any field rests on the sustaining energy these motives provide. As they achieve their own natural unity under growing awareness, perhaps they constitute the general motive that would be called "truthfulness"—the aspiration for cognitive integrity.

But unfortunately for our wish to simplify, there are also motives that in the decisive respect we now have in mind are ambiguous. A prominent instance is the desire for the approval of other people. Such a feeling obstructs a thinker's quest for truth insofar as it makes bold pioneering difficult, renders him easily upset by criticism, and makes him distrust ideas that are not quickly shared. It supports that quest insofar as it facilitates his putting himself in the place of others, entering into their experience and aspirations, and seeking a conceptual framework that will provide a place for the universe which each of them inhabits. Another instance is rebelliousness against the parental generation. This is a very constructive force in the readiness it fosters to question the presuppositions of that generation; it is not so in the often accompanying readiness to throw overboard everything prized by one's forebears.

A third distinction is between motives that merely affect the thinking of a single individual and those that are shared by a larger or smaller group. For our purposes the former can be neglected, except that their existence must not be forgotten. When one reflects on the latter, the question naturally arises as to whether any philosophically important interests are universal—shared by all men—and if so, what interests the list would include.

A fourth distinction relates to the time during which a given motive influences whatever thinker or thinkers are concerned. Some affective feelings are transitory, and thus differ from the rather prolonged ones that we call "moods"; and these in turn are distinguished from the still more enduring states referred to by such words as "propensity," "disposition," "attitude," "temper of mind."

This distinction is more significant than it might seem to be, for it leads to a quite vital question: Are there any motives that, once they have risen to an influential position in a thinker's mind, can be maintained permanently? This question is vital on its own account and also because it is involved in such further questions as: Are there ultimate presuppositions that can be maintained permanently? If so, what part have they played in philosophy, and what part should they play in the future?

Merely to survey this list of distinctions indicates that some complicated problems lie ahead. But through their aid a few promising guidelines take form. For example, with regard to the motives that are important for philosophic understanding, it is clear that we will mainly be concerned with those that support the quest for truth instead of those that oppose it, those that are widely shared rather than those limited to a single person or small group, and those that are capable of endurance instead of those that are transitory. Moreover, with each realistic facing of difficult problems, grounds for hope also appear. The essential reason for this hope is simple but fundamental: To become aware of motives that conflict with truthfulness is to begin to grow *beyond* them under the guidance of that awareness; to become aware of motives that accord with truthfulness is to grow *in* them.

II

These distinctions were drawn without any reference to the process of revising our presuppositions under the influence of whatever motivations are active at any given time and place. Now, two further distinctions which require that we have that process specifically in mind are essential. The main task for which all these distinctions are needed is the task of wisely mastering that process as it goes on both in each philosophic mind and in the history of philosophy at large.

The primary distinction of this pair arises from the causal relation between motive and presupposition when the former leads to a thinker's adoption of the latter. It has already been mentioned and illustrated. There are motives that make no difference to the content of the presupposition they thus influence, such as a strong attachment to any presently held presupposition, and motives that affect the content itself, such as impatience for a quick and simple solution of our problems. Because this distinction is very important we shall need further illustrations, of both kinds, that have been philosophically significant.

For cases of the first kind, consider the following passage from Lewis S.

Feuer, in which he describes some motives that have led in the past to the adoption of philosophical ideas. In his terminology they are presented as exhibiting certain characteristic "principles."

> First, there is what we may call the principle of *counter-determination*. . . . We tend to reject the opinions and ideas of persons to whom we are opposed. . . . When American conservatives in the early nineteenth century wished to define themselves in a way distinct from the deistic democrats, they were led to reject Locke, the democrats' philosopher, and to adopt Coleridge's transcendentalism in his stead.

But when a thinker is moved to reject a philosophy in this way there is always more than one alternative to which he can turn; he selects among various possibilities. Hence a second principle, over which we need not pause, is invoked to explain how that selection takes place.

> We are then led to a third principle—the principle of *the life cycle* of philosophic ideas. Philosophic ideas tend to go through a life cycle. They begin as liberating, offering a fresh perspective, stimulating new experiences and scientific advances with their live idiom and images. But as time goes on, as the philosophic system becomes a hereditary creed, it ceases to exercise this evocative function. It becomes an official philosophy. . . . Trace . . . in modern times the transformation of Marxism from a revolutionary philosophy into a bureaucratic ideology.[1] [Italics mine]

Feuer's point about this third principle is that the philosophic ideas that at an early stage of their evolution expressed an adventurous motive may at a later stage express a conservative one, the content of the ideas remaining unchanged. The more general conclusion supported by both principles is of course that there are motives that influence the adoption of presuppositions without affecting their content. In the case of "counter-determination," it is evident that when one is moved by hostility toward a social group the presuppositions he adopts will depend on the system of thought held by that group. If it is an empirical philosophy, some form of rationalism will appeal to him; if it is a materialistic philosophy, some anti-materialistic doctrine will be attractive. Other motives that act in the same fashion are reverence for an admired teacher, eagerness for approval by one's associates, and an itch to startle people by a clever refutation of some widely held belief. The content of the presuppositions adopted under the stress of such motives depends not on the motives themselves but on the beliefs thus respected or attacked.

Turn now to some motives that do affect the content of the presuppositions to whose adoption they lead. Two obvious illustrations, important historically, are the longing that the universe fulfill our moral aspirations and the desire to anticipate and control future events. Each of these motives will make a difference to the cosmic order presupposed under its influence; a thinker dominated by the former will conceive the universe as a teleological order of which philosophy and theology have seen many examples, while the latter will require a predictive order of causal conditions and consequences like that of modern science.

With this distinction in mind we can raise a fundamental question about the process of revising presuppositions, namely: What happens to the motive and to the presuppositional content in the course of that process? A general answer would seem to follow from the above reflections. On the side of the content, plausible alternatives to the presuppositions previously accepted are glimpsed; new ways of conceptually organizing our experience are being considered. On the side of the motives at work, a suspicion arises that other forces besides the desire for truth have played a part in the adoption of the presuppositions now questioned; no thinker wants such forces to determine his beliefs, hence the gamut of motives in his mind undergoes a change under the guidance of this suspicion. If one comes to realize, for example, that he has adopted a certain presupposition because of admiration for a philosopher who championed it, the influence of that emotion begins to weaken; for he knows that no philosopher is infallible.

But a more detailed answer is needed, and to reach it still another distinction must be introduced. This is the distinction between the process of revision as it takes place under the play of accidental forces, and as it becomes a conscious and systematic quest to reconstruct our basic presuppositions. Unpredictable circumstances prod philosophers to change their presuppositions from time to time, but we may expect that in the future purposeful reconstruction will be more and more in evidence.

In the first situation the new content apparently takes form in a thinker's mind first, awareness of the motive that is no longer acceptable only occurring afterward if at all. How does that content take form in his mind? This may happen in various ways. Perhaps he has been criticizing another philosopher and has elicited a reply that makes him aware of a weakness in his own position. He suddenly realizes that an idea he has previously taken for granted is not as sound as he had assumed. An alternative that promises to remedy that weakness then occurs to him.

In the other situation, when a thinker is consciously reconstructing his presuppositions, it would seem that either order could be exemplified. He might have formed the habit of periodically questioning his presuppositions and locating the motives expressed in their adoption. On the other hand, he might seek to uncover any motives in his mind that conflict with truthfulness; in that case they will become the objects of awareness first. He will then recognize how they have influenced his adoption of some presupposition, which he sees is questionable for that reason. When this order is exemplified, the reconstruction of the presuppositional content will follow and be guided by the new emotional awareness.

But something crucial has been omitted. It may be that even in the first of these situations the temporal relation between motive and revision of content appears as we have described it only because attention was paid merely to what occurs on the conscious surface of the mind. When the process going on underneath is recognized, does it become highly probable that some unconscious change in the thinker's dominant motivations has taken place, and that otherwise he would not have seen the inadequacy of his earlier presupposition and become receptive to the new one? That this would be the case is naturally suggested by the very conception of motivation as filling a causal role.

Consider a pair of controversies that will test this suggestion.

What is a "relation"? This question was hotly debated by the analytic realists and the idealists fifty years ago. Here is an important relation—say, between the root and the trunk of a living tree. There is sharp disagreement as to what its essence is. The idealist is impressed by the fact that the two entities are conjoined in a single organism, which as such possesses a distinctive character. He holds that the relation "synthesizes" them into that organic totality; it is therefore a "unifying ground" in virtue of which they constitute a systematic whole. The realist notices these same things, but he interprets them otherwise. His basic concern is an accurate analysis of the complex situation thus presented—that is, a careful description of each of the elements and connections involved. When that is accomplished, he regards his job as done. He means by "relation" merely a distinguishable link of some kind disclosed by descriptive analysis of the facts.

Turn now to the other controversy. Does consciousness exist, or is a behavioristic interpretation of mind fully adequate? This question was raised a generation ago by J. B. Watson and is still in vigorous dispute, although varying interpretations of what "behaviorism" means have appeared. James B. Pratt, among many others, insists that consciousness exists. He roundly condemns behaviorism as palpably inadequate; certain facts of mental life, in his judgment, absolutely require the concept of "consciousness" for their explanation.* But those who champion the other position find no identifiable facts that are not facts of behavior. For them, consciousness is not a given fact but a very dubious interpretation of certain facts.

Here are two instances of a typical philosophical impasse. How can such a conflict be understood in terms that will illumine the dynamic relation between motive and presupposition? And since we will soon need to reflect on a group of motives mentioned earlier—those that are capable of being permanently maintained—can we understand it in such a way as to throw light on them as well?

In answer, I offer this twofold thesis: (1) Each of the contending philosophies has already committed itself to a distinctive controlling motive or interest, and (2) in all cases that interest is such that it can never be defeated by any observable fact. Hence its champions always find what they are looking for; and their dominant interest can be permanently maintained. We shall test both halves of this thesis.

In the first controversy the idealist is saying in effect: Look for an inclusive synthesis; that is what is important. The realist is saying: Engage in a thorough dissecting analysis; that is always worth accomplishing. And nothing stands in the way of following either proposal. The realist's aggregate of terms and their linkages can always assume some sort of organic unity for the idealist. The latter's systematic whole never forbids the detailed dissection of the realist, and under it becomes a pattern of elements in whatever specific connections are found. This means—and here we recall the historical survey in Chapter II—that the proposal of each includes its own criterion for deciding what is a fact and what is not. As a result, the realist's atomic entities have no factual character for the idealist, since they are absent from his universe, nor do the idealist's unifying syntheses seem to be facts to the realist. Unless something happens to modify their dominant interest, neither will perceive the distinctive realities perceived by the other.

In the second controversy the decisive difference is a difference between two motivating commitments as to what is the wisest way of studying

* *Can We Keep the Faith?* (New York: Ryerson Press, 1941), p. 185.

mental phenomena. The behaviorist prizes the outcome reached when all facts about mind are so explored that they constitute a publicly observable realm; and if such facts are what one is always concerned to discover, this recommendation can never be defeated. His opponent values the result reached when mind is so conceived that a major part of it, at least, constitutes a private realm open only to subjective observation. Since such a realm can easily be found if one looks for it, this proposal can never be defeated.

The lessons taught seem to support my thesis; let us state them.

The primary lesson is that the decisive role in the dynamic relation between motive and presupposition is always played by the motive. Each of these four philosophies has its distinctive criterion for identifying and interpreting facts, which its champions have come to value as the most promising and fertile criterion, deserving unlimited employment. Adoption of such a presupposition is the effect of the rise to a dominant position of the appropriate motive; and any change in the presupposition would be preceded by a change in the motive. If this is true without qualification, then even when awareness of alternatives to a presupposition previously taken for granted appears to come first, a shift in the underlying valuation has already taken place and could be detected were one consciously alert to the occurrence of such a shift.

But another lesson is taught also. Each of these philosophies is convinced that its criterion is universally applicable, and in each case this conviction appears to be confirmed. The idealist has adopted the way of synthesis in a larger whole as the essential route to the understanding of all facts; the realist, by contrast, has chosen the way of analysis into distinguishable elements and their orderly connections as always suitable. How could either position fail to find confirmation? For the behaviorist the way of publicly verifiable description is the sound route to the understanding of all mental facts; everything reported by introspection must be construed within the framework it provides. For his opponent the distinctive nature of mental facts is what is revealed about them to a private view. As long as each adheres to his value commitment, how could his position be refuted?

We need now to give systematic attention to this second half of the thesis—namely, that the motivating interest expressed in each of these philosophies is such that it can never be defeated by any observable facts. Everything becomes grist to its mill; therefore once such a motive has been adopted it can be permanently maintained. Are there then presuppositions that can be permanently maintained? If so, what role do these motives and presuppositions fill in philosophy? To answer this pair of questions, the idea that there are motives which affect the content of the presuppositions adopted under their influence needs further examination.

The word "affect" is vague, and it has been used for this reason. A basic presupposition may be quite simple or it may be rather complex. When it is complex there are likely to be features of it which do not specifically reflect the motive that led to its adoption. By careful analysis, however, it is possible to disentangle these features, and what will then be left is a presuppositional content wholly generated by that motive. So far, for example, as a teleological cosmology pictures the universe as realizing generally approved ends it reflects a moral motivation, but such a conception will normally contain other features as well. When we have before us, either directly or as the result of this kind of analysis, a content wholly generated by the controlling motive, the two are so intimately connected that it is often natural to refer to both by the same phrase. Expressed in psychological terms it is the motive; expressed in logical terms it is the content of the presupposition. In the idealist position, for instance, the controlling motive is that of seeking an inclusive synthesis; the presuppositional content is the belief that such a synthesis can always be found, and that it provides the explanatory reality needed.

This truth in turn has a vital implication. Any presupposition wholly generated by a motive that never needs to meet defeat will also never need to meet defeat. No refractory facts will ever be observed; no conflicting considerations will be compelling. If a philosopher who holds such a presupposition decides to do so, he can maintain it no matter what happens.

Some perennial philosophical problems are clarified by this conclusion— for example, the problem of the a priori in its contrast with all that is contingent in human experience.

The fact that there are motives and presuppositions that never need to meet defeat enables a philosopher to discover the realm of the a priori and to give it systematic articulation. The reason is that the concepts in which such presuppositions are expressed appear, when one has adopted them, to be universal categories naturally required for the description and explanation of anything. Prominent among the categories emphasized in the past are time, space, number, causality, substance, and quality, along with those of formal logic. Each theory of these basic concepts reflects some dominant interest that a philosopher or school takes for granted as capable of being permanently maintained.

A theory of time, for example, gives stable form to our experience of sequence as interpreted under the influence of such an interest. But no dominant interest is shared by all philosophers, nor does any remain dominant through all historical periods; and it is now no mystery that several interests can fill this role with high success. The outstanding difference revealed in the history of Western thought is the difference between time conceived as a dimension of living growth and time as a dimension for measuring change. The former reflects a concern to understand life as experienced from the inside; the latter a concern to gain exact knowledge of objects in motion. A theory of space gives stable form to our experience of the togetherness of things, likewise under the influence of some persistent valuation. The outstanding difference that has appeared here is the difference between space conceived as a network of simultaneous relations between objects, and space conceived as an infinite room in which objects move. The category of causality gives form to our experience of one thing or event as capable of explaining the existence or occurrence of another— the mode of explanation chosen again reflecting the influence of some deep-seated valuation. Whenever an interpretation of these categories that has been widely influential for a period in some culture-area is replaced by another, my thesis would hold that this is because a significant change has taken place in the controlling interest of thinkers in that culture-area. The realities involved have come to be differently envisaged and need a different conceptual framework for their interpretation.

An important philosophical implication of the preceding chapter is thus specifically brought out: Our criteria of form and of fact depend on our ultimate values, and on the way they evolve from time to time under growing awareness.

III

Let us return at this point to the strong attachment of philosophers to their present presuppositions. The outcome just reached enables us to see this emotion in a completer setting. When it was examined earlier its irrational aspect stood out prominently. But a more rational aspect is evident when we recognize that presuppositions may be such that they never need to be defeated. In their case, why should one not be strongly attached to them? We know, of course, that a philosopher's confidence that his presuppositions are of this kind may be deceptive. However, if he has adopted them with sufficient skill, they might well be capable of being maintained without fear of running into any upsetting experience. Moreover, since the universe tolerates contrasting sets of presuppositions in this fashion, it would be unfortunate if various sets were not championed with sufficient zest to clarify their bearing on all major problems; in that case the resources on which future thought can draw would be impoverished. With the idealist and realist in mind, for instance, not only is there no contradiction between the demand to seek a further synthesis of whatever facts are at hand and the demand to engage in their further analysis; each of these schools is making a contribution that would be lost if it did not persistently apply its dominant interest and adopted presuppositions. Future philosophy will not wish to be deprived of syntheses that the realist would never have taken seriously, nor of analyses that slip through the idealist's net.

But these considerations have not eliminated the irrational side of this attachment. We must now bring that side out more fully, hoping that by doing so in the present setting we can see a wise resolution of the problem posed by this powerful motive. Two facts are pertinent here.

One is the simple fact that nobody wants his fellow philosophers to be rigidly attached to their presuppositions, for he is eager to convert them to his. It is clear that if all cling firmly to the presuppositions now held, there is no chance of success for anyone in this enterprise. Thus, if he adopts such a policy, he is assuming a special privilege that he is sure would be out of place in others.

The second is the lack of any assurance that he will not find himself weaned away from his present philosophical orientation, no matter how strong his attachment to it. In the past a philosopher could usually expect to stick to whatever position he had adopted after reaching adulthood; the pace of change was relatively slow and he could more easily isolate himself from criticism by other philosophers. But this situation exists no longer. The clash of ideas insistently presses on everyone, and it takes place on a worldwide forum. In this dynamic interaction with other thinkers, it makes a great deal of difference whether or not a philosopher has oriented himself in advance for a shift in his basic presuppositions.

If he has not done so, he can hardly avoid being harassed by disturbing emotions when such a shift takes place. He will be aware that he has been trying to convert other people to ideas that he was not going to hold very long himself. In this poignant awareness feelings of guilt, resentment, and futility easily arise. He feels guilty because he has misled his students and readers—he has persuaded them, more or less successfully, to adopt a position that he now sees to be inadequate. He may be consumed by half-conscious resentment toward those who had induced him to believe the ideas he has now come to reject. This resentment can easily be extended to the ideas themselves; he will feel an urge to punish them for having maliciously deceived him. Gilbert Ryle provides a convenient example. He realizes that some readers of *The Concept of Mind* will be puzzled by his blunt summary of the Cartesian dualistic conception of man in the phrase, "the ghost in the machine." Hence in the Introduction he makes a frank confession: "Some readers may think that my tone of voice in this book is excessively polemical. It may comfort them to know that the assumptions against which I exhibit most heat are assumptions of which I myself have been a victim." [2] As for feelings of futility, when a radical change of presuppositions occurs late in a philosopher's career it is hard to avoid a haunting sense that the main work of his lifetime has been in vain.

If, however, he has oriented himself to the change before it occurs, there will be no place for these distressing emotions. To be thus oriented does not of course mean that he must keep silent about the presuppositions that seem to him sound. An active mind naturally expresses whatever position it has reached at any given time; it cannot help illustrating Hegel's taunt about Schelling: "He carried on his philosophical education in public." Indeed, Hegel illustrated it himself, as one who reads his early philosophical writings quickly realizes. But it is not necessary to do this in words implying that one thinks his education is complete. In the present setting what this orientation does involve becomes clear, and a solution of our dilemma about philosophical attachment emerges. One can conceive and publish the ideas that intrigue him, not as assured truth but as promising possibilities in the quest of philosophy to advance from where it now is toward the fuller truth. No feelings of humiliation will afflict him in this case. No regrets arise when one exemplifies the spirit of openminded and openhearted searching—the unqualified readiness to make the most of every available set of presuppositions while never allowing oneself to be imprisoned by it.

This readiness obviously characterizes the history of philosophy, as it deals with the varied and competing sets of presuppositions that are championed from time to time. On the one hand it never commits itself to any particular rival in this competition; it insists on keeping itself open to whatever is of value in all sets. On the other hand it refuses to be limited to the viewpoints that happen to be available at any given time; it always leaves room for new ideas that go beyond what philosophical insight has already achieved.

Why not identify ourselves with this inclusive historical process that absorbs the contribution of all philosophical movements as they appear on the scene, rather than with the particular presuppositions that happen now to appeal? Why not welcome continuing revolution in our philosophical presuppositions as a natural and normal process, to be fostered under conscious guidance—taking it for granted that no matter how satisfying or successful our present presuppositions seem to be, they are always capable of being replaced by a more adequate conceptual scheme?

Suppose that this orientation were to prevail in the arena of philosophical discussion. How would the rise of a new movement differ from what has been usual in the past?

In that situation the leaders of the movement would be free from the unjustified assurance that they have found a final key to the solution of all philosophical issues, and its opponents would be free from the equally deceptive urge to reject it out of hand so that they might remain in peaceful bondage to their own pet presuppositions. Indeed, in that situation there would be neither champions nor opponents in the sense with which we have been familiar. Those who propose a novel insight would do so tentatively, under no need to make exalted claims or to defend it with anxious heat; and others would feel no need to whip it off the stage. All philosophers would combine their talents to discover and unfold its promising possibilities—drawing the distinctions required to make it clear and tracing its systematic bearing on problems in every field. What proves unsound in its presuppositions would quickly be laid bare and left behind; the enduring contribution would emerge and find its happiest articulation.

But a crucial question has not yet been met. In what sense can this continuous reconstruction of presuppositions be called progress? Is there evidence that the outreaching awareness that guides it becomes a more inclusive awareness, and that the outcome of such reconstruction is a better, not just another, set of presuppositions?

When the course of history is surveyed with this question in mind it seems clear that philosophic awareness naturally reaches out in two directions, which may appropriately be called the horizontal and vertical directions. On the one hand, philosophy draws freely upon all insights that are available at any given time, and in doing this it is always seeking a broader perspective that will contain everything of constructive value in them. On the other hand, it never restricts itself to integrating the promising values in ways of thinking already available. As new dominant interests and ideas emerge, new clues to the structure of reality are suggested and keen philosophic minds are ready to seize and make the most of them.

Moreover, the philosophies of the past that illustrate with marked success these two modes of expansion are the ones that history accounts the great philosophies—especially the few whose achievement is high in both of them. Some possessed an unusual power of pioneering alertness, and were thus geniuses in the vertical mode; some displayed an unusual power of hospitable responsiveness to the presuppositions of other philosophies, and thus were geniuses in the horizontal mode. The former sensed among the kaleidoscopic phases of human experience some that might be significant for philosophical insight but had never provided the key to such insight before; the latter sensed the constructive possibilities in the various schools of thought competing in their day and could disentangle them from their unpromising accompaniments. Plato, Descartes, and Locke are outstanding examples of the philosophical pioneers; Aristotle and Kant of the philosophical synthesizers. Indeed, these two thinkers achieved their syntheses in such a fashion that they were successful pioneers also—they initiated ways of thinking that many generations following them found fruitful.

Where and how do these modes of outreach reveal an inclusive as well as an expansive awareness, and demonstrate progress as well as change?

Consider first the horizontal expansion, where these features are most easily visible. When we examine the syntheses that are achieved from time to time it appears that they can establish a perspective that embraces a wider range of experience and reflection than any previous perspective. Evidence of such a revision of presuppositions, and clues as to how its success was won, come to light in more than one area of philosophical history; we shall pick an area for detailed illustration that is especially illuminating. The philosophical issues that emerge there center around competing definitions of this or that philosophical concept, and the syntheses consist in replacing narrow definitions by broader ones which take account of the considerations that seem compelling to each of the opposing schools. The partisan definitions, previously assumed by their champions to be universal, are cut down to size and become species under one or another of the broader definitions thus established.

The procedure exemplified in this kind of synthesis might be appropriately called a "formation rule" for determining the meaning of the major concepts that provide the medium of philosophical discussion.*

---

* In my earlier writings I have referred to this procedure by the phrase "generic definition," and that phrase has some advantages. See my paper on this topic in *The Philosophical Review*, Vol. LXII, No. 1, (January, 1953). I have applied

The outstanding instance of this procedure in ancient philosophy is Aristotle's way of defining "causality." In his time there were various schools disputing hotly about the nature of the causal relation. Some insisted that real causality lies simply in the matter out of which an effect appears; some, in the form that comes to be exemplified; some, in the end that is realized through the process; some, in the action of a productive agent. Such argumentation could have been maintained indefinitely, and doubtless there were those prepared to maintain it indefinitely. Each school would merely have had to keep on claiming that what it was seeking is the only causal factor worth seeking, and that its definition of causality is the only justifiable one. No school would have been forced to abandon its claim. Aristotle rescued the category from this futile dogmatism by assigning it a more general meaning, under which the possible truth in each of these contentions could be given a recognized place as species. We have a right, he said in effect, to look for what each of the disputants is looking for; the material cause, the formal cause, the efficient or the final cause; and when we look for them within this impartial instead of some partisan perspective we can tell what sort of explanation each provides and how they can contribute together toward our total understanding of an effect.

The most striking instance in early modern philosophy is the gradual emergence of an inclusive definition of "knowledge." Here no single philosopher is responsible for the achievement although Leibniz, with his distinction between "truths of reason" and "truths of fact," played an important part. The historic conflict between rationalism and empiricism centered around two contrasting beliefs as to how this concept should be defined. The rationalists presupposed that all knowledge must be capable of cogent deductive demonstration; any ideas incapable of being established in this way do not count as knowledge. The empiricists presupposed that knowledge of factual phenomena can be established through sense-perception, even though deductive proof is in the nature of the case impossible. Indeed, the extremer empiricists were ready to reduce all knowledge to this type. But each of these definitions proved to be too narrow. Gradually a more adequate conception of knowledge, making a place for both kinds, was adopted. Thinkers realized that the rationalistic ideal of knowledge is appropriate in logic and mathematics, while the empirical defini-

---

tion is entirely justified in the realm of observable fact. A comprehensive and neutral framework was thus established within which all issues about knowledge could be discussed without being hampered by dogmatic claims and partisan prejudices.

During the last seventy-five years the procedure illustrated in these two cases has been exemplified in the emergence of a new and fruitful use of the word "value," especially in the ethical field. The utilitarians had been asserting that the major problems of ethics can be adequately analyzed only in terms of an ultimate end; the followers of Kant had contended that this is possible only in terms of a universal law; and other theories were appearing in addition to these. By taking over the concept of value, which had already been filling a quasi-impartial role in the science of economics, ethical philosophers have put themselves in a position where this impasse can be ended. When a utilitarian and a Kantian state their positions in terms of this neutral and more general category, the theories become objectively comparable; it is possible to clarify in an unbiased way the kind of value that is realized by pursuing the end of human happiness and the kind that is realized by applying a universal rule. In what situations each is an appropriate guide can become clear.

Certain important virtues of the use of this formation rule will be obvious from these illustrations. After the more impartial definition or concept has been established, no philosopher need deprive himself of the light thrown by any of the alternative positions thus synthesized; in the last illustration, for example, neither the "right" nor the "good" need be subordinated to the other as a moral category. Not so obvious is the vital virtue that is best revealed by asking: In the absence of such a formation rule and the conceptual framework established by it, what linguistic medium can be employed when one is discussing a fundamental issue with an opponent? Evidently, he must either use his opponent's concepts, defined in terms of the latter's presuppositions, or his own. A philosopher might be willing, for the sake of propitious discussion, to adopt the first of these alternatives and try to express his own position in terms of that unaccustomed medium. But he would find that with the best will in the world this is not always possible. Some issues that seem relevant to him, and perhaps quite important, cannot be stated in the linguistic resources provided by his opponent.

This is in fact the case with the conflict in the field of ethics between utilitarianism and Kantianism. If a utilitarian should attempt to explain his position in the language of Kant, he would meet no difficulty in stating, in that medium, his insistence that the happiness of every man is to count equally with the happiness of every other; for this is one of the implications of Kant's categorical imperative. But it would be a sheer impossibility to state in that language one of his major problems as a utilitarian—how to evaluate, comparatively, different kinds of happiness. For to the Kantian this is not an ethical problem at all. He would have to break it up into two questions: first, a psychological one—How do people actually decide between alternative modes of conduct that promise satisfaction? and second, an ethical one—How should they decide which mode of conduct, if any, is right? In this dissection the problem as conceived by a utilitarian has disappeared. Similarly, a Kantian would be unable to state in utilitarian language the basic feature of his own position which holds that each man possesses indefeasible moral rights, so that the happiness of all other men must be regarded as subordinate to them.

These inherent limitations bring out clearly the fact that until appropriate neutral definitions are established fruitful discussion of the issues involved is drastically hampered. Either the contending philosophers remain at certain points in linguistic isolation from each other, or else one or the other disputant must abandon problems that are genuine and important to him because of inability to state them in his opponent's language.

When philosophers join forces in applying this formation rule to such indispensable concepts as "experience," "truth," "reality," "meaning," "value," and the like, the horizontal expansion of awareness at the level with which philosophy is concerned should be greatly accelerated as compared with the way it has occurred in the past. The long-run aim in employing it methodically and cooperatively would be to make available a philosophical language as comprehensive, impartial, and fertile as possible, so that all problems troubling any inquiring mind in the present or the foreseeable future can be stated in its vocabulary and can advance in the medium it provides toward a wise solution.

Of course there are limits to the acceleration that is possible. No definition of a major concept that has any chance of proving more adequate can be concocted on demand. The search for it takes time, and requires a stretching of awareness under the guidance of an interest in achieving the most universal perspective that might be achieved.

But philosophical insight also expands in the vertical dimension. It reaches out toward promising ideas that are not bound in any way to the present philosophical scene. Can this kind of expansion exemplify a more inclusive awareness and bring progress as well as change?

Here speculative imagination obviously has a freer play. It acknowledges no responsibility to any set of ideas already at hand. Yet, if such an out-reach is to succeed in its aim, there must be as genuine a continuity with the present and the past as in the case of the horizontal expansion. There is a difference between a promising philosophical idea and a fantasy; and we can distinguish between them, although not as confidently as we might wish in advance of their systematic elaboration. The former exemplifies in its own way the quest for synthesis, for it has no chance of succeeding unless it is such that the total body of knowledge and insight now at hand can grow toward further fulfillment through it. And sometimes success is achieved.

IV

Progress, at the deep level with which we are concerned, does not consist in gradually coming closer to a defined goal, but rather in continued improvement at whatever stage and in whatever setting is now present. But faith in it and commitment to its achievement imply an unqualifiedly dynamic orientation toward the universe and everything in it—an orientation that acknowledges the ubiquity of change and is always ready to make constructive use of the opportunities change brings. Is this creative orientation the one that can most successfully be maintained?

Let us reflect on it in the widest setting in which it might be viewed, surveying the whole adventure of man on the surface of this planet and observing how he has dealt with the challenge of change. I see in this setting a growing ability on his part to accept its pervasive presence, to improve on the past by learning new lessons as they are needed, and thus to master the art of transforming change into progress.

During the vast era preceding the rise of civilization primitive man must have learned new lessons by which he became better adjusted to his changing environment; otherwise the obvious achievements won in that period could not have been won. But significant achievements came so infrequently that he was almost unaware of their coming. With the rise of civilization this was no longer quite the case; thinkers realized that salutary improvements had from time to time been introduced—for tradition kept alive the memory of a discoverer of agriculture, an inventor of a counting system, the initiator of a more efficient type of political regime—and that such reforms were occasionally occurring in the present. As yet, however, this realization was dim, and it remained so for many centuries.

The orientation of intellectual leaders in this regard at any given epoch is most clearly revealed when we measure their ability to question established beliefs and to open their minds to the possibility of novel solutions. In the primitive mind the painful tension of doubt about established beliefs can hardly be tolerated at all. As civilized societies develop, there is an unmistakable increase in the ability of people to tolerate this tension. Ancient and medieval thinkers were able with equanimity to entertain alternative answers to minor questions, although they were sure that their logical and metaphysical principles were grounded in eternal truth. This need of decisive commitment still persists in the areas of theology and politics; sects may diverge on nonessentials without risk of damnation, but on the fundamentals of doctrine no skeptical doubt or criticism can be allowed.

A revolutionary change of attitude dawned with the appearance of modern science, a change not yet fully assimilated by the civilized layman. It involved a shift from the prevailing ancient assumption that all additions to knowledge really needed by man have already been made, and that therefore the main task of thinkers is to demonstrate to the ignorant what is already known by the wise, to the awareness that more truth always lies ahead and that the task of science is steadily to widen the frontiers of the conquered area. And the modern scientist realizes that even the most soundly verified knowledge may not be final; he assumes that it is always capable of being improved.

Such a drastic reorientation naturally led to the conscious emendation of men's ways of living as well as their ways of thinking. Technicians and engineers learned how to apply the knowledge won to that end, and what had been in earlier ages a slow and unconscious transformation became a rapid, purposeful, and systematic process of revision.

The impact of this momentous revolution on the business world of today is increasingly evident. When President Harlow Curtice of General Motors was asked in 1956 by members of the congressional committee investigating that industrial giant what the secret of its success was, he replied that it was an "attitude of mind." This attitude consists, he said, in bringing the "research point of view" to bear on all phases of business enterprise—assembling of facts, analysis of the lessons they teach, and readiness to follow the trail indicated even if it leads into unfamiliar and previously unexplored territory. The guiding assumption in this point of view is simply that "anything and everything can be improved," and the best single phrase by which to describe the underlying attitude is, in his words, "the inquiring mind." [3] Change can be for the worse, but it can also be for the better; the task of the inquiring mind is to find out how to realize the latter of these two possibilities.

If this bold and optimistic assumption is sound everywhere, it applies to philosophical presuppositions; they too are always capable of being improved. The distinctive and exciting role of the philosopher is to exemplify the inquiring mind in its most basic and general form. By reconstructing from time to time the conceptual foundations of our thinking, he expresses in that difficult but inescapable realm the radically progressive orientation exemplified by the scientist in his specific revisions of knowledge and by the industrial researcher as he utilizes these revisions in meeting more efficiently men's practical needs. The logical principle underlying this orientation is that any statement whatever that has seemed or now seems to be true under all possible conditions may prove to be true only under certain conditions.

Thinkers in the West are familiar with the idea of "alternative conceptual systems" and have gained facility in its application to various realms of thought. In realizing that alternative sets of ultimate presuppositions are always possible, have we not discovered the realm of its widest, indeed, of its unlimited application? When one applies it here his mind becomes an active crucible in which all conceivable ways of interpreting the universe can be envisioned, articulated, and compared. Indeed, philosophers are coming to realize that in the long run there is no tenable alternative to adventurous inquiry in this realm as in others. Said former Justice Holmes: "To have doubted one's first principles is the mark of a civilized man." [4] And what Morris R. Cohen affirms of presuppositions in the field of history surely applies everywhere: "The safeguard against bias in the writing of history, as in the natural sciences, is not to indulge in useless resolutions to be free of bias but rather to explore one's preconceptions, to make them explicit, to consider their alternatives." [5]

Moreover, some philosophers realize that the unqualifiedly dynamic character of science requires full acceptance of the same dynamic role for philosophy. If never-ending and unrestricted innovation is to be welcomed in the sciences, it is also essential in philosophy. In the words of J. P. Corbett, if science is "the permanent revolution of all the ideas and principles in terms of which we order, interpret, and explain the world," [6] modern man's acceptance of science carries a trenchant consequence for his attitude about everything—theology, economics, political ideologies, metaphysical ideas—namely, that he must be ready for revision everywhere. For the only real alternative to innovation about everything is innovation about nothing.

The position of those who are opposed to innovation [in any area] is only impregnable and beyond discussion so long as it is kept consistent— so long, that is, as all kinds of innovation are rejected in theory and blocked in practice. If, for example, science is exempted from the ban, then . . . also, as experience shows, amounts and kinds of knowledge will eventually be released into society by science which will make the task impossible of keeping its structure, and so the moral and social principles which it embodies, unaffected. When science is pouring out new kinds of knowledge, and therefore making possible new forms of life, it seems that no institution can be strong enough to keep society from moving off in new directions however destructive to the system they may be. Hence the opponents of innovation must oppose all innovation or else they will find themselves to be both theoretically and practically inconsistent. . . . But to oppose all innovation is much more than the great majority of those who are committed to so doing by the logic of their system can really stomach. The value of scientific, if of no other kind of innovation, is admitted by them all, both for itself and for some at least of its practical advantages. . . .

The real choice therefore is not between acceptance of innovation and its flat rejection, but between a confused and partial acceptance and one which is complete and clear. It is the fundamental task of philosophers at the present time to work from the first toward the second.[7]

If Corbett is right, innovation elsewhere inevitably entails unresolved conflict until thinkers unreservedly accept philosophical innovation. Man is capable of continued growth, not only in the particulars of his experience but in the underlying process that transforms his experience as a whole; and the former kind of growth requires the latter. Whether or no he lives in an expanding physical universe—which is an intriguing scientific theory —he does live in an expanding universe of human awareness, which is even more fundamental. In fulfilling this creative role, philosophy becomes the culmination and completion of the spirit of inquiry—of searching, of pursuing truth beyond every present horizon. Other intellectual disciplines by and large seek the detailed truths that can be discovered on the basis of a given set of presuppositions which they take for granted as sound. But the function of improving our presuppositions themselves must also be filled, for the only adequate adjustment to dynamic reality would seem to be an open, free, and adventurous adjustment, ready for innovation at every level.

So the philosopher who pioneers in this fashion will gladly leave it to other thinkers—scientists, mathematicians, theologians, engineers—to elaborate in whatever way may be needed the specific implications of any prevailing set of presuppositions, to enlarge our knowledge under their guidance, and to give practical direction to those who live for a while in the world whose structure they define. His own role in the expanding universe is like that of the research staff of a large corporation in the limited field of its responsibility, whose task is constantly to improve machines and methods while leaving it to the production staff to supply the market by the machines at present in operation. He identifies in mind and heart with the total evolutionary process that goes on in the history of thought, not with any particular framework of ideas now and then deposited by its ceaseless flow.

Two serious objections can be raised to this radically dynamic orientation: a practical one that may trouble psychologists and social scientists, and a theoretical quandary in which logicians may try to engulf us.

First, let us put outselves in the place of thinkers who are irked by what we seem to expect of this thoroughgoing revisionism. "Is it not quite fantastic to suppose that people can achieve such flexibility? Is not the power of tradition and habit, the need to feel secure in what they already believe, the longing to rest on authority, so potent and pervasive that it would be quixotic to expect in any but a few intellectual leaders this unreserved welcome to change?" And indeed we have acknowledged, throughout, the strength of man's tendency to cling to his present presuppositions and to the self of which they form the core; most intellectuals have succumbed to this tendency along with others. The forces of lethargy, tradition, and conservatism are very powerful.

The general answer to this objection is that people who are diffident of their own mental power and who therefore need to depend on authority will continue to do so; they will ignore the disturbing pioneers and will turn to such authorities as they believe can be trusted, finding in them the guidance and emotional support they seek. Not a few, however, are open to novel ideas even at the deepest level, and their number is gradually growing. Moreover, when we survey the accelerating process of change around us, is it not clear that the dogged and fanatical faith of many people in the absolute rightness of their presuppositions, and their slothful reluctance to open their minds to other possibilities, is the most perilous obstruction to success in the human venture? To cling with such grim determination to whatever ideas they already hold leads to dire evils in theory and sometimes to catastrophic ones in practice. Shall we not tactfully encourage, everywhere, the most flexible adjustment to the changing universe that can be realized? And here a more specific answer emerges.

Innate in man is a power of expanding awareness, of himself and his world; he has a wish to know the truth and to realize the conditions of dependable well-being in reality as it is. His fear of losing the cozy moorings of his present presuppositions, and his longing for the transitory satisfactions they assure despite their conflict with reality, are not the whole of his makeup. Because of this innate power, the long-run advantage is on the side of truth. No matter how intense any given motive may be, or how appealing the presuppositions that express it, if they are incompatible with reality man can become aware of that fact and can revise them accordingly.

In any case, people who insist on living by error when truth has been glimpsed gradually pass from the scene; the future lies with those who are not imprisoned by their present motives and presuppositions and can wisely reconstruct their way of thinking in detail and as a whole.

But the brows of some logicians are still furrowed; they are troubled by the theoretical difficulty. "You just can't have it this way," they are waiting to say, "for a reason you have not yet mentioned. Any consistent course of thought implies some presuppositions that for it are beyond question. You cannot avoid committing yourself to the presuppositions of your own conception of philosophy. Some of these are quite obvious. Your position presupposes, for example, that the whole framework of a person's present thinking can be discovered to stand in a definite relation to something beyond it—e.g., some describable motive in his own mind. Would not any such presupposition have to be accepted, on your own showing, as absolute?"

The answer to this objection is simple. There are two ways of "committing oneself" to an ultimate presupposition. One is the way of making it an absolute dogma. The other is the way of taking it as a relative guide, at present superior to any available alternative. Today, I see no reason to replace any presupposition of which I am aware. But there must be many of which I am not aware, and even in the case of others there must be some that will prove to need revision. While, however, they continue to withstand criticism and seem superior to available alternatives, it is sensible to stay with them. Perhaps a few will keep this advantage indefinitely.

Looking toward the moving horizon of our experience, can we find any wiser guiding maxim than this: If under the stress of searching criticism by oneself and others a given presupposition succeeds in maintaining itself, well and good; continue to hold it. But do not insist that even the most obviously acceptable axiom must remain so forever. The expectation should rather be that a more adequate replacement will be found for it, later if not now.

If one is always open to new insight he can be quite happy when it proves, for a while at least, not to be needed; if he is not open he will unhappily and anxiously resist when reality inexorably calls for change. The one thing to avoid is an imprisoning attachment to any presupposition and the motive behind it, lest growth in philosophic understanding come to an end.

7

Science and philosophy

How does science fit into this relativistic and dynamic perspective? What role has philosophy filled in relation to science, and what role can it wisely fill in the future? In view of the vast territory involved in these questions, my hope is only that I may have caught some insights that will aid our search for understanding.

The most serious problem confronts us in the realm of the natural sciences, when we think of the relativities described in Chapter V and especially of the relativity of all perception and explanation to human interests. How does the scientist meet the challenge posed by these relativities? He cannot escape that challenge, and no one doubts that he meets it successfully. Scientific conclusions are objective. As N. R. Campbell says: "Science is the study of those judgments concerning which universal agreement can be obtained." [1] What is the secret of its success?

I

The core of my proposed answer is this: Science achieves objectivity by making its own certain vital interests that all people share, and by setting itself to learn and follow the most effective way of satisfying them. A scientific law is not a description of how things behave when isolated from human motivation; we have no means of imagining what such a law would be like. Any description that can occur to a thinker and become a candidate for verification reflects the operation of forces in himself, and the ultimate force is his motivating interest. My proposal then is that a scientific law describes how this or that part of nature behaves in its dependable relation to some universal interest (or interests) of man.

In exploring this proposal, it will be best to give "science" the broad meaning in which it covers any sincere and persistent attempt to discover truth about the world; only thus can the varied conceptions of this enterprise that have appeared in the course of history be understood and impartially compared. With a narrower definition, it is easy to attribute a dogmatic absoluteness to the presuppositions of present-day science.

We begin with a very instructive fact—namely, that the whole development of science through the ages provides the most striking testimony to man's ability to become aware of the influence of emotional motivation on his way of observing and explaining events, and to replace a misleading way by one freer from deceptive distortion. When primitive man described the world around him he saw in it an unpredictable medley of spirits, whimsical wills, and magical powers; he did not yet know that these were the projection of his own anxieties, hopeful longings, and fearful apprehensions onto the natural events on which life and well-being depend. The most notable achievement of science to date is that through it our conception of how physical objects behave has been freed from the confusing presence of these subjective entities. As the latter are recognized in their true character they are detached from the external world and become mental processes, to be described in impartial psychological terms as soon as this becomes possible.

Our social science is now gaining the same emancipation; it is gradually learning how to view human behavior objectively instead of in terms of forces projected by the scientist. The process is slow, for the emotions naturally expressed in these forces, which resist unbiased awareness of our social relations, are very potent. But the emancipation steadily goes on, and no thinker has any serious doubt of the direction in which it is advancing.

Look at what has happened in the scientific study of anthropology. Entities that two generations ago were regarded by anthropologists as objective features of the various cultures they were investigating are now seen to be projections of an emotional need to view our Western civilization as superior to all others. Influenced by that need, scientists assigned to every culture its place in a supposed unilinear evolution from the crudest beginnings toward this "highest" form of social life, and that place was thought to be a property essential to it. Today the scientific study of human societies has largely been freed from the perverting effect of this conceit.

Thus the historical evolution of science demonstrates the encouraging fact that while the cognitive enterprise cannot be separated from the constant play of motivation it can gradually be liberated from motives that are superstitious, provincial, and otherwise unreliable. By exemplifying more and more clearly the qualities required for this liberation—open mindedness, respect for evidence, patience, and impartiality—science has become the great teacher of men in their quest to master the conditions essential to reliable knowledge.

Next, we shall try to detect the most general presuppositions that have been held as to what constitutes a scientific explanation, and to identify some of the interests expressed in them.

First, both primitive and civilized attempts to explain nature reveal at least one general interest and basic presupposition in common. They both confidently believe that there is intelligible order in the universe, by grasping which man can win the security and power he seeks in a perilous environment.

Second, all civilized conceptions of science seem to reflect another common interest; it may be present in primitive thinking too, but is not so obvious there. This is the interest in achieving economy in our explanations; the accompanying presupposition is that sound economical explanations are attainable. Whenever a scientist offers a more complicated account of some group of events than is necessary he presumably does it for temporary amusement; the task of understanding a baffling world is difficult enough without adding needless complexities. So science seeks simple explanations of intricate processes, and wherever two explanations are equally satisfactory on other grounds the simplest one is adopted. We need not pause over the question as to what the criterion of simplicity is.

But besides these universal interests and quite general presuppositions there are others that are clearly relative to historical circumstances, and among them are some that until recently have been relative to the particular culture in which they arose. In their presence one realizes that intelligible order can be conceived in many different forms and that each reflects a somewhat distinctive interest or set of interests. We must omit a comparison of Oriental with Western conceptions, although such a comparison would be very revealing.

Confining ourselves to what has been happening in the West, a casual glance at certain presuppositions widely held in ancient times, and almost universally during the medieval period, quickly discloses a striking difference from the presuppositions characteristic of modern science. Regarding causality, for example, two prevailing assumptions in those days were that an "infinite regress" in any causal explanation (i.e., refusing to postulate when tracing a chain of events backward that there must be a first or absolute cause) is irrational, and that a cause must be at least as perfect as its effect. How did such ideas arise, and why have they now been abandoned? My answer is that the dominant interest of intellectual leaders in Europe prior to modern times was different from that which now motivates scientific minds, and that therefore their whole conception of science, except for the general presuppositions mentioned above, was different.

The motivation that dominates contemporary science is in essence, I believe, a concern so to describe and explain events that the behavior of similar events in the future can be predicted and controlled. Its other activities fill their role under the influence of this concern. To live successfully in any environment depends on man's ability to anticipate correctly what is going to happen so that he can modify it in the direction of his desired ends where that is possible and adjust himself to the inevitable where it is not. Hence the results that science reaches, in its systematic endeavor to discover truths that will serve this purpose, gain objectivity. People everywhere can agree upon them. Hence, likewise, all can agree on the categories employed by science—space, time, causality, motion, matter, energy, function, correlation—when other meanings are set aside and they are defined so as to harmonize with that interest.

The most prominent instance of this redefinition appears in the history of the category just used for illustration—the category of causality. Aristotle's concept of "efficient causality" corresponds most closely, in his thinking and that of his ancient and medieval followers, to the concept of causality that came to be generally accepted in modern thought. But he does not envision a causal explanation as serving the purpose of predicting effects on the occurrence of their causes; in fact, temporal sequence is not essential to the causal relation in his mind. In modern science, however, temporal sequence has become an essential part of its meaning. Modern man is convinced that through intelligent prediction he can make nature serve his ends, and when effects are conceived as regularly following in time upon their causes an effect can be confidently predicted on the occurrence of its cause; otherwise it cannot. Indeed, several recent thinkers have frankly defined the causal relation in terms of the predictability of one event on the occurrence of another.

It is vital however to avoid construing this central idea of predictability in too narrow terms. An impressive illustration and therefore a natural paradigm is forecasting in the field of astronomy, where exact predictions reaching far into the future are possible. But the general meaning is much broader than this; it is better exemplified in a typical scientific experiment, or a series of observations aiming to detect a significant correlation between one occurrence and another. The basic idea might be expressed as follows: We gain predictive knowledge whenever we learn what else will happen if such and such conditions occur or are brought about; for then that happening can be predicted on the appearance of those conditions.*

To clarify this idea, two important distinctions need to be drawn.

One is the distinction between the role of predictability in the establishment of scientific theories and its role in dealing with particular connections between one event and another. In the former case its role is revealed in the circumstance that no theory can hope to win the acceptance of scientists unless it makes possible the prediction of facts and relations that are then discovered to take place as predicted. Especially significant are facts that had proved stubbornly resistant to attempts to explain them by alternative theories, and facts that had previously not been noticed at all.

In the latter case, where a particular event is predicted on the occurrence of another, a second distinction is important. It concerns the temporal relation between the two events. In many situations, especially in the natural sciences, the predicted effect follows after its causal condition, and this

---

* Stephen Toulmin, in his otherwise perceptive and illuminating book *Foresight and Understanding* (Bloomington, Ind.: Indiana Univ. Press, 1961), rejects the idea that prediction plays such a central and decisive role in scientific explanation. This is because, in my judgment, he conceives prediction in the limited sense of "forecasting." He rightly points out, however, that some scientific enterprises (e.g., the fertile classification of facts) precede predictive explanation and have their own independent value, and also that scientists are often influenced by explanatory paradigms lingering from the past.

sequence in time is directly observed; then the predictive relation can be thus expressed: Whenever A happens at t_1, B will happen at t_2. But often, especially in the social sciences, the two phenomena thus related seem to occur at the same time. In this situation the objective sequence is determined by the scientist's interest in controlling what happens. Which of the correlated occurrences is the "independent," which the "dependent" variable? That is, through which of them can one, when interference is feasible, control what happens in the other? Here the predictive relation can be thus expressed: Whenever a change is brought about in A a correlated change occurs in B.

But our survey thus far has left out a very important interest—an interest that has been a notable connecting link between ancient and modern science. This is the interest in discovering a mathematical order in the world of nature, enabling us to describe that world in terms of exact quantitative relations.

In ancient times the prime branch of mathematics was not arithmetic or algebra but geometry. Also, except for a few pioneering figures like Archimedes and Aristarchus of Samos, who would have been happier if they had been born two millennia later, mathematicians did their work in the setting of one or another of the prevailing cosmologies—that of Pythagoras, or of the atomists, or a teleological cosmology such as Plato and Aristotle championed. And although astronomers viewed their realm as essentially that of celestial geometry, they were by no means free from astrological presuppositions, while among the Pythagoreans and Neo-Platonists ideas about the magical potency of mathematical forms in general were never quite abandoned.

In early modern times a new epoch in the fulfillment of this interest dawned, marked by the persistent and successful effort to apply mathematics in measuring the motions of physical bodies. Among other things, a more exacting standard in the formulation of causal laws could now be realized; when the motions of objects are conceived as subject to quantitative measurement they can be explained in terms of "functional" instead of merely causal laws. This enables prediction of events to be far more precise than was possible before; given a certain set of causal conditions the scientist can predict not only that a specified effect will follow but just what its quantitative structure and relations will be. When, for example, a projectile of a certain description is launched under such and such circumstances he can foretell, not only that it will fly in a given direction but also what its initial velocity will be, how far it will travel, at what angle it will fall, when it will reach its target, and what the force of its impact will be.

The fundamental place of the interest in prediction and control in modern science is vividly revealed in the transformation undergone by mathematics as it has become acclimated to the setting dominated by this interest. Look at the tasks that occupy a modern mathematician. Of course he will at times just play with intriguing forms, but he is often doing more than this—in his own way he is participating in the predictive enterprise of science. Instead of seeking axioms that can be plausibly viewed as self-evidently true and tracing their quantitative implications (as with few exceptions was the case until a century and a half ago) he now experiments with various postulate-sets, moved in some measure by an interest in their possible applications. Sometimes problems faced by other branches of science explicitly guide his imaginative search. Whether this is the case or not, he will be aware that novel problems in other fields are met from time to time and that by filling his role in this experimental fashion he may sometimes provide a mathematical pattern in which those problems can be fruitfully stated and resolved. He may thus anticipate significant applications in other scientific fields; models of exact analysis that can be used in various situations become available.

I I

Leaving this preliminary survey, let us now reflect on the proposed view of science and of the motivating interests expressed in it. On the one hand, if that view is right, the successive cosmic pictures that science offers us tell something important about reality, for each picture is as objective as the tested methods available at the time make possible. On the other hand they tell something important about the evolving nature of man—his power to grow from one set of dominant interests to another and to reconstruct his scientific presuppositions, along with others, in harmony with that growth.

A question naturally posed by the second of these two assertions gives us a good starting point.

Some dominant interests can last a long time. But we know that even those that are pretty deep-seated may change sooner or later, and when they change everything else changes with them. Radical possibilities thus arise; we can hardly avoid asking if a wholesale revolution in the interests and presuppositions reflected in contemporary science is likely. Howard Becker boldly says: "Of one thing the scientist can be sure: namely, that the working postulational system of today will be the museum piece of tomorrow." [2] It seems clear that this could happen only as the result of such a revolution. Is he right?

If he means to raise a serious question about the presuppositions evident in all sincere attempts to decipher the world, and likewise those revealed by the search for truth in every civilized culture—such as economy and systematic unity in the explanations reached—he is surely mistaken. These appear to express a universal and permanent need of the human mind. Can any situation be imagined in which we would gain by abandoning them?

But the particular interests and presuppositions emphasized in modern Western science—especially the interest in gaining the kind of knowledge permitting successful prediction—do raise a question. In the long evolution of influential conceptions of science this emphasis is a relatively recent affair. Whether its sway is likely to be brief or enduring is a question worth thinking about at some length; light will be thrown on all the major problems that we wish to consider.

Many significant facts attest the great importance of predictive knowledge. One such fact stands out in the experience of every family. Watch the growth of a child toward adulthood, and observe the difference that appears according to whether he is surrounded by a high degree of predictability or by its absence. When a boy or girl finds his parents dealing with him consistently, even though the rules he is expected to obey are quite restrictive he feels secure, and he easily becomes adjusted to the requirements of orderly social life. He can anticipate with confidence what will happen if he does this or that. When his parents vacillate in enforcing the family's rules of conduct he feels insecure and lost. He cannot anticipate with any assurance; he finds himself living in a very erratic and confusing world.

Another such fact stands out in human experience at large. Although the scientific emphasis on predictive knowledge appears to be quite recent, the quest for this kind of understanding has by no means been limited to the areas now occupied by science. In many other areas man has been enlarging his ability to anticipate the consequences of what is happening, so that he can live more confidently as he looks toward the future.

Consider a few examples. The anxious concern of the Hebrew prophets was to predict the catastrophic consequences of radical moral failure to a community. Hindu and Buddhist thinkers discovered laws of spiritual growth, resting on the conviction that the sequence of stages which a person needs to pass through in that process can be predicted. Pioneering seers of various religions have offered predictive insights, some of which sound paradoxical: "Hatred is not conquered by hatred at any time—hatred is conquered only by love"; "They that take the sword shall perish by the sword"; "He that saveth his life shall lose it, but he that loseth his life shall save it"; "Gentleness overcomes strength." And turning to quite different spheres, people around us boldly predict the swings of the stock market and the outcome of football games, horse races, or national elections; often they do this with considerable skill.

Such facts are a trenchant reminder that prediction is simply conscious and articulated expectation; and men have never been blind to the truth that if they are to live successfully in any environment they must have expectations about the future that can guide action reliably.

How then did it happen that only in recent centuries has science given a central role to predictive relationships in the knowledge it seeks to establish? To answer, we must look back over the whole history of man's quest for knowledge, trying to gain a wise perspective on the evolution of science from its very beginnings. Such a perspective will also provide the larger historical setting in which the methods of revising common sense discussed in Chapter II can be more fully understood.

Thomas S. Kuhn in his thought-provoking book *The Structure of Scientific Revolutions* portrays the history of science as a sequence of revolutions from the dominance of one major theory to that of another, interspersed by (often lengthy) periods in which "normal science" is occupied in elaborating the then prevailing theory and achieving a closer fit between it and nature. Except for the earliest revolutions mentioned, those that he has in mind—connected with the names of Galileo, Newton, Lavoisier, Einstein—can be seen, however, in a long-run view of history, as minor rather than major transformations. In that view, vaster upheavals are also visible, each of which takes centuries or even longer to be completed and in which no single thinker or group of thinkers plays more than a quite limited role. Two such upheavals can be identified in the course of man's age-old quest to understand his world, and the revolutions with which Mr. Kuhn is mainly concerned have occurred within the scientific orientation that came to prevail as a result of the second upheaval.

The essential difference between a major revolution, or upheaval, and these minor transformations is that in the former the dominant interest governing the search for knowledge changes, and with it the whole conception of what scientific explanation requires; whereas in the latter the dominant interest and conception remain unchanged, and all that happens is that the theory which had served as a model in guiding the work of normal science under that conception is replaced by another. To call the latter "minor" transformations should not be taken to mean that they involve no significant changes in the scientists' methods and way of looking at the universe. It does mean that the major transformations involve far more drastic changes—one might say that when such an upheaval has taken place scientists find themselves living in a different universe than they had lived in before, and picturing the truth they seek in different terms. The meaning of all their categories has been revised.

If two of these upheavals can be confidently identified, it should be possible to describe three major stages in the evolution of science, each with its characteristic dominant interest, its corresponding view of the form that knowledge takes, and its conception of the universe. We shall see if historical evidence enables us to do this.

The first stage is that of the typical orientation of primitive man, with its (to us) queer mixture of aggressive magic and humble supplication of the powers believed to control events. The magical element reflects the bold presupposition that man can know nature in such a fashion as will enable him to make it do whatever he wants it to do. The element of supplication reflects the sobering realization that there is something in nature which cannot be thus controlled and to which he must submit. Primitive man could hold the two elements together without feeling any serious inconsistency between them because his dominant interest, in the historical situation that he had to meet, was a concern to get the forces in and behind nature to be favorable rather than hostile to him. Moved by this concern, it did not matter to him whether an incantation or a ceremonial prayer worked by magical coercion or by inducing a quasi-personal power to do the right thing; what was important was simply to find the successful technique. That there was an earlier period almost everywhere in which the methods of magic reigned alone is a plausible speculation.

The form that knowledge of the world took for him might be described by the phrase "associational apperception." Primitive man perceived events in terms of the laws of association mentioned in Chapter V, only very partially corrected by the lessons experience can teach. That is, he saw things happen mainly as he expected them to happen under the influence of his wishes, fears, and other constant sources of vivid association. What we would call "counter-instances" to his expectations were either not noticed at all or were explained in the simple fashion always open to primitive metaphysics—some opposing magic was at work, or the will of the animistic spirit involved was intractable. In many kinds of situation, indeed, the power of these forces affecting perception was so strong that there were no counter-instances—the expectation generated could become a self-fulfilling prophecy. This must have been especially the case with the techniques for inflicting or curing disease. Primitive man thus lived in a universe whose varied happenings were held together partly in the fashion required by the presuppositions of sympathetic and contagious magic and partly by those of early theology, with its belief that personal wills determine how things happen.

The revolutionary transformation which in course of time ushered in the second major stage—that generally prevailing in Greek and medieval science—involved several sub-processes which we must now try to describe.

For a long period the main need was for thinkers to lose confidence in the assumptions of magic and to learn the lessons implied by employing the other method—that of humble supplication. It was necessary to perceive quite clearly that "nature can only be conquered by being obeyed," and to realize that the techniques suggested by an undisciplined acquiescence in the principles of association do not dependably work. This realization slowly came. Although the appeal of magic on the human mind is so strong that its hold was only partly broken in the second stage, and continues to assert itself even in the third, leading thinkers did become aware of its fundamental error and followed the clue given by more promising ideas. In the setting of primitive thought this meant increasing emphasis on the idea that the powers responsible for nature's behavior are personal entities, operating behind the observed events rather than in them. They were pictured as superior to man in every important respect; among other things they are assured masters of all the magical arts that man would have liked to practice but had not been able to master. The beneficent divinities were gradually separated from the malicious demons, and as this happened one of the major ways in which their beneficence showed itself—according to the natural and growing belief—was in graciously revealing to man the knowledge he sorely needs to live life successfully.

These developments continued during the early rise of civilization. In that altered setting they paved the way for two further decisive aspects of the transformation which issued in the second stage in the evolution of science.

On the one hand men found themselves living in large empires with a single central authority whose laws every citizen had to obey. This experience facilitated the process through which the recognized divinities coalesced into a single, all-governing Deity—God as conceived by Judaism, the

Greek philosophers, Christianity, and Islam—who was believed to reveal, in the nature he created as well as in sacred scripture, the truths man needs to fulfill his vocation in this life and beyond. On the other hand the increasing division of labor had a significant effect. In any primitive society the intellectual leaders are never very far removed from active participation in the techniques of trying to make nature serve man's needs, and their conception of knowledge reflected this fact. As civilization evolved, however, this participation was gradually lost. More and more, the men who were intellectual leaders took no part in these processes, which were assigned to artisans without any social prestige. This meant that the relation of thinkers to events in their physical environment became that of a mere spectator; no longer was it that of an agent. There were outstanding exceptions among the Greek scientists, of course—exemplified by such men as Archimedes, Hippocrates, and even Aristotle in his biological investigations —but these exceptions had no apparent influence on the assumptions about cognition which in this situation came to prevail. That scientists had now become passive spectators was especially important in view of the fact that the thinkers of ancient civilization remained ignorant of most of the relativities that pervasively affect our perception and interpretation of events. Because of this ignorance, they naturally took for granted a rather naïve realism in their picture of how an observer gains knowledge of the world —he was assumed simply to apprehend the forms and laws that are already there for him to apprehend, revealed by God or nature.

The basic interest that dominated the second stage is readily understandable in the light of these historical factors. When thinkers have abandoned magic and feel themselves living in a world that they cannot control, their primary and persistent need is to find security in that world—intellectual security at least, and if possible, emotional security as well. With the universe now viewed as a single system, ordered by an ultimate Divine Being or cosmic principle, the way in which they sought to satisfy this need also becomes understandable. They were guided by a concern to reach infallible truths about the structure of the universe as a whole, and to demonstrate how every particular truth depends on those assured axioms. When man believes that he has achieved this kind of certainty he feels secure; he knows his place and the place of everything around him in the all-encompassing fabric of reality.

How was scientific knowledge conceived at the stage dominated by this interest? A twofold answer is needed.

So far as concerns its distinctive character, it took the form of a final explanation of the cosmic whole and all that it contains. In this setting it was no accident that the science of geometry provided the model of acceptable explanation in all fields where it could possibly be applied. The ideal of a deductive system grounded in self-evident axioms is the natural guiding ideal when, above all else, men seek security in the possession of assured truth. This does not mean that the ancients had no concern for successful prediction, but such concern as they felt played a very minor role. Astronomical forecasts were made, usually for astrological purposes, and in the field of medicine there was an interest in anticipating the future course of a disease on the basis of present symptoms, as also the effects of applying this or that remedy. This kind of interest, however, seems to have had almost nothing to do with scientific explanation; only when these detailed temporal sequences were seen in their relation to the ultimate causes did science achieve what was felt to be a real explanation.

When thinkers are moved by this demand for a final explanation, especially when they take for granted the teleological presuppositions of Plato and Aristotle, it is easy to appreciate why they adopted the presuppositions about causality mentioned above; the essential aim is to trace all secondary and finite causes back to an absolute and perfect cause.

So far as concerns the method by which knowledge is gained, the prevailing conviction at this stage was that it comes to man as *revelation*. Such a conviction is quite understandable in the light of the historical processes we have sketched. The transition from the first stage to the second left as its stable deposit the presupposition that man must submit to powers controlling his world, on whose beneficence he depends for whatever truths he discovers. What is instructive is the vigor with which the picture of knowledge as revelation persists, not only in this stage but beyond.

As the second stage led to the third, the revealer of truth came more and more to be conceived as nature rather than God, but this made much less difference than one might expect. Even when God faded into the limbo of a distant First Cause and sacred scripture was no longer regarded by scientists as a source of truth about the environing world, the same picture of how knowledge is gained remained dominant in the minds of thinkers. Nature continued to be viewed as revealing the forms and laws that constitute her truth to the apprehending mind of man, which receives in humble dependence whatever she reveals. Even today many scientists talk as though their task is that of plodding along from one revelation of nature to another, slowly filling their filing cabinet with the truths thus apprehended. Their expectation apparently is that sooner or later the files will be filled;

for the proper goal of science from this viewpoint is to establish a complete system of knowledge, in which every true proposition will have been discovered and assigned its proper place.

But as science advances into the third stage it has undergone a major revolution, as a result of which a quite different orientation toward knowledge and how it is won has emerged. The essence of the difference is that in place of humble submission to a world that must be accepted as simply given, man now feels confidence in his power to master it by his own resources and to change it in the direction set by his growing aims. The emotion dominating the second stage—a pervasive sense of being at the mercy of largely unpredictable forces surrounding him—has been replaced by an assurance that he can fill an active and creative role in dealing with his environment. The need to interpret the universe so that he can feel secure in it—to relate everything that happens to an eternal and hence dependable ground of reality—has given way to the buoyant feeling that he has already won his basic security so far as the physical world is concerned and can now learn how to remake it according to his desires. In this growing assurance, the changes going on around him no longer appear to be a threatening danger but become instead the medium through which hopeful possibilities can be realized. The confident attitude of the primitive magician is thus regained, but on the firmer basis provided by a sounder understanding of the conditions under which a really significant mastery of the world can be achieved.

The interest that seems more and more to dominate the scientific mind today, and promises to be characteristic of the third stage, is the one that naturally arises from this orientation and this new attitude toward change. It is an interest in steadily expanding our knowledge through new discoveries and thereby increasing man's control over the world. And the accompanying picture of how knowledge is gained, which seems destined to replace the long-prevailing revelational picture, reflects this interest and the historical setting dominated by it.

It might appropriately be called the *interactive* picture of knowledge. Thinkers are coming to realize that the gaining of knowledge takes place in and through a dynamic interaction between the human inquirer and his environment, and that the very nature of cognition is profoundly affected by that fact. This interaction becomes evident whenever the relativities involved in perception and explanation are fully recognized—especially the relativities to factors in man—but it becomes more strikingly evident when through his aggressive self-reliance the modern investigator engages in the diverse experimental and creative activities that are characteristic of science today. For several hundred years scientists have been systematically interfering with nature in their endeavor to make her fit their theories and their theories fit her; now they are even creating new substances—e.g., plutonium—possessing desired properties and capacities that were not possessed by any of the substances at hand before they came on the scene. In the presence of this enterprising involvement of the scientist with the world he is coming to control, the idea of knowledge as revelation seems quite out of date. Far from being a passive reception of what nature graciously or reluctantly reveals, cognition now appears to be the intellectual aspect of this dynamic interaction of man with environing reality. The pursuit and discovery of truth has become intrinsically bound up with his adventurous probing, testing, and remaking of the world, which presumably will continue without end. Knowledge is the conceptual product ever emerging from this process.

How shall we describe the distinctive form taken by scientific knowledge when viewed in this interacting setting, so that its contrast with the associational apperception of the first stage and the ultimate explanation typical of the second will stand out clearly?

It takes the form of predictive understanding of man and his world. When thinkers look toward change with hope instead of fear, and seek greater power over nature rather than security in it, this is the kind of understanding inevitably sought. Adopting such a self-confident orientation, their eyes are on what will happen in the future instead of on the supposedly changeless structure of the universe. Their concern is to anticipate as accurately as they can the effects that will follow from causes presently at work and to learn how to bring about the effects they desire. Only through the steady pursuit of this aim and the achievement of this kind of understanding can their bold interaction with nature attain maximum effectiveness. As science thus moves into the third stage, explanation and prediction, which had previously been separated in scientific thinking, come together in a firm and forthright union. All categories of description and explanation are now revised so that they will harmonize with this orientation; we have already observed the change required in the category of causality.

Minor revolutions of course occur within the larger process of consolidating this stage; they are the revolutions instructively analyzed by Mr. Kuhn. But the major revolutions must never be forgotten if we are to understand science in the widest and most illuminating perspective that can be attained. One trenchant reason why they need to be recognized is that certain important truths are likely to remain invisible if we are content with a more limited perspective—for example, the truth that these scientific upheavals involve a decisive change in the dominant interest of thinkers.

Suppose we ask how it was possible for modern man to find himself in the vast immensity of time and the unimaginable immensity of space that have now entered his awareness. He is today aware—as until a century ago he was not—of the evolution of life for half a billion years and of his own evolution for several hundred thousand years; he is also aware of billions of galaxies like our Milky Way, in manifold stages of development. We easily think of these achievements simply as great scientific discoveries. But scientists have to be ready for such achievements; and this readiness depends on the right conditions. Should we think of them instead as the outcome of periodic surges of man, in emotion as well as intelligence, beyond his previous horizon? For when they are viewed in the perspective just sketched, it is hard to understand how thinkers would have been open to these "discoveries" while they were dominated by the need for security in a finite and even cozy universe, and by a narrowly egocentric orientation such as was typical of the ancient and medieval period. A less adventurous interpretation of the observed data is always possible if our presuppositions require it. In short, it would seem that a revolutionary surge must be prepared for by some measure of openness to a more capacious orientation than has been taken for granted; in the absence of such openness how could anyone think seriously of inventing the instruments—e.g., the telescope—needed to explore that vaster universe?

We return from this historical study to our question about the possibility that the predictive emphasis of modern science may not long endure. An essential part of the answer is now clear. It is hard to imagine any time or circumstance when it will not seem important to predict the future as accurately as possible, or to imagine that, once man has become assured through many victories that increasing mastery over nature and guidance for life can thus be won, this assurance will ever be lost and the orientation grounded in it ever abandoned. Indeed, today we see the science and technology that express this orientation spreading their influence everywhere and entering into the thinking of all cultures; such a development would seem to attest their claim to a permanent role in man's quest for the most adequate understanding of his world.

And yet—it would be unrealistic not to expect that in time a major revolution, bringing radical changes, will again take place; the perplexities that have been haunting us are not yet resolved.

III

First, it will be fruitful to reflect further on this interest in successful prediction.

Our discussion thus far may have seemed to suggest that it is a self-sufficient interest, capable of being satisfied apart from others. But this is clearly not the case. The quest for predictive knowledge is normally influenced by other interests than the interest in successful prediction itself, for one engaging in such a quest is interacting with a complex of factors, human and nonhuman, in relation to which he has a variety of motives and concerns. Some of these are quite specific, some more general; but each of them implies an end that may affect the detailed form taken by whatever knowledge is gained. This means that there are many strands of predictive connection in any medley of facts we seek to understand, and that our selection among them is decided by the ends we want our predictive knowledge to serve.

Take a simple illustration. I am thinking of buying a house, and am trying to anticipate the consequences of this or that possible purchase as a guide to my decision. Whatever chain of consequences I select, I have an interest in successful prediction—I want my anticipations to be as accurate and dependable as possible. But more than one chain can be selected because there are several ends that I want this purchase to serve: it should provide comfortable living quarters for my family; it should facilitate my professional work; and it should be a sound investment. As I look at a house for sale, now with one of these ends in mind, now with another, the detailed predictive connections that I follow up are different; each set reflects its controlling end.

Applying this important principle to the scientific enterprise, there are always prospective ends—usually very general ones—which, consciously or unconsciously, scientists are eager to achieve and envision man as capable of achieving; these inevitably determine the predictive relationships selected as they probe any group of facts to be described and explained.

Thus applied, the principle throws light on our question about future changes in science and how radical these changes might be. Even assuming, as we probably may, that the concern for successful prediction continues to be effective, these collateral ends can hardly be expected to remain the same. They are subject to all the social forces that play upon every member of society, including scientists. In a period when certain ends are widely shared and therefore taken for granted by almost everyone, it is hard to realize that the forces reflected in them change. But they do, and when this happens with the deeper forces, even ends that have seemed most stable may change. Indeed, when one looks thoughtfully at the ends that have recently guided scientific activity it is not hard to imagine possible changes and the circumstances in which they would be likely to occur.

Let us make this suggestion concrete by turning for a moment to the important word "control." We have said that man is concerned to learn how to predict the course of nature successfully, so that he can modify it in the way he wishes to wherever that proves possible* and adjust himself to the inevitable where it does not.

What sort of modification do scientists have in mind?

During the modern era they seem to have taken for granted an interesting answer to this question; it reveals the kind of control they have aspired to achieve in their interaction with nature. That answer is well expressed by the word "manipulation." Pure science unconsciously and applied science consciously have been aiming at power to manipulate the world of objects as efficiently as possible—to bend their behavior into harmony with purposes imposed by man. The appeal of such an aim is easy to appreciate; emphasis on it expresses the growing awareness throughout this era of a wide gulf between the way in which nature has been serving man's needs and the way in which it might be made to serve them through greater predictive mastery of his environment. Will this general end continue to exercise such a dominant role? We shall focus our attention first on predictive knowledge of objects in the physical world and then on predictive knowledge of men in society.

For a long time to come scientists will doubtless be eager to learn how to manipulate the varied forces in the world of nature so that they will serve men better. Yet even in this area it is not hard to imagine a future in which that concern would change. Suppose an era when organized war has been ended, the world's population problem solved, and the standard of living everywhere sufficiently raised through the techniques then available so that people are assured all the material comforts that it is reasonable to

---

* Scientists (especially in the social field) sometimes use this word in other senses too—e.g., they speak of a causal condition as "controlling" its effect, or of a set of conditions allowed to operate without interference as the "control" of a set interfered with in a specific way.

desire. Would not the settled methods for providing these be so completely taken for granted in that situation that they would drop out of sight as a matter of conscious concern? Technicians would already be manipulating the forces of nature as fully as there seems any sense in doing. In such an era some different value expressing another human need and capable of guiding the further development of physical science may be expected to emerge into prominence and reshape scientific presuppositions to accord with it.

What value? One possibility readily comes to mind. The value of esthetic and mystic rapport with nature might replace the present zest for greater manipulative control. If that were to happen, the structure of science would presumably be altered so as to provide a prominent place for predictive laws by which men can be guided in realizing this rapport. The artist lives in such a relation with nature now; he is ever telling us that the physical world is far more than a system of instruments for satisfying our practical needs. And the "pure" scientist would very likely find it easier to do his work in such a setting, for it is a historical accident that his urge to understand the world has in the recent past been entangled with the manipulative ideal.* We would expect of course that a large measure of continuity with the scientific structure we are now familiar with would be preserved through such a change, for science always seeks to retain everything in its past achievements that does not conflict with the newly adopted presuppositions.

How about the scientific study of man himself? At this point a vital issue must be met. Thinkers in the democratic tradition (as well as those in the tradition of each of the great religions) realize that the kind of control over other people that is morally justifiable differs radically from the kind that seems permissible with subhuman objects: a human being is not to be manipulated. It follows that the kind of predictive knowledge needed is also radically different. But this realization has had to contend with a powerful rival. The seductive urge to apply everywhere the exact techniques of physical science, combined with the aggressive wish to control other people as though they were chattels, insinuates into the sciences of man a method that flatly contradicts our humane ideals. The "behavioral sciences" are caught today in the dilemma of wanting their knowledge to serve these

---

* The reader should not miss a provocative passage discussing from a psychoanalytic viewpoint the motivations behind physical science, and the ways in which they are likely to change with the growing maturity of man. See N. O. Brown, *Life Against Death* (New York: Modern Library paperback, 1959), p. 236.

ideals and also wanting the kind of knowledge that a dictator can put to effective use in "conditioning" all people who fall under his power. Such a serious conflict will have to be resolved, and any enduring resolution will involve a revision in the ends now governing the scientific study of man, and thus in the predictive relations on which it concentrates.

IV

Next, a very fundamental question arises. What is the scope of our power to achieve successful prediction? Apparently it can be exercised wherever temporal regularities of any kind are detectable, so that future events can be reasonably anticipated by careful observation of past and present events. Does the region in which this is possible have any limits?

A specific form of this question is especially interesting. In view of the emphasis we have placed on major motivations and the presuppositions adopted under their influence, are they capable of being predicted? The interests that dominate thought in any part of the world appear in temporal sequence; is this kind of sequence such that an interest that will prevail in the future can be predicted through clarified awareness of present interests?

I have just implied that this is feasible in the case of the interests that exert an influence on the physical sciences. In Chapter VI a similar conclusion appeared plausible in more general form—namely, in the idea that as awareness of our basic motivations expands, the blinder interests give way to ones more alert to the likely consequences of pursuing them, and the interests that clash with truthfulness are gradually replaced by ones in harmony with it. If these ideas are sound, some measure of predictive understanding is possible even in this difficult region of our controlling aims as they change from time to time.

To what extent then can successful forecasts be made in the area of human motivations and the beliefs they affect?

In the case of specific motives there is no serious problem. Advertisers obviously accomplish this or they would go out of business; they learn how to forecast the conditions under which a given product will appeal to consumers and induce the belief that it is what they want. Also, any adult can predict certain powerful interests that a youth will show at this or that stage of his growth, such as an interest in the opposite sex when he becomes an adolescent, together with the changes in his beliefs that will be involved.

But our main concern is whether the more deep-seated interests by which men are moved, and the ultimate beliefs that reflect their influence, can be predicted.

One essential and instructive limitation appears. It is clear that no one can predict the novel basic interests that will in the future take form in his own mind, nor the presuppositions in which they will find expression. In this area prediction becomes intrinsically impossible. Could a person anticipate them they would already exist—they would have replaced the ones now dominating his thinking. Their gradual emergence in each individual marks the advancing horizon of his experience, and their gradual emergence in all individuals marks the advancing horizon of human experience as a whole. But this may be the only limitation. Even in the case of such basic interests, if one is a rare genius—both in sensitivity and in breadth of perspective he may be able to predict with significant success their emergence in thinkers around him, and to glimpse the kind of presupposition needed to express them. There is evidence, as we have seen, that pioneering minds have been able to sense the concerns destined to appeal to the coming age and to formulate the conceptual framework in which they could be wisely articulated.

A daring idea now becomes plausible. Perhaps man's entire quest for knowledge and insight can be fruitfully organized, for the foreseeable future, around the emphasis on successful prediction.

Assuming that such a development is a significant possibility, and that in any case it will be enlightening to see what it would involve, let us mobilize the conceptual resources needed to think effectively under the guidance of this idea. What major distinctions must be recognized if one is to explore by their aid the whole region included in man's search for predictive understanding, clarify the promising possibilities that open up, and deal wisely with any problem that he might confront? The analysis that I shall offer is far from perfect, for the distinctions listed overlap each other; it is hard at present to see how to realize the neatly organized system that is desirable.

To begin with, a few elementary but vital distinctions. One is the distinction between predictions made with careful regard for the pertinent evidence and predictions otherwise grounded. The latter often reveal mere wishful thinking, or they may rest on some traditional authority. A second is the distinction between predictions that are quite certain and those where the predicted event is only more or less probable. At the extreme in this direction are mere conjectures about the future. A third is the distinction between predictions made within a well-established system of knowledge, such as mechanical physics, and predictions in areas not yet systematically unified. A fourth is the distinction between short-run predictions and anticipations of the more distant future. In some fields, e.g., astronomy, this does not seem to be a very significant distinction, but in many it is. It is sure to be significant wherever relevant changes in collateral areas, capable of affecting the predicted event, are likely to take place before the event occurs. A fifth is the distinction between prediction in situations where the predicter can modify the causal conditions at hand and thus the consequences anticipated, and forecasts in situations where no such modification is possible. Eclipses of the sun and moon illustrate the latter. A sixth is the distinction between predictions that may affect their own outcome and those that make no difference to the outcome. Many predictions in the area of human behavior exemplify the former; an important class of them consists in what are called "self-fulfilling prophecies." If a recognized investment authority publicly forecasts an advance or decline in a certain group of stocks, the prophecy will almost surely bring about such an advance or decline.

To these elementary distinctions a couple of others need to be added; they are especially valuable when we try to clarify the larger implications of the idea now guiding us.

One of these is the distinction between predictions made by the scientist that take for granted the presuppositions determining his current criteria of fact, and predictions that involve the reconstruction of these presuppositions. The latter envision revised criteria, which the predicter believes will come to be accepted as superior to the present ones. The other is a distinction that falls within the former group of predictions. In our increasing awareness that the scientist is always interacting, not only with environing nature but also with other members of his society, it is evident that two possibilities need to be distinguished here. When he has gained a given bit of knowledge he can of course predict what will happen, under certain conditions, in the physical world; this is his habitual form of prediction. But it is also possible to predict, in some measure, how people will use the knowledge thus gained—how man and society will be affected by such an achievement. As scientists and others reflect on the momentous events in the international arena today, predictions of this latter kind are assuming a more and more significant place.

Stated thus abstractly, these distinctions may appear rather opaque, but they will gain clarity as we put them to work. Let us concentrate with their aid on two problems—one especially revealing and the other especially timely. The first is vividly suggested by the feats of speculative geniuses who have boldly engaged in reconstructing the presuppositions of science; if the proposed solution is sound, it will show that not only can successful predictions be made in that difficult region but that they have an indispensable value for science itself. The second is suggested by the last of the distinctions just drawn; and its solution will have a vital bearing on the relation between science and the pressing social issues of our time.

V

Recall, as we take up the first problem, the major questions that arose in our discussion of objectivity and how it is attained. At a very important point the verb "objectify" was introduced. Our subsequent explorations show more fully why, if objective truth is to be attained, some responsible enterprise must accept the arduous task of objectification. The universe does not present us with objective truth on a platter; it has to be won by the strenuous exercise of creative imagination. This has a crucial implication—namely, that the long-range process of objectification is essential to the short-range achievement of objectivity.

The underlying reason for this is that over and above the problems that lead from common sense to science, with its trustworthy methods for interpreting the factual evidence before us, there are also the problems arising through the claims of contrasting criteria of fact and evidence. Just as we often learn through the scientist that the facts we perceive need a different description, so we sometimes learn through the pioneer in this long-range process that our way of telling what *is* a fact needs to be replaced by another. A speculative idea is thus, when it originates, the proposal of a new world in which men might live and think; it is saying: "Here is a better way of conceiving objective reality than the way you are familiar with." The language naturally used to describe this pioneering function implies that in its own fashion it involves successful prediction. The speculative genius proposes a novel conceptual framework which, he believes, is destined to replace the present one; and sometimes his proposal succeeds. Since this is the case, the scientist's power of prediction depends in a specific way on the power of prediction exercised by such a genius. To see how this is so, we must note certain conditions that are required for successful prediction in science; they pose an interesting and illuminating problem.

When the scientist predicts some event in the future he couches his prediction in the conceptual framework to which he is accustomed, assuming that whoever observes the event will perceive and describe it in terms of that same framework. He can do nothing else. And usually this assumption is justified; even if the predicted event is to occur several generations in the future, the chances are that no radical change in the presuppositions of science will take place before it occurs. But our analysis shows that this is a fortunate case of a more general situation that is not so favorable; such a change may occur at any time. It would occur if the dominant interests reflected in our present scientific concepts should undergo a major change. In that case the new concepts adopted may be sufficiently different from those now employed so that even though the event might take place as predicted, no one would be able to observe it. Whatever is observed by persons contemporary with the event will no longer be described in the categories taken for granted when the prediction was made.

For a vivid illustration of this important truth we need to go back to a period preceding the adoption of present scientific concepts and presuppositions—that is, to the second stage in the evolution of science. Think of the momentous shift, between ancient and modern times, from the widespread assumption that the heavenly region is a more perfect realm than we find on the earth, to a belief that uniformity of law reigns throughout the whole of physical nature. One of the convictions made plausible by the ancient assumption was the belief, systematically expressed by Aristotle and shared by many other thinkers, that the sphere of the fixed stars (and each of the planets) is informed by a nonmaterial entity which, as a final cause, accounts for their regular and unchanging orbital motion.

Suppose that an ancient astronomer who held this theory had predicted some celestial event due to occur in the twentieth century, the prediction being naturally expressed in the concepts appropriate to that theory. Could such a prediction be verified? The answer is that so far as it involves features of the behavior of the celestial bodies that are still regarded as real by modern astronomy, e.g., motion in space, it is verifiable;* so far as it involves features that have been left behind—such as the activity of these final causes—it has become meaningless and is incapable of being tested. Nothing could now happen that would be observed and described in those abandoned terms. This reminds us of a crucial fact—namely, that any sci-

---

* Although even then it may need to be translated into concepts now regarded by scientists as the appropriate ones. For example, some problems earlier articulated by the concept of "ether" are still meaningful, but have had to be translated into other terms.

entific prediction of a future event is a prediction of what some person who is contemporary with that event would, if the prediction is correct, be able to observe. Usually he will be able to observe anything that could be observed when the prediction was made, but not always; given a radical change in the conceptual framework of science during the intervening period, everything capable of being observed and thus verified will change accordingly.

A more recent illustration can be drawn from the history of modern chemistry. An eighteenth-century chemist interested in problems about combustion might have predicted that under certain circumstances, to be expected several decades later, the "phlogiston" of a given substance would separate from its "calx" in a specified way. After Lavoisier's work, however, nothing that happened would be interpreted in these terms. The concept of phlogiston had disappeared from scientific thinking.

But it might be possible to save a prediction of distant future events from such a defeat. Suppose one could predict, say for the year 3000 A.D., not only specific events due to happen at that time, but also whatever changes will occur between now and then in the interests that dominate scientific ways of thinking and in the conceptual framework expressing them. In that case one could anticipate how the event would be described by an observer contemporary with it, and hence how its occurrence or nonoccurrence would at that time be tested. Possessing such a power of prediction, the range of his successful forecasts would be greatly widened as compared with ours; they would not be limited to the epoch of science during which its present framework continues to be accepted, but would also include the epoch that will succeed it. One would live with confidence in a larger time-span and would be at home in a vaster universe.

This answer has a trenchant implication. The ultimate kind of prediction that thinkers are challenged to make is not prediction of specific events, important though that is, but prediction of changes in the dominant interests that govern all prediction and verification of specific events—forecasts, that is, as to how future generations will wish to describe and explain the world. The basic laws that underlie all intelligent exercise of man's prophetic power, understanding of which is needed if we are to extend the range of our forecasts as far in the future as possible, would seem to be laws of the evolution of man's dominant interests.

It is true that our capacity to achieve such understanding is severely limited; however, the pioneering geniuses of history prove that we do not wholly lack it. They gained insight into the kind of presupposition destined to dominate thought for a lengthy period after them; and unless we have gone seriously astray, this required sensing the appealing values that would naturally be articulated in this way. Scientists in subsequent generations found that they could fit everything significant in their experience into the inclusive picture of reality that these pioneers offered them. Think of the great metaphysicians of ancient and early modern times—Plato, Aristotle, Descartes, Hegel. These men envisioned possibilities and organized ideas that proved fruitful for a long period in the quest of inquiring minds to comprehend the environing universe.

What is the specific bearing of these reflections on the theme of objectivity and the indispensable function of objectification?

Observing the historical achievement of such geniuses in our present setting, we can see how the subjective and the objective are interrelated in the evolution of human thought. Every conceptual framework widely accepted in a given epoch for interpreting the world sooner or later proves inadequate. New interests emerge and new features of reality open up for which it makes insufficient provision. Original minds, sensing its increasing inadequacy, glimpse novel cosmic structures which, existing as yet only in their own imagination, are obviously subjective. Whether they will become more remains at this stage to be seen. A proposal articulated by the author of such a vision may turn out to be incurably bound to his individual foibles, but if any among these pioneers has met the challenge wisely, his vision will be shared by many of his successors. As it achieves systematic form it provides a more dependable framework within which all facts that are important to them find their place. This framework will supersede the one left behind; thus what might have proved a mere subjective fantasy has become objectified. It is now the fabric of the real universe, and is confirmed as such so long as it continues to function as a reliable guide; when the time comes for some alternative insight to give more reliable guidance that insight is confirmed in its place. Filling this prophetic function, these geniuses have played their distinctive part in revising the cosmic structure taken for granted in their day.

The scientist easily forgets that this profoundly transforming process is going on. It is especially easy to forget it when he is seized with enthusiasm about some theory for which he has just found substantial support. "Here," he is tempted to exclaim, "is the answer we have been looking for all these years. When it is worked out we will have the complete explanation of this group of puzzling facts." But by the time it is fully worked out a change may have taken place in the conceptual framework presupposed in the explanation, a change that will lead to a somewhat different set of discoveries about the same facts. The principle underlying this reminder is instructively applicable to thinkers who are confidently voicing a radical determinism in terms of present-day computer-oriented research. "If we could build a perfect computer," they say, "all our present information might be fed into it and it would then predict all changes that will take place in the future." The difficulty with this expectation is that by the time significant progress in that direction is made scientists will almost surely find themselves building a different kind of computer, which will handle its information in a different way. That is, it will be built in accordance with altered interests and presuppositions.

Will this reconstructive function continue to be filled? Yes, indeed—how could it be dispensed with? And it will be as thrilling a role in the future as it has been in the past. One who ventures beyond our present horizon in this fashion is seeking nothing less than to survey the possible worlds in which coming generations might live and to envision the world which, when coherently portrayed, a long succession of them will choose to inhabit because it gives room to the emerging energies for whose fulfillment the time is ripe. By what interest will such a pioneer be moved as he fills his ambitious role? Surely not by a desire to manipulate the world, nor by any other obviously limited concern. It would seem that the most general interest naturally expressed in the quest for successful prediction is simply an aspiration to transcend the narrow temporal limits of our present experience so that one can live and think in a wider time-span than before.

In the past the philosopher has usually filled this role. But the day when he can expect to make an important contribution toward revising the conceptual framework of science is probably over. The vast proliferation of scientific knowledge and its accelerating growth pose a baffling handicap. And so it is not surprising that ever since the accelerated proliferation began, this aspect of pioneering has been more and more performed by theoretical scientists themselves. The old scientific concepts—motion, causality, space, time, matter, energy—were created by philosophers. The new basic concepts—field, gene, relativity, space-time, behavior—have been created by scientific theorists who are familiar with the rapidly expanding background as philosophers can no longer be. This means that the progressive revision of our criteria of fact and of its wise explanation has mainly passed into their hands. So far, however, as concerns problems of scientific method and how it might be improved, the contribution of philosophy will continue to be needed. Analytic philosophers are more familiar than scientists with the standards of logical rigor that have evolved, and especially when criteria of evidence are undergoing reconstruction they can offer valuable aid.

But this change frees the philosopher with a streak of pioneering genius for other problems that arise as we search beyond the present horizon—for example, the varied problems attacked in this quest for inclusive understanding. These involve their own kind of predictive orientation. The thinkers who engage in such a search would seem to be the clearest examples in our day of man's urge to overcome, so far as is possible for finite minds, the limitations of specialized knowledge through unified insight.

V I

Turn now to the second problem, which is thrust upon us by the last distinction drawn above. This is the distinction between predictions whose scope is confined to anticipated events in physical nature and those that take into account as fully as possible what people do with such mastery of the environment when it is gained—how man and society are changed by the increased possession of verified knowledge. In the past, scientists assumed, almost without exception, that they were responsible only for the effects brought about by their work in the external world. Today, in view of the revolutionary impact of their activities on every phase of human life, a growing concern is evident as to whether they are not also responsible for the other effects as well.*

Is this concern justified? If so, what revision of our traditional presuppositions will be needed to express it?

Facing these questions, let us begin with a reminder that the basic em-

---

* A. T. Waterman, in a paper on "Science in the Service of Man," *Bulletin of the Atomic Scientists* (May, 1963), pp. 3, 5, states clearly the traditional assumption and its plausible justification, and then states also the essence of the situation which is bringing that assumption into question:

"The pure scientist, working in his laboratory, usually cannot foresee or predict the uses to which his work may eventually be put. Indeed, such is not his aim. . . . Science, in its pure form, is not concerned with where discoveries may lead; its disciples are interested only in discovering the truth. . . . It is society that makes the ultimate decision as to the uses to which new discoveries shall be put.

". . . The reduction of poverty, disease, malnutrition, and illiteracy requires the combined intellectual resources of the physical sciences, the life sciences, and the social sciences, as well as the humanities. We need the humanities to help us to see and feel these problems, and the sciences to help us solve them. Fortunately, all these great areas are finding it increasingly possible to share techniques and processes and to work together."

phasis on prediction in present-day science is an expression of the increasingly confident interaction of modern thinkers with the world around them and their growing realization of what that interaction involves. And it clearly involves not only the scientist's activities in relation to physical nature; his relations with other people and their pressing concerns are also involved. He is interacting with them, directly or indirectly, in everything he does.

When in this setting we examine the connection between the accumulating discoveries of science and what men do with them, the fundamental truth that stands out is this: Every act of a scientist in his role as scientist has varied and complex effects. Traditionally, he has restricted his attention to the effects in the physical world, for it is there that he looks for the outcome of an experiment or a set of observations that provides an answer to the question he has asked. Other effects, which do not belong to that world, he has excluded from the realm of science and from the scope of his responsibility. Such a narrow view of science reflects the lengthy period in its history when these other results could be easily neglected—when the knowledge sought was the knowledge of natural forces whose understanding and harnessing (where possible) seemed clearly beneficial to all concerned. One thinks of the forces present in the action of windmills, pumps, falling bodies, and magnets, the resistance met by moving objects, the circulation of the blood, the revolutions of the celestial bodies. Indeed, behind that long-accepted limitation of the realm of science there may have been an unconscious wish to protect its life and growth against persecution by religious, social, and political institutions. Such persecution might have been too severe had scientists not kept discreetly quiet about the larger impact of what they were doing.

This traditional line between science and what lies outside it is surely convenient for many purposes. But can it be plausibly retained when we observe the whole network of effects that appear as men make the energies of nature serve them and their fellows in more and more impressive ways? The scientist doing his job is not an isolated experimenter with these energies but a full human being; when he enters his laboratory he is still the breadwinner of a family, a staff member of a university or an industrial corporation, a citizen of a community, a researcher for the government of a nation, a man in interaction with all other men on the surface of this planet. His every act not only bears on progress in our understanding and control of the material world but also on the life and well-being and prospects for the future of all these social entities. In many cases the effect on such groups of what he does is minute; in some cases it may spell the difference between larger life and death in a nuclear holocaust. He cannot limit his awareness and his sense of responsibility to the physical effects of his acts. The results produced in the laboratory or even in the physical realm as a whole are a small fraction of the results that can be intelligently anticipated from his work.

"But," the reader may strenuously object, *"are* the effects of scientific activity on human society predictable?"

The frank answer would seem to be: "As yet, perhaps very little, and with only a low degree of probability. However, some prediction in this area is possible, and the stakes are so enormous that we cannot escape the responsibility to recognize the causal relations present and to increase our predictive power as rapidly as possible." Indeed, there are indications that this is already taking place. Realization of the inevitable social ramifications of scientific discovery has been playing a significant part in such rapidly developing fields as industrial engineering and military technology. In the light of such developments, the line traditionally drawn between the concern of science and what lies beyond it appears quite artificial. As we form the habit of seeing the scientist's work in this larger network of consequences, the only relevant difference would seem to be a comparative one: the physical effects of a given scientific act can be predicted with greater assurance than the social effects.

The upshot is that in today's world the physical and social consequences of scientific activity cannot be separated. They form an organic whole, and all of them alike fall within the realm of our capacity for predictive understanding. There is not, and cannot be, any such thing as "pure science," if we mean by that phrase a form of scientific activity that has no foreseeable social consequences. When this truth is fully recognized, will not every investigator accept the obligation to orient himself toward the entire future that his work is helping to bring about?

Moreover, there is a very poignant reason for accepting that obligation; whether the scientist himself will have a future is at stake. The world has entered the nuclear age—a momentous event that is itself an effect of his work. In this age he cannot escape a sobering realization, namely, that the principle of the self-fulfilling prophecy is fatefully relevant to his own career. That is, his ability to continue his work depends on conditions that are now threatened, while his conception of what science is, and what his scientific responsibility includes, may be a decisive factor in whether or not the threatened doom falls. Simply and starkly put: the adoption of one conception of science will tend to create the conditions under which it can continue to exist and grow, while the adoption of another (or rather the preservation of an outmoded one) will tend to destroy those conditions. The scientist has produced weapons of such lethal power and swiftness of delivery that they have brought to an end the era in which any nation can really defend itself against others that possess or will possess them; this means that a national policy which menaces any people anywhere is now a peril to all people everywhere. In this situation a conception of science that evades responsibility for its larger human effects, and thus allows those who adopt it to promote by their work the interests of one nation against others, is a self-destructive conception. If scientists are to assure the survival of science, they must leave behind the tempting idea that they can obediently carry out political orders, whatever those orders may be.

Nonetheless, it is not easy for scientists to see their activity in this total human setting and to be vividly aware of the effects on their fellows of what they are doing. The difficulty does not lie merely in the uncertain nature of prediction when these effects are concerned. The same forces are active here that account for the slow rate at which men have learned to distinguish realities from emotional projections, and social thinkers to free objective knowledge from subjective distortions. It is important to understand how these forces work in the situation we now confront.

When a man of science does see what he is doing in this total setting and accepts the responsibility which thus becomes obvious, he is extending to the whole social arena the same maxim that he is guided by when he anticipates the physical results of a scientific act. This is the maxim that *causes have their predictable effects.* In following it he is fulfilling more completely than before the intrinsic nature of the scientific enterprise, i.e., the systematic quest for predictive knowledge wherever it can be gained. He is viewing each of his acts as a causal force at work in the social as well as in the physical world; his aim is to forecast realistically what effects of every kind any act is likely to produce, so that he can judge before acting whether those effects are desirable or not.

But in the arena of these social consequences of an act there is a strong tendency, in scientists as in other people, to think unscientifically. How does this happen? What alternative orientation has enticed him?

The appealing and popular alternative today is exemplified in the political leader. His orientation, as we see it revealed in various situations, is grounded in the belief that one can perceive clearly the end that ought to be served by human action and in its light pick the right means to achieve it.

How does this alternative work out? What happens is that a man who adopts this belief sets his eyes on what appears to be a noble or sacred end and selects means that have come to be associated in his mind with that end. His guiding maxim is that *the end justifies the means.* Now the dangerous consequence of following this alternative is that one who does so can easily deceive himself on a vital matter—namely, whether the relation he sees between means and end is really a dependable one or is due mainly to the potent emotional appeal of the means that entices him. It is especially easy to forget that in dealing with human beings, no means "leads to any other goal than that which is like it" [3]—violence breeds violence, threats engender counter-threats.

What may mislead a scientist (and others) at this point is the fact that in the areas already mastered by exact knowledge this orientation is quite proper—it is the essential orientation of the technician. That is, when cause-effect relations have been precisely identified and can be fully controlled, a cause *is* a reliable means to its effect as end. But to concentrate on choosing means for alluring ends in other situations is a very unreliable way of thinking; one easily believes that he is reasoning validly when he is rationalizing an impulsive mode of action that satisfies some strong but deceptive emotion.

In sum, through both of these orientations men seek to achieve understanding and guide action by the aid of dependable temporal relations between one event and another. But to think in terms of means and ends may in social situations turn out to be quite undependable, while to think in terms of cause and effect is as dependable as the present stage in the evolution of truth-seeking inquiry makes possible. The reason for the difference, as we have seen, is that the latter way of thinking has become purged, by fuller awareness, of the variable, blind, and transitory emotions that are likely to infect the former; it is what the former becomes when these are replaced by more enlightened, impartial, and enduring motivations. To realize the difference does not weaken one's effort to envision wise ends and to investigate the conditions of their attainment. Such effort was never more needed. But one will know that when honestly appraising those conditions one must follow the causal way of thinking. When scientists with their present prestige exemplify this way everywhere, science as the quest for the most responsible and accurate predictive knowledge that can be won will exert the salutary moral influence on man's social evolution that its genius is capable of exerting.

One more important question arises. Suppose that the reorientation of scientific thinking just described were to be generally accepted. What transformation would this require in the meaning of "science"? Would the word be stretched so as to cover the entire fabric of man's predictive knowledge? To stretch it thus would be a natural step to take. Scientists would express in that way the belief that the function of science is not merely to be a model of predictive understanding in its most rigorous form, but also to guide thinkers in realizing the distinctive virtues of such understanding wherever it can be achieved. And there are advantages in a conception of science that embraces all modes of explanation grounded in detectable regularities through time.

But the consequences would be pretty radical. The consequence for the detailed structure of science would be that it would then include the many kinds of predictive thinking it has thus far left out—at least all that show a conscientious concern for relevant evidence. The general consequence, however, would be still more radical, and to our established habits of thought rather startling. When we ask what would give science its organic unity in that enlarged structure, the conclusion seems unavoidable that all science, physical and social, would then be unified under the principles gradually taking form in the latter. The reason is twofold: (1) The attempt to forecast the effect of scientific activities on society is clearly a part of social science; and (2) the periodic reconstruction of scientific presuppositions under the influence of newly emerging interests also belongs to social science, so far as the process can be predicted by wise insight. The physical sciences, without losing their distinctive character, would thus become a branch of the science of man. It is the task of the latter to understand all that men do in their interaction with the environing universe, including their adoption from time to time of whatever presuppositions seem promising for explaining the physical world. The ultimate key to all predictive understanding, however strange it may sound, is human understanding.

This conclusion naturally leads to a different conception of the relation between science and the human adventure as a whole than has usually prevailed. The words of Eugene Rabinowitch seem fully justified: "Science [is] part of a broad human striving for the achievement of a better and more perfect state of man." [4] Its contribution toward that striving has distinctive features, of course, arising from its special cognitive responsibility, yet no claim of independent and final authority for it is plausible. It takes its place beside art, religion, philosophy, and statesmanship in their quest to realize the highest fulfillment of which man is capable. Each of these pursuits exemplifies its own mode of interaction between man and man and between men and environing reality, and each contributes in its own way toward the richer life that man aspires to achieve.

But as we peer ahead in the light of this conception, other significant possibilities can be glimpsed—especially the possibility of a drastic revision of our presuppositions about social science, and through it of our presuppositions about the scientific enterprise in general. We earlier took note of the attempt to gain predictive knowledge of people on the assumption that they are subject to manipulation like physical objects, and a basic moral question had to be faced. An equally important practical question also arises: Is any such attempt, in the long run, futile as well as inhumane? It may be, in an age when men are no longer cowed by threats and are less captivated by clever propaganda than they used to be, that successful prediction in the realm of our social understanding requires sensitivity to human beings, and a respect for each individual that is quite alien to this eagerness to manipulate him. Perhaps it can be achieved dependably only through alert responsiveness to the real concerns and growing aspirations of those one seeks to understand.

In short, the whole fabric of our predictive knowledge may fulfill its promise only when it is unified under a dominant interest that at present might easily appear irrelevant.

8

Awareness, truth, and communication

When a thinker is exploring within the framework of a given set of pre-suppositions he is using his faculty of reason. When he is reaching out toward a more adequate framework he is seeking insight.

The main danger in the quest for insight is the strong temptation to take an appealing insight as self-vouching, and to regard its systematic articulation as the final truth about the area with which it deals. The main danger in using reason is the temptation to identify the essence of reason with some particular set of presuppositions about it. When that happens, to cling zealously to one's present theory of reason seems to be simply the expression of a quite appropriate loyalty to reason. One forgets that any theory of reason reflects underlying motives which, when they become the object of clear awareness, may need to be revised. Thus among the insights that should, and do, dawn from time to time are clearer insights into the nature of reason, revealing inadequacies in whatever conception of it has previously been dominant.

But we cannot get along without both reason and insight. Reason saves us now and again from the seductive strategy of trusting in some sectarian faith, or of turning to some rebellious cult of unreason. Insight saves us from permanent bondage to some limited framework of presuppositions—presuppositions about reason as about everything else. And as these two cognitive faculties continue to fill their function, it is clear that there must be both continuity and discontinuity between them. Continuity is necessary because no trustworthy insight can be achieved by flouting the standards of meticulous reasoning thus far won; moreover, the capacity of any insight to win objectivity can only be tested by the systematic development, through reason, of its implications. But discontinuity is unavoidable too—the discontinuity that arises from placing in jeopardy our present presuppositions about reason, with no assurance in advance as to what will replace them.

These reflections remind us that man has a more general power which underlies all his cognitive activities, and which can guide his thinking both in its adherence to any given framework of presuppositions and in its adventurous quest for a wiser framework. Reason and insight alike are expressions of his unlimited power of expanding awareness. Of the reality of this remarkable gift of awareness there can be no doubt. It is actively present whenever one's mind is awake and alert. Taken in abstraction from all possible objects, it seems to be the one assured factor in our experience that transcends relativity. We cannot conceive or imagine what any universe would be like, or any entity within it, of which no one is aware. It is equally present in any perceived fact and in any imagined possibility. But more remarkable still is our capacity to stretch and thereby to expand our awareness. So far as I can see, there is no such thing as *bare* awareness—awareness separated from all striving, all interest, all interaction with the surrounding world. It naturally reaches out toward *full* awareness. This reaching out goes on constantly, if haltingly; any person who has not lost his memory and whose mind is not completely torpid participates in it. And because this is true in some degree of every normal individual, it is also true of every living society and of the course of human history at large, which is just the evolving experience of all individuals.

Expanding awareness acknowledges no limits; it is bound by no rules. Yet, in virtue of the open and alert sensitivity intrinsic to it, it can give us the guidance we need. This capacity is most vividly revealed in its power to uncover defects in any previous insight and in any presuppositions about reason, thus pointing the way toward their constructive replacement.

However, experience constantly teaches us that awareness—whether in the form of reason or of insight—can expand dependably, and that it can expand (or seem to) undependably. The words traditionally employed to denote these two outcomes are "truth" and "error" (or "falsehood"). What is truth, and how do we tell when we have it? By what criterion can it be clearly distinguished from error?

Here we find ourselves in a dilemma. On the one hand, our analysis of the relation between motivations and presuppositions in any cognitive quest strongly suggested that truthfulness is more basic than truth. There have been many theories of truth, and there will be more; but they, like other sets of ultimate presuppositions, are revised from time to time through the enduring concern of thinkers to be truthful. On the other hand, does not truthfulness always imply truth, in the form of an ideal of cognitive reliability by which our concern for it is guided? Is not such an ideal present in all sincere searching, beckoning us beyond the best exemplification of truthfulness now achievable toward the better exemplification that is always possible?

II

I propose that we tentatively adopt the orientation usually taken for granted by Western philosophers when treating these issues. They have said very little about truthfulness but much about the nature and criterion of truth. In this orientation they have found it easy to ignore the general ideal just described and to concentrate on the truth of propositions or statements, where "not true" is equivalent to "false" in the simple sense of "erroneous" or "mistaken." And indeed it seems clear that any insight or reasoned conclusion is naturally expressed in the form of a proposition. But serious difficulties appear when this course is followed, especially when we are dealing with truth in philosophy.

Let us begin to work our way out of the dilemma by seeing what happens when, in view of these difficulties, we try to dispense with the concept of truth. Many modern thinkers have done precisely this, so far as philosophy is concerned. They have become persuaded that the concept of truth can properly be applied only in areas where a method is available by which differences of opinion can be resolved. Such a method is usually available in the areas of common sense and of science, but not in philosophy. Hence the widely accepted conclusion that in distinctively philosophical issues truth is not attainable; the concept thus does not apply there.

Yet this drastic conclusion seems to lead us into equally serious difficulties. How about the social sciences? If the consideration just mentioned is decisive, the same conclusion becomes inescapable there. For in that field too there are frequent differences of opinion as to whether a given statement is true or not, and they are refractory in the same way that disagreements in philosophy are. How should such an unsatisfactory situation be met?

Two decades ago some of the logical empiricists faced this question frankly and proposed the radical solution of abandoning the concept of truth in a broad area of social science as well as in philosophy. By what then would it be replaced? The only proper course they could see was that instead of referring to a statement as "true" or "false," we should simply say that this statement is "accepted by us [i.e., a certain group of scientists] at a certain time and a certain place." *

But is not the baby now thrown out with the bath? The natural answer to a renunciation of *all* claims for a statement responsibly made is: "Why then should I be one of those who accept it?" After all, a person who has reached a conclusion through careful inquiry means to say more than that some respectable people believe it; he wants others to face fairly the facts that he has observed, and to take into account the considerations that lead to his conclusion. He is aware of something that others as well as he need to know if they are to think and act wisely in the presence of the realities involved, and he wishes them to share his awareness.

So wherever any sincere cognitive quest is going on it is hard to dispense with the ideas traditionally symbolized by the words "true" and "false." To boast that one is now in possession of the truth may in many situations be presumptuous, but the claim that no responsible investigator can avoid making, however it be verbally expressed, is the claim that what he has found contains something that deserves to play a part in the comprehensive understanding of reality which through the labor of all thinkers is being slowly achieved.

Where should we turn for further light?

These continuing disagreements in philosophy and in social science give

* See Otto Neurath, *International Encyclopedia of Unified Science*, Vol. II, No. 1, *Foundations of the Unity of Science* (Chicago: Univ. of Chicago Press, 1944), pp. 12 ff.

us a clue. And it becomes a hopeful clue when we survey again the history of Western philosophy and see what has happened in the course of its long wrestling with the problem of truth, for the most persistent idea that emerged in the evolution from ancient to modern philosophy is the idea that an essential criterion of truth is just the bringing of disagreement to an end in agreement. This did not mean an abandonment of the hoary conviction that a true statement must agree with the relevant facts, but it meant a growing belief that agreement beween one thinker and others is an indispensable further criterion. The underlying presupposition evidently is that a solution which proves acceptable to all sincere thinkers is *for that reason* a sounder solution than one which does not.

At first sight this idea seems queer. One naturally asks if a person cannot often tell by himself whether a given statement is true or not. So let us consider for a moment what he *can* do by himself.

Were he living in a world without other people, and capable of alert discrimination, he could presumably learn to distinguish between a belief about how things happen that gives dependable guidance to action and a belief that does not. With the former he can act confidently in the flux of events so far as they recur from time to time; where he is condemned to the latter he cannot. But this kind of belief would be very meager as compared with what men achieve as social beings; ought we to call such a solitary achievement "true"? In that case there would be no connection between truth and agreement. Perhaps, however, the word registers the difference between that kind of belief and the cognitive feats of our collective experience; what is merely true for me or for you is not yet true, however satisfactory it might be were we existing in lonely isolation. If this is so, the idea of agreement as a criterion of truth becomes very plausible.

We shall trace the instructive evolution of this idea in Western philosophy and ponder the questions that inevitably arise.

Agreement seems to have played little part in ancient notions about truth except in the limited form of the Stoic *consensus gentium* ("agreement of [all] peoples").

Only the aristocratic experts in philosophical reasoning—so it was generally assumed—could be expected to attain truth; others would naturally disagree with them and with each other because of their lack of rational competence. But if one's peers in the philosophical aristocracy also disagree? This is disconcerting; however, it was easy for ancient thinkers to assume that any such disagreement would disappear when each of them exercised his mental powers more carefully. And agreement among those capable of thoughtful reflection came to appear quite important; there is strong evidence that the Socratic dialectic was conceived as essentially a technique for securing it. As the main discussion about justice in the *Republic* gets under way the question is raised as to whether it should be carried on as a contest for debating supremacy between Socrates and Thrasymachus or with a different aim, and on this question Socrates says:

> If, then, we give him speech for speech and recount all the good things which the just man has, and let him make another speech, and then make another speech ourselves, we shall have to count the good things, and measure them, in each of the speeches, and then we shall need judges to decide; but if as before we come to some *agreement* between ourselves, we shall be ourselves both pleaders and judges.[1] [Italics mine]

As we pass from the ancient through the medieval period, the idea of agreement as an index of truth finds wider though still limited expression. Vincent of Lerins was sure that in the field of Biblical interpretation what has been believed "always, everywhere, and by all" Catholic Fathers must for that reason be true. Mohammed is supposed in Moslem tradition to have said, "My followers will never agree in an error," and thus to have made consensus, in this negative form, a criterion of religious truth. And when we come to the early modern philosophers, whether rationalists or empiricists, we find that disagreement among thinkers has become a matter of persistent concern. As they set themselves to establish a new and more adequate method of gaining knowledge their basic aim was to find a way of reaching universal agreement.

At the beginning of that period Descartes expressed this orientation by turning to mathematics for a key to the right cognitive method. Disagreement, he saw, especially on underlying principles, reigns in all other branches of supposed knowledge, but it is overcome in mathematics; if we can seize what is common to the mathematical sciences and apply that key to the search for knowledge everywhere, this distressing state of affairs would be ended.* Leibniz and Locke were also moved by this solicitude; the former spent many years endeavoring to perfect a "thought alphabet," which would be able to settle any dispute between two thinkers, while the latter was sure that the way to agreement can be found in an empirical method. Kant explicitly affirmed that agreement between different investigators is one of the two criteria by which we can tell whether any given

* *Discourse on Method,* Part I; *Rules for the Direction of the Mind,* Rule II.

intellectual discipline, such as metaphysics, has entered on the secure path of a science.*

When we turn from these pioneers of the modern era to the leaders of the philosophical schools prominent during the last century, we find that this emphasis on a procedure capable of leading to agreement continues.

Charles S. Peirce, father of pragmatism, insists that "the opinion which is fated to be ultimately agreed to by all who investigate, is what we mean by the truth," [2] and for him appropriate methods of inquiry are determined by their ability to guide us toward that opinion. Bertrand Russell, explaining the method of logical analysis characteristic of the British realists, holds that it is the one capable of winning agreement; after calling attention to the conflicts between philosophers in the past, he affirms: "I believe that the time has now arrived when this unsatisfactory state of things can be brought to an end." [3] And similar confident claims are made by leaders of other recent schools.† Indeed, so widespread had this urge to find a way of achieving agreement become that even Bergson joined the chorus. Defending the method of intuition—one that the historian of thought would judge least capable of leading to any such outcome—he nevertheless offers the promise of doing so as its main virtue.‡

This is impressive testimony. All these philosophers are sure that in some sense universal agreement is a valid criterion of truth. But the idea is still puzzling. Many are the instances of widespread agreement on erroneous beliefs; the Ptolemaic astronomy and the pre-Darwinian theory of the origin of man are outstanding illustrations. Höffding's reminder is quite in

---

* *Critique of Pure Reason,* Preface to the Second Edition, p. 1: "Whether the treatment of that class of knowledge with which reason is occupied follows the secure method of a science or not, can easily be determined by the result. If, after repeated preparations, it comes to a standstill, as soon as its real goal is approached, or is obliged, in order to reach it, to retrace its steps again and again, and strike into fresh paths; again, if it is impossible to produce unanimity among those who are engaged in the same work as to the manner in which their common object should be obtained, we may be convinced that such a study is far from having attained to the secure method of science, but is groping only in the dark."

† Dewey believed that empirical method as conceived in his form of pragmatism would "procure for philosophic reflection something of that cooperative tendency toward consensus which marks inquiry in the natural sciences." (*Experience and Nature,* first ed. [Chicago: Open Court Pub. Co., 1925], pp. 35 f.) Moritz Schlick maintained, after describing the essential character of the "verifiability principle" adopted by the logical positivists: "And it is of course only in virtue of this character that the strife of systems can be brought to an end." ("Die Wende der Philosophie," *Erkenntnis,* Vol. 1, pp. 10 f.)

‡ *Creative Evolution* (Mitchell translation), New York, 1911, p. 238. Bergson holds, however, that intuition needs to be supplemented by "dialectic."

point: "Let us remember that 'facts' are not more real or 'ideas' more true because the number of those who believe in them is a large one." [4] In what sense, if any, can this proposed connection between truth and agreement be persuasively established? Several searching objections must be satisfactorily met.

Progress in the sciences indicates that agreement on the part of every Tom, Dick, and Harry is of little consequence. So far as this concept points to a real criterion in that area it takes the form of "agreement of the competent." We know how to tell competence in science, but by what standard can we determine its presence in philosophy? Here everyone, and no one, is competent. And how avoid the seductive temptation implicitly to restrict competence to those who agree with *us?*

Agreement can be secured by various means. When gained by some of them, such as coercion through the exercise or threat of force, it is obviously no sign of truth. Today we are aware that many subtle as well as overt modes of coercion may be employed, ranging all the way from gentle brainwashing—with no mention of penalties for continued refractoriness —to the taking of life itself. Chauncey D. Leake recognizes this factor, and suggests the needed addition to the above criterion, in the following passage: "Voluntary and uncoerced agreement among reasonble competent scholars in a field, on the basis of the objective evidence available, constitutes the only 'authority' which science can recognize." [5] But it is difficult to say when agreement on philosophical issues is free from coercion. Is the attempt by aggressive argument to render one's own presuppositions convincing to others a form of coercion?

A serious problem arises from the fact that agreement may be secured at once, or its attainment may take time. In common sense and in science it is often achieved quickly, by following a specified course of inquiry or by making a few observations. But it appears that where truth in philosophy is concerned, time is of the essence—indeed, consensus in this realm is always *coming to be* and may never at any given time be fully attained. Moreover, in the case of philosophical issues, not only is there no hope of settling the matter immediately, but also it may be impossible to tell just what needs to happen for it to be settled. A new perspective on everything may be required. Clearly, to recognize in this fashion that agreement must be postponed to the indefinite future means that it cannot function in the way one naturally expects of a criterion of truth. No controversy can be decided by appeal to it.

III

Nonetheless, these difficulties do not mean that the ideal of universal agreement, voluntarily achieved, must be thrown overboard as of no relevance to philosophy. Its persistent appeal through the centuries surely indicates that it has an important lesson to teach. Two considerations are especially illuminating.

Recall in the light of that ideal the method discussed in Chapter VI for resolving philosophical conflicts. History shows that the resolutions reached were successful. But they did not win immediate agreement among the philosophers participating in those conflicts, and full agreement has never been won. However, the form they assumed seems to have been determined by a search for the conditions under which agreement would be reasonable and continued disagreement unreasonable. They took account of all relevant factors in the conflict; they were impartially fair to both sides; they asked no disputant to give up anything that seemed important to him—he only had to give up the claim of absolute truth for his own position.

Recall likewise our earlier analysis of objectivity. We concluded that objectivity is irretrievably social in essence, and hence the ideal of agreement would seem to be presupposed in any responsible judgment, aiming to be objectively true, about anything. Let us examine some instructive situations.

When alert observation enables us to correct subjective errors about an object, as it often does, what happens is not that we just stare more intensively at the object. Such staring would do no good; we would simply continue to see what we had seen before. What happens is that we achieve a more impartial mood, in which our individual habits, demands, and fears about that object lose their previous potency; we perceive it in socially sharable terms. And the role of agreement in the work of the scientist is revealed by the fact that he must always be on guard against the "personal equation." Ordinarily, in carrying out his observations and experiments, he will see what other scientists would see in the same circumstances; but there is always the possibility that his own emotional bias may stand in the way. Science must be assured that any results reached will command agreement; if a careful check by others is often dispensed with, it is because everyone is sure that the nature of the problem, and the disciplined habits of the scientist in question, are such that any other trained inquirer would reach the same result.

In the light of such situations, we shall try to describe the essential function of agreement in the achievement of objective truth and in any quest for objectification.

The basic fact seems to be that when two thinkers disagree in their interpretation of some reality, this indicates that in one interpretation or the other—perhaps in both—some personal idiosyncrasy or group peculiarity has not been transcended; whereas agreement, reached voluntarily, shows that the conclusion thus agreed upon is independent of factors that vary between one thinker and another. Disagreement means that although the entity about which they are talking may be located by each of them in the same spatio-temporal setting, one person is talking about something that varies with him and the other is talking about something that varies with him. In short, they are talking about two different things—and they may simply let them remain different. If and when, however, they advance toward agreement, this means that they have decided to overcome these idiosyncrasies, confident that each can come to understand as the other does, so that at the end they will find themselves in the presence of the same reality —enriched to include whatever is significant in the experience of both. In this process their attention is of course turned toward the entity under discussion as well as toward each other—here is where the presence of external reality is clearly revealed. However, the goal of mutual agreement to be won would seem to be the determinative factor throughout. Were it absent, further observation would accomplish nothing; but if each is open to see what the other sees, a more inclusive reality can emerge, capable of a common description and an interpretation acceptable to both.

It is essential to distinguish two aspects of this process; one is logical and the other psychological. Logically, it involves precisely the same features that appear whenever in the pursuit of accurate knowledge we find that a statement previously supposed to be unqualifiedly true is true only under certain conditions. The difference is that here the unexpected complexity is due to the presence of two or more active centers of observation and explanation. What is to be done? Just what the scientist naturally does; discover the factors responsible for the variation, and allow duly for them. In the present situation this means to become aware, through sensitivity to each other's interests and presuppositions, of the conditions under which the object disagreed upon reveals one character to one experiencer and another character to another.

With these conditions thus recognized, the psychological aspect becomes obvious; when agreement is achieved in this fashion there has been a mutual sharing of experience, so that each thinker has come to appreciate everything significant to the other. The presence or persistence of disagreement, however, is not such a clear and unambiguous indication. It may of course mean indifference to each other's experience or a hostile refusal to share it. On the other hand, it may mean: "I would like to agree with you, but I can't do so till this important consideration is taken into account or till that serious objection is met."

Thus when two thinkers find themselves in disagreement on any issue, two alternatives always lie open. They can remain in their present opposition, making no effort to overcome it; or they can regard their disagreement as a positive opportunity, assuming that each can be sensitive to the considerations that are important to the other and that progress can thus be made toward a common understanding. This alternative was described in religious language by an early Quaker, John Saltmarsh, when he said (in his "Smoke in the Temple") "Another's evidence is as dark to me as mine to him . . . till the Lord enlighten us both for discerning alike."

I V

Men find that they agree or disagree through communication. And any shared quest for truth that aims to overcome disagreement depends throughout on communication. So, to complete our understanding in this area we must understand communication. What happens when one person communicates with another, and under what conditions is the communication truthful?

In our day this theme has taken its place on the center of the intellectual stage, and is being approached from many angles and through the resources of many fields—mathematics, sociology, and psychology, as well as logic and linguistics. I shall attempt simply to clarify those aspects of the process of communication that promise to throw special light on the problem of truth in general and philosophical truth in particular.* And the key to the

---

* Its important role in fields where little used to be said about it is now explicitly recognized. According to Professor Edmund S. Morgan, the two essential qualities of a true scholar are curiosity and a compulsion to communicate, and the second is inseparably connected with the first. "Communication is not merely the desire and the responsibility of the scholar; it is his discipline, the proving ground where he tests his findings against criticism. Without communication his pursuit of truth withers into eccentricity." (In the *Yale Alumni Magazine* for November, 1959, pp. 12 f.) According to Elizabeth Janeway, writers of novels are "basically . . . trying . . . to learn the truth and to *tell* it (or as close as they can come to the truth) about the way things happen, the way the world

clarification lies in a thought implicit in all that has been said about language and objectivity as well as about truth and agreement—what is primarily capable of being true or false is not a set of propositions but *speech;* long antedating and implicitly grounding our theories about truth in science and philosophy is the time-honored locution "telling the truth." How can one be as sure as possible when speaking to another person that he is telling the truth?

If truth is both attained and expressed through communication, a very illuminating consideration is this: the state of mind of those to whom a communication is made cannot be ignored. Thinkers seem to have often retained, unconsciously, the primitive idea that words somehow have a power and authority in themselves, irrespective of what they achieve in communication. But it is impossible to communicate successfully—i.e., with any chance of mutual understanding and of progress toward agreement—without perceptive contact with that state of mind. This means that truth is relative to the experience and conceptual framework of the person or persons to whom the truth is being spoken. So we must explore this relativity and see if we can grasp more clearly, in its light, the nature of truth.

It quickly appears that it was a wise step to free ourselves from dependence on "truth" as an abstract noun. Through the centuries that abstraction has gathered many associations, some of which are a deposit of fruitful insight and some of which are misleading. We turned for help to the unsophisticated adjective "truthful," and it will continue to be used. But as we think about communication the adjective "true" and the adverb "truly" can also serve as well if we let them find their natural meaning in our present setting. What is true speech? When is one speaking truly?

Suppose we forget our philosophical puzzles and reflect on the simple relation between "true," "truly," and "truthful" that emerges when we think of the familiar daily uses of the adjective "true." What is it to be a true man? The unrehearsed answer would presumably be that it is to measure up to the ideal stature of manhood—to fill the role that in view of his distinctive capacities a man might fill. Why not the same answer in the

---

works. . . . They believe that they can show other people how it works." (*Cf. The Authors Guild Bulletin* for May, 1959. [Italics mine].) According to the most comprehensive mind among the philosophical existentialists—that of Karl Jaspers— two of the five distinctive features of the philosophical role of reason involve communication between one thinker and another. (See his *Reason and Anti-Reason in Our Time,* tr. by Stanley Goodman [New Haven: Yale Univ. Press, 1952], pp. 42 ff.)

case of speech? Speech is true—is it not?—when it performs the function that speech at its best is capable of performing. If this clue is followed, the adverb "truly" will find its corresponding meaning. Surely, to speak truly is to share with others the most trustworthy understanding that the speaker has won and can communicate. And is there any difference between doing this and expressing, in the fullest measure possible, the supreme virtue of truthfulness?

I believe we have discovered the perspective in which the essential interdependence of truth, communication, and reality can most clearly be seen. "The problem of being honest," Peter Bertocci says, "is the problem of conveying to each person involved what each needs to know in order to plan and act with reality in mind." [6] That is, what I say is true in the circumstances in which I say it if it helps the hearer achieve wise accord with the realities there to be met, while a false assertion is one that fails in this respect. Whether it succeeds thus or not obviously depends in part on his present state, and how, in virtue of that state, he responds to my assertion and to the realities we both have in mind. Speaking to another person is an *act,* and like every act is a cause producing its natural effects. When I speak, the effect of what I say in the experience of the hearer is conditioned by all the circumstances that have made his state what it now is. If I am to speak the truth, I must then be sensitive to those circumstances so that I can anticipate the likely effect, in his experience, of making this or that assertion. Only thus can I judge whether what I say will help him meet wisely the relevant realities or not—whether it will play the constructive and trustworthy role that it might in his subsequent thinking.

Here the unavoidable relativity of truth confronts us squarely—and here we also find that it unavoidably transcends relativity.

Truth is relative because, in view of the great variety of human situations in which a given question can be asked, the truthful answer to it must vary accordingly. For this reason truth-telling is in many cases a very difficult art. The variability that cannot be escaped is revealed most vividly in the relation between a psychoanalyst and his patient. The same question, raised by different patients or by the same patient at different times, must be answered differently—and sometimes radically so. For the analyst must answer in terms that each patient can accept in the light of his own experience and the progress toward self-understanding he has thus far achieved. The analyst would not be speaking the truth if he were to answer without taking full account of this relativity, for he is speaking to a person—he is not just pouring items of information into a cognitive receptacle.

Truth transcends relativity because, except in communications that are confidential and can be trusted to remain so, this relativity to the immediate situation is not the whole story. A person who communicates cannot be sure, except in very unusual circumstances, that what he says will forever be confined to the limited social context in which it is spoken. It may reach anyone at any later time. So if he is to be truthful he must say it in such a way that it will not be misleading to any person anywhere; he must make it, so far as he can, a universally valid servant in man's quest for true understanding.

How reconcile these two contrasting requirements? How can a statement be unqualifiedly relative to a specific and limited situation, and also fulfill its obligation to universal validity? To answer this question adequately, the reconciliation must be achieved from both directions. Let us try them, one at a time.

First, look at the requirement of relativity—that truth must be spoken so that it can be experienced as true by the person to whom it is spoken, in the situation in which he finds himself. If we remember that his experience is not static but is always evolving, we will have our clue to the reconciliation from this direction. He is in that particular situation now, but he is also in process of moving toward whatever larger experience awaits him. Realizing this, one who tells him the truth must do so in such a way that it will not only be confirmed in his present experience but will also guide him toward a fuller grasp of similar situations in the future. And since the larger experience toward which he is moving is at least a broader social experience, a fuller grasp would take account of what other men who have inquired into the area in question have found. It would need to embody the trustworthy lessons they have learned. When one endeavors to speak truly he must, therefore, not only be aware of the immediate situation and speak appropriately to it; he must also be aware that that situation is being transcended, and that he will be a truth-teller only if what he says guides the process of transcendence wisely.

As an illustration, consider a tribe of primitive people who are disturbed by every occurrence of an eclipse. In terms of their traditional ideology, what happens in such a portentous event is that a celestial monster—Rahu,* let us say—swallows the sun or moon and then after a time disgorges it.

Suppose that a Western astronomer is visiting this tribe; he knows that

* This is the name of the mythical monster that, according to an old Hindu tradition, swallows the moon.

an eclipse of the moon is due in the near future. Imagine a conversation between him and an astrologer-priest. The priest asks: "Is it so that you can tell beforehand when Rahu will try to swallow the moon?" What should he answer, if he is wholly concerned to tell the truth? He cannot answer "No," as he would at once if this question were asked in the West. But he cannot answer simply in the language of Western astronomy. As an attempt to communicate truth to the priest, this would be speaking inappropriately rather than truly. In fact, if the circumstances were such that there was no chance for any further explanation, he might be quite sure that his answer should be "Yes." It is the answer that would enable the members of this society to anticipate reality correctly, in terms of their established conceptual framework. However, although his wish to be truthful would be satisfied by this answer, he would be unhappy if he had to leave the matter thus. His responsibility to truth would not have been fully met. He knows that scientific astronomy is not just a peculiarity of Western culture. It takes account of more of the observable facts than mythical explanations do; it makes possible more exact and confident prediction of eclipses, at whatever time or place, in all the details of their behavior, than those explanations even attempt to achieve. Thus, although it is not absolute truth, beyond improvement, it is the expression of a fuller understanding of eclipses than pre-scientific explanations provide, and it would give any people more dependable means of accommodation to their occurrence than presently available alternatives do. When its concepts and methods have been mastered by those who now interpret eclipses in terms of the voracious Rahu, they too will talk about sun, moon, and earth in their capacity to throw shadows on each other as they move in their orbits. Whatever further explanation such people may feel that they need will be built on this foundation.

So the astronomer would only be quite happy in this situation if he could say: "Yes, in terms of the presuppositions to which you are accustomed, Rahu will swallow the moon; in fact, I can tell you just when the swallowing will occur, how much of the moon will be engulfed, and how long it will be before the moon is released once more. Now the reason why I know these things is not that I have any magical power of precognition; it is that where I live we have found a better way of understanding all celestial events than the way you are familiar with. I will be glad to explain this better way if you would like to learn about it. But the explanation will take much time, and it will call for a drastic readjustment of your ways of thinking about everything."

Pause a moment to generalize from this lesson. Telling the truth requires respect for the immediate social circumstances of the telling, which include the present state of mind of those to whom it is told, with their cultural background; and it also requires respect for the universal experience of men as, through sharing the quest for knowledge, they gradually achieve more thorough and dependable understanding. Since those to whom it is spoken are growing toward a wider experience and more reliable modes of cognition, the first of these maxims leads inevitably to the second and cannot be separated from it. And the two maxims, taken together, have an obvious bearing on the function of language as a medium of truthful communication. The truth-teller cannot dispense with words that are already current in the community in which he is speaking; and it is his task to make into current coin, as best he can, whatever words promise to lead toward a fuller mastery of reality than those to whom he is speaking had been able to win before.*

Try the quest for reconciliation now by starting with the requirement that truth transcends relativity—that it must be valid for all minds at any time. The crucial clue here is that this universality can never be achieved if the truth-teller ignores the special circumstances of those to whom he is speaking. What is said will not be true for them if it is spoken in words that they do not comprehend and that their experience cannot verify; but if it is not true for them how can it be true for all? The universality of truth thus depends on its being so expressed that it can guide people anywhere from whatever beliefs they now accept toward an understanding sharable by all; there is no way to catch it in a formula abstracted from this process. The most esoteric report in a scientific journal must be capable of translation into terms that any person who appreciates what science is about can comprehend, so far as concerns the essential discoveries reported. Were no such translation possible in the case of this or that truth, its claim to unlimited validity could not be made good.

* An important earlier conclusion is thus confirmed in a new way. Can the truth always be told in ordinary language, or is an ideal language sometimes needed to communicate it? Our answer now is: So far as telling the truth requires effective contact with each variable human setting in which it occurs, and assures the guidance of each hearer from where he now stands toward fuller understanding, ordinary language must be used; no other medium can fill this role. So far as it requires anticipation of the more exact and reliable insight that corrects the inadequacies of his present perspective, it must use whatever words provide the medium in which that superior mastery can be gained; and these will constitute a more perfect language. But again it is clear that these two requirements do not conflict.

Again, we realize the vital sense in which common sense provides the goal as well as the starting point of the scientific and philosophical reconstruction of human knowledge.

V

How would the outcome of this analysis bear on a fundamental question about *demonstration?* Demonstration is a distinctive and important form of communication, in which one person is trying to make a statement that seems to him true persuasive to another person. What conditions must be met if this goal is to be attained?

This is a very poignant question for a philosopher. He is ever trying to demonstrate his convictions to other philosophers and rarely succeeds. Indeed, in that situation effective communication is often not achieved; each participant in the discussion unconsciously expects others to proceed on the basis of his own presuppositions. Thus the attempted demonstrations actually form a set of "crossed monologues," * with only bits of authentic dialogue feebly appearing here and there.

However, when a philosopher faces the question just raised, he usually forgets his own difficulties and turns to situations in logic or in empirical science, where the ideal of demonstration that perennially entices him is exemplified. He thinks of an inference whose conclusion clearly follows from its premises, or of a scientific law unimpeachably verified by the relevant facts. It is easy to assume that demonstration in other situations must be neatly assimilated to one of these models if its demonstrative character is to appear genuine. But perhaps by this approach a quite essential requirement is in danger of being left out. Since demonstration is a form of communication, it can only take place through the medium of a shared experience. What are the necessary conditions of such a medium being present?

The essential requirement stands out clearly when we turn to the field of values. Here it is obvious that any demonstration will fail unless a common value has been established between the demonstrator and the person to whom the demonstration is made. To prove to anyone that something is good is impossible in the absence of a mutually accepted standard of goodness.

* A phrase used by Richard P. McKeon in commenting on the speeches concerning freedom and value at the International Congress of Philosophy in 1960.

In the light of this truth let us examine what is needed for a formal or empirical demonstration. There must be a common value here, too; if it is not mentioned, that is because it can ordinarily be taken for granted. In formal reasoning the common value is respect for logical validity, as contrasted with the emotional appeal of this or that invalid transition from one idea to another. In empirical reasoning it is the value of readiness to revise the beliefs one now holds in the light of factual evidence, instead of remaining attached to them because of a strong wish to believe. Whenever these common values are absent any attempt at formal or empirical proof is futile. In short, do we not have here a necessary condition of successful demonstration everywhere?

However, an important issue arises at this point, and a possible misunderstanding of this requirement must be avoided. There are keen thinkers who insist, with their eyes on the fierce ideological controversies of today, that the essential need in the presence of disagreement on basic values is not to try to establish a common value, but to cooperate in meeting the urgent practical problems that both parties to the dispute recognize. No agreement on a common value is needed for such cooperation, and the attempt to establish it is likely to be futile or even to exacerbate the disagreement.

Quite so; it is true that this is the most promising way to make progress in such a situation. Nonetheless, to proceed in this way clearly implies that a common value is present—indeed, two common values. When cooperative action begins, both parties have tacitly agreed on the value of getting along together in harmony. They are also implicitly committed to the value of understanding each other's interpretation of the practical problems to be met and the interests reflected in that interpretation; otherwise, insuperable difficulties are likely to arise in adjusting the two ways of meeting those problems so that the cooperation may be effective. If these common values are not really present, or fail to be maintained, cooperation will come to an end.

The instructive truth in the position of these thinkers is that as long as cooperative effort continues on both sides, the essential common values do not need to be explicitly acknowledged but can be presupposed—and this is better than to argue about them. Until fuller mutual understanding has been achieved, argument will almost surely be futile; each side will wish to articulate its conception of those values in its own way and will be sure that no other articulation is sound. The conclusion is that common values are present in such a situation, although any attempt to demonstrate them is premature.

Yet—it may be that thus far a too narrow notion of demonstration has been taken for granted. We have assumed that it is the kind of process that can only go on where a common value is already present. But a further question must surely be asked: What needs to happen if the common value and the shared experience it makes possible are not already present?

The obvious answer is: They must be brought into being, so that it will then be possible to proceed on that foundation. And would it not seem that to bring them into being is itself a form of demonstration? Indeed, not only is this the case, but it also becomes the primary form, necessary to the success of any other form whenever the condition required is not at hand. This process likewise involves communication, of a very special kind. From the viewpoint of the one who initiates it, his task is to throw a bridge across whatever gulf intervenes between his own and the other person's mind, so that a common experience and a common value may arise.

How is this creative task accomplished?

One way is evident; it is simply an application of the principle involved in the dependence of truth on successful communication. Truth can only be spoken, we have found, when the speaker is sensitive to the hearer's experience of reality and to all the factors that make it what it is and what it might become. One of those factors—and a very important one—is the set of values now dominant in the hearer's mind. To attempt to change them by aggressive argument, and thus to make the speaker's values the common ones, is futile; if the hearer is not a skillful debater, he may be silenced but he will not be dependably convinced. However, when the speaker shows that he is open and responsive to the hearer's values, he has begun to build the needed bridge. There are times when this is far from easy. In the most difficult situation that may arise—when the hearer is so emotionally attached to his own presuppositions that his mind is closed to any alternative—the speaker will have to begin by becoming himself the hearer. By his own willingness to listen, he enters into a tacit contract. He is saying: "I will be open to whatever you have to tell me; then perhaps you will wish to listen too, and we can converse together."

Showing thus an unqualified sensitivity to the other person's values, the one who initiates the shared experience naturally evokes a similar attitude in response. A common value has then emerged, and fruitful communication has become possible. When the foundation thus established is firm enough—which may take time—all the facts perceived by one of the participants will become perceptible to the other, and all the evidential considerations that loom large to one will also loom large to the other. A significant measure of agreement is already present; progress toward fuller agreement in a common universe is under way. The primary and ultimate form of demonstration has been exemplified.

9

Love, creation, and reality

There is a way of classifying the kinds of knowledge man can gain with which all thinkers today are familiar. It locates them on a spectrum ranging from the most exact, dependable, and certain knowledge at one end to that which is most deficient in these respects at the other. The possible kinds of knowledge thus fall into a revealing hierarchy.

But this way of describing that hierarchy encourages the idea that the most exact knowledge provides a model to be imitated by all other kinds, and that its virtues can be realized in each of them if the right method for applying the model can be discovered.

A very tempting idea—but also a deceptive one. It may be that a more valuable and instructive classification is found when we describe that spectrum in different terms. The two ends have other characteristics than those above emphasized. Suppose we view the spectrum as ranging from the most abstract knowledge to the most concrete, by which is meant—in the perspective that has been taking form in these pages—from the knowledge that is freest from the influence of unstable emotional forces in ourselves and others to the knowledge in which those forces must constantly be taken into account. To put this proposal in another way, it may be illuminating to recognize that the exercise of curiosity in our search for truth goes on at several levels, differing in the degree to which the objects we are trying to know can be abstracted from the play of changing interests and warping emotion. The level whose objects are least affected by this play can be assumed to be shared by all people capable of cognitive discrimination; hence the entities existing on that level are necessarily bare, skeletal, and objective. The most concrete level consists of entities that are radically different in these respects.

Let us survey the various fields of knowledge from this viewpoint.

The most abstract level is obviously exemplified in formal logic and mathematics. Here one is dealing solely with conceptual relations; once their unique nature is grasped, truths about them can be discovered and communicated with maximum ease and freedom from misunderstanding. When a thinker roams in this realm he can forget the emotional disturbances of ordinary life; nothing need upset his assurance and equanimity. He is in calm mastery of all he surveys. And the compensation gained by excluding everything that does not belong to this safe and tidy realm is very appealing; a high standard of precision, rigor, and certainty can be achieved. Somewhat less abstract is the knowledge gained in the realm of physical facts, for in their case concentration on the logical structure of a causal law must be accompanied by openness to changing experience, with all the unexpected anomalies and perturbing possibilities that it may bring. Less abstract still in most situations is the realm studied by the social scientist, where knowledge of the statistical regularities of group behavior can never be wholly detached from recognition of individual members of the group and the varied forces revealed in their spontaneous acts.

The field that lies at the other extreme, being therefore richest in its content but also quite unprotected against disturbing change, is that in which one gains understanding of another human being as a person, with all his distinctive interests, emotional energies, and protean potentialities.

It is vital now to note that this level is not only the most concrete but is also the most inclusive. It is so for two reasons. First, every such person is an individual; he has his individual set of values, and therefore also has a framework of presuppositions for interpreting his experience that is not identical with the framework of anyone else. There is much, of course, that he will share with others, and this common area will presumably include the field of mathematical knowledge and that of the empirical sciences so far as he has become acquainted with them. But in virtue of his uniqueness he is the center of a universe that is never the same as that of any other person. To come to understand him requires openness to this previously unknown universe and readiness to enrich one's own experience by discovering all that is different in his. The second reason is that when one is really open to any person in this way he is also open to others; he will then be exploring, however feebly, the unlimited realm that includes all centers of experience and all the limited fields that they may share.

Because of the striking contrast between these two levels, when one passes from the former to the latter he passes from an exercise of outreaching awareness that is thin, austere, and safeguarded from disquieting surprises to one that is full, expansive, and pregnant with infinite possibility. When seeking truth in the former realm he is applying his intellectual powers to a desiccated conceptual order in which he can move securely step by step. When seeking to understand in the latter realm he has to be ready for challenges of any kind; his mind must respond freely and alertly to the totality of other minds, and to every less-inclusive realm as it is structured by their values and presuppositions—for he is dealing here with persons in their full actuality and inexhaustible potentiality. To seek truth in this region is by far the most difficult but also the most rewarding mode of cognitive outreach. It is difficult because really to open oneself to another person is an adventurous and humbling matter. It means laying aside one's protective cloak; if one is to understand another he must be willing to be understood himself, in his foibles and weaknesses as well as his virtues and talents. It is uniquely rewarding because the path toward knowledge of other people as persons is the path toward the fullest realization of oneself as a person.

In this perspective it is apparent that thinking at the abstract level depends in a particular and inescapable way on thinking at the most concrete level. When the normal freedom of the former from emotional disturbance is lost, as it sometimes is, we would expect that even that realm of conceptual relations can no longer be explored with the assurance and impartial concentration that otherwise can be taken for granted. And we find this to be the case. Glance again at the mathematicians whose abstract kingdom has just been surveyed. The conclusion drawn applies to them only when their cognitive relation to the objects with which they deal is all that needs to be considered. But this relation is embedded in others and is affected by them. Mathematicians are persons. When they talk with each other they talk not as logical machines but as persons. Their intercommunication can usually be easy and fertile because they share each other's values as mathematicians. At times, however, these common values are driven into the background by feelings of rivalry or by claims and fears about priority in this or that achievement; then they meet difficulties in communicating freely and investigating fruitfully their mathematical universe. Only when the play of these distracting emotions comes to an end, and the common values resume their place, can the normal exploration and intercommunication also be resumed.

But the fundamental insight toward which these thoughts converge is that among the various kinds of knowledge of which man is capable, the most inclusive and full-bodied is knowledge of persons. The quest for such knowledge is the quest for truth in its richest possible form. The universe that comes into being through the growth of persons toward mutual understanding is the all-encompassing universe; nothing can be conceived that falls outside it. And any less extensive cosmos leaves out a part of reality; it is a truncated universe—the present world of some individual or limited group.

The next important insight needed is that the most inclusive and full-bodied knowledge of persons is an understanding of them in their growth toward fulfillment. Any static apprehension or cross-sectional acquaintance is clearly incomplete. The basic reason is that like everything else in the universe people are changing; they do not stay as they are. Each person is always evolving from what he now is to what he is going to become; and if so he can only be truly known as changing in this way. It would be a serious error to restrict our attention to what can directly be observed about him; account must be taken of the inner forces that are slowly at work and take time to be revealed. Just as knowledge of a physical object requires a grasp of the potential energies in it as well as of its directly observable qualities and relations, so knowledge of a person requires discerning his as yet unrealized potentialities; otherwise it cannot possibly be adequate.

The area into which these insights lead us is today witnessing significant developments in psychology and the social sciences. These developments are throwing much light on this dynamic aspect of human experience, especially on the interaction between one person and another, and on the knowledge that is gained through such interaction. In addition to the theories of personality in its social aspects that are always appearing, new theories are being elaborated; notable illustrations are game theory, bargaining theory, theories of role-taking, theories of conflict resolution, and theories of psychodynamics in general. But a philosopher should not hesitate to enter this area too. For its thorough exploration, the resources of all conscientious thinkers are needed. Moreover, there is the serious danger—which a philosopher can point out—that many thinkers who are concerned with knowledge about people fail as yet to understand their own psychology, and especially how unconscious motivations influence their psychological and sociological theories. My aim in this complex and rapidly changing situation is the modest one of sketching a framework of ideas that may guide us toward the more adequate conceptual system needed.

I I

A crucial fact now turns up and leads to a third important insight. This fact is that the way in which a person is known makes a difference to the way he changes. Coming to know him is not an otiose contemplation that makes no difference to its object; it is an active process that has its natural influence on the one who is known. Even though any given episode of cognitive acquaintance may be very meager, it becomes a cause that has its effects in the subsequent experience of the person known. He will be, in some measure, a different person because of it. We shall not forget that much knowledge about people is indirect; it is gained from reports secured by someone other than the present knower. But there must have been direct acquaintance at some point, and knowledge of a person as a unique individual is quite impossible without it.

The more general implication of this fact is that the interaction through which man comes to be understood cannot be separated from the nature of man as understood; it is part of the total process through which his nature takes the form that it does. Such a conclusion is what we would expect from the interactive conception of knowledge developed in previous chapters; everything is known in the character that it acquires through its interaction with the knower.

But to appreciate the full force of this fact a vital distinction needs to be recognized. It is a distinction whose presence is evident not merely in man but in all living creatures. It arises from the very nature of the sensitivity with which an organism reacts to objects in the environing world, and which is thus the basis of its ability to gain knowledge of that world. Any response to an object takes either a negative or a positive form. There may of course be a period of wary hesitation before one or the other form becomes definite, especially when it is uncertain whether or not the object is an immediate threat, but such a period usually does not last long. The negative form is exemplified in a reaction permeated by fear and the need to guard against danger; it will be shown by a withdrawal from the apparently menacing object or by a violent attempt to destroy it. The positive form appears in any reaction marked by a desire to come closer to the object and to realize some of its potentialities; this requires a capacity to discover these potentialities and to anticipate the consequences to which an act expressing such a desire will lead. How to draw the line between the positive and the negative is a difficult problem, and several degrees of each may have to be recognized. Here it will be sufficient to note that the line must be drawn differently in the case of physical objects and in the case of persons; what is a positive response with the former may be negative with the latter.

Consider this sensitivity now as it is shown in the reaction of human beings to their fellows. The negative form naturally appears in the guise of suspicious or hostile feeling, and the positive in open responsiveness to the actualities and possibilities in them. When the negative dominates, the characteristic reaction is an apprehensive shrinking from the person toward whom one has such feelings, or an aggressive attack on the source of danger that seems to be embodied in him. In the grip of these urgent emotions, one is blind to the long-run consequences to himself and to others from acting in the way he does. When the positive dominates, the reaction expresses a sense of the varied abilities in the person toward whom one is thus responding. There is an effort to put oneself in his place, so that one can share his experience and his aspirations. In simple terms, the former reaction says: "I'm afraid of you; let me escape"—or, "Get out of my way lest I destroy you." The latter says: "I want to know you; let me in, so that I can see all that you see and all that you have it in you to be." *

When the positive and negative reactions to another person are thus described, it becomes evident that one who exhibits the positive reaction is aware of the truth expressed in our second insight, namely that the other person is a growing self. He realizes that there is much more in that person than appears or is able to appear at any given moment, and he responds accordingly. The negative reaction, by virtue of the emotions intrinsic to it,

* This is not to imply that a positive reaction is always possible, especially in cases where the threat of danger is real and serious.

lacks this dynamic awareness. One's attention is limited to the immediate situation; his concern is wholly focused on his own protection or aggrandizement. He inevitably misses significant realities that the one who reacts positively is able to take into account.

Our present task is to explore this difference, specifically as it bears on the gaining of knowledge by one person of other persons, and to formulate the third insight as we do so. Not only is such knowledge always gained through a process of interaction, which has its influence on the person known, but also the nature of that influence is different according to whether the one who actively seeks the knowledge is exemplifying a positive or a negative reaction to the other.*

A concrete case will illustrate these conclusions. Person A is seeking to know person B, and is responding to his presence in the typically positive or typically negative way. If it is the latter, B will sense A's hostility, however well it may be repressed, and will be hampered in some measure—by the need to guard himself—from realizing his creative possibilities. Thus A will be blocked from coming to know those possibilities. If it is the former, B will sense A's openness to his potentialities and will be encouraged to reach out toward their realization. A will thus be enabled to know them, as fully as the circumstances of the interaction permit.

The essence of the third insight then is this: True understanding of a person is gained only through the positive response to his presence. Only when one's interaction with him becomes an active participation in his growth toward fulfillment can one come to know his full self, because only in the medium of such a response is that full self coming to be.

But two serious objections are naturally raised against this trenchant outcome. We shall try to meet them, and in doing so, to provide whatever further justification can be provided for the soundness of the insight. The less fundamental objection will be considered first.

Is it not the case that in any man at any time there are manifold potentialities, and that any interaction with another man will facilitate the fulfillment of some of them? If so, is not his fuller self being achieved whichever of these potentialities is realized? Let it be interaction with a person who wishes to know him better, and we will grant for the moment that such a person must exemplify either a positive or a negative approach. Are not two directions of change equally open and hence two possible forms of com-

* In the following discussion we shall neglect the fact that when one comes to know another person he also becomes known, in the same way, to the other and to himself.

pleter understanding? This appears to be the familiar situation of the self-fulfilling prophecy, with the dual alternatives that it always involves.

This reasoning would be expanded as follows: When one's approach to another person is permeated by animosity or distrust, the person thus approached is more likely than he otherwise would be to act in a way that verifies such a malevolent or suspicious judgment. He will then be known in terms of these characteristics; the hostile mode of understanding him will confirm itself. When that interaction expresses openness to his positive capacities, and faith in their realization, he will thereby be energized to see, develop, and realize those capacities. He will then be known in terms of the qualities thus awakened and developed; this mode of understanding will confirm itself. It would seem that each of these ways of interacting with him has its own natural effects, and each will lead to its own form of verified knowledge. Do we have any right to say that in the one case a fuller self is realized and known, while in the other it fails to be realized and known?

Here is the crux of the problem posed by this objection. And the answer implied by the third insight is this: While a self-fulfilling prophecy is indeed at work in both approaches to another person, they are not on a par. Only the positive approach fosters the emergence of the full self that we wish to know; the negative hampers that process. Fear, suspicion, and similar emotions obstruct the vision of the would-be knower and obstruct fulfillment in the person known. One who is swayed by them sees only what they project on their objects; other realities and more hopeful possibilities, no matter how important, are blotted out from his vision. Unobstructed sensitivity, however, can envisage all the realities and possibilities that are present in any situation. One who expresses it is open to all that the hostile or fearful observer sees; if he is free enough from the negative feelings he can even be sensitive to the need of another to withhold himself, to be wary of all advances. He understands what lies back of this need; thus, even in such a situation, he will see possibilities that a negative approach makes it impossible to see.

The conclusion then is that the positive response to another person creates, and in understanding grasps, a fuller reality than can appear and be known to the negative emotions. It tends to release and energize the versatile capacities in the other that may previously have been hidden but can now move toward their fruition. The man who is understood in the medium provided by this response is the whole person that is coming to be;

the man who is known in the medium of the contrary feelings is a cramped or distorted fragment of a person.

But an even more fundamental objection must be faced. Is it justifiable to assume an exhaustive dichotomy between the positive and negative approaches? In any interaction between persons, including the interaction involved when one is seeking to know another, it might seem that a neutral attitude must be possible; one should be able to enter the presence of another simply as an indifferent spectator. Psychology and the social sciences appear confidently to assume that this is possible; are they right? Or is it so that whenever two people are in each other's presence everything that each of them says and does inevitably has its positive or negative effect in the experience of the other—either tending toward the fulfillment of his potentialities as a person or toward their obstruction?

The answer may well be that no neutral approach is really possible. Let us ask what neutrality would actually mean in the interaction of two persons. It could hardly mean the absence of all responsiveness; in that case each would ignore the other and no knowledge of any kind would be gained. And a revealing word has just been used. Does it not mean what, in emotional terms, we call "indifference"? Now indifference is surely a form of negative feeling. Like hostility, it too erects a wall of protectiveness in the person thus treated; and the supposedly neutral observer thus blocks the potential self that is there from being realized, and blocks himself from discovering it. Just as truly as animosity or suspicion, this attitude contrasts with Marcel's "availability," in the presence of which the other person finds the freedom and courage to become the full self he has it in him to be.

Consider, in the light of this pregnant thought, the method of understanding people that is oriented around the concept of "behavior"—the popular method today among psychologists and social scientists in many parts of the Western world.

Nothing could be more plausible than this reduction of the knowable reality of people to their behavior in an age zealously seeking truth about man and powerfully influenced by the ideal of objectivity as it is revealed in the natural sciences. When one studies human behavior, taking the word in its most generous meaning, one seems to leave out nothing that an objective approach can possibly use. Thus full continuity is secured between the responsible procedures of physical science and the scrupulous study of people; their behavior is the closest analogue to the observable changes of a physical body. And indeed a wide range of dependable truths has been discovered, many of which would never have turned up in the absence of such an approach. Moreover, this way of understanding man provides a much needed corrective to both the sentimental and the cynical views of human nature with which philosophical and theological theories in the past have been replete. As for people's complacent judgments about themselves, canny observers in all ages have learned that "your deeds speak louder than your words," and the behavioristic theory of man is a systematic articulation of that lesson.

Nonetheless, it may be that this salutary method fills in the long run a subordinate rather than a primary role in our quest for an adequate understanding of man. It yields information but, by itself, no comprehension. To put the crucial weakness bluntly, if one says implicitly to another human being, "So far as I am concerned, your behavior as I can now observe it is all that you are," he is saying something both false and hostile.

Why false? Compare such an assertion with the long influential but now outmoded way of explaining the physical world through its directly observable qualities and motions. These are obviously there, and to note their orderly relations is to grasp a modicum of truth about that world. But to understand the important changes in physical objects was impossible without recognizing potentialities of change, which are real but incapable of being directly observed; they are inner forces, which reveal themselves gradually through time. Surely it is the same with a human being. What is disclosed in his present behavior falls far short of his full selfhood; to understand the latter, one must glimpse the reality slowly coming to light as he grows from what he now is toward whatever fruition of his powers lies ahead. And no one who meets him and seeks to know him can be unconcerned about these powers; all will be affected by them in some measure, either for good or for ill.

Why hostile as well as false? Because, when one is interacting with another person, if the aim is merely to observe his behavior and nothing more, he is being treated not as a human being but as a thing; and to treat him thus is an expression of hostility. It is to say, in effect: "I do not care whether or not you fulfill your capacities as a person; I am only interested in watching how you tick." This is to erect a wall between observer and observed, with only a narrow window through which the latter can be examined as an external object. Since he is aware of himself as more than an object knowable through observation, he resents being reduced to one; he feels it an unfriendly act, for his most basic need is to be accepted as a person and to be treated as such.

Of course, the study of human behavior in the laboratories of psychology and social science is by no means fated to exhibit the aloofness just described. The investigator himself is a person as well as a behavioral scientist, and he often establishes a quite positive relation with his subjects. When such is the case he will not only observe their behavior but will also show respect for the personalities before him and concern for their growing fulfillment. These are happily not incompatible; there are many situations, in fact, where objective study of a person or group is a prerequisite to wise action seeking their good.

Still, however, a serious difficulty lies in the fact that if the investigator presupposes that people are really known only through their behavior, the most significant bits of understanding gained through this relation easily drop out of sight and find no place in the verified conclusions reached. A creative intercommunication between knower and known may have developed, but the rudiments of real comprehension that it makes possible are likely to seem nothing but vagrant and unreliable intuitions. Were the limitations of this unfortunate presupposition left behind, would it not be obvious that a human being is always more than objective science can verify about him, and that reliable knowledge of his behavior is a subordinate domain in the quest for adequate understanding? He is not just an aggregate of activities; he is a person.

Let us return now to our main theme and draw these varied threads together. One who seeks to know another person is thereby interacting with him, and every interaction has its characteristic effects on the one who is known. Being the process that it is, causal action and the quest for understanding are intrinsically bound together in it. If the seeker for knowledge exemplifies a positive response to the other's presence, the causal action and the quest for understanding are in harmony with each other; action is eliciting the emergence of the self to be known. If he exemplifies a negative response, they are in conflict; action is obstructing the emergence of the full self to be known.

III

Do we need to avoid any longer the appropriate word for what has been called the "positive response" to another person? Thus far it has seemed wise to avoid it because of its deep-rooted and pervasive popular connotations. When the question is asked, what love is, people naturally think of the watchful concern of a parent for his children, or of the romantic attachment between man and woman, or of the mutual affection of two friends; these are prominent ways in which the affinity of a person with other persons reveals itself. Because of the strong influence of such associations, one is tempted to speak instead of "sensitivity," or "openness" to others, or "responsiveness," as we have been doing. Each of these has its advantages, but each has its limitations too. I believe that the wise strategy is to clarify the word "love" and then use it freely, rather than surrender it to vague and confused thinking.

The crucial reason for believing so stands out clearly when we examine these popular connotations and realize that to identify love with sentimental or romantic attachment is to run the risk of violating the true meaning of the word instead of being faithful to it. Such an identification encourages the assumption that something is essential to love that is not essential —something that may even be incompatible with it. Those emotions can be present when respect for the one loved is lacking. And they almost always harbor exclusiveness and dependence: exclusiveness by being an attachment to this person as against others; dependence by expecting a requital for one's devotion as the price for continuing to feel it. But is love truly such if it can only be felt toward one person by hating others, or by threatening to hate him too if he does not respond as the lover demands? Is it not evident that we need a sounder conception, which will include these familiar forms of love but will give them their proper place in a wider and more reliable perspective?

We look then for the primary meaning. May it not be this: Love is freedom from self-centeredness, and hence from the demands and limitations that self-centeredness involves. So far as a person is not thus free, what he calls love is likely to be partly or wholly something else—an eagerness for approval, a desire for comforting gratification, or an urge to control another person to make him serve one's needs. So far as he is thus free, his liberated feeling for others will flow in every direction and ask no recompense for its outreach. How else could that freedom reveal itself? To be sure, the flow must begin with much less than a universal outreach; a child needs an intimate few to enfold in feeling and by whom to be enfolded. But if it is love that is taking root in him, it has the seed of unlimited expansion. If this is so, then exclusiveness and dependence have disappeared; it becomes clear that love by its very nature embraces unconditionally all men. Such an insight does not conflict with the patent truth that love will show a deeper tenderness and a more constant thoughtfulness toward those who are bound to us by special ties of family or friendship than toward others.

In its true meaning, love is then just what we have described as free and open responsiveness. And this identity becomes more obvious when we examine a perplexity that might be suggested by the all-embracing character of love. A keen thinker can get entangled in it if he takes for granted the tempting presupposition that loving a person always means helping him achieve his present ends. Reasoning thus, he is likely to ask: Since one who loves universally is responsive to the values that any other person seeks to realize, will he not be hamstrung when he finds it necessary to support one in preference to another? Will he not love the man who is acting unjustly as well as the man who is unjustly treated? How can he take sides, resisting the former and aiding the latter? But this weird paralysis could appear only if love were stupid—and of much sentimental and romantic attachment this is doubtless the case. However, if we think of love as involving by its very nature an outreaching sensitivity, this quandary disappears completely. Love has its inherent implications for the guidance of action, and complete support of the person loved is not necessarily implied. One who truly loves will be concerned so to act as to bring about the conditions under which love can realize itself more fully. In the presence of exploitation he will act in such a way as to induce the perpetrator of injustice to become aware of what he is doing. To love is thus to seek wisely the "common good"; indeed, it may be that this concept, so indispensable in legal and political thought, gains its meaning through the existence and intrinsic universality of love. A common good can hardly arise except where concern for the well-being of every person in the community is effectively present.

In short, these varied considerations point toward the conclusion that love for a person and openness to all his actualities and potentialities are one and the same thing. And in virtue of this openness love is intrinsically universal; it will express itself in respect for and responsiveness to every person in whatever situation he may be. True knowledge of men and love of men cannot then be separated; neither is possible without the other.

Looking back in the light of this identity, it now appears that love was really contained in the meaning of several concepts that have proved indispensable.

For example, the objectivity sought by the scientist reveals his insistence that any acceptable result of his work must be capable of verification by other competent inquirers; and without sensitivity to the experience of others and to standards generally approved in his field, how could such a result be intelligently sought? Another example is agreement between investigators, which became more and more influential in the course of history as a criterion of truth. The very word implies that a quest for mutual understanding through openness to each other's experience has been going on and that it often achieves its goal. A free responsiveness is even more obviously involved in the basic condition of successful communication, which is necessary to the gaining and speaking of truth. Only when such responsiveness to the state of mind of the person communicated to is present, can one speak the truth—that is, make an assertion to him that will reliably guide his wise adjustment to the realities which are being discussed. Telling the truth, in short, is one of the ways in which love is expressed; and we well know that when love is absent words can and will be used to deceive. But the most vivid illustration of this intrinsic bond appears if we turn to the distinctive kind of communication called demonstration, and especially to the form of demonstration that fills a primary role in relation to all other forms. When, in the presence of disagreement on fundamental values, one person takes the initiative in building a bridge of communication to another person, he is revealing the freest and most positive response that can be revealed in any human situation.

In the light of these instructive links between love and the various concepts through which the meaning of truth and of knowledge is clarified, we can fully appreciate what Bertrand Russell meant when he wrote: "The impartiality which, in contemplation, is the unalloyed desire for truth, is the very same quality of mind which in action is justice and in emotion is that universal love which can be given to all." [1]

If this outcome still seems strange, perhaps the further step needed is to note that the principles which have emerged as essential to true knowledge of persons are essential to true knowledge of everything. Just as the negative emotions of fear, hate, suspicion, and indifference block the way to understanding a human being, so they block the way to any form of understanding.

Observe first how one's attitude toward another person inevitably affects one's power to comprehend anything when in that person's company. Watch two congenial people converse about matters of mutual concern. Each is open to learn from the other's experience and judgment. Watch two who dislike one another. Each is alert for some warrant to disagree and reject; instead of reaching out toward the larger truth that might be gained, his mind is imprisoning itself more tightly in its narrow opinion. Remember what happens to the mathematicians, when the shared orientation usually present is lost because distrust and hostility have crept in. They are seriously handicapped in exploring their mathematical realm together.

But the maxim applies always and everywhere. Its negative implication is trenchantly stated by Smiley Blanton when he says:

> Expressions of hostility so distort our outlook that we are unable to view life in a clear and objective manner. Fear paralyzes our natural impulses to explore and investigate, while resentment causes us to misinterpret what we see. Anxiety prevents us from accepting the normal experiences whereby we grow. . . .
>
> Against these hostile emotions neither laws nor logic can prevail. They hurtle us on to repeated errors despite ourselves—for love is the only true source of knowledge and without it we lose our ability to learn and to understand.[2]

Its positive implication is that we can respond in open and free sensitivity not only to other persons but to any object attracting our attention, and that such a response is the necessary medium for attaining the truth about it. Every exercise of unobstructed curiosity about the world is then an expression of love, and no stretching of the proper meaning of the word is required. "For love, in its widest meaning, is simply *an intense, positive interest in an object.* When we love a thing, we become deeply engrossed in it with all our senses. This is true whether the thing we love is a woman or a flower, a food or a landscape, a song or a philosophical theory. In each case we want to come into the closest possible contact with it—to look at it, touch it, listen to it."[3] Indeed, Rudolf Steiner flatly affirms: "Nothing can reveal itself to us which we do not love."[4] In the absence of an open heart there cannot be a fully open mind.

The intrinsic bond between love and the quest for truth holds then with no qualification. Whenever complete and undistracted attention is given to an object, the same kind of outgoing absorption in it is realized that is present in love between persons. Love is at work wherever awareness expands freely—that is, without allowing its expansion to be blocked by any negative emotions.

IV

We return to the less general theme of knowledge of persons. Erich Fromm has said:

We know ourselves, and yet, even with all the efforts we make, we do not know ourselves. We know our fellow man, and yet we do not know him, because we are not a thing, and our fellow man is not a thing. The further we reach into the depth of our being, or someone else's being, the more the goal of knowledge eludes us. Yet we cannot help desiring to penetrate into the secret of man's soul, into the innermost nucleus which is "he."

There is one way, a desperate one, to know the secret: it is that of complete power over another person; the power which makes him do what we want, feel what we want, think what we want; which transforms him into a thing, our thing, our possession. . . .

The other path to knowing the secret is love. . . . Love is the only way of knowledge, which in the act of union answers my quest. In the act of loving, of giving myself, in the act of penetrating the other person, I find myself, I discover myself, I discover us both, I discover man.[5]

Let us concentrate on the central thought, vividly confirmed by these words, that since such knowledge is always gained in a process of interaction, it unites by its very nature causal activity and the quest for understanding. Being able now to use the word "love" for this process when it leads to true understanding, let us reflect on each of these two aspects while not forgetting their essential union. What is implied about the knowledge of a person, as knowledge, by the fact that it is gained through love? What is implied about the causal action, as action, by the fact that its mainspring is love?

Through love a person is truly known—so we have said. But a philosopher will insist on asking how one can be sure that the knowledge gained is true. One reaches out toward another person, seeking to know him—yet how can one tell when this goal has been achieved? Indeed, aware of his inevitable limitations, would he not be presumptuous ever to allow himself any such assurance?

Yes, there are limitations, and he can have this assurance only under one condition—but does not love by its very nature provide that condition? To love is just to be open and responsive to the experience of others—to share it, to make it a part of one's own experience. When one is not blocked by self-centeredness, he can perceive what they perceive, feel what they feel, and discover what, as they grow toward a larger universe, they are discovering. If this responsive identification were lacking, love would be lacking.

The power of mind thus exercised is the power we call imagination. "To send one's imagination forth to establish a beachhead in another man's spirit, and from that vantage-point so to blend with the other's landscape that what one sees and feels is authentic—this is the great adventure in human relations." [6] Through the medium of such an outreach the universe of one person and the universe of another do achieve a wider and richer intersection.

But there is a most illuminating paradox in this coming to know a person through blending with his landscape. The understanding thus gained is true understanding, and can be known to be, but if it were *claimed* as such it would become false. The broadened and deepened experience won does approximate the normative experience which confirms its truth, but to claim that character would be to lose it. The reason is simple but rather subtle: In this area any claim to truth inevitably expresses a dogmatic assurance that is incompatible with love. To make such a claim is to insist that one's present insight into another person is true as it stands, while to love is to quicken his growth toward a fuller selfhood, to which no insight already gained can possibly be adequate. We are aware that in other areas, too, a thinker is gaining dependable truth only when he is open to more truth; but, in common sense and science, to claim validity for the results reached by well attested methods need not conflict with such openness. Here, however, any insistence on the truth of a present insight does conflict with the openness to further insight that love intrinsically implies. The price of continuing to progress in the knowledge of persons is then to avoid claiming that one already has it. To make such a claim is to ensure that it will be false.

We have said also that coming to know a person is an active process, and we are aware that behind any such process there is always a motivating interest whose nature the action will reveal. What then is revealed about love when it serves as the mainspring of action? One naturally pictures love as a special kind of interest or motive that can be set off from others; and of some familiar forms of love this is the case. But is it the case when the love we have in mind is universal sensitivity and full responsiveness to persons? How should its relation to other interests that express themselves in action be described?

Love in this most authentic form is *all* interest finding its real fulfillment, and *every* motive realizing the dependable satisfaction that can be realized when destructive conflict within a person and between persons is overcome.

This is true because, on the one hand, if love is the kind of motivation just portrayed, it has no special interest of its own—it identifies itself with all interests of every kind so far as they do not annul each other, and seeks their richer fulfillment. On the other hand these varied interests, with the values they project, can avoid suicidal conflict and achieve enduring fulfillment only as they accept the place that love gradually discovers for them in the totality of man's aspirations. Viewed thus, love is the energy ever organizing that totality into a stable, freely shared, and effective whole.

A trenchant corollary is that one who loves can make his own the optimistic insight won by our religious pioneers; he knows that good is victorious over evil in the long run of human experience. In the absence of open responsiveness to the concerns of others, one's criterion for telling whether progress is ultimately real or not is whether he sees evidence that the universe is realizing the good as he now conceives it. When this criterion is taken for granted, a lurking pessimism is unavoidable. When such responsiveness is present, one's criterion is whether the universe is realizing the good of all, as through imaginative sensitivity that good is gradually clarified and in growing cooperation pursued. One who has adopted the latter criterion and is participating in this creative process knows that the energy expressed in the clarification and cooperation is always at work—though it works slowly.

This insight will be strengthened, and our understanding of love as mainspring of action will be enriched, if it is placed in a wider historical setting than any we have thus far occupied. There is an instructive relation that can be seen between love and forces perennially at work in the subhuman world. At each stage in the vast process of cosmic evolution there are forces that maintain whatever unifying order has been achieved at that stage, and there are forces that create novelty and diversity. But besides these there are also forces that make for diversity in unity, seeking the maximum of individual freedom that is possible consistent with the stability essential to continued existence.* All these forces reveal their presence in the inorganic world; they are likewise at work in the biological realm out of which man has developed.

In what do we find the third kind of force exemplified at the stage of evolution marked by interaction between persons, with the distinctive potentialities there disclosed? Love is the power that realizes the maximum of freedom consistent with stable order at this stage; that is its very nature. Did it fail to respect individual freedom it would not be love; did it fail to

---

* For example, a suitably located planet of a solar system fills its place in the order of that system while providing favorable conditions for the variegated forms of living and nonliving matter that develop on it.

reach out toward unity with all men and thus toward an inclusive world-order it would also not be love.

V

But each of our statements employing the word "action" has been an understatement; and the bolder word needed has occasionally been used. If coming to know another person is a dynamic interaction in which the one known is energized to reach out toward a greater and fuller life, the process is not merely action but *creation*. Love as an active power creates.

What does it create?

Primarily, a new value; and then everything that naturally grows from that value—the aspirations, hopes, and imaginative insights that are thus awakened, and all the manifold modes of fulfillment that are fostered. When a person is aware that he is loved, he realizes: "I have a value that I didn't know I had before—and a value not as an instrument for someone else's ends but to discover and seek my own ends." Love is the creative medium in which a person can find the self that he has it in him to be, and can perceive that he is the potential center of a vaster universe than he has yet experienced. Seeing himself endowed with this new value, his self-esteem is enhanced—and it is vital to note that it is esteem for the self that is evolving in the medium love has created. This means that along with whatever else comes into being a responsive love is born, with the greater freedom to reach out and explore and create than had been present before.

Such a response may not be evident immediately, or in the short run; the counterforces are sometimes very strong, and they may not have been rightly appraised by the one who elicits the response. We need to understand better than we now do how this creation of love takes place and the conditions of success. But the basic law is clear. We know that when an animal is treated with fearless love it responds in kind, even though we also know that such an approach is likely to fail with a lioness protecting her young. And some important features of the creative process are also clear. If the love thus expressed is narrow and blind, the one loved will identify with it in its narrowness and blindness, till he is disillusioned by wider experience; if it is universally sensitive and alert, he will identify with it—so far as he is able—in its all-inclusive sensitivity, and in that case no disillusionment will need to arise.

The power that is love is thus the power to create, in the domain of the full actuality and infinite potentiality of man. The joy of loving is the joy of creating, in the most expansive realm in which creation is possible—as Plato discovered long ago in his *Symposium.*

With this word filling its appropriate role, a more venturesome insight looms ahead than any that would earlier have seemed plausible. Already we have seen persuasive evidence that, ultimately, growth in each individual and in the human race is growth in unobstructed sensitivity and alert responsiveness—that is, in love. The essence of the cosmic evolution at the human level would seem to be unending progress from the greatest love yet realized toward the greater love that always lies ahead.

Dare we envisage the possibility that this progress may be—as the seers of religion have also held—the inflow within our present horizon of a more perfect love beyond, which is slowly creating us in its image and at the same time re-creating our universe?

Our study of the process of demonstration and of how value-concepts gain new meaning reveals the way in which this creative inflow takes place, however we interpret its ultimate source. A new ideal of love is born in the heart and mind of some spiritual pioneer. He then communicates it to others—but how does he do this? It cannot be done merely by words, for any words he speaks are old ones and by themselves will convey their habitual meaning. Yet he must use words; how do they acquire the novel meaning needed? The answer is that he exemplifies the new ideal he has glimpsed, and as his action elicits in others its natural response, the words that accompany this process gain in their minds the intended meaning. They will then begin to exemplify it too, and the new meaning becomes more widely shared. The Gospel of John describes Jesus at the Last Supper as teaching his disciples such a new ideal. He led them beyond the meaning of love rooted in their experience of family life and in their concept of the kindly but stern God of the prophets. How was this achieved if not by his exemplification of the new ideal in the loving acts that accompanied his words? Responding to these acts, though feebly at first, they gradually came to understand the new meaning and make it their own. Without his persuasive example, could they have freed themselves from the limitations of the traditional meaning?

But power of creation varies, and in several dimensions. It varies of course in the degree of transforming energy revealed. The highest degree of which man is capable is revealed in such great souls as Jesus. Near the low point on this scale is the creative power shown in the simplest experiences that are familiar to everyone. The homely perception of a common object always contains its bit of individual interpretation; if so, every such act of perception is in part a creative and not merely a receptive process.

But it also varies in another important dimension, namely in the scope of the insight that arises from the new value created. And here we think again of the philosopher's role. Is he a creator as well as a seeker for inclusive understanding?

When a philosopher (or a theoretical scientist) proposes to reconstruct a prevailing framework of presuppositions he is surely engaging in a creative adventure of the most comprehensive scope. He is not gaining insight into truths already there and waiting to be discovered; he is creating a new conceptual framework, which, if it succeeds, will guide thought in the centuries that follow and give a new unity to the experience of those thus guided. Later thinkers would never have hit upon just his vision, but once it has been caught and expressed they find it the answer to their own quest. That vision and insight bring into being a new universe in which they will live, so far as its basic structure is concerned.

Henry Sigerist maintains that "the philosophers are the most powerful makers of history." [7] Whether this is so or not, they do play an essential and unique part in the total process of creation that is ever going on. Their genius is the genius of unusual sensitivity to the needs of the epoch that is coming to birth, combined with unusual power to articulate in systematic form their interpretation of those needs. Such a seer shares the thrill of the creator in any other field, but his is the distinctive thrill of creating in the unlimited realm of human progress as a whole.

Philosophers have been filling this creative role for many centuries. Can it be filled in the future with more prophetic discernment and more energy of creation than it has been in the past?

VI

To understand is to understand reality; to create is to bring into being some reality; philosophy unites the quest for truthful understanding with the creation of reality.

We have observed that the word which ends each of these clauses points, when reliably construed, in two contrasting directions. On the one hand thought is always confronted by some reality beyond itself which it must respect; and on the other it continually reshapes reality so that the thinker comes to live in a different world than he did before. When looking in the first direction we are aware of the sense in which all who sincerely seek truth are "realists." When looking in the second we are aware of the intrinsically pliable and social nature of reality. And the implications of this second awareness have proved pretty radical.

For the reality to which thought is responsible to conform is not merely that which exists before us in the domain of observable fact. Common sense naturally identifies it with that domain, for the latter constitutes the environment in which most people now live. Nor is reality limited to the ranges of phenomena that make up the vaster domain of science. In accepting either of these limitations we would be recognizing only a cross-section of reality, for the prophetic genius appears from time to time and when he plays his part successfully he reconstructs both of these domains for those who come after him.

The intelligent realist will, then, require his thought to square with what the universe is becoming; if he limits himself to the realm of facts as they are now perceived and explained, with no alert sensitivity to the direction of change, he will miss the most important realities that might be discovered. Viewed as a whole, reality cannot be less than the all-inclusive process in which new criteria of fact—and of form and value as well—arise, remold our experience, and pass away in favor of their successors.

In virtue of the second of these two directions that determine its meaning, reality is always reality from the human standpoint, or rather—to invent a word that accentuates its dynamic character—reality from the human "growth-point." When we seek to know what is real we are seeking nothing that can be separated from the dynamic experience of man—from the widening sphere in which perception by human faculties, articulation by human thought, and communication by human speech are possible. If one allows himself to suppose the contrary, what actually happens is that he erects some limited human perspective into an illegitimate and illusory absolute.

We have now reached the point where this aspect of reality can be seen in the setting of the major forces that determine its evolving structure. In that complex setting, let us turn to the hoary branch of philosophy that has made the adventurous enterprise of understanding reality its own. The metaphysician is the thinker traditionally concerned with this task. Through his distinctive talent he has attempted to achieve what the poetic or religious seer achieves in a less coherent form. The latter opens before his unimaginative fellows glimpses of new territory to be explored, but it is no part of his task to provide a map in which such glimpses are logically connected with the rest of their experience. The metaphysician draws a map by which, he hopes, men can be wisely guided as they try to capture with systematic understanding what the seer leaves as inspired intuition. This role is intrinsically continuous, of course; before any given map of reality has fully served its purpose, thinkers will be venturing beyond its confines, guided by some new insight. The moving horizon thus revealed is the growing-point of human experience as it seeks rational interpretation; for that reason the category of reality can never be wholly freed from vagueness and ambiguity. The metaphysician, however, wants to sharpen its meaning as best he can and to draw all the distinctions that are essential.

In assuming this function, he finds himself in a unique relation to common sense as well as to science. The man in the street always has an ideology in terms of which his major interests find their place and the scattered strands of his experience are bound together in an inclusive whole. That ideology is his map of the universe. If the metaphysician fails to offer the kind of map that his breadth and impartiality make possible—and in a form communicable to others—people have no alternative to the seductive but specious maps that warp the facts of their experience and guide action in ways that lead to disillusionment.

VII

How does he draw such a map, meeting thus the need for a wise and well-organized perspective on the universe?

In general, by achieving a vision, and then by articulating the conceptual deposit of his vision. He is a person especially sensitive to the territory stretching beyond our present horizon, and especially capable of giving whatever insight he gains the systematic form without which it could not be communicated. Few can fill this function successfully, for it requires creative imagination and the skill of an artist as well as the rational talent that a philosopher would naturally possess. But when one does succeed, and his vision wins wide acceptance, it will no longer be regarded as a vision; it will have become to those who adopt it the structure of the real world in which they live and think. The word "vision" is naturally used only when it is still visionary—when it is just the glimpse of a possible universe about which no one yet knows whether it will pass from the status of hopeful individual fancy to that of objective reality.

In particular, by finding a distinctive use for the category of "reality"; at least, his role seems to have been filled most auspiciously by doing so. How has that happened? Through what process does this category gain its metaphysical meaning? We shall have to restrict our answer to the way in which it has happened in the Occident; the orientation of Eastern thought on this problem has developed differently.

A twofold responsibility must be met. Any adequate definition of the word must reveal obvious continuity both with the relevant uses in daily life and with the use typical in metaphysical tradition. To secure the former continuity it is wise to center attention on the adjective "real" and the verb "realize"—even the adverb "really"—instead of on the abstract noun "reality," for the same reasons that led us to turn in the preceding chapter from the abstraction "truth" to the unsophisticated correlates "true," "truly," and "truthful." If the adjective "real" is chosen, we will have to avoid the influence of specialized meanings, which appear in such phrases as "real number," "real property," etc., and likewise cases where "real" is synonymous with other adjectives like "existent" or "genuine." To secure the latter continuity we must look for current uses of "real" which support the traditional philosophical assumption that reality occupies an ultimate position in relation to all other categories of thought.

By this route we shall examine reality in its significant interaction with the Western categories that have already been found to fill a basic role— namely, logical form, empirical fact, and value. A metaphysician may limit himself to revising the framework in which the realm of fact is interpreted. But he is often more ambitious than this, projecting a revision of our criteria of form and value as well as of fact. Contemplating this ambitious enterprise, we recall that when the process of lifting unconscious presuppositions to awareness is taken into account, some value always plays a determinative role in relation to forms and facts as well as to other values—that is, in such a situation value is the ultimate category. But in the historical process with which we are now concerned these categories are on a par; each fills a similar function. In this setting values interact with the realms of form and fact, and the category of reality plays the ultimate role.

Viewed against the background of philosophical history, my proposal is that through the concept of reality philosophers revise the meaning of each of these three categories when this becomes necessary from time to time, and also express their growing insight into the dynamic interdependence of the realms denoted by them. It is clear that when problems that fall within any one of these realms are dealt with, nothing but confusion results from introducing concepts that gain their meaning in another. A problem in formal logic, for example, is never advanced toward solution by appealing to factors distinctively revealed in the verifying observation of a fact. But the metaphysician is concerned with the total arena in which each of these realms has its place, and in which a fruitful interaction between them is going on. In the comprehensive issues he confronts, verified facts, logical necessities, and appealing values may all be relevant; we might say that he is dealing with reality in the very process of being dissected into these realms.

Consider then, from this angle, these three categories. In Chapter II we sketched the course of evolution by which each of them came to be conceived as it is today in Western thought. We now need insight into their significant interrelations—to see how their essential independence is compatible with their interdependence, and with the ways in which it is revealed. Let us briefly retrace their historical emergence, with our attention first on a special aspect of the process that will clarify their independence of each other. It will also throw light on the distinctive nature of the realm dealt with by the metaphysician and the reason why its problems cannot be evaded.

During the long period dominated by rationalism, when mathematics supplied the model of knowledge for most influential thinkers, it was natural to assume that if any intellectual achievement were to count as knowledge it must be logically demonstrable—like a mathematical proof. As it seemed evident that statements about the facts of sense perception do not satisfy this criterion, there was a strong tendency, especially in the Platonic tradition, to disparage such statements as mere "opinion" falling far short of true knowledge. But by the late medieval period these statements had become quite important, because they were needed to guide effective action in the environing world; how, in that altered situation, should they be viewed? Naturally, different attitudes appeared. There was a negative attitude, expressing a pessimistic and conservative judgment on all assertions that fail to measure up to the traditional standard. From its standpoint no knowledge is really attainable in this imperfect region. If perceived facts cannot be known by deductive proof from assured axioms, so much the worse for them; the mathematical standard must be maintained. But fortunately there was also a positive attitude, expressing a forward-looking orientation. In essence, those who exemplified it were saying: "Let us seek the best-evidenced statements that prove possible in this region, giving dependable guidance to our activities in it; if we can distinguish them from less reliable ones, there is no need to worry about whether they satisfy the criterion of knowledge that our forebears took for granted."

In time enough thinkers adopted this positive attitude so that a new criterion of knowledge could emerge—namely, the criterion exemplified by empirical science. The quest for conclusions that give reliable guidance in its realm was successful. As such conclusions were distinguished from assertions about perceived facts that lack their dependability, the appropriate criterion in this realm became clear, and it was generally accepted. All statements that met its requirements won their title to the status of knowledge.

At this stage statements about values were left in the lurch; they did not appear to satisfy either the mathematical or the empirical criterion of knowledge. Earlier, they had been validated in terms of the rationalistic perspective, which in its own way gave them an honorable place; but now, with the radically altered presuppositions about knowledge that had come to prevail, they were gradually orphaned. It became clear that the assertion "to act thus and so is right" can be established neither as a theorem in a mathematical system nor as a verified relation between observed facts.

However, as in the case of empirical truths, it was in due course realized that these statements are vitally important—for human life and thus for philosophy. Hence, during the modern period, there has appeared a divergence of attitudes similar to the earlier divergence. There has been the negative attitude, again expressing a pessimistic and conservative judgment. From its standpoint no rational results, and therefore nothing that can be called "knowledge," are attainable in this area. Assertions about values are simply expressions of emotion;* to be counted as knowledge, they would have to be reduced to verifiable factual statements. If there are any values that cannot be known in this way, so much the worse for them; the now-established criterion must be regarded as absolute. But, fortunately, the positive attitude has been present also. Its maxim, as revealed by those who exemplify it, is similar to that of the empirical scientist earlier: "Let us seek the most dependable statements that are possible in this area, and so far as we succeed there need be no worry about whether they meet the criteria of mathematical or of empirical science. If they give us trustworthy guidance in distinguishing the right from the wrong and the better from the worse, that is enough."

Since intelligent choice between values needs guidance by concepts different from those of form and fact, the positive orientation in this area has likewise appealed to an increasing number of thinkers. The result is that a new and distinctive criterion—if not of "knowledge" at least of wise "judgment"—is achieving clarified formulation. The search for dependable

* This is one influential theory expressing the negative attitude.

normative principles has met with success, as thinkers in all ages who have seriously dealt with the problems of ethics and of legal theory know; they can be discriminated from supposed norms that are seductive but lead us astray. Valid criteria are thus attainable in this vital area, and statements that respect them acquire a status comparable to that of the reliable conclusions of mathematics and empirical science in their fields.

There remains a fourth realm besides these three. It has already been recognized, and parts of it have been surveyed; now we see that it is the realm with which metaphysics is specifically concerned. In it, too, a distinctive problem appears, irreducible to the problems dealt with by any of the other realms. The statements that express the outcome of attempts to resolve it do not satisfy any criterion of formal validity, nor of factual evidence, nor of comparative value as these are applied at any given time. What makes them different and irreducible is that in the case of these problems the adequacy of previously accepted criteria in one or more of those realms has been thrown in doubt, and there is a search for new and wiser criteria to replace them.

It is not surprising that when thought ventures into this enticing but mysterious region, a divergence of attitudes appears among philosophers similar to the divergence that has appeared in each of the historical situations just described. There is the negative attitude, expressing a pessimistic and conservative judgment on any assertions that may be made in this region. Those who exemplify it say, in effect: "It is obvious that no rational procedure is possible here; whatever is asserted reflects an absolute presupposition that can only be adopted or rejected—our cognitive faculty can do nothing with it. For if an assertion is to be regarded as rational, it must conform to the criteria now employed in one or another of the above three fields, and this is impossible in these exploratory gropings."

But fortunately there is also the positive attitude, expressing in this difficult region the constructive and forward-looking orientation. Metaphysicians are the thinkers who have taken it. Through much of past history it was easy to take it because they believed they were simply completing on sound rational principles the edifice of scientific truth. Now that the long reign of that belief is over, our task is to reinterpret their positive attitude so that a promising foundation may be laid for the metaphysical enterprise today. And a natural way to describe this attitude is in words analogous to those we have put in the mouth of the forward-looking pioneers of empirical science and of a reasoned theory of value: "Let us seek the most reliable insights that are possible in this obscure region, without worrying whether they satisfy any criterion that would be applied elsewhere." The sensible aim, in short, is to clarify whatever criterion actually offers help in this quest, and to use whatever method gives guidance in distinguishing results that prove trustworthy from those that are deceptive. The same basic situation is present here as in the other cases; the main difference is that in the others an appropriate criterion gradually takes definite form, whereas in this case difficulty in defining the needed criterion can never be quite overcome.

VIII

Before we journey into this fourth realm and clarify the metaphysical meaning of "reality," we must look at the emergence of the other three realms once more, with our eyes now on an aspect of the process that reveals ways in which those realms are interdependent. Notice two instructive relations of dependence.

In the first of these, the dependence of a more complex realm on a simpler one is obvious. The mathematician, as such, passes no judgment on problems of empirical science or of comparative value. The empirical scientist passes none on problems of value, but he is responsible to respect the criterion of formal consistency as well as that of factual evidence—his inferences must be logical. The thinker in the realm of values is not free from responsibility to these two criteria; he also must render his thinking consistent and must respect all facts that are relevant. Indeed, he often finds it necessary to explore some empirical facts that no one had investigated before, but which prove vital to his quest. Studies in the field of social policy frequently illustrate this truth; the values that can be realized in a given situation are largely determined by those facts. But, in addition, he is responsible to compare any pair of alternative values between which choice must be made, in the light of the clearest vista of human good that he can attain. In his case a threefold criterion must be satisfied; none that is less complex would be adequate.

The other relation is the converse of this; it reveals a dependence of each of the simpler realms on the more complex. Although the rules of validity in formal science are independent of the other two areas in any given application of them, the adoption of such rules is influenced in the long run by the circumstance that we wish to reason validly *about* facts and values. This is clear when one traces the historical succession of logical and mathematical theories. Similarly, while the rules of empirical method, in any particular case of their employment, are independent of the investigator's preference for a particular outcome, the choice of such rules is determined in the long run *by* value commitments. Men desire to explain facts in such a way that certain values they count important can be realized by the kind of explanation reached.

When one is vividly aware of these modes of dependence he is prepared to recognize the ultimate interdependence that the metaphysician finds he must take for granted. We shall examine two illuminating ways in which it is revealed. The first is a natural consequence of the mode of dependence last described; in the second, the metaphysical meaning of "real" with its cognate words comes clearly to light.

When the metaphysician searches for more adequate criteria of form, fact, or value he feels no need to keep these three realms from intruding on each other. A promising criterion of logical form may be suggested by new discoveries in the realm of empirical fact or new ways of explaining them. Conversely, a wiser criterion of fact and how to describe it may be suggested by a novel conception of logical form. Either of these may be suggested by a change in dominant values. And new values are often suggested by the discovery of facts that make their realization for the first time possible. Consider briefly two examples of this kind of interdependence.

An outstanding case in which newly noticed or emphasized facts led to a revision of presuppositions about logical form was the shift, in the late nineteenth and early twentieth century, from the Aristotelian logic to its present successor, and to the resulting union of logic with mathematics which found its most notable expression in Whitehead and Russell's *Principia Mathematica.* The former theory reflected the subject-predicate grammar of the Indo-European languages and the way of ordering facts emphasized by our ancestors under its influence. The latter reflects the growing influence of modern science in its zeal to explain the enlarging realm of fact by relational categories that ancient logic had neglected or treated as unimportant exceptions—such as the categories of distance, time, motion, and predictive causality. Underlying the increasing use of these basic concepts was the insistent demand that the empirical realm be described mathematically. This meant among other things that physical objects and events must be so conceived that quantitative relations are essential to them and no longer subordinate to the qualitative distinctions that can be expressed as predicate terms in Aristotelian logic. Thus an epoch-making revision of logical presuppositions and a more general conception of form was gained, as a result of persistent concentration on a range of factual material that could not be handled in terms of the formal framework previously taken for granted.

The other example is an instance in which a change of dominant values led to a new way of interpreting empirical facts, and to a new definition of a vital category used in explaining them. I mean the emergence of the modern concept of causality. Philosophers since Hume have accepted this concept so completely that they have hardly noticed how radically it diverges from the orthodox notion of causality in ancient and medieval thought; and a more detailed comparison of the two notions than we have thus far attempted will be very instructive.* Hume finds three necessary and sufficient conditions for applying the category of causality: (1) the cause and its effect are closely connected in time, (2) the cause precedes the effect, and (3) the cause has in the past been regularly followed by the effect. But turn back to Aristotle's conception of causality, the most influential earlier conception. What he calls "efficient causality" is the closest analogue to Hume's concept, and his definition of an efficient cause reads: "That from which the immediate origination of movement or a state of rest comes." † He typically illustrates the relation by such situations as that in which the cause is the activity of an artist and the effect the work of art he produces, or where the cause is the labor of a builder and the effect is the building he constructs.

Observe that in these situations not a single one of Hume's conditions is present. As for the first two, the cause and effect occupy the same period of time; for as soon as the cause becomes active the effect begins to emerge, and the cause continues to be active until the effect assumes final form. The crucial difference, however, is that there is no dividing line in time between the occurrence of the cause and the occurrence of the effect, which is vital to Hume's conception.‡ As for the third condition, from the Aristotelian viewpoint a thinker would never refuse to apply the category of causality where an agent is creating something for the first time. No repetition of what has happened in the past is essential; one can see a new product

* See my paper in the *Journal of Philosophy*, Vol. XLIV, No. 7 (March 27, 1947), pp. 169 ff. Also the following passages in my *Types of Religious Philosophy*, rev. ed. (New York: Harper & Brothers, 1951), pp. 200 f., 208–212, 425–429.

†See W. D. Ross, *Aristotle* (New York: Charles Scribner's Sons, 1924), p. 72. This is Aristotle's definition in *Physics*, 194b. There are complexities in Aristotle's view of efficient causality that are here neglected.

‡ Some of Aristotle's illustrations do involve a temporal separation between cause and effect, but he evidently does not regard such separation as essential.

taking shape under the activity of its maker just as easily as he can see something produced that has been produced before.

What explains the shift from the earlier to the later conception of causality? The answer seems obvious. The dominant value expressed in the pre-Humean conception was the value described briefly on p. 168 f. The dominant value expressed in the Humean notion is the one that is central in science today—the value of successful prediction. If causal explanation is to serve this value a temporal line is required between cause and effect, for only then can the latter be predicted on the occurrence of the former; and if the prediction is to be a confident one, the effect must have been regularly observed to follow the cause in the past.

So, in performing their distinctive task of revising our present criteria, metaphysicians use as grist to their mill whatever promising ideas are suggested in any realm of experience.

Turn now to a second illuminating way in which this ultimate interdependence of the three realms is revealed. Indeed, it becomes a pair of ways rather than a single one, for it can be clarified either by probing prominent examples from the history of thought or by examining the quest of an individual for self-realization. In both cases the metaphysical function of the category "real" with its opposite "apparent" is brought out in especially vivid form. We shall explore each of these instructive situations, beginning with the historical endeavor of philosophers to interpret the arena of man's experience as a whole. And although the meaning of "real" that we are now investigating is present whenever prevailing criteria in any realm have been thrown in doubt and more adequate criteria are being sought, it is best revealed in problems that specifically involve two or more of these realms. There are such problems; by their very nature they can only be solved by bringing the realms in question together in a unified perspective.

For the first example, look at a problem not traditionally regarded as metaphysical but which can serve as a useful introduction to those that clearly are. This problem has been a perennial one for theology; it involves the radical conflict that appears from time to time between the highest moral ideal man has glimpsed and the claims of fundamentalist religion. The classic discussions of the conflict are found in the ethical criticisms of the religion of their day raised by the Hebrew prophets and by the Greek dramatists and philosophers. There are three possible types of solution, each of which reflects the adoption of a basic principle; and the main principles that have been historically championed are familiar to everyone.

On the one hand there is the principle that God is not to be judged by man—i.e., that if our moral thinking leads to conclusions at variance with those of the current theology it is thereby shown to be fallacious and the ideals envisioned delusive. On the other hand, there is the principle expressed so vividly by Euripides: "If the gods do aught that is base, they are no gods." Which of these is valid, or is some third principle superior to both of them valid?

These solutions can be readily formulated in terms of the ultimate metaphysical categories. Are man's moral ideals "really" subordinate to what God is now conceived to approve, or should man's conception of God be revised so that it will harmonize with his clearest insight into what is "really" good and right? Or are both these solutions only "apparently" sound? Is there a third principle superior to them, expressing a more comprehensive grasp of the "realities" involved? Whether these specifically metaphysical words are used or not, the issue is being assessed in terms of the categories of reality and appearance. And what do they mean in such a situation? The answer seems to be: When the conflict between these two proposed criteria is viewed in the broad perspective now required, in what principle can we find dependable guidance, so that the wisest harmony of moral idealism and religious insight will be "realized"? And the required perspective can be more definitely described: It is a vision of the growing experience of men as capable of moral sensitivity and also of spiritual awareness, and thus as always seeking the fullest contribution that both morals and religion, with due regard to each other's presence, might make toward the "realization" of man's potentialities.

Were we limited in resolving this conflict to the first two alternatives most readers would doubtless pronounce in favor of the second, for history seems to teach that when religion does not revise its concept of God to accord with the highest moral ideal available it can become a terrible source of evil. However, the third alternative is always relevant, and unless it is kept in mind as a live possibility the perspective adopted may be inadequate for a wise solution. If the highest moral ideal at hand fails to exemplify impartiality, expressing instead some racial or national or class bias, religion at its best can teach a lesson that moral sages may have missed. A vital general truth thus comes to light—namely, that when a metaphysician breaks free from previous presuppositions about such issues and is open to their replacement, he finds that the third alternative provides the key to ultimate understanding of every problem he confronts. Even if in a given case he reaches the conclusion that the demands of one

field should be wholly subordinate to the claims of the other—as he sometimes will—this is because his appraisal in the wider perspective opened up
by that alternative leads to such a conclusion.

Let us take an example now from issues universally recognized as metaphysical. Consider the persistent conflict between religion and science. In
attempts to resolve it, the categories of reality and appearance have long
been standard coin. Indeed, the traditional metaphysical systems in the
West are largely an elaboration of principles prescribing how we should
decide in the presence of such a conflict. Is the world disclosed by scientific
investigation unqualifiedly real as it stands, or is it a world of appearance—
a "phenomenal" realm merely—in contrast with a more ultimate and comprehensive reality grasped by religious insight? In terms of the major distinctions we have kept in mind, how can one bring together coherently the
realm of facts this side of the horizon, structured by our present scientific
presuppositions, and the realm beyond the horizon? Since the latter is usually conceived in some sense to embody supreme perfection, the problem
intrinsically involves both fact and value. And again, is not the essential
meaning of the categories of reality and appearance clear in this situation?
When the issue is viewed in the total setting of man's pursuit of knowledge in the realm of sense perception and of his quest for a reliable transcendent vision, what principle points toward a solution that can endure
because it takes account of all that each of these cognitive endeavors can
contribute toward wise understanding?

Today, all philosophers and most theologians would agree on the right
principle were we asking merely what should be done when the issue concerns detailed truths capable of being tested by scientific method. But since
it also concerns the criteria of fact, of truth, and of sound explanation, the
situation is different. The third alternative is here clearly relevant, as it
was in the case just discussed. A new insight into reality, leading to a
revision of theological ideas, has often arisen from scientific experience;
and an insight that leads to a reconstruction of scientific presuppositions
may have its source in religion. An outstanding instance of the latter is
worth mention. In early modern times thinkers rejected the prevailing presupposition that the celestial region is a complex hierarchy of degrees of
perfection as one ascends from the earth toward the empyrean, and adopted
the contrary presupposition that it is an order of uniform law. The
former idea rested essentially on Aristotelian metaphysics, whereas a major
source of the latter—as is evident in such pioneers as Copernicus, Kepler,
and Bruno—lay in the religious conviction that God is omnipresent and

unvarying in His action, so that the entire universe created by Him must conform to the same general laws.*

It is interesting to examine an issue analogous in every respect to those just discussed, except that it involves the realm of value alone. That realm includes both artistic and moral values, which are sufficiently different so that reflective treatment of them divides into two branches of philosophy, esthetics and ethics.

Thus, besides the many problems that fall entirely within one of these branches, occasionally problems arise that involve a conflict between an apparently valid esthetic criterion and an apparently valid moral one. Consider a familiar illustration. Artists are often inspired to create works that violate the moral sensitivities of their contemporaries, as in the free treatment of sex by present-day novelists. Or esthetic values that were consistent with the moral standards of an earlier day become inconsistent with the ideals established through a period of moral progress; one thinks of the classic discussion of this theme in the third book of Plato's *Republic*. In such a situation the same three alternatives that have appeared above become relevant. One will be the puritanical principle championed by Plato himself—namely, that the demands of art are subordinate to the moral values involved; another will be the principle toward which artists naturally incline, proclaimed in the formula "Art for art's sake." The third will be the principle that neither field can wisely be regarded as always having supremacy over the other. The issue is easily stated in terms of the metaphysical categories: Is art "really" subordinate to morals, or independent of moral claims, or do both of these principles only "appear" to be sound guides? The third alternative reminds us that what is needed may be an enlarged insight—one that is sensitive to the total experience of men as beings capable of moral excellence and also responsive to beauty in nature and art—and thus always seeking the fullest "realization" that morals and art together can make possible.

In each of these five instances except the last, the problem confronted by philosophers brings together in one way or another two of the three realms of form, fact, and value. And the third and fourth instances show how the category of reality gains a distinctive meaning in such a comprehensive setting; it serves our need for an adequate criterion that embraces and transcends the criteria now accepted within each of the realms involved.

---

* It is true that the former idea also enjoyed a certain religious support. Since heaven was God's special abode it was naturally pictured as free from the corruptions caused by human sin.

But once the appropriate meaning for "real" and "apparent" has gained clarity in such a setting, we can see (as in the fifth instance) that it is also present in any situation where a previously prevailing criterion of form or fact or value has been thrown in doubt and a philosopher is searching for a more adequate one.* It does not matter whether his solution is suggested by some other realm than the one he is concentrating on—as in the first and second instances described above—or whether it arises within that realm itself; in either case his quest will naturally be expressed by using the metaphysical categories. In the first instance, for example, one might say that the Aristotelian conception of form has appeared to be adequate but is not really so; by contrast the modern conception, because of its greater inclusiveness and other virtues, provides the real category needed.

The general problem in all these cases can be put thus: All relevant considerations being taken into account, what criterion "really" enables us to deal wisely with the total field that is involved, and which criteria tempt us to adopt them but only "appear" to be adequate?

I X

It remains to probe the role of the metaphysical categories in the second of the two ways in which their meaning comes plainly to light—that is, by watching them at work in the growth of an individual person toward his fulfillment. When one seeks to understand this process, in himself and in others, he naturally employs the distinctively metaphysical concepts, and adopts a perspective similar to that taken for granted in these historical situations.

As a person, each of us is an evolving individual with many potentialities pressing toward realization. These reflect the same phases of experience that on the larger scale appear in the realms of form, fact, and value. We have our share of curiosity about facts, which finds expression in deference to the discoveries of science; we respond to the ideals and virtues that approve themselves in man's mature experience; we play our part in the conquest of unstable transitions of thought by respect for the norms of

---

* Indeed, the metaphysical meaning of "real" can be and is extended further in the direction of restricted fields; when this happens, the meaning approximates that of more limited concepts such as "actual," "important," "changeless," and the like. We may ask, for example: Does the railroad track really converge in the distance or only appear to do so? This is a synonym for: Is it actually the case (in terms of accepted factual criteria) that the track thus converges, or not?— except that the associations of a metaphysical perspective are not wholly lost.

valid inference; we have our capacity for religious feeling, attested by the echo in every human being of the voice of the mystic seer. In a given individual, unfortunately, any one of these powers may develop like a tumor at the expense of others, and distortions of personality, which block him from growing freely toward his true destiny, may appear. But every individual is also *one* person, and this unity of selfhood is progressively "realized" only through a balanced fulfillment of all his positive possibilities—a fulfillment such that the further growth of each fosters rather than hinders the continued growth of the others. And the quest for such a balanced fulfillment is a gradual discovery of reality in the same essential sense that the word carries in the larger historical setting just surveyed. Indeed, how could it be otherwise, since the progress of the human species simply gathers into a totality the growth of all individual persons?

That this close analogy between macrocosm and microcosm actually holds is shown in certain ordinary uses of the word "real" (with its cognate words), which are likely to puzzle a philosopher unless they are viewed in the perspective we are exploring. After a person has undergone a religious awakening, or has achieved a deeper self-understanding, he will often say: "I thought the life I was living before and the things I was giving myself to were real, but I see now that they were not." Moreover, one of the basic principles of psychoanalytic psychology is naturally stated by using this category. Freud saw that the overcoming of inner conflict in the search for health and integrity is a process of passing from domination by the "pleasure" principle to unqualified acceptance of the "reality" principle.* Most adults have successfully made this passage in dealing with the more obvious physical and social realities around them; otherwise they would be hopelessly maladjusted to life. But it is one thing to gain this measure of liberation from unrealistic demandingness, and quite another to achieve responsiveness to all the realities present in man's entire environment.

Hence every individual in his personal growth is as familiar with the problem naturally expressed by using the word "real" and its associates as the expert metaphysician. And there is another significant parallel. In a sense everyone is dealing with that problem every moment of his conscious life, but it faces him with special vividness when he meets issues in which more than one side of his personality is involved and needs to be taken into account. Choosing a marriage partner is one of these; another is decid-

---

* The pleasure principle might better be called, I think, the "wish-satisfaction" principle—the emotionally grounded assumption that the world must satisfy one's wishes.

ing on his vocational career. Reflect for a moment on the latter case. Several conditions must be met by a wise decision; they arise from the varied potentialities mentioned above. An individual should respect his major and persistent interests, his skills and aptitudes as given facts, his sense of moral obligation to family and society, his ultimate spiritual values, and his power to draw sound inferences about these factors. In short, here the balanced well-being of his whole self is at stake, and he most simply acknowledges his sense of this fact by saying: What career do I "really" want? What vocational goal do I wish to "realize"?

Reality thus reveals its essential metaphysical meaning, whether we approach it on the scale of history at large as it guides philosophical insight through the centuries, or on the less conspicuous scale of each person's quest for self-realization. Let us now draw the significant threads together and state, as best we can, the major generalizations that this survey seems to teach.

First, what does the word "reality," in its contrast with "appearance," mean when it is used in resolving these ultimate issues? The answer is: It orients our search for the most adequate perspective which, when clearly envisioned, enables us to distinguish between what we will accept as real and what by contrast will be pronounced merely apparent.

Second, by this answer we readily understand the statements employing the category of reality that have been fiercely argued for and against in the history of metaphysics: "God is a real being"; "Only matter is real"; "Time is unreal"; "The Absolute alone is fully real." The word "real" is indispensable in these assertions because no other adjective, such as would be natural in dealing with more limited areas, is quite synonymous with it. It transcends what is meant by "valid," "existent," "true," "genuine," "important," and the like, for it points beyond the present horizon of the realms in which they have an established use. To employ them would imply a narrower context than is "really" present.

Third, when we compare reality in its role as criterion in this pioneering endeavor with criteria that are sufficient in more restricted fields, a vital difference appears. It is unique in that it is never definitely clarified in the sense in which other criteria can be; it is always emerging from the mist and never fully emerges. It has no distinct form itself, for it is that in relation to which other basic concepts take form, gain definition, and in course of time are revised.

A philosopher is tempted to give it a precise definition, hoping thus to domesticate it within a tidy system. But any who succumb to this temptation must be met by the warning: How then are we to talk about the unmapped realm into which thinkers are constantly advancing? When exploring under its guidance we do not know just what should be meant by the words we have to use, and are fumbling for an appropriate meaning; we are not sure just what should be taken as given fact or valid reasoning or controlling value and are seeking a better criterion for one or more of these; we have recognized as inadequate the cognitive methods applied before and are trying to find wiser ones—in short, this is the kind of adventure in which our very foundations are undergoing re-vision. The category of reality in this role cannot lose the character of horizon-transcendence; its function is to lead us from where we now are toward the uncharted infinite. But it proves its reality by rewarding our search with glimpses of a sounder base than we had previously been building on.

Fourth, in this setting a distinction can be drawn between two important aspects of reality. That to which the metaphysician or growing individual responds in this pioneering process is reality as creator—the dynamic source of each new vision and each new universe that emerges through it; that which is deposited as a result of the process is reality as created—the novel structure of experience as it takes form from time to time in the course of history or of personal fulfillment.

In the light of these summarizing thoughts we shall venture a succinct description of the unique role that reality fills in its relation to the criteria at work in more limited fields. A condensed and abstract formulation might be this: Reality serves as our criterion of criteria—that is, as the criterion by whose aid we tell what other criteria are relevant in any situation, how they need to be revised, and how the claims of each should be weighted and balanced when they point in incompatible directions. More fully and concretely expressed, so as to bring out the human concerns at stake, the task of metaphysics through its interpretation of reality is to enlighten man's continued progress in the sciences and the arts, in morals, religion, social statesmanship, and law—i.e., in all the varied aspects of human culture—and to enlighten it by achieving the most comprehensive attainable vision of the totality of man's powers in relation to the totality of his universe, to the end that each of these phases of his growth may make the maximum contribution that in this infinite perspective is possible to the enrichment of human experience. In the first of these formulations we are defining reality as a cognitive category; in the second we are thinking of that to which the category refers.

Metaphysicians often attempt much less than this, and rightly so. But the greatest among them have met precisely this need; and the value of the less ambitious tasks they perform can be seen in fullest clarity against the background of this creative vocation. Metaphysics, thus conceived, is the supreme exercise of our power of adventurous searching. It fills the unique role of bringing the wholeness beyond the horizon within the horizon, so far as this can be accomplished by the finite mind of man.

10

Eastern and western philosophy

Our search for philosophic understanding need not be confined to the resources that have emerged in the evolution of Western thought. We are
living in a period when ways of thinking in the East and in the West have
for the first time been thrown into wholesale, intimate, and provocative
interaction with each other. History has given our century an unprecedented opportunity.

Since the beginning of Neolithic times, at least, human evolution has in
general consisted in a gigantic process of cultural differentiation, as men
have migrated over the habitable areas of the earth and have settled down
to solve their problems of survival and progress under diverse conditions.
As a result, the civilized cultures of the world have developed in sufficient
isolation from each other so that the distinctive genius of each—in art and
religion, in morals and statesmanship, in science and philosophy—has had

its chance to unfold without being hampered by a too insistent and therefore confusing challenge from the genius of others. This isolation has been
less than a superficial study of history might suggest, but the handicaps to
intercommunication were formidable enough so that a large measure of
independence was realized. The differing philosophies of mankind are an
expression of the distinctive insights that appeared in the various cultures
because of this segregating process; each of them embodies some core of
wisdom that has proved significant and without which the world would be
poorer.

The Chinese became a great people because at an early period of their
evolution in the Far East they learned certain major lessons in the art of
living wisely. The genius of the Chinese mind has perennially been shown
in its full acceptance of man's essential social relationships and the inescapable practical problems of life in face of the realities he has to cope with.
It has thus won firm and durable moral understanding. The Indians became
a great people because at an early period their seers poignantly sensed the
unbearable limitations of this mundane life and began to fathom the art of
exploring the infinite reality beyond. The genius of the Indian mind thus
lies in its power to discover man's deep and mysterious potentialities as
they lead into a realm far transcending his present experience. Both these
peoples, along with others, are now eagerly absorbing important ideas from
the West, especially in the areas of science and technology. But we may
take it for granted that the core of their long-developed philosophical tradition will not be lost. It will modify what they are absorbing fully as much
as the latter will modify it.

Today, however, a turning point has come in this vast movement. Cultural differentiation, to be sure, is still going on and will doubtless never
cease. Nonetheless a reversal has appeared in the course of evolution as a
whole. Humanity is no longer an aggregate of separate cultures; it has
become a single organism, moving either toward more abundant life as a
viable world community or toward early death. In virtue of this reversal,
intercommunication between individuals and interaction between peoples
all over the world has now become so constant and so intense that whatever positive values have emerged in each of these cultural patterns can
now enter into the far richer experience that all men might freely share.
Our elaboration of this possibility will have to be limited to the major
Eastern and Western philosophies. But it is well to remember that these do
not exhaust the panorama. There are other civilized cultures; also there are
many so-called primitive societies, some of which seem able to maintain

themselves in health even under the impact of civilization. Each of these societies has its own language, structured in a distinctive way, and underlying that structure is a unique framework of categories and presuppositions. In many primitive cultures this framework diverges markedly from what the metaphysic underlying any of the civilized languages reveals: distinctive ideas of time, space, matter, motion, causality, and the like are involved. Probably no such framework would in the long run prove superior to any system of categories developed among civilized cultures. Yet some of them may have an illuminating light to throw on particular problems.

Why is this novel situation a significant and challenging opportunity for philosophy? One reason is that it opens up a more inclusive and adequate perspective in which to solve philosophy's own perennial problems. How this is so will soon be illustrated in the setting of two of these problems. Another and more important reason is that mutual understanding between peoples must be achieved at the philosophical level if man is to progress successfully toward stable coexistence and peaceful growth in a world community.

This is so because the kind of understanding required to guide this progress has two dimensions, both of which are equally essential. The first points to the wealth of detailed facts in which the nature of a living culture is displayed, the second to the framework of basic categories through which those facts gain coherent meaning. When seeking to understand a culture in terms of the former, we are absorbed in a mass of particular items in their political, economic, religious, and sociological diversity; when trying to master it in terms of the latter, we are led to the enduring hopes, the accepted values, the comprehensive ideas that give unity to these details. The importance of the second dimension is obvious so far as concerns moral ideals and their influence on the political and social aspirations of a people. But we have seen that the same conclusion applies to their logical and metaphysical categories. These ultimate concepts do not merely serve as principles of explanation, of truth, of reality; they express the prevailing decisions of a living culture as to what sort of thing an explanation should be, what kind of truth is worth seeking, what type of event it is wise to take as real.

Appreciative mutual understanding between cultures must then be won at the philosophical level if solid foundations of trust and friendship are to be established. Otherwise the supreme values and organizing ideas to which one people is committed will remain alien, opaque, and therefore unreasonable to those who have grown up in a different cultural background. Not that the absence of sharp cultural differences guarantees harmony between peoples, as is evident from a glance at the history of the West. But their presence exacerbates other sources of fear, distrust, and discord, and makes any conflict far more difficult to resolve. So the unique and indispensable contribution of philosophy toward realizing the world community of the future consists in creating a communion of minds in this second dimension and in breaking down the age-old barriers to mutual understanding which exist at that level.

How can this shared understanding be gained? The general answer we already know. It would be quite unrealistic to hope for a world community in which the members of each culture respond appreciatively to all that is good in the achievements of every other culture if the human mind were a separate, purely individual entity. But while every person *is* an individual—and his individuality never needs to be lost—through his power of unlimited sensitivity he is also universal. Vigorously or feebly, he can stretch his awareness beyond every present boundary, including the boundary set by the presuppositions of the culture to which he belongs.

A more specific answer is needed, however. And the best, perhaps the only, way to develop a satisfactory answer is to engage in this stretching ourselves. We will see as we do so how a more adequate solution of certain issues faced by both Eastern and Western philosophers can thus be glimpsed than could have taken form in the narrower setting of their traditional presuppositions.

I propose a twofold experiment of this kind. The first issue concerns the power and limitations of reason. Western philosophers, with few exceptions, trust this faculty to grasp whatever truth and insight are attainable, whereas Eastern thinkers, likewise with few exceptions, have been convinced that the most important truths can only be reached by transcending reason. This is a very basic divergence. Communication and mutual understanding at the philosophical level between East and West can only be realized if a way is found to bring together these contrasting convictions in a perspective that includes them both and indicates how a stable reconciliation is possible.

Before we probe the heart of the issue we must see how this radical divergence came about.

One clue appears in the sharp difference between the primary concerns of Eastern and Western philosophy. The persistent concern of the West (except during the medieval period) has been to understand the external world; hence it tends to approach the study of mind and society with a criterion of sound explanation borrowed from its successful mastery of our natural environment. In the East, especially in India, the controlling interest has been to comprehend the inner self of man, in its capacity for growth toward wholeness. The ultimate nature of the surrounding world is grasped in its subordinate relation to this quest for self-understanding. By this approach the Eastern sages quickly became convinced that such understanding cannot be gained by viewing the self as an object, like an external thing; it can only be gained in and through the progressive realization of the self one has it in him to be. Thus the confident expectation of the West has been that we can know man, in others and in ourselves, by making him an object and gradually learning how to allow for the differences between a person and a thing, while the conviction of the East has been that true comprehension of any entity can only be won in the radically different setting of a quest that leads beyond the realm of knowable objects.

Both sides have taken for granted that reason is the cognitive power that does its work through systematizing the manifold distinctions that mind is able to make whenever it analyzes and interprets any object. Hence, from the viewpoint of the West, it naturally follows that reason is the faculty to trust in the pursuit of truth everywhere, while from that of the East the most important understanding can only be gained by passing beyond the limits that reason intrinsically sets.

Another clue appears when we look at the evolution of philosophy in East and West and observe how it has met the main challenge that seemed to be posed by its cultural and historical setting. Western philosophers have been vividly aware of man's long struggle against the forces that lead to wishful thinking, and they see thinkers in all fields frequently tempted into cognitive irresponsibility. Nothing has entered their ken that they feel able to trust as a better guide than reason. The alternative guides with which they are familiar—intuition, faith, the authority of tradition—seem clearly less trustworthy than reason, and when any question is raised about the full competence of the latter they easily imagine that one of these alternatives is vaulting into its place. They fear that all the hard-won gains of conscientious truth-seeking in the past would be lost if thinkers were to succumb to the seductive assumption that the ultimate forces moving man to think what he thinks are nonrational, and hence that no integrity of the reasoning mind, in its relation to all that impinges on it from within or without, is possible. Their prime duty, as they see it, is to guard people against turning to any blind faith, against any submission of the inquiring mind to partisan commitments, against any blurring of the difference between honest acceptance of truth and wily propaganda—in short, against any surrender to this or that cult of unreason. Eastern philosophers, on the other hand, have faced a rather different challenge. In their search for a sound way of reaching beyond the horizon of our present experience they have concentrated their energy on discovering a mode of insight that transcends reason and yet can prove itself to be trustworthy—that is, can reach results that are essentially agreed upon by the sages who have sought them. Thus, despite their transrational character, these results appear to have achieved an appropriate kind of objectivity. Eastern thought believes that it has thus fulfilled its prime responsibility.

II

Is reason competent to grasp all truth? If not, why not?

Let us first listen to an Eastern philosopher as he tries to make his viewpoint on this issue intelligible and persuasive to the West.

"To cognize anything is always, in one way or another, to grasp a stable unity in the midst of changing diversity. In daily experience the most frequent example of this axiom is the perception of an enduring object as it unites its manifold and fluctuating qualities—e.g., a distant mountain with its shape, height, color, light and shadow. In scientific discovery it is the apprehension of a constant law which reveals its presence under varying circumstances. Now the same axiom holds in coming to know a person in his full selfhood, and also in apprehending the total reality in which the growing experience of all persons finds its unity. But there is a special problem about the unity in diversity exemplified in these cases. Here we are seeking to grasp, not that which binds together a limited whole, but that which unites an unlimited whole. It is hardly surprising that distinctive features appear; and if they are not understood, the nature of cognition in these cases can hardly be understood.

"Consider the process of coming to understand a mural that one confronts for the first time. Suppose that it is large enough to cover a long wall of a room in a museum. At first it cannot be seen as a whole. An observer has to begin by noting parts of it in their separation from each other. He notices, let us say, a man on horseback in the center of the wall, then a banner held aloft far to the right, then on the left a stream of people winding into the distance. After another partial scene or two has caught his attention he can stand back and survey the whole mural. Suddenly the meaning of the entire panorama is perceived: it is a procession of pilgrims on their way to the celebration of some sacred rite. He could not grasp this meaning or apply this concept before, but once it has taken form in his mind it cannot be lost; it discloses the real unity of the entire scene. Earlier, all that he had been able to see was a collection of distinct parts, each with its own character and form; he could describe their spatial relations to each other but could not perceive any more significant connection. That stage is essential, because apprehension of the nature of the whole depends on it— it is the whole *of* those parts. But everything in the mural is now seen in its relation to the unifying insight he has won. Nothing that had been perceived before is lost; but over and above the relations that separated one part from another, a concept that transcends these separations and binds all into a single entity is now grasped. That entity constitutes the "reality" of the mural; everything seen before is now confidently interpreted, not in terms of the relationships noticed earlier but in terms that depend on this reality. Moreover, unless the observer has made an unusual mistake, the inclusive meaning he apprehends is not subjective; a similar insight attained by others will confirm its truth.

"Suppose now that in the presence of this mural someone who has seen the parts but has not yet grasped the unifying whole were to demand of one who has: What evidence have you that this unity you talk about is really there? Prove to me that it is there, and that it gives the correct meaning of the scene. What can be the reply? One who has caught the total panorama can only wait until the skeptical questioner has done the same; at most he may say something—and presumably he will try to do so—that will facilitate the needed insight."

Enough for this analogy. In the light it throws, why do Eastern thinkers insist that when the vision of ultimate truth is concerned reason must be transcended? Is not what they are saying this: In the quest to understand reality in its wholeness—and the same applies to a person in his individual selfhood—one experiences something of this kind; he advances in his view of the totality before him from the indispensable work of reason, in drawing distinctions and noting relations, to the realization of a comprehensive unity that gathers all of them in a total meaning, which, once gained, cannot be lost. He has transcended all the distinctions so far as they divide one thing from another, and is no longer limited by them. He has passed beyond reason—not in the sense of succumbing to any irrational caprice, but in that of grasping the unity at which reason aims in its systematizing endeavors but which by itself it is impotent to achieve.

Yet, at two points this analogy—and any analogy—is inadequate. There are crucial differences between a limited whole, such as the mural on the museum wall, and an infinite whole. A rational concept can be applied to the former—namely, "procession of religious pilgrims," but not (in the same sense) to the latter; moreover, the former is apprehensible in a merely cognitive unity while an infinite whole will integrate all the resources of the perceiving self. Thus in the former case there will still be a separation between the subject of the unifying intuition and the object he is trying to understand, whereas in the latter case this separation will have disappeared. But these two inadequacies can be partially overcome if we ponder modes of experience that engage a person far more deeply than this perception of a religious procession is likely to.

Think first of the most complete case of esthetic absorption one has ever felt. Such an experience is intellectual, of course, for one's cognitive faculties are at work; but it is more than intellectual, for one's entire emotional nature finds fulfillment in it. And all sense of separation between experiencer and experienced has faded away. To an external view there is a subject and there is an object, but to the inner realization there is no such division at all. An identity of subject and object is achieved, which is just what we express by saying that the former is "absorbed" in the latter. An even more vivid illustration is found in sexual union between a man and woman who love each other so deeply that all their resources of body and soul are engaged in mutual giving and receiving. The sense of duality is transcended, and when the consummation comes it is not experienced as two separate joys of two separate persons but as one joy uniting them both.

These illustrations attest the instructive truth that our rational discrimination of one thing or person as inherently separate from another, and of ourselves as separate from both, is born of fear and self-centered desire. We are afraid of what objects and people may do to us, and each of them threatens us in a different way. We want them to serve our needs, but one thing or person is capable of satisfying this need, another of satisfying that. It is clear that when we are moved by such feelings, alertness to the difference between objects and to the distinctive modes of behavior that each reveals is necessary. But when these self-assertive and self-protective emotions are transcended in an experience whose very nature is to break down the walls of separation, one catches a glimpse of the union that the mystic philosopher of the East is trying to describe. To be sure, these experiences too are limited. In esthetic absorption there is always a boundary; unity is realized within the scene to which one is responding, but not beyond it. In sexual union the world outside the two lovers is excluded, even though their sensitivity to everything beyond themselves may be enriched. But it becomes plausible from such situations that man is capable of an experience of oneness that equals these in intensity and is all-inclusive in scope, admitting no boundary and transcending every horizon.

Moreover, these illustrations may help to resolve a perplexity that seriously troubles some Western thinkers. Recall that when one gains insight into the unity of a limited whole such as the mural in the museum, there is always some intellectual concept that can be applied to it, a concept suggested by similar scenes that have been experienced before. But when one realizes the unity of *the* whole, this is naturally impossible. Such an experience is unique. It makes use of all the rational distinctions available and carries to completion the quest that they have served, but the final step is intrinsically beyond conceptualization. *The* whole is incomparable with any of its parts, because it embodies a new value and meaning of the parts. This is why the theology of the mystic is inevitably a negative theology. What he has experienced is *in*effable, *in*describable, *in*comprehensible, *beyond* what rational thought can grasp. And this is why, when he employs words to describe it, he seems to contradict himself. Not only does he use such negative terms as these, but also words of positive import; he refers to that which he has experienced as One, as Good, as Real. What does he mean by saying such things? Is this not a serious contradiction?

Perhaps, however, the answer is simple. These concepts as he uses them would be contradictory in one sense but not in the sense he intends. When the mystic employs them he is not describing the Ultimate as it is in itself; that is beyond conceptualization, as he well knows. If those to whom he speaks take him to refer to unity as, in their non-mystic experience, it is opposed to plurality, unity will be a rational concept and will not properly apply. Similarly with goodness and reality. What he hopes for is that people will take these words as revealing the direction in which they need to advance if they are to share his experience and realize the Ultimate for themselves. And when he speaks about what he has found, it is this that he is concerned to accomplish. He is offering guidance, not giving information. The Ultimate is beyond unity, goodness, and reality as concepts, for it signifies an inexhaustible flood tide of awareness that these abstract categories cannot even suggest. But what it promises can only be realized by turning away from their opposites—by resolving conflict, by commitment to what is dependably good, and by seeking that which is more real within the range of our present experience.

The message of Eastern thinkers then, if it has been rightly interpreted, is that while it is essential for reason to achieve all that it can by its capacity for discriminating analysis, what is most important cannot in the nature of the case be attained by reason. This is the realization of a unity within the self, and a merging of the self with its universe, that transcends all rational distinctions. And it transcends them, not by blotting them out—indeed, one may find that his power to take wise account of the differences between one object and another is even heightened—but by grasping the whole in which these separations are overcome.*

In this philosophical perspective Eastern thought brings into intimate union the two approaches to the metaphysical meaning of "reality" which in the typical perspective of the West can be parallel but still remain separate. One is the approach by way of the historical quest for more adequate criteria of fact, form, and value; the other is the approach by way of the individual's quest for self-fulfillment. From the viewpoint typical of the East these are two sides of the same approach, for only the self that is achieving inner integrity is able to apprehend outer reality in its wholeness. Just as the scientist needs perfected instruments in order to perceive the world of phenomena aright, so, according to the Eastern way of thinking, the philosopher needs a perfected instrument to perceive reality aright—namely, a mind purged of all the emotional forces that conflict with full devotion to truth. As long as one's cognitive powers are clouded by biased and unstable motives one cannot see reality as it presents itself to an impartial vision. In S. K. Saksena's words, "a *niskama* (non-attached) mind . . . appears to be a necessary qualification of an ideal philosopher, whose task is to perceive the truth about reality with undefective and clean instruments of reason and heart."[1]

But is the East entirely in the right on this basic issue? To assume so

* Although this orientation is foreign to the dominant trends in Western philosophy and psychology, it is by no means unknown to the Occident. Besides the naturalistic theories of man, which express the belief that he can be rationally understood as an object, there are theories that take seriously the experience just sketched (as in mystical theology) or that stress by some other route the wholeness of human personality (as in psychoanalytic psychology).

would surely be a mistake; there must be something valid in the dominant orientation of the West which the East has been apt to miss. Its central conviction—strong and persistent through the centuries—is that reason fills a more general function than Eastern philosophers have clearly envisaged, and that in performing it a value is realized that is part of the unique perfection of which man is capable.

To understand this orientation, one must bear in mind that a different relation between philosophy and religion evolved in the West than has been the case in the East. In the East, by and large, these two quests were pursued in harmonious collaboration, philosophy being the reflective interpreter of religion as it gradually freed itself from primitive superstition, and religion being the expression in daily life of philosophical vision. But in the West a prolonged conflict between them proved unavoidable: first in the Greek period, because of the revulsion of philosophers against the immoralities of both popular and state religion; and then in the Christian period, because of obstructions erected by authoritarian faith against the free growth of science and the right of philosophy to attack irrational traditions. In this different historical situation Western philosophers were naturally tempted to place an extreme emphasis on the virtues of reason and were encouraged to make the most of the values that could be found in it. Through such an emphasis the West became convinced that the development of man's rational power is in the broad sense of the term a spiritual and not merely a secular enterprise. This conviction is revealed in the fact that in the periodic syntheses of Christian insight with philosophical ideas, the religious goals of the former as well as the cognitive ideals of the latter were transformed; the supreme quest culminates for St. Thomas in the vision of Divine Reality which is the perfection of human intelligence, as it does for Spinoza in the intellectual love of God.

The outcome of the whole evolution was that Western thinkers came more and more to believe that through reason's fulfillment of its proper role an ultimate, not merely a subordinate, value is realized. This belief was readily construed, under the influence of associated presuppositions, as implying that man has the capacity for rational mastery of the universe as a whole, of the physical world around him, of the social order in which he lives, and also of himself—viewed as an intelligent and active individual facing both world and society. We shall listen then to a Western philosopher as he tries to make intelligible to the East his confidence in reason.

"Notice carefully what it is about reason that we regard as so precious. Happily, a single word gives its essence. Rational mastery is an ultimate value because it is a *universal* value—and the ideal symbolized by this word can be explored in several directions. It will be enough to look briefly in two directions—one leading to an appreciation of the universal value in the achievements of Western science; the other to a vision of the moral and social meaning of universality.

"When scientific progress over the centuries is surveyed in this perspective, three ways in which reason as employed by science realizes a universal value can be distinguished.

"First, its essential categories, and the conclusions stated in them, are communicable to all thinkers, whoever and wherever they may be. By reason, we are thus able not only to preserve in conceptual form the distinctions needed for a reliable description of the world, but also to share them throughout the entire community of human inquirers. Second, its conclusions, if justified, must be valid for all minds, and hence convincing to any mind that grasps the problem involved and has gained the background needed to understand the solution. Third, through the shared meaning of scientific concepts and the persuasive power of the conclusions reached, reason can assure an unbroken temporal continuity in the advance of knowledge from generation to generation. And there is every justification to expect that this advance can continue without end, because whenever any inadequacy in rational understanding becomes evident, reason can locate its source and remedy the defect by a needed distinction or an improved conceptual system. In the light of these virtues, it appears that the major accomplishment of modern science does not lie in its conquest of the environing world, important though that is; it lies rather in the universality of the truths it establishes, so that they can enter into the cognitive heritage that is becoming common to all human cultures.

"In this setting one can understand and appreciate the instruments that we in the West have developed for realizing these universal values. The two outstanding instruments are logic (including mathematics) and empirical method.

"Logic is one of the magnificent creations of our ancient period, embodying the outcome of the search for a dependable pattern of inference about any reality. Such unquestioned success has crowned this search that it is easy to assume that our present logical presuppositions constitute an absolute framework which the human mind must necessarily respect. But if that error is avoided, may we not affirm that the conception of a universal pattern of valid inference is one that *deserves to be absolutized* as fully as proves feasible? The aspiration toward this ideal is sound. That is, any proposed articulation of such a pattern ought to be freed as completely as possible from the limitations of particular subject matter and particular interests, so that it simply expresses the conditions of truthful understanding as such.*

"The inductive method of the empirical sciences is the main universal instrument developed in our modern period. Along with the variations that appear as one passes from this branch of science to that—and especially from the physical to the social sciences—there are certain common features that express the essential nature of inductive reasoning so far as it has achieved clarity to date. Thus its development has also been inspired by the hope that a rational pattern validly applicable everywhere can be found —in this case, a sound method for describing and explaining empirical data of every kind. The ambition expressed in this quest is revealed most vividly in the fact that the procedure sought is self-correcting—i.e., is such that if error turns up in the outcome of any given investigation it can be corrected by a further application of the same principles. And does not this ideal likewise deserve to be absolutized as fully as possible, so that our quest for reliable explanations of nature's behavior may proceed with maximum assurance? The aim, as aim, is universally valid.

"But the reason why this capacity for rational universality can be regarded not merely as an intellectual but also as a spiritual endowment, comes most clearly to light when we pass from the first to the second direction it opens up. The unique ideal implied by it has become for us an ultimate ethical and social value. And no one familiar with Western history can miss the passionate aspiration that has been expressed as it fills this role. The fundamental moral axiom it implies has been formulated in the

---

* It is an interesting question whether this conception of logic quite came to full clarity in the East. It would seem that there any proposed model of inference derives its validity from some controlling value other than the value of universal validity itself.

For example, the Nyaya theory of the syllogism in India, which was generally accepted by other philosophical schools, differs in obvious ways from the Aristotelian analysis of valid inference; when these differences are examined, it is evident— and indeed this point is explicitly recognized—that they reflect the characteristic values that have dominated the major trends of Indian thought. Theories of inference in China differ both from those in India and from those in the West. When one examines these differences carefully one finds again an obvious reflection of typical interests of the Chinese mind—in particular its interest in moral understanding, and in general its concern to enlarge the reader's insight instead of trying to coerce him by a display of demonstrative finality.

Golden Rule, which takes persuasive form initially as a religious command and is later (at the hands of Kant) explicitly interpreted as a universal law of reason.

"So interpreted, its meaning is that every man, just because he is a man, is always to be treated as an end, never merely as a means to another's end. As a legal principle it appears in the increasingly influential maxim that impartial justice is the right of every human being, whatever his status in society; the Hebrew prophets and the Stoic philosophers and jurists were the chief ancient champions of this meaning of universality. As a political principle it is clearly revealed in our democratic insight. Every man, simply by being a man, has a right to participate with other men in the processes and institutions that determine the conditions under which his life is lived. And when this moral implication of universality is examined to discover what constitutes its core, we soon find the underlying idea and ideal of *equality*. All men are essentially equal, however much superficial appearances and transitory inequities may belie this truth. Why are they equal? Through the centuries Western thought has converged on this answer: Because all alike share in the power of reason. To answer thus is not to express a belief that intellectual keenness and sagacity are equally distributed. Rather, just as the universality sought in logic deserves to be absolutized even though no formulation of its axioms can pretend to be absolute, so universality in its moral and social meaning deserves to be absolutized even though no definition of what that involves is beyond correction. This is to affirm that the conditions required for the equality of all men in exercising their power of reason ought to be realized, however relative any description of them may turn out to be and however serious the obstacles that stand in the way."

Let us return to the central question raised when we embarked on the present issue regarding the capacity of reason. We now understand how and why the typical Western thinker today views the competence of this faculty as he confidently does. Both his persistent hope and his successful experience strengthen the conviction that reason can always win new conquests wherever they are needed—over physical nature, over the perplexing problems of society, even over his own self.

"Over his own self?" Here is the heart of the disagreement; here we confront the boundary of reason's domain insisted on by the East. Is this a justifiable hope? Is something essential to an insight into man's selfhood lost when this task is attempted by our rational faculty alone? Eastern thinkers, almost unanimously, are sure that the answer is yes. And they are equally sure that the same reply holds of any attempt by reason to master reality as a whole. Who is right?

We had better resist the temptation to answer this question and to propose the wise definition of "reason" that an adequate answer would need. Each reader will explore beyond this point in his own way.

But his exploration will be more hopeful if we now observe that the Eastern and Western presuppositions involved in this issue do not conflict; the two orientations are complementary rather than contradictory. They agree completely on the basic conviction that there is no limit beyond which reason cannot go *in knowledge of objects and whatever can become an object.* The difference is that the typical Western thinker is satisfied with this conclusion, seeing nothing beyond or other than the realm of objects to investigate. He concentrates his energies upon what can thus be known; he even defines "consciousness" as always implying awareness of some object. By contrast, the Eastern thinker sees something of vital importance beyond and underlying all objects—namely, the universe that encompasses them, and the self that apprehends them—the knower, which by its very nature is the subject of consciousness and always eludes us when we try to make it an object. In fact, he is sure that when its essence as knower is fully realized—and "realization" rather than "knowledge" is the proper word here—the separation between subject and object that is necessary for rational knowledge is transcended, and the self becomes aware of itself as a unity in which that separation has been overcome. He is likewise sure that consciousness—so far from disappearing in this realization—only then becomes freed from its prison and fulfills its intrinsic nature. Convinced that while the self as knower is indispensable and creatively active in all inquiry into objects of every sort, it cannot itself be known as an object, the philosophical genius of the East has through the ages been largely devoted to the task of exploring the way in which its nature can be truly apprehended. In describing briefly his own philosophy, President Sarvepalli Radhakrishnan summarizes this major aspect of Indian thought:

[The] highest knowledge transcends the distinction of subject and object. Even logical knowledge is possible because this highest knowledge is ever present. . . .

We use the direct mode of apprehension which is deeper than logical understanding when we contemplate a work of art, when we enjoy great music, when we acquire an understanding of another human being in the supreme achievement of love. In this kind of knowledge the subject is not opposed to the object but is intimately united with it. By calling this kind of knowledge integral insight, we bring out that it does not contradict logical reason, though the insight exceeds the reason.[2]

III

Turn now to the second issue. What is the essence of human freedom—a fundamental value for both East and West? As in their approach to the role and competence of reason, each of these two ways of thinking has its characteristic and confident answer, but the answers are different.

This is a rich theme indeed, which could be canvassed from many angles. We must confine ourselves to the contrasting conceptions of what freedom is freedom *from,* omitting any elaboration of the implied ideas as to what freedom is *for.* A virtue of this limitation is that it will emphasize a significant continuity with the first issue. There too we were concerned with freedom; our main question might have been: Do we need freedom *from* reason as well as freedom *through* reason? Western thinkers have been the pioneers in realizing the freedom that man can achieve through reason, while the Eastern sages have led the way in realizing the freedom that needs to be achieved (if they are right) from the limitations of reason.

But we want to face the more general problem of the essence of freedom. The West has explored this problem in many directions, and diverse solutions have as usual been proposed.* A perennially influential conviction, however, is that man has the liberty he seeks when he is free from external constraint, so that he can make his own choices and proceed hopefully to satisfy his own desires. Most theories of freedom imply this conviction; whatever blocks man in either of these two ways is an obstruction that must be overcome if he is to be truly free. It is recognized that some constraints are necessary for the sake of social order, but they are limitations on freedom. According to the dominant orientation of the East, one who is merely free from external constraint is by no means really free; for this he must be liberated from the internal forces that drive him to make wrong choices or are revealed in unrealistic and ego-centered desires.

* A recent comprehensive treatment of this theme is given by Mortimer J. Adler in *The Idea of Freedom* (New York: Doubleday & Company), Vol. I, 1958, and Vol. II, 1961.

When an inquirer asked Sri Ramakrishna, "When shall I be free?" the saint replied, "When the 'I' shall cease to be." He meant the ego that is in bondage to these forces; only when liberated from this bondage is a man truly free.

From both points of view freedom poses a theoretical and also an inescapable practical problem. In detail these take quite different forms in the East and in the West. But in general the theoretical problem, for each, consists in showing that man has by nature the capacity for or an intrinsic right to freedom, while the practical problem consists in overcoming whatever obstructions prevent his achieving it. It is important to note that when one concentrates on the theoretical problem freedom naturally presents itself as an absolute; man either has or lacks the capacity that the concept is believed to involve. When one is concerned with the practical problem freedom is always a matter of degree; under any given set of conditions a certain measure of it is realized, which with a change in those conditions would be increased or diminished.

Why is this so? The answer is: Thinkers on both sides realize that ignorance means bondage, whereas knowledge spells freedom. From the Western viewpoint as to what is important, knowledge of the physical world brings man greater freedom in his relation to it; instead of being in bondage to its forces so that he must submit to whatever effects they produce, he can control nature's doings so that they will serve his ends as they otherwise would not. Likewise, knowledge of the political and social forces around him brings man greater freedom as a citizen; when he gains this understanding, instead of remaining in bondage to institutions that unjustly suppress his power of action he can change them so that they become his servant instead of his master. From the Eastern viewpoint, it is knowledge of one's self that brings true liberation. Nothing else can achieve this result, for the bondage the Eastern philosopher is concerned about is bondage to one's own inner drives and emotions. While ignorant of them one is inevitably their captive, but as one becomes aware of their presence and nature he no longer needs compulsively to express them in thought and action. And a significant link becomes obvious with the position of each side on the competence of reason. The freedom from external constraint emphasized by the West can plausibly be sought under the guidance of reason, while freedom from inner bondage cannot be achieved by reason alone; this faculty itself easily falls captive to the subconscious urges from which liberation is needed.

The major questions perennially discussed by Western and Eastern thinkers when they deal with the concept of freedom grow out of the orientations just sketched and reflect the contrasting sets of presuppositions. The pervasive conviction of Western philosophers has been that man realizes the best life by fulfilling his present desires so far as their goals appear justifiable; he must then have freedom to do so. "The best," says George Boas tersely "is that the future will satisfy our present desires." [3] But Eastern sages have strongly maintained—and religious pioneers in the West have done so too—that even the desires that seem most reasonable are not unqualifiedly good. Like others, they may need to be transformed through clearer awareness of their true place in our growing experience as a whole; only the aspirations of the self that is achieving unity through such awareness can be wisely and safely satisfied. The freedom discussed in the East reflects this different setting.

The two questions which vividly reveal the characteristic approach of the West appear in the metaphysical controversy about free will and determinism, and in the political controversy about the rights of a citizen in relation to his government. In the first of these the champions of freedom are concerned to prove that man is not a puppet of fate—he is free, they hold, from the constraint of causal forces that are external in the trenchant sense of being ultimately beyond his control. If the determinist is right, every choice a man makes and every apparently voluntary act he performs has its prior causes, given which it had to happen as it does; when this chain of causes is traced backward, we come sooner or later to foredooming events that happened long before he was born. In the second controversy the champions of freedom are concerned to defend the individual's right to take part in the decisions that affect for weal or woe the conditions under which he lives, and to transform social institutions so that this right can be more fully exercised. Here the constraint from which he needs to be freed is the tyrannical exercise of political power, flouting his claim to equal justice and enslaving his life to the arbitrary will of other men.

Is this conception of liberty, as essentially freedom from external constraint, a sound one? Listen again to an Eastern philosopher—one who is well acquainted with the social history of the West—as he gives his answer:

"Such a conception expresses a natural human demand, especially among those in each generation who rebel against the traditional restraints of family and society, and in general among all who have come to realize how precious is the value of individuality and of real opportunity for its fulfillment. But it surely requires careful limitations and harbors serious dangers. It is one thing to hold that freedom from external constraint is an important relative good; it is another to exalt it to the position of an ultimate good. Placed in that role, it threatens divisive and disastrous consequences; except among those strongly moved by humane concern for others, it naturally fosters the feeling: If I am to be free I must bring and keep other people under my control as fully as I can, because that is the only way to keep them from bringing me under their control.

"The most dangerous consequence is the one just implied. When liberty from external constraint is made the supreme value, men easily detach it from a live sense of social responsibility—they seek to maximize their individual liberty. Thus detached, freedom can turn into anarchic license, and become a terrible evil instead of a good. There are situations in which all are aware of this danger and realize that it must be overcome. Every parent wants his children to grow into the acceptance and conscientious fulfillment of their adult obligations. Every democratic society wants its members to share the complex responsibilities of a modern nation, each citizen acquiring independence of judgment and respecting the rights and freedoms of others. Unless a majority do meet the minimum standard required, such a society cannot survive. But when the primary emphasis is on liberty it is easy to lose sight of this truth. And even when that standard is fully met in the life of a small group—a family, a town, a vocational community—there may be no vivid awareness of the needs and rights of any larger whole on which the group depends. The upright local citizen may place the interests of his small region ahead of those of his country, and the zealous patriot readily places the wealth, power, and ambition of his nation ahead of the interest of mankind. In the face of such seductive temptations the only sound solution is to make a sensitive oneness with the needs and hopes of all people the primary value; then freedom and responsibility are harmoniously united.

"The second danger looms sharply before us when we see men and women becoming apathetic about their freedoms, or when freedom is suddenly given to people long accustomed to being ruled from above. An enthusiast for liberty may be astounded to realize that many adult persons do not want it. They are emotionally dependent; they prefer important decisions to be made for them, so that they need not engage in the difficult task of forming their own judgment. When complicated issues must be faced, they evade the obligation of free citizens, falling back on the comforting but deceptive confidence that "father knows best" (whoever "father" may be in the situation in question). Moreover, if political freedom is suddenly bestowed on people long cowed by those in power, fear of expressing dissent is added to this emotional dependence. We now know that a "free" election among such people will be overwhelmingly won by the party holding the reins of authority; few dare to register a contrary opinion. When this second danger is frankly recognized, it is clear that the political liberty prized by the West cannot really be exercised unless those who possess it have become free from their ingrained feeling of incapacity to judge and from fear of reprisals by those in governmental control.

"A third danger arises from the failure of many persons to achieve wise adjustment to the inevitability of many external constraints, and readiness to accept them without pining. The world was not made for us, and we cannot accomplish anything valuable in it without recognizing what is beyond our powers and learning how to make use of the opportunities it gives. In the absence of this adjustment one will be a prey to anxiety, frustration, and querulousness; these emotions can poison one's way of exercising whatever liberation from arbitrary constraints he may have won. His basic need in such a situation is to become free from the unrealistic demandingness that is the root of such emotions.

"So when a responsible thinker asks in the light of these fundamental considerations: What kind of freedom do we really want? can he avoid the answer: The freedom that is essential above all else is inner freedom; it is required if men are in truth to be outwardly free. When we confront the realities encompassing human life, and clarify the true good of man in relation to the universe and to his fellows, the enticing traditional ideal of the West cannot stand as an ultimate value. Man's primary need is freedom from the forces within himself that tempt him to evade responsibility instead of fulfilling it, to remain the prey of dependence and fear, to refuse to accept in serenity and cheer his place in reality. On the foundation of this freedom alone can the liberties prized in the Occident be dependably gained and exercised. And the conclusion applies to those who wield political authority as much as to others. Without inner freedom, they are in bondage to forces that make their power a source of sorrow and calamity to their fellows and sooner or later to themselves. Only when liberated from that bondage can they become true democratic leaders, using their persuasive and organizing skill to establish conditions that foster increasing liberty for all. The freest man, whether ruler or citizen, is the man who has ceased to be subject to blind and undisciplined forces within himself.

"Now we in the East have since ancient times been concerned precisely with this inner freedom; philosophy has been conceived in our tradition as basically a search for the systematic understanding that can guide men toward its realization. We have dared to believe that a person may grow from the stage in which this or that urge can toss him about like a piece of driftwood on a stormy sea toward one in which his liberating awareness will be so alert that as soon as a motive appears its nature will be realized and whatever phases of it are unacceptable to his mature self will fade away. Our thinkers have been sure that as he gains this freedom he thereby becomes serenely and creatively adjusted to whatever forces impinge on him from the outside—the forces at work in physical nature and in the behavior, whether dark or enlightened, of his fellows. The latter achievement is involved in the former. Of course the East has had no monopoly on this orientation. It has entered the religious insight of Western seers; they have told us—however difficult it may be to fit the idea into their traditional theologies—that God is the Infinite Reality 'whose service is perfect freedom.'

"A very important implication is that the practical problem of winning more freedom is intrinsically prior to all theoretical problems about it. The decisive reason for this conclusion is that if one assumes the contrary—if his primary aim is to prove the reality of freedom, or to analyze the concept, or to study current uses of the word—the results he reaches will naturally reflect whatever state of inner bondage and of liberation he is now in. Only a free man's idea of freedom is likely to be an authentic one. Hence we are sure that the supreme task for every person is to become more free; as he does so his presuppositions about freedom will change, and change for the better. Consider, as an especially instructive example, how this principle bears on the issue of determinism. One who has experienced liberation from a certain form of bondage can no longer believe that he was always free from it, nor can he believe a theory of determinism which implies that such bondage is inevitable."

Does the East then provide a wholly adequate philosophy of freedom, needing nothing that the West has to offer? No, indeed. Here too the West has learned something that the East needs—and is now eagerly striving to master. So we shall listen once more to a Western philosopher—one acquainted with the history of the Orient—while he tries to explain his insight to the East. And we must remember while listening that it is an assured conviction of both East and West that freedom in its true meaning is the rightful heritage and destiny of all men.

"Under the economic and political conditions that in the past have prevailed in the East, the concept of inner freedom could and did shape the ultimate ideal that became accepted as valid for everyone. But it led to a division in society between those who were ready to subordinate all else to their quest for this freedom, and those who were not yet ready to do so. The former renounced family responsibilities and retired to the forest or the monastery; the social institutions around them were thus left as they were except insofar as they might be reformed from above by a wise ruler who had been touched by the message of the saintly pioneers. Since, if all people followed the former, the daily needs of society would not be met, there appeared a strong tendency to perpetuate this division and to develop doctrines that justified its continuance. The Indian doctrine of *karma,* or reincarnation, encouraged the masses to accept their present lot in life and not to protest against it or try to change it. The doctrine told them that this lot is the result of their own conduct in previous lives, and it fostered the hope that humble performance of their duties would lead to rebirth in a form enabling them to pursue the ultimate goal with greater zeal and hope.

"In this historical setting there was little chance for systematic progress toward realizing the conditions required if the vast majority of people were to discover and fulfill their potentialities—of freedom or of any other appealing value. Indeed, in the absence of hope that the lot of the masses can be bettered, it was hardly possible even to see clearly that they cannot become full human beings unless they are liberated from ignorance, from fear of starvation, injustice, and ruthless oppression, and from the pressure of long hours of dull physical toil. Spiritual freedom for the few can doubtless be won under any conditions, but real freedom for the many depends on steady progress toward emancipation from arbitrary political power and from age-old economic bondage to the pressing elementary need for food and shelter. It is now obvious to all thinkers in both East and West that any widespread sharing in spiritual values, however these be defined, can only be achieved through a rise in the standard of living, which requires mastering the technological victories gained in the West.

"Thus the contribution that we in our part of the world have made is indispensable. Ever since the time of the Hebrew prophets Western religion has expressed a passion for justice toward all and a zeal to realize it in man's social institutions. Western ethics has included its branch of political philosophy, in which democratically minded thinkers have been concerned to clarify what freedom from injustice and oppression means, and to defend the rights of individuals and minority groups. They have engaged in trenchant criticism of current political, economic, legal, and educational practices, seeking to reveal the conditions under which every person would have the maximum opportunity and encouragement to fulfill his capacities. Men of action have aggressively transformed the institutions around them, guided by the ideals religion has emphasized and by the patterns of social organization that ethical thinkers have clarified.

"The goal toward which these efforts have converged is most clearly expressed in the ideal that loomed before us when we were probing the moral meaning of universality—the ideal of equality, equality of all men before God and in their relation to each other. How to define this ideal has always been perplexing, but that handicap has not prevented it from exercising a strong and persistent appeal. Of course what is meant is not equality of possessions, nor equality of talents, nor even equality of opportunity, although it is incompatible with drastic inequalities in these matters. Increasingly our thinkers see its basic meaning as equality of dignity or worth as a human being—the right to be respected because one is a man, and to be treated on the basis of that dignity. On the negative side it means the rejection of all condescension in human relations, of every hint of self-righteousness, superiority, or aloofness. It implies that true freedom from external constraint is freedom from all forces whose expression is irreconcilable with this equality of worth. The West is sure that only as progress in this direction is achieved can people really come to believe in themselves and their infinite value, and to seek with hope the varied forms of fulfillment that thus open before them.

"The wise champion of freedom in this sense well knows that the opportunities it brings will often be misused, and that only through constant alertness will the conditions under which it realizes its promise be more clearly envisioned and more securely established. But this is the inescapable practical challenge; it does not derogate from the universal validity of the ideal."

Where lies the right synthesis of these two insights into the nature of human freedom? Again, it is best that each reader search for his own answer. Let us not even try to anticipate the answer that history will give, as men continue their quest for greater freedom and for greater clarity as to what it means.

What we may well do is to raise the now familiar question: Are the two insights compatible with each other, or do they intrinsically conflict? And it seems clear that there is no contradiction between them, either theoretical or practical. Neither denies what is essential to the other. When a man seeks freedom from inner bondage he can also be concerned—in fact, today he will surely be concerned—with freedom from outer bondage too; unjust dependence of one person on another is a flagrant form of inner bondage for both. Likewise, when one seeks freedom from external constraint he will also, if he is alert to the realities involved, be concerned to win inner freedom; for he will see that without it outer freedom is sadly incomplete and may be self-destructive.

Indeed, our analysis implies that in the long run each of these quests contributes indispensably toward success in the other; inner freedom saves outer freedom from becoming an empty form or a social peril, while outer freedom saves inner freedom from remaining permanently the privilege of a few.

IV

The East has a special gift for the West—indeed, for thinkers everywhere. It is made possible by the East's ideal of freedom, and by the major lesson learned in the persistent endeavor to realize that ideal. The West is now beginning to find a partial substitute for this gift through the techniques of clinical psychoanalysis, and in course of time it may become a significant alternative.

All thinkers prize power of concentration. So far as one has it he can steadily focus attention on whatever subject occupies his mind at any given time. So far as he lacks it he wastes his mental energy, frittering it away because of inability really to control it. Eastern philosophers have from ancient times sought to understand and master the conditions under which steady concentration is possible. In fact, this is to them a vital part of the spiritual quest; they have often described the goal of that quest as the achievement of genuine and stable "mind-control." Western philosophers, in view of their very different presuppositions, have been conscious only of an occasionally vexing practical problem of no philosophical significance.

What has the East discovered in the course of this search? Following our accustomed pattern, we shall listen to an Eastern sage as he offers his answer:

"Suppose we imagine ourselves in one of the typical situations in which the achievement of concentration is a real and serious problem. A thinker is trying to give unqualified and continued attention to the topic he has chosen. He is focusing his mental power on it as best he can. But what happens? He succeeds for a while; then his mind wanders—it is enticed in other directions, and before long he is exhausted by the effort to pull it back and make it obey. If he reflects on such an experience, he realizes that he has only been able to offer a feeble part of his reasoning power to the subject on which he wanted to concentrate. His capacity for mind-control is evidently very weak. To overcome this weakness would surely be a boon to any thinker; his mental alertness would be freed from a discouraging and obstructive force.

"First, we need to ask why it is so hard to gain real mind-control. And the primary answer may well be that it is because of our blithe readiness to deceive ourselves. Despite constant proof to the contrary, we persistently assume that we already have it. Almost everyone casually speaks of his mind as *his* mind, implying thereby that in some real sense he possesses it and is able to direct its operations. Is this an honest way of speaking?

Let us take an example from ordinary life. I think this house belongs to me; how am I to verify if it is really mine? I write on a slip, "This person, the bearer, is my friend; he is entitled to stay in this house for five minutes." My friend takes this slip and enters the house; but to his horror, twenty people come from somewhere and unceremoniously push him out! As this fate overtakes him every time he enters the house, I have to conclude, for the present at any rate, that I have no control over the house. I must take suitable steps and establish my claim over it, before I can call it *my* house any more.

Let us now substitute the surface mind for the house of the example. And to test our control over it, the permit and our friend will correspond to a well-selected thought "A," which we shall expect to send "in" and retain "there" for five minutes. The thought "A" can be of a flower or a picture or whatever you please. If we honestly try to do this . . . we shall find that within a few seconds our thoughts wander, and that a number of unexpected mental pictures or thoughts rush in, preventing "A" from occupying the field. Let us call these intruders, for convenience, "B to Z." Repeated experiment will convince us that our inability to keep "A" inside, according to our intention, means that the surface mind is "bound" by the unwanted forces "B to Z." What religious books call spiritual bondage is verifiable in this manner as psychological bondage. . . .

We learn one important lesson from this experiment. We find that our will is ordinarily helpless to resist the "attacks" of unwanted and unexpected forces in the inmost recesses of our personality.[4]

"Our second question is: What accounts for this bondage? The answer quickly appears when we look for the source of these unruly and distracting intruders. They arise from our fears, hopes, longings, resentments, and other emotional forces that are at work under the surface of the mind and whose objects are always competing for our attention. These objects, uninvited, seize possession whenever they can. By strenuous exertion we can usually chase them away for a while, but they are not in this fashion brought under dependable control. They subtly regain their hold at a weak moment; enticing images occupy the center of attention; the deep-lying forces expressed in them thus reassert their sway. We might suppose that our faculty of reason would provide the needed remedy, but it does not; we are already using it as vigorously as possible in achieving whatever continuity of attention we are able to. Confronting this poignant plight, a philosopher will remember Hume's conclusion that 'reason is, and ought only to be, the slave of the passions.' * He will hardly agree however about the 'ought to be'—in this situation he wants his reason to be able to think, and to think with persistent concentration. Yet, as long as anyone is subject to the vacillation just described, this is impossible; he will fall prey from time to time to irrational forces that he can only very partially master.

"The third question is obviously: How can freedom from this bondage be won? It is evident that the problem of making our minds truly our minds is just the problem of achieving control over these distractions, so that our mental energy is no longer wasted or perverted in this way. And how does one make confident progress toward such control? We in the East have for many centuries been trying to find out. The most influential solution is the practice of disciplined meditation, which we have learned by experience will lead toward that goal. In meditation the feelings at work when a thinker is unable to concentrate are progressively revealed to him. As he sees them clearly for what they are, those feelings gradually weaken and fade away; their place is taken by other motives that are acceptable

* *Treatise of Human Nature,* Book II, Part III, Section 3. The modern reader should have in mind that Hume means by "passion" in this passage any feeling that operates as a motive.

because they harmonize with his aspiration for truth. Thus stable mind-control is slowly achieved; one no longer needs to identify, even for a short time, with whatever emotion or desire pops into his mind. He can reach a position where the part of himself that he really wants to rule does rule. And once significant progress in this direction has been made, one realizes for the first time how large a part of his time and energy has been wasted on objects that he knows are not worth bothering about. He also realizes that what made possible the degree of concentration he has been capable of in the past was not a pure desire for truth. Combined with this desire was some potent motive of which he was not aware; the two together were able for a longer or shorter time to keep out all rivals. But that motive may be no more acceptable, once its nature is clearly seen, than the miscellany of irrational feelings it helped to keep in check.

"The price of this freedom—and it is a price he is then most happy to pay—is that he will exercise his realized power of concentration on the themes chosen by his liberated self, and these may be rather different from those that appealed to him before. Not that anything, from any source, that could enrich his life will be shut out. But whatever enters his experience will now be subordinate to the overarching concerns of the self that has won its unity. No longer is he pushed and pulled by trivial objects and transitory feelings. If he is a philosopher, the distinctive reward of winning this freedom is that he finds his philosophical energies heightened from more to more, so that instead of being weakened by hidden conflicts they function with all the vigor and efficiency that at their best they can command."

11

Philosophy and the future of man

The widest and most difficult setting for our enterprise still remains.

Everything of human concern is of concern to philosophy. We must therefore pursue our quest for philosophic understanding in the setting of the human venture as a whole, not only looking back toward the vast stretches of its past but also ahead toward its hidden future. The full nature and promise of philosophy can be revealed only when its role in this total perspective is revealed. And there is a special reason for placing ourselves in this perspective as the world of the late twentieth century opens before us. Man has entered the nuclear era, and we are awed by the inexorable challenge that has not yet been met but must be met if human life is to survive and continue to fulfill its promise. In this unprecedented scene with its momentous stakes, can a philosophic orientation contribute to our understanding, helping people to learn how to live in this era? Can it play a part in guiding the creation of the world community toward which men have aspired through the ages?

I

For a wise starting point, let us identify the crucial problems that man has had to face in the course of his long career on the surface of this planet. In the last analysis the course of history is guided by the persistent needs of men and their unflagging endeavor to satisfy them. In this broad perspective, is it not clear that there have been just two such problems, each reflecting a basic human need? The word "basic" is pertinent here for a very simple reason: these needs are so inescapable and so urgent that if man fails to find a way of satisfying them he does not survive, and therefore will not be able to satisfy any other need or solve any other problem. Hence the whole course of history may be confidently viewed and wisely interpreted in the light of these two needs and man's persistent striving to meet them successfully. The reason why it is hard to view history in this way is that we are now so entangled in the second need that only through clarified insight can we observe it from the outside and thus catch a stable vision of the whole. The two are so related historically that the second only became an insistent challenge when the first had in essence been met.

Generally speaking, the first need was the dominant characteristic of primitive human existence. For ages men lived in small and relatively isolated communities. During that protracted period they were struggling to win a secure existence against the imperfectly mastered forces of their non-human environment. It was a long struggle. Hundreds of thousands of years passed while they lived mainly by hunting, gradually learning the arts that enabled them to spread over the habitable globe and to gain their livelihood more efficiently. Human societies were often swept away in the course of that arduous and uncertain effort; in fact, during the early part of this period all manlike creatures may more than once have perished, so that a new species had to evolve.

By the opening of the Neolithic age ten thousand years or more ago men had sufficiently mastered the domestication of animals and the growing of major crops so that they could live in relatively large herd-raising and agricultural communities. After another five thousand years still larger political units, able to organize an extensive group of communities living in the same river valley, were appearing. At some time in the course of this more recent period it became fairly certain that so far as human life as a whole is concerned the first major problem had been solved. Enough knowledge of the way nature's forces behave and enough skill in controlling those forces had been gained, so that no longer did man need to fear destruction by his nonhuman environment, at least for millions of years. And today this success has culminated in the discovery of methods for releasing nuclear energy and placing its inexhaustible power at man's disposal. He has available now, in his relation to the physical world, a dependable foundation on which to achieve whatever else in his growing experience he wills to achieve.

But our poignant anxiety about this culmination reminds us vividly that the second basic need emerged into challenging form as a result of victory over the first. This has characterized man's quest for a truly civilized existence; it is the need for each group of men to learn the art of living successfully with other groups. The achievements that made possible a solution of the first need thrust people into increasingly complex interaction with and interdependence on each other. This interaction and interdependence led to threatening conflicts on a scale previously unknown, both within each expanding society and between one society and another. By about three millennia ago this transition had sufficiently taken place in several areas of evolving civilization—in the valleys of the Yellow River and the Nile, in Mesopotamia and India—so that this second need had begun to compete with the first in importance.

In each of these areas there was a large and growing agricultural community, in possession of dependable methods for assuring a fairly regular food supply and for guarding against the varied threats to life that had haunted primitive man. Within such a community there rapidly developed a process of specialization and hierarchical stratification, which was necessary but which made the problem of harmonious social adjustment more difficult than it had been in the life of a small and isolated tribe. Distinctive functions multiply—in the production and distribution of goods, in political administration, in religion, in supplying professional services—and with them the interests of the varied groups thus competing for security, prestige, or power. Those who perform these functions and feel these interests are dependent on each other for their continued existence and well-being, but the membership of each group transcends the ties of family and clan, ties that in a primitive society create a spontaneous sense of emotional unity. In this strange and disturbing situation the groups and their members have to find some way of achieving efficient cooperation with each other, despite the absence of any feeling that they naturally belong together.

In the relation of each of these communities to its external environment the same problem appears in another form. More territory is needed to meet the requirements of a swelling population and an increasing diversity of activities; surrounding peoples are absorbed, and what had originally been a local clan becomes an empire. Roads and canals are built, and it is now possible to maintain an army in the farflung corners of the spreading realm. Sooner or later two such empires come into conflict with each other, and war in the modern sense appears for the first time in history—war for conquest and control of the larger area that each power can effectively reach and which it covets to assure its prosperity. At first these wars are geographically small—they are fought for mastery of a limited area in the Near East (which is the arena where such conflicts first occurred)—but they gradually affect wider territory; today—this is the sobering destiny of our century—they have become world wars from whose impact no people can hope to remain aloof. Weapons of more and more lethal power are invented and used; this phase of progress has now reached its peak in man's achieving the ability to destroy, along with his enemies, the whole of civilization and even of the human race.

Such a survey of this vast historical process brings out vividly the fact that while the basic source of insecurity for primitive man lay in his relation to the forces of physical nature, the basic insecurity of civilized man lies in his relation to his fellows—in his and their aggressive urges and hostile acts. Primitive man had achieved sufficient discipline of his dark emotions so that life in the tribal pattern could go on from day to day with a high degree of concord; civilized man is still struggling to achieve the discipline needed in the setting of the increasingly intimate interaction of people throughout the whole planet. He has won his victory over the environing world, but not yet over himself. All his other hopes and aspirations now wait on the removal of this insecurity, for unless it is removed he will not survive as civilized man.

But the ominous threat to survival is only the negative side of the challenge man is summoned to meet; it has a breathtaking positive side as well. Civilized life opened up new possibilities in man himself—possibilities of a kind of satisfying fulfillment that could hardly be glimpsed when his mind was mainly focused on the uncertain, harassing struggle for the means of continued physical existence. Cities were built, breeding new and perilous problems, but also creating new opportunities. Alert minds were brought together; this fostered a stimulating intercommunication and a richer sharing of ideas and ideals. Art, technology, and philosophy could develop at a rapid pace. Above all, speculative and religious pioneers, devoting their powers to the novel perplexities of their day and providing the wise insight needed to meet them, could appear. Through their vision an ideal of brotherhood and equality in freedom between men everywhere began to loom before all who could respond to it, and knowledge was slowly gained as to the essential conditions of its realization. It gradually became clear that man is not condemned to permanent control by the tribal orientation that cramps him in primitive life nor by the frustrated emotions let loose in the groping quest for civilization; he is capable of a will to justice and to friendship that is not confined to his clan, race, creed, or nation, and of finding joy in the creative relation with others that can result. His true good, it came more and more to be seen, does not lie in the aggressive assertion of himself *against* other men—as if all outside his enfolding and protecting group are merely external obstacles to the satisfaction of his desires but rather in the realization of a unity with them in virtue of which the good of each person becomes for that reason the good of all, and the good of all becomes the freely accepted good of each. We now begin to see that once the pattern of existence in separate tribes is left behind there can be no stopping place short of a world community of this kind.

The crucial and increasingly insistent problem of these few millennia of civilized life has become, then, the problem of achieving the sensitive awareness required on a wide enough scale so that the threat of universal catastrophe can be averted and these appealing possibilities realized.

II

What are the most serious handicaps man has been under in meeting these two problems, and what have proved to be his major resources in the effort to solve them? As we search for an answer we discover a very illuminating truth—namely, that the persistently obstructive handicap and the fundamental resource have been the same in both cases, even though the detailed form they take is naturally quite different.

The major handicap is the potent influence of undisciplined emotions on man's way of perceiving and explaining the world, with the result that he interprets objects around him in terms of those emotional projections instead of in terms of objective reality. This is not the only handicap; there is also, for example, his strong attachment to his present presuppositions and his eager demand that they must be capable of bringing him security. Moreover, the search for wiser beliefs is difficult, and the uncertainty involved in the stage of doubt and questioning that has to be passed through is very painful.

His major resource lies in his deep-seated drive toward life and well-being, and in his distinctive capacity to be aware of the difference between deceptive and dependable ways to life and well-being. Led by men of pioneering genius who exemplify this power of expanding awareness in whatever form is crucially needed at the time, he learns how to achieve reliable understanding of the realities he has to cope with, replacing the blinder emotional projections by more objective knowledge. And along with the slow development of this positive capacity, an inexorable negative force is always at work. The peoples less able to learn the needed lessons are constantly weeded out in the struggle for survival; their place is taken by those with greater energy of awareness and greater ability to use it in meeting any challenge that must be met. In the course of biological history, as we know, nine-tenths or more of the species that have appeared are now extinct; the surviving fraction consists of species in firm possession of the talents through which they are able to cope with the conditions they face. The same principle applies to the history of man, in his endeavor to find the way to survive and progress.

Turn briefly to the age when the first need and problem were dominant. The obstructive handicap appears vividly at that time in the ideas and practices of primitive religion, and the saving resource in the slowly gained anticipations of scientific technology.

The objects and processes in the world on which primitive man depended for the necessities of continued existence were viewed by him under the compulsive projection of his fears and hopes. Nature was pictured accordingly as the domain of mysterious powers that need to be magically coerced or humbly persuaded to show him beneficence instead of hostility. He was familiar of course with the obviously regular features of things and events around him, but since he was not anxious about those features they did not occupy the center of his conscious attention. Thus he saw in the sun not only an object with certain quite dependable properties such as its shape* and daily revolution, but also an unpredictable power whose behavior in relation to the crops people were trying to grow is very undependable; sometimes its genial warmth nourishes them to fruitful maturity, while at other times it burns them up with its fierce and scorching heat. He saw in the rain not only drops of water descending from the sky in the habitual fashion of any falling object, but also a strange power that could not be counted on; sometimes it falls gently and frequently during a long growing

* Of course eclipses occasionally occurred, and aroused much anxiety.

season, but it may fail entirely for months at a stretch or sweep down in violent storms that destroy or wash away his crops.

But keen thinkers gradually learned how to correct the distortions in this picture of physical nature and thus to master the distinction between an emotional projection and an objective fact, in the form then desperately called for. They detected, more and more clearly, the causal relations that must be taken into account if man is to deal with the physical world successfully, and freed them from the mysterious powers that were merely the reflection on external objects of his longings and apprehensions. Their efforts must have been sadly obstructed by the strong wish among their fellows, and even in their own minds, that the fundamental presuppositions already held must be right and can guide their commerce with nature successfully. But in time these pioneers in the quest for scientific knowledge succeeded, and such unpredictable entities as the rain-god faded away from the universe of civilized man. Today we see the world around us as the scene of regular law, and allow our hopes and fears to distort the scene only in unusual situations.

Turn now in the same way to the second need and problem, insistently pressing for solution under the conditions set by civilized life.

The core of this problem lies in the fact that as science successfully met the first challenge it threw people all over the world into increasing de pendence on each other, while their pervasive feelings still largely reflected the isolation that had characterized their existence throughout the long ages of the past. The primitive clan or tribe is an extension of the family; it *is* a larger family. Its members sense that they belong together. The good of the clan is felt to be the good of each member. Whatever disputes may arise or antagonisms develop, they are encompassed and limited by the atmosphere that this spontaneous feeling creates. Other members are in the nature of the case allies; all are bound together by the bond of a common blood. With the bigger and more complex groups that appear with advancing civilization this sense of mutual belonging is absent, and only takes form slowly.

The difficulty posed by such a state of affairs is serious even within the boundaries of any civilized society. Neighbors in a modern city may live close together, but they have only a weak sense of any common concerns. The point is revealed in provocative form by a group crowded into a subway car; they jostle against each other and are dependent for life or death on the same forces, but they feel nothing that really binds them together.

Now a person who does not belong with me I perceive as an *alien,* and an alien is someone to be excluded and ignored if possible—if not, to be feared, distrusted, forced into a submissive position. No wonder that this dark and dangerous feeling of alien-ness is especially strong when I have to confront members of another society, and more especially still when between the two societies there are barriers of language, culture, race, religion, ideology. Such men are *ipso facto* felt as enemies. But the modern world is inexorably thrusting all people into each other's presence; increasingly we have to deal with one another even while still dominated by this deep sense of alien-ness.

Here is the most fertile field that one could imagine for the play of emotional projection, and for the most formidable difficulty in breaking free from its distortions. Here it is other people that we perceive and interpret in terms of the images thus projected instead of in terms of the reality that is there. And, again, the emotions reflected by these projections are largely our unrealistic hopes and our equally unrealistic fears.

Consider international relations as an instructive example. With our allies, even though they are but temporarily such, we feel ourselves in the presence of friendly forces and construe what they do on that presupposition, while our enemies we feel to be sinister demons and interpret their behavior accordingly. The parallel with primitive man's perception of the beneficent and hostile powers in physical nature is almost exact. The dedicated Communist perceives the Western world as ruled by wicked capitalists; everything that happens in it he sees as the direct or indirect expression of capitalistic exploitation, hypocrisy, and greed. The aggressive anti-Communist responds in kind, and just as completely; every move on the part of the Communist leaders he perceives as an expression of a diabolical aim to bring the whole world under their mastery. And those distortions are pregnant with ominous possibilities, especially in the case of the demonic projections. Instead of anticipating the consequences of present decisions and acts that are actually likely, both participants in this bizarre process foresee outcomes that express their biased emotions. They thus concentrate their energy on guarding against these outcomes instead of those that are really taking form.

But the most instructive aspect of this kind of emotional projection is that when our relations with other people are concerned, the projections may embody a self-fulfilling prophecy, with its tremendous possibilities for both good and evil. The most insistent challenge today to our expanding awareness of the effect of emotion on our perceiving and interpreting activities is the challenge to realize how such prophecies work in the interaction of man with man, and to express that realization in every human situation. As we know, the influence of underlying motivation on everything we do cannot be avoided; however, there is a decisive difference between the blinder emotional projections and those that express a more reliable and objective understanding.

Nothing quite corresponds to these self-fulfilling prophecies in the play of emotion as revealed in our dealings with the first problem. Physical nature does not seem to care what predictions we make about her doings; she continues to behave in her accustomed way, unaffected by them. But we know that in human affairs this is often far from the case. An act expressing a suspicious or hostile prediction is likely to elicit the kind of response that verifies the prediction. Similarly, an act expressing the wish for a friendlier relation, at least if it is guided by alert awareness rather than naïve gullibility, is likely to lead to the consequence wished for.

In personal relations this truth is frequently illustrated in the experience of everyone. A man approaches an interview, expecting that the person to be met is difficult to deal with. In this expectation he will present a tense and defensive posture, and the other person reacts by being difficult to deal with. If, instead, he expects to meet a genial person, he will feel at ease and be relaxed; the other person reacts by being more genial than he would otherwise have been. The important difference is that the one outcome is bad for both participants while the other is good.

In international relations the world is constantly witnessing the way self-fulfilling prophecies operate, and sometimes the outcome is good. Under Gandhi's leadership India achieved independence from Great Britain, and this might easily have led to an unfortunate relation between the two after that goal had been won. Gandhi and his followers, however, always made it evident that they felt no hostility toward Englishmen, but only toward the chains that were enslaving India. As a result the relation between the two countries since independence has been one of mutual trust and friendship. All too often, however, in relations between nations, self-fulfilling prophecies and the acts to which they lead express fear and hate; then the tragic outcome is that the feared event happens, as it might not have done otherwise. The United States fears that it will lose a friendly foothold in Southeast Asia through the hated expansion of Communist China. Dominated by these emotions, it tries to force the people of South Vietnam to take its side in its war against communism instead of (as the basic policy) taking their side in their struggle against poverty, disease, illiteracy, foreign interference in their affairs, and continued military devastation. As a result it gradually loses most of the popular support it originally had, and other nations of southern Asia, in heightened apprehension and distrust of American policy, enter into closer relations with the Communist countries than they had been ready to accept before. Premier Chou En-lai doubtless had this process in mind when he said: "Once we worried about Southeast Asia. We don't any more. The Americans are rapidly solving our problems for us." [1]

What form, then, does man's basic resource for meeting the challenge of this second problem take, compounded as it is by the inescapable presence of self-fulfilling prophecies? How does he show here his capacity for clearer understanding of the forces at work and thus for mastering the lessons essential to continued life and growth? More specifically, what corresponds in this situation to the replacement, in solving the first problem, of the kindly or malicious powers in nature by an objective scientific picture of the world?

No single process provides the answer. In the area of our dynamic interrelation with other persons and groups—some of whom we feel to be friendly allies and others alien enemies—various transforming forces that tend to replace distorted images by a more objective way of perceiving people are perceptible. Travel has this effect in some degree; after Mr. Khrushchev's visit to the United States in 1959 the ghoulish caricatures of him in the American press largely gave way to more realistic cartoons. Economic trade is a very significant factor. Interchange of goods with the prospect of mutual advantage tempts men strongly, even when the other party to the transaction is a hated rival; this is illustrated today by the gradual expansion of trade between the Communist bloc and the West. In the course of the interchange, less-prejudiced knowledge of the other side inevitably develops; projection of diabolical motives gives way, in some measure, to awareness of people's real needs and concerns. Political relations too—especially through such a worldwide organization as the United Nations—can play an important part.

But these modes of expanding social awareness, by themselves, are weak; at every stage they are severely limited by the power of emotional projections, especially the hostile ones. When suspicion, fear, and pugnacity are strong enough they can dominate any kind of contact with people felt to be alien. There must be some other vital force at work, filling the major constructive role. Where do we find it?

Those who most clearly exemplify its creative possibilities are the pioneers of the great civilizied religions—Zoroaster, Buddha, Confucius, the Hebrew prophets, Jesus Christ, Mohammed. Consider briefly the momentous contribution these rare souls have made. The earliest among them responded to the emergence of this second need when in the sixth century B.C. it first became an inescapable challenge, and all of them have done so with insight and compassionate understanding. Their consuming concern was to gain the ultimate vision and practice the way of life whereby it can win an enduring solution. They discovered that union with the divine and oneness in spirit with other men are the same experience. Hence they broke down the wall of emotional separation so far as their own attitude toward people was concerned. They transcended the cautious limit set by other constructive forces in an all-embracing love and respect for their fellows, without regard to differences of race, nation, sex, or social status. The deeper insight thus realized they expressed in courageous, hopeful, and imaginative action.

These men were geniuses in the supreme art of making creative use of the principle of self-fulfilling prophecy—they acted with any other person, friend or foe, so as to elicit the most auspicious responding action that might be elicited. They realized that this art expresses the way of transforming emotion now needed—transforming it from narrow group-centeredness toward universal sensitivity. They understood the dark forces that break out from time to time and could face them without despair. To "love your enemies," fantastic though it sounds to a man still caught in his pugnacious emotions, is simply to express one's vivid awareness of how self-fulfilling prophecies work, and of the crucial difference for weal or woe between their constructive and their destructive use. Thus out of evil in human relations these great souls could bring forth good, and out of good a greater good. They opened up unlimited capacities in man for growth and happiness—capacities that had no chance even to be discovered during the first period, when people almost everywhere were absorbed in the laborious struggle to maintain their existence against the threats of physical nature.

These pioneers have surely been the greatest explorers of human history. In the obscure, convulsive, and tangled region of the emotional energies of men they have filled the role that the resolute geographic or scientific explorer fills in his less difficult realm. Just as the geographer surveys the vast topography of the earth, discovering the varied resources of its most remote regions, and the scientist probes beneath the surface of events, revealing the hidden forces on which successful technology depends, so the even bolder adventurers of civilized religion explore the mysterious psychology of man—penetrating hitherto inaccessible areas in his capacity for demand-ingness and acceptance, fear and hope, suspicion and trust, hate and love, despair and joy, and learning how to achieve the freedom, vitality, and assurance that integration around the constructive emotion in each of these contrasting pairs can bring. They realized clearly centuries ago what the nuclear age is now compelling all men to realize—that not only is the good of others one's own good but also their evil and peril is one's own evil and peril. They caught the vision of an ideal community embracing all the inhabitants of the planet, in identification with which each person finds true harmony in his own soul and satisfying union with ultimate reality. They perceived clearly one of the most trenchant truths about man that can be perceived, namely that when he is in unresolved conflict with other men he is in unresolved conflict with himself; he cannot understand himself or others, nor can he realize the joy, serenity, and strength of full accord with the universe that enfolds him.

From these men an energy was released into subsequent history that has never been lost and continually grows. The ecclesiastical organizations that preserve this energy have diluted the insight won through compromises with the world around them; yet in every generation many individuals have been transformed by it—their sense that all people belong together in a universal community has been awakened and deepened. Through their in-fluence political and social institutions are gradually being reformed. While the citizen of a modern state can still, in time of tension, believe that his nation is the chosen people and that God is on his side, he is haunted by guilt when he does so; this reveals how far he is separated from the typical member of a primitive tribe, who was quite sure that the divine powers he worshiped always made his enemy their enemy.

III

Where does the world now stand in its long endeavor to solve these basic problems? What has been accomplished? What remains to be accom-plished?

The first major challenge has been met. The regularities in nature that might serve man's ends but are still hidden are being ferreted out with increasing acceleration; the breathtaking promise of a victorious scientific technology opens before us. No longer is it a utopian dream to picture human life freed from the age-old prison of a scarcity economy through

mastery of the infinite energies of nature—and freed also from the drudg-
ery of menial labor and toilsome routine through the unlimited possibilities
of automation.

The second challenge is the critical one today. The form of awareness
that urgently needs to expand is awareness of the deep-seated motivations
active in one's relation to other people, for they are the forces decisively
affecting man for weal or for woe. The greatest danger to his future lies in
the distorting emotions and destructive passions that he has not yet overcome; the greatest promise lies in his capacity for a sensitive understanding
of himself and his human fellows, and his power to enter the inclusive
universe in which the creative aspirations of all can move freely toward
their fulfillment. A realistic assessment of where we now stand with regard
to this challenge reveals both hopeful and perilous possibilities that are
vaster than ever before.

The hopeful side appears at once when we compare our present situation
with the early plight of man as he began to lose the cohesion of the primitive tribe and took his first fumbling steps toward civilization. One can
hardly help seeing a halting evolution from suspicious and hostile divided-
ness, with all the handicaps to a fully human life that were involved, toward a larger unity with its promise of high fulfillment. What has been
going on over the centuries is a gradual consolidation of the human race,
each stage of which was essential to its survival and growth. Take a quick
look at this evolution, especially as revealed in the relations between social
and political entities.

For long eons the functioning social unit—and the unit sufficient under
ordinary circumstances for survival—was very likely a small family. Then
it slowly became the larger clan or tribe. As this occurred, families incapable of merging in that more inclusive and efficient unit because of their
intense jealousy and distrust were swept away in the relentless struggle for
existence or were driven into remote pockets where no one else would live;
such pockets still exist in a few parts of the world, e.g., the high valleys of
Peru east of the Andean watershed. The process of consolidation very likely
paused here for a long time; the clan or tribe was the largest social unit
that could readily maintain itself under the conditions of primitive technology and means of communication. Then the tribe grew into a nation or
empire when enough of the techniques of civilization were mastered to
make this second transition possible; and viewing the progress of mankind
as a whole, this stage is still the most prominent one. The peremptory need
almost everywhere is for a potent sense of national belonging unobstructed

by tribal and local differences. This is especially evident among the newly independent countries of Africa, which are now striving to achieve a super-tribal unity comparable in emotional force to the bond that unites a primitive clan.

But the process of unification does not stop here, and men are more and more sensing that the nation is no longer a viable unit for survival. Under the pressure of the same forces that have brought the world to its present degree of consolidation, accelerated today by the rapid increase in means of communication, nations and empires are feeling their way toward the formation of supernational units. This is happening under various compelling motives, and the units thus arising take more than one form. When we contemplate this whole evolution—from the stage in which any stranger from beyond one's clan is viewed as an enemy to the stage where there is as much peaceful intercommunication and cooperative interaction as there is today—we are aware that a radical transformation has taken place, and we realize the enduring strength of the creative forces at work.

Nonetheless, in the nuclear age the unit of survival is no longer the nation, nor even a limited alliance of nations; it is the human race as a whole, which will now either live or die together. As we frankly face this truth the sobering side of the picture confronts us. Civilized man has only feebly begun to move toward a world society possessing the stability in filling its all-embracing role that the isolated tribe could possess in its narrow milieu. Yet nothing less than such a society can meet his need. His most perilous handicap is the sluggishness with which he achieves the capacity to put himself in the place of other groups, nations, creeds, and races, so that he can foresee how others will respond to this or that course of action and can choose the action that will serve the long-run good of all.

In this sadly imprisoning plight the dominant urge of most people is to overcome their galling sense of personal weakness by identifying with the power and prestige of their nation. No dependable and widely shared feeling of emotional unity transcending national loyalty—and loyalty to the ideology for which one's nation stands—has yet been achieved. The American and the Russian, the Westerner and the Oriental—each feels the other to be an alien menace, just as the member of a primitive tribe feels the outsider to be a menace. In any international situation each presupposes that the present interests of his nation have a right to be satisfied; instead of expanding his horizon to appreciate the values of other people, he is ready to impose his own upon them if he can. Insensitive to the promising and the fearful possibilities in self-fulfilling prophecy, his mind is caught in whatever emotion possesses him at the time, with hardly a minimal aware-ness of the consequences of acting under its compulsion. Only in scattered individuals and small groups has the wall of emotional separation been broken down, and the feeling of hostile alien-ness replaced by a sense of brotherhood in a single world community. Indeed, even within a nation or a bloc men have thus far, in general, realized an effective union only in the presence of a common enemy or a common danger; when the outside peril no longer threatens, their clashing local and sectarian interests come to the fore again.

This side of the picture becomes even more sobering when we recognize fully the other threatening changes now going on besides the emergence of the possibility of nuclear destruction—such as the population explosion and the increased tension between "haves" and "have nots." But the change that most seriously compounds the nuclear threat may well be the tearing of people away from their traditional roots, so that they are groping in anxi-ety, frustration, and confused uncertainty for a new and more dependable foundation. Men and women everywhere are losing the patterns of living familiar for many centuries, together with the social controls embedded in them; these roots in the past have provided their needed guidance and emotional support. In this unprecedented upheaval even our most funda-mental institutions are drastically affected. For example, the tribal and na-tional patterns of marriage and family life, successful for many ages in ordering that basic phase of social existence, are passing away, while as yet we are far from establishing a new pattern that would be really adequate to the needs and possibilities of civilized life today.

As a major part of this bewildering transmutation, the metaphysical framework that people have for centuries taken for granted is also breaking down. Within that framework their deep longings and aspirations found unified expression, but it can no longer serve as an acceptable background for life in the novel world of the twentieth century. In times of apprehen-sion they still try to find comfort and reassurance in the hoary ideas they have inherited, but it proves increasingly impossible really to believe them. This change is startlingly revealed when we compare the medieval picture of the astronomical world with the picture to which modern man must somehow accommodate himself. Our medieval ancestors looked out on a cozy cosmos with the earth at its center and the sphere of the fixed stars not far away; all was embraced by the infinite power, wisdom, and good-ness of God, whose presence assured them that everything that happens has its place within the eternal Divine plan. Modern man looks out upon a stupendous immensity of material existence; he peers into the unending vastness of the nebular universe in which his solar system is an insignificant speck, with distances of space and epochs of time that baffle his imagination. This is an exhilarating scene to all who are open to its breathtaking possibilities, but to those who hanker after the protecting cosmos of the past it is very frightening. Yet even they dimly realize that the comforting assurances of the past are now gone and that they must somehow find their home in this awful immensity.

The bearing of this wholesale upheaval on our moral foundations must not be forgotten. In large areas of the world, especially in the West, the laws of conduct necessary for social survival and growth have traditionally been accepted as valid because they are commandments of God, conceived as the authoritative governor of the universe. That traditional support is rapidly weakening. Not only has "the old man in the sky" faded away, but the theistic conception of God in general is losing its persuasiveness. The result is that in many quarters, for example, among young intellectuals, the restraints of the past have been rejected and the atmosphere is pervaded by moral confusion. The fundamental questions—*Are* there any moral laws? On what are they grounded?—have not been convincingly answered. As yet only very partial glimpses have appeared of ways of living and ideas of the Divine that promise to give men and women a stable adjustment to the new physical and moral universe in which they find themselves. In the long run this loss of ancient roots is not only inevitable but good; it will lead to a more dynamic orientation, which can adapt itself to all evolving realities and be fully open to new possibilities. But in the short run it is bound to be very upsetting and in not a few cases shattering. The fact that a large part of the world has now become an affluent society is itself a peril as well as a promise. Life in such a society gives scope for the expression of emotions which in a primitive tribe were kept in check by the need for everyone to spend most of his thought and energy in providing the daily necessities of existence.

It may well be that for some time to come the fabric of human society will be weakened and rent more than strengthened. The forces at work will release the destructive as well as the constructive possibilities of which man in possession of the instruments of civilized technology is capable. It is in this setting that the inevitable proliferation of weapons of mass annihilation comes into the picture. There is no need to assume, of course, that all nations having the capacity to develop nuclear weapons will do so; some almost surely will not. But so long as the great powers obviously think that these weapons are needed for their safety many others will think so too.

We naturally long for some cosmic guarantee that the human race will avoid the threatened catastrophe. But how can there be any such guarantee? Man is always hurtling forward into the unknown; and the unknown includes the outcome generated by his turbulent and frustrated emotions as well as the destiny to which the generative processes of physical nature are leading. And there is a more specific reason for the absence of any guarantee. This is that the virtues making for survival and progress under one set of historical conditions are rather different from those required in another (even though certain basic virtues, such as alert awareness and human sensitivity, are essential in all); the fact that man has mastered the virtues needed in the past gives no assurance of his power to master those needed in the present.

We must dwell for a moment on this pregnant reminder. During the long epoch of pre-civilized life the virtues that made for survival and progress were physical courage, capacity for endurance, keenness of perception, prudential intelligence and resourcefulness, along with a strong sense of family and tribal responsibility. In the age of developing civilization these virtues were still important; but the emphasis then fell on growing responsiveness to the needs of all one's fellow citizens in a complex society, thus fostering loyalty and mutual support throughout a farflung empire.

What virtues are imperatively called for today? Many of those vital in the past are clearly still vital, especially the ones that express man's indomitable energy, his widening sense of social responsibility, his insistence on the maximum viable scope for freedom and initiative, and above all his readiness to run whatever risk needs to be run for the sake of the goals he envisions. We must not forget that thus far in human history the forces of evolution have mainly been accomplishing the same result that they have in the age-long development of life, and that this result was required as a sound base on which a great future could be built. They have been weeding out or pushing off to the periphery those types of humanity that are lethargic, overcautious, and prematurely contented, in favor of the types that are alert, inventive, and daring. But in the age we have now entered, the peoples with the best chance to survive and to lead the way toward the future are the ones who combine these dynamic qualities with a sensitive understanding of their fellowmen and a growing ability to make creative use of the power of self-fulfilling prophecy. Such are the virtues that foster the harmonious coexistence of nations great and small, that evoke voluntary cooperation and promote mutual trust between peoples. The policies that lead to survival and strength are now those that reduce fear, suspicion, and hate on the part of others, not those that arouse them.

In short, if man is to live on into the future he is irrevocably summoned to unite the bold, energetic, far-seeing qualities that led to success in conquering physical nature and forming ever larger political units, with appreciative responsiveness to the values and aspirations of all his fellows, and increasing wisdom in following the policies that express this responsiveness.

However—as we know to our pain and sorrow—to realize this truth and to practice these virtues is hard. The world has not been trained for the nuclear age. Man is still the pugnacious patriot and the aggressive champion of a dogmatic creed. He is still prone to blame his frustrations on the malicious failure of other people (especially those whom he regards as alien) to do as they should, instead of seeing their source in the blithe greed or zealous righteousness of himself and his leaders; he easily persists in the emotional projections that express this proneness. There is no assurance that in the convulsive and ever-shifting tension of our day between the reckless urge toward acts that lead to destruction and the creative search for community, the former will not precipitate an irretrievable catastrophe before the latter has led us over the hump.

Man may not make it much longer; he could perish, by his own suicidal act, at any time. One dare not contemplate what this means, lest he be overwhelmed by the magnitude of the agony that would be undergone before the last man, woman, or child has breathed his last. Nonetheless, if this proves to be our fate, should we complain? It has always been clear that man's life on the surface of this planet will not be everlasting; it depends on conditions that can hardly be preserved forever. In his career thus far he has engaged resourcefully in a magnificent adventure, and he is doubtless capable of far greater achievements such as today cannot even be imagined. But in the case of an individual we know that as soon as he is born he is old enough to die; his life may be cut short at any moment, with many of his talents unexpressed and his high potentialities unfulfilled. Is it not inescapably the same with the human race? * Elsewhere in the vast celestial spaces intelligent beings have presumably appeared who were

---

* There are many other ways besides nuclear annihilation in which the human race might meet a premature death. See Teilhard de Chardin, *The Phenomenon of Man*, tr. by Bernard Wall (New York: Harper and Brothers, 1959), pp. 274 f.

snuffed out long before their career had developed as far as man's has already done. Have we any right to demand of the universe that homo sapiens live out his threescore years and ten?

I V

But having said this—having faced the fact that universal annihilation is possible, that some nation or group may in frustration and rage carry out the dour will that if it cannot have its way in the world everything must perish—let us dare to be optimists. Let us have faith that man will come through. Not that he will escape anguish and tragedy—even, it may be, dire devastation—but that in and through whatever suffering may be his lot he will learn the lessons required to choose life in the nuclear age instead of death. Let us dare to believe that as he proved able to conquer the weird distortions of physical nature caused by projecting his compulsive emotions, he will conquer them also in relation to his fellowmen—the form of projection now so fraught with peril to his continued existence. Our sun—so scientists tell us—will continue to shed its light and warmth for at least a billion years longer; let us trust that man will live on into the distant future, that he will yet realize his promise, that he will become fully himself. When the time arrives for natural causes to end his career, may he have given to whatever larger cosmic reality can receive the gift the most splendid contribution that his endowments make possible.

Is there any sane alternative to this faith?

In adopting it we need not be naïve about the evils that harass man in the present or will haunt him in the future. We can realize fully that when the evils that seem so appalling today have been victoriously met, others will surely arise—some of which may well seem equally appalling to our successors. Reality seems set on testing man's powers to the limit as long as there is any danger of his lapsing into lethargy; and the perils that assail him in each age may be the necessary condition of significant progress. In any case, progress does not consist in leaving all evils behind; it consists in the growth of alert and prophetic sensitivity, which is expressed in conquering the sources of present evil for the sake of creating the finer humanity that is to be—a humanity with greater power of creation, and thus more capable of meeting whatever evils may threaten and of realizing whatever goods become possible.

The challenge to our generation is the challenge to transform an unparalleled crisis for man into an unparalleled achievement. Never was the maxim embodied in self-fulfilling prophecy more vividly relevant. If too few men and women make this faith their own, our doom is sure and will not be long delayed; if enough do share it and act resolutely on it there is a chance—and a good chance—that the hopeful prophecy will be realized.

Must it be a sheer faith, or is there perceptible evidence to support it? When we survey the scene realistically, can we see signs that man's constructive energies are gradually mastering the destructive forces of self-centered greed, angry passion, and narrow loyalty? Do we find encouraging corroboration for the maxim that "love is stronger than hate, strong as that dark passion may be; and love will create more than hate can destroy"? [2]

To make any prognostications for the short run would surely be a mistake; such a precarious enterprise is for others than philosophers. Let us concentrate our attention on the forces that are obviously the ones on which survival and growth in the long run depend. When we surveyed life in the total sweep of its evolution, there seemed sound reason to believe that through the play of the stupendous vitalities at work, the forms most likely to survive in any crisis are those whose nature is exhibited at the human level in expanding awareness. In terms of the "negative" and "positive" reactions to the presence of another living being, the line of evolutionary progress is set by the forms that keep the negative subordinate to the positive—i.e., do not allow the fullest exercise of sensitive discrimination in whatever situation is involved to be blocked by the fearful urge to shrink or the angry urge to destroy. When we survey the narrower panorama of human experience, the conclusion toward which our whole course of thought leads is that only through growth in love does one grow in understanding, and that only through increased understanding can one guide action wisely in the presence of whatever realities must be met.

But these are very general considerations. More specific grounds of hope can also be found. Let us reflect on the promise that can be discerned in the two basic relations into which human beings enter—basic because they are those on which man's continued existence and progress depend.

The first is the relation between man and woman as mates. The potent need of the sexes for each other underlies and preserves all society, primitive or civilized. And throughout the ages this has been the crucial experience for breaking down the wall of separation between one person and another and for the gradual achievement, in equality, of satisfying union. It is true that sexual longing can be tied, more or less strongly, to any other emotional urge of which man is capable—deceptive or honest, destructive or creative. Yet, whatever else it may be, it is the longing for union with another person; and it can grow in awareness, especially awareness of that person's needs and hopes. By virtue of this growth men and women slowly learn that in the sexual relation the highest satisfaction is impossible so long as either partner is using the other as a means to his or her self-centered pleasure. Any hint of this exploitation constitutes a block to the free and spontaneous mutual accord that is necessary to the complete happiness of each. It is also true that where the ideal of equality between the sexes is not yet widely accepted, many bad patterns can long be maintained. Nonetheless, these are temporizing solutions. Only when each partner is seeking the fulfillment of his mate as well as of himself, and has come to feel his sexual power as an instrument toward such fulfillment, can perfect harmony and a dependably happy union be achieved.

In the course of learning this lesson men and women gradually learn another, namely that sexual love attains its perfection only when it is in full accord with all else that is good in their growing experience. Then the delight of sexual embrace becomes the joy that can be realized when the sensual is integrated with the spiritual. All the riches of their total sharing will permeate each episode of loving union.

As these lessons are more widely learned, the transformation of attitude and habit thus achieved spontaneously spreads. The ideal of unity between persons in freedom and equality, having revealed its essential meaning and satisfying value in the intimate union of husband and wife, can penetrate all other forms of human interaction in the way appropriate to each.

In this relation between mates nature dictates that the initiating and guiding role be filled by the male partner. In the second basic relation, that between parent and child, the corresponding role must be filled by the woman, as mother. Her urge to nourish and protect the little ones she brings into the world provides a firm foundation on which the sensitive understanding that needs to be mastered by both parents can be dependably learned.

With husband and wife, the ideal guiding their fuller realization intrinsically involves mutuality and equality, but with parent and child the capacity to express unfailing responsiveness is for a long time all on the side of the former. The child begins life with an imperious demandingness for himself; whatever power to give himself to others he succeeds in realizing depends mainly on the unfailing reality of the parents' love during his years of growth. On this account the evolution of parental emotion toward its ideal takes a different course and exemplifies another phase of man's moral progress. It becomes clear in the setting of family life that it is unrealistic to expect children to love their parents, except in the self-centered form determined by their need for protection and approval. The prime lesson that they should learn in these early years is that of a basic trust in their social world. So the instinctive concern of parents for their children while the latter are still young must take the form, under the pressure of this inescapable fact, of a love that does not demand any love in return. The wise parent knows that he cannot withhold his giving till he is sure that the child will respond; his love flows out, making no demands, and trusts in doing so that the power will be awakened in those upon whom it flows to become good parents in their turn.

Is it not a justified expectation that over the centuries, despite many relapses, parents will realize these essential truths earlier and more widely than now, and children will grow more rapidly and surely toward maturity under their guidance? Furthermore, in this experience of parenthood we have the enduring natural source of whatever power men and women achieve to give love freely without any conditions. Just as the attitudes developed in the marriage union increasingly affect all other human relations, so when parent-love in its perfected form becomes dominant in a person it molds his orientation toward every other person. Free from the obstruction of demandingness for himself, he can realize more and more fully his capacity to overcome hate with love and evil with good.

But a serious doubt may arise about the important conclusion just drawn. *Can* the attitudes gradually developed in family life permeate other human relations, and the social institutions in which they are organized? Especially in the case of political institutions, it is hard to believe that the ideal possibilities for an individual in his intimate relations are also the ideal possibilities for a nation. And there are truths that seem to support this disbelief; for example, in fulfilling one's responsibilities as a citizen or agent of society one will accept moral compromises that a high-minded individual in his relation with other individuals will reject. Must then the ideal for a political entity diverge from the ideal for an individual or a family group?

For a partial answer, reflect on the obvious fact that every social group, including every nation, is composed of individuals whose fulfillment is achieved, not in isolation but by sharing with other individuals as they build together ever larger types of effective organization. The same basic laws of growth that are at work in the individual must then operate in every social entity. Each society, like each person, is a theater in which kaleidoscopic forces are struggling toward a liberating and integrating harmony under the guidance of expanding awareness. Indeed, the world as a whole can today for the first time be seen as such a theater; it is an aggregate of interacting groups, now opposing each other in fierce conflict, now uniting in cooperation.

Let us see if this answer is confirmed when we observe in unbiased perspective the trend of social and political evolution.

That lengthy historical process clearly teaches a most significant twofold lesson: (1) As ambitious men seek power they find that they must appeal for support to a wider and wider segment of their fellow-citizens; only thus can such men in each succeeding age hope to displace those now in power and inherit their authority. (2) In order for this support to be genuine and enduring they must become aware of the hitherto unsatisfied aspirations of those whose support they need, and must be ready to change social conditions so as to satisfy these aspirations. It follows that political power achieves its aim successfully in proportion as it becomes the power of love; or—put in different words—that sensitive awareness of and responsiveness to the growing needs of people is in the long run the greatest power. Apparent power that lacks this wise alertness and understanding proves to be weakness instead of power.

Such an implication may sound rather startling. But look at two of the many evidences of its truth from the course of history.

One is the radically transformed role of the common man. In the early millennia of man's quest for civilization the masses counted for nothing and could easily be manipulated by clever rulers. Ignorant and disunited, they submissively accepted their dismal lot. Now we have begun to see the end of the period when the welfare of the common people can be ignored. Increasingly, through the quest of potential leaders for wider support and with other forces aiding the process, all people are being brought into participation in the social and political life of their nation. Those hitherto submerged are becoming aware of their massive strength. The outcome today is that throughout the world there is an insistent and swelling demand that the millions who have thus far been excluded from the good things that life makes possible now have the opportunity fully to share in them.

The other is the obvious transition, over this long period, from reliance on harsh and insensitive methods of winning support to the use of more humane and enlightened ones. It has gradually become clear that enduring allegiance can only be won by a government that assures for the people it rules a large measure of security, justice, and opportunity to satisfy their growing interests. And if its pattern of social order is unusually enlightened for the era in which it emerges into dominance, the successful political entity can unify a wide territory and last a long time—witness the significant transformation in the ancient world as the rule of the Hittites and the Assyrians passed away and was succeeded by that of Persia and of Rome. It is true of course that the relapses are frequent and sometimes devastating—as in the case of Nazi Germany.

A most instructive feature of this secular process is the gradual shift from the use of *threat* as the main principle for establishing a viable social order to an ever greater use of the principle of free *exchange.** The essence of the former principle is: You give me what I want or I'll do something you don't want. The essence of the latter is: You give me what I want and I will give you something that you want. This significant change stands out for all to see in the history of commerce through the ages and in that of diplomacy in recent times. The broad course of evolution from slavery through feudalistic serfdom to the present relation between capital and labor is an excellent illustration, as is the passing away in our day of colonial exploitation in favor of voluntary exchange between economically developed and undeveloped peoples—to their mutual advantage. Compare the practice of the European colonists a century ago with the semi-colonialism of the United States since the Second World War, based as the latter is on the lure of financial rewards rather than on outright military control. Political pressure still exemplifies a combination of the carrot and the stick, but those who make the latter too obvious and wield it too blatantly fail to build an enduring social fabric in competition with rivals who have better learned this vital lesson. Attempts will doubtless be made for a long time yet to master people by terrorism and fear, but there is ground for hope that the era of Hitler and Stalin will prove to have been the last in which this was tried on a grand scale.

In short, an epoch has emerged in which the statesmen who persist in trusting the principle of threat in their dealings with other people soon lose out in the quest for prosperity and power, while those who pioneer in the direction opened up by the principle of exchange are far more likely to achieve their ends. The latter show a clearer awareness of the long-run consequences of their acts. In this epoch a vast arsenal of destructive weapons is becoming a source of weakness rather than of strength. Look at

* See Kenneth E. Boulding, in a paper read at a meeting of the American Economic Association on December 29, 1962; also Chapters I and IV of his *The Meaning of the 20th Century* (New York: Harper and Row, 1964).

America and Russia during the decade of the 1950's. Pugnacious brandish-
ing of their nuclear "deterrence" quickly reveals their impotence in relation
to each other, for the threat is either incredible or suicidal; whereas, in
their relation with other nations, it is increasingly clear that each of them
can hope to win lasting support only as its policies promise to meet the real
needs of those whom they are wooing. When America insists that the
countries of Western Europe accept the status of satellites under her nuclear umbrella she begins to lose her allies; and Russia in turn finds that
she must come to terms with the persistent demand of the countries in her
orbit to pass from domination by the Soviet Communist party to an alliance in which that party will be merely *primus inter pares.* In fact, she has
now found it wise, in her struggle to maintain ascendancy over China, to
promise them full equality.*

But even more prophetically revealing are the clear signs in this novel
kind of international competition that a third principle, which transcends
the principle of exchange as the latter transcends the principle of threat, is
emerging. A nation that hopes to win such a race must not wait too cau-
tiously for a good bargain to be struck; while it hesitates and dickers, its
rival may steal a march by a more generous offer. The essence of the third
principle might be thus expressed: I shall do something that you want—
something that will serve the well-being of both of us, and indeed of the
whole world—without waiting to be sure that you will reciprocate.† When
a government puts this principle into practice it will hope of course that
those whose support it is seeking will respond in kind, and it believes that
they will more readily do so if treated in this way—but its initiating act
will not depend on any bargain to this effect.

The gradual appearance of this third principle means that statesmen are
beginning to learn the full implication of the radical change brought about
by the advent of nuclear weapons: namely, that danger to anyone anywhere
in the world—especially to those whom we feel to be enemies—has now
become a danger to us. In the past, when a Socrates asked: What does it
profit me to act so as to make another person worse, even if he is my
enemy? it was plausible to answer: He can't be any worse than he is, and
the safest thing is to act so as to make him dead. But in the age we have
entered a different answer is called for: If you act so as to make him dead,

* See *The New York Times,* April 13, 1964, p. 1.
† Was not this principle exemplified in America's Marshall Plan for Europe,
along with the self-interest that led in the same direction?

you will almost surely be dead too. When you realize this you will consider before acting whether he is as bad as he might be, and how you could act so as to make him better rather than worse.

That statesmen are aware of the negative implication of this change is already evident. They clearly show the influence of the maxim: Act so that neither of us will need to be dead. Leaders of small nations with no atomic weapons in their arsenal are often ready to run the same risks that were run in the past; hence "brushfire" wars will doubtless occur for a long time to come. But the leaders of the nuclear powers—America, Russia, China, Britain, France—are displaying more restraint than ever before and are following policies guided by caution. When we watch their deeds instead of listening to their bellicose words, it is obvious that while they wish to gain the advantages that capacity for horrendous destruction seems to promise, the prime consideration with all of them is to avoid an all-out conflict. It may be that by this prudential self-control they are already creating the most peaceful world order that is possible while human animosity, suspicion, fear, and cockiness are still such potent factors.*

But there is a positive implication too, and the third principle just enunciated embodies it, although in limited form. That principle only needs to be generalized to become the expression, in political relations between nations, of the positive maxim that is valid for a person in his relation with other persons: Act always in the way that is likely to call forth the most farsighted response on the part of those affected by your action. The ultimate ideal toward which this principle points—for international as well as for interpersonal relations—is that of alert perceptiveness and ready cooperation in freedom and equality. Statesmen are coming to realize that only by leading their people in this direction can there be hope of survival and progress. True strength, for a nation as for an individual, is not military force or financial power or propagandistic skill, but growing capacity to sense the needs and aspirations of all people throughout the world and to act accordingly.

V

Our thoughts turn to a vision of the ideal community, and of how each individual and group would live within it. The quest for such a vision can

* See W. Millis and J. Real, *The Abolition of War* (New York: The Macmillan Company, 1963), especially Chap. 6.

encourage sentimental dreaming, but—when it plays its proper part in a total perspective—it can be an indispensable aid. We shall remember the inevitable relativity of such a vision; by the time significant progress toward it has been made, a more adequate ideal, growing out of that achievement, will have emerged. But it will clarify our hopes and guide our active participation in the cosmic adventure if we put into words, however feebly, the best vision we can now grasp. Let us follow three clues as we embark on this task.

First, we can survey some of the trends of change in the world-scene before us and ask what constructive promise each of them holds for the future. Two of the most obvious examples are the rapid acceleration in the gaining of knowledge and the annihilation of distance, with the more intensive interaction thus made possible between peoples all over the world. Taken together, these changes open the way to an unprecedented flowering of man's intellectual, artistic, and spiritual life, fed by the emotional energy that has in the past been weakened by isolation and fragmented by destructive conflict but that in the setting of the ideal community could be enhanced without limit.

As for the pursuit of knowledge in that community, Teilhard de Chardin gives us a succinct picture of the possibilities. "We can envisage a world whose constantly increasing 'leisure' and heightened interest would find their vital issue in fathoming everything, trying everything, extending everything . . . a world in which, as happens already [with many], one gives one's life to be and to know, rather than to possess." [3]

This emphasis on the wresting of nature's secrets would not exclude the application of the knowledge thus gained to better the lot of man and to improve man himself. Quite the contrary. And here a cooperative quest within the world community, to serve the well-being of all in freedom and equality, obviously becomes the essential foundation. When this quest can be taken for granted, we need no longer hesitate (as we surely must in an era of aggressively self-interested nation-states) to realize the fullest measure of control over the physical forces around us, and over man himself. The resources of the globe can be distributed to maximum advantage and far more effectively used; the powers set free by automation can be intelligently and happily employed; the weather everywhere in the world can be brought under control; new substances with novel and promising properties can be created; even a humane science of eugenics, aiming at the emergence of the noblest personalities and the finest social institutions, can become possible. Man will have won, and will be able to put into practice, trustworthy insight into how he may wisely remake both his world and himself.

As for the flowering of spiritual life in the ideal community, the unhampered interaction between people everywhere and the responsive sharing of values then taken for granted would usher in a thrilling advance such as can now hardly be imagined. All dogmatic attachment to the past and all sectarian defensiveness will have been left behind, and the saintly leaders of that era will fill their role in full command of the resources offered by every branch of our religious heritage. They will recover, and communicate to others, a sense of the infinite preciousness of every person—now so tragically being weakened in an age when masses of people can be slaughtered at a distance. Those among them who are contemporaries will freely learn from each other, and thus form a pioneering brotherhood which would serve as a dynamic model for the beloved community of all. They will be aware that the process of uniting the enduring truth in each of our present religions with the enduring truth in the others, thus bringing them all together in a single panorama of man's search for the Divine, will be gradual; and that the ways of realizing this unity will be varied. It will take its natural form in the heart and mind of everyone who is eager not to miss any possibilities of spiritual greatness that might be glimpsed. And the process will be continuous, for the pioneers of the future, like those of the past, will not be limited by the clues to religious understanding already grasped. Their adventurous searching will reach out beyond every horizon, no matter how impressive and rewarding the wisdom that their predecessors have won.

Second, we can turn to the fiercely competing ideologies of today, aware through our search for truth wherever it can be found that their basic ideals are complementary rather than contradictory, and that what man needs is not the victory of one ideology over the other but a wise balance between them. Our challenge is to gain a clarified vision of that balance.

At the heart of the ideal of Western democracy lies reverence for the individual person—for his right to pursue his own goals so long as he respects the equal right of others, and to play his part in the progress of society toward wiser goals than those embodied in present policies. It thus provides the sole way of organizing political and social life that accepts human experience as having the radically dynamic character that in fact it does have. Other forms of government assume that certain presuppositions are absolute and therefore never to be abandoned; the consequence is that when (as sooner or later always happens) they have to be abandoned, this can usually only occur through a violent revolution, with its accompanying chaos and destruction. By protecting individual liberties and minority rights, democracy provides a method of passing peacefully from the control of a country's policies by one set of presuppositions to control by another set, and encourages the emergence of new parties and policies to meet the needs of a new day. It places its trust in the greater truth that always lies ahead and is sought through the free clash of ideas in the open market. It thus implicitly accepts the arduous task of maintaining the political, industrial, legal, and educational conditions necessary for such peaceful passage —conditions exceedingly difficult to maintain. If one believes that certain moral and social principles are absolute and must be preserved come what may, he is no democrat at heart; he may accept democratic ways as a temporary convenience, but if and when he has the power to enthrone or defend those principles by force he will do so.

It is true that a dictatorial regime is unavoidable in certain historical circumstances; when people who have never participated in democratic institutions are freed from past forms of bondage their only hope may be to find leaders who are committed to their long-run good and who will wisely exercise political power to establish its foundations. An attempt to practice democracy prematurely, on the assumption that all members of any society can exercise freedom responsibly under any conditions, only leads to paralysis or disaster. But this fact does not derogate in the least from the essential rightness of the democratic ideal, as expressing the true nature of man in his growing accord with dynamic reality.

Consider the serious weakness of totalitarian communism in its contrast with the basic method of democracy. Two ultimate presuppositions of the former are the essential validity of the Marx-Leninist dialectic and the sacredness of the "party line" once it has been determined. Consequently, when practical necessities require the revision of that dialectic, or new contingencies force a drastic change in the party line, elaborate maneuvers of rationalization are needed; inconsistency cannot quite be hidden, nor bewilderment in the minds of many followers avoided. Moreover, different interpretations of the dialectic inevitably appear, and different party lines are adopted in the various Communist countries; in the combative atmosphere engendered by their confident claims we witness the very revealing phenomenon of the heretic being hated with greater virulence than the infidel.

Unless a significant measure of freedom is increasingly allowed, it seems inevitable that this divisive weakness will become more serious with the expansion of education; trained minds cannot help ranging widely and asking critical questions, and they will be less and less ready to believe that whenever their party leader changes his tenets it is essential for everyone to change in the same way.

But is it not equally clear that another ideal—that of a community united in spirit and feeling—is also ultimately valid? Duties to the encompassing social whole are as fundamental as rights for the individual or the smaller group. In the heat of the Cold War Western thinkers have found it hard to realize the nature of the vision that inspires their adversaries and gives it a moving appeal all over the world. They easily identify communism with a feared strategy of revolutionary expansion and fail to appreciate its forward-looking ideal. Indeed, the Communists themselves often seem not to understand that vision fully; they are apt to describe it by the narrow and negative concept of the "classless society." But if one probes beneath the surface for the real source of their strength, one sees that what elicits their sacrificial commitment and arouses their impassioned devotion is a goal far broader than this—and in clarified form, a goal that is surely sound. Mr. Khrushchev gave it simple and homely expression in describing the new educational system adopted by Russia: the aim is to substitute "we" for "I" and "ours" for "my" in the basic feelings of each child. In the light of this goal one realizes why, of the various words available from our heritage, "communism" with its distinctive associations was chosen.

Glimpses of this appealing goal have been caught by the seers of all ages and cultures; every generation in Christian history has been taught its intrinsic meaning by the text: "Ye are members one of another." The verbal symbols that have conveyed these glimpses through the centuries are those of "brotherhood," "fraternity," the "more perfect union," etc.; but the most deeply appealing symbols are those hallowed by their religious associations: the "beloved community," and (as we peer beyond time toward eternity) the "communion of saints." No wonder that youthful enthusiasm is stirred by this ideal and that boundless energy is mobilized for the building of a model society on the foundation it implies. No wonder that the new China fosters through its communes—often pictured in the West as achieved only by ruthless regimentation—a radical stretching of the Confucian family loyalty so that every person will feel himself a dedicated member of a much larger clan and, through it, of the united community of his people and of the world. Such loyalty and dedication cannot be realized quickly in dependable form, but when they are thus realized a society can actually live by the Marxian maxim: From each according to his ability; to each according to his need. To state the valid essence of this ideal, is it not a universal brotherhood in which every individual realizes his true self, and every lesser group finds its true good, in responsible commitment to the good of all?

Westerners, moved by their vigorous demand for individual liberty and absorbed in the unprecedented opportunity to satisfy it that has been their lot, find it easy to forget two important truths. One is that liberty as they conceive it has thus far been a rare luxury for man, whereas a stable society is absolutely necessary for survival. Freedom for the individual is only tolerable and can alone preserve itself where established habits of cooperation are sufficient to maintain social unity, so that in matters of major concern expressing one's freedom and serving the larger whole go harmoniously together. The other truth is that the primary emotional need of men is not for liberty in the Western sense but for security, justice, and the feeling of being welcomed by their group. The freedom for which all deeply long is freedom from the threat of starvation, from ignorance and disease, from injustice, and from isolation. Only when these freedoms have been won and are protected, can men begin to prize the freedom of thought, of expression, of conscience, and of the ballot that are central in the Western ideal of liberty.

Communists, moved by their zeal to establish a just social order that will leave behind the cruel exploitations of the past, have also found it easy to forget two basic truths. One is that any social order grounded in a set of rigid dogmas is doomed. If the conditions essential to progress are not assured, a society will fall by the wayside in competition with others that are more adaptable to changing reality. Now a fundamental requirement of such adaptability is an atmosphere that supports imagination and initiative. Men must arise in each generation who have the freedom and courage to criticize the maxims of the present and to proclaim new ideas that may point the way to a happier future. The other is that no social revolution, no matter how thoroughgoing, and no process of conditioning, no matter how persistent, can by itself change human beings in the way Marxism has assumed. Even after such a drastic experience people and their rulers can still be moved by obstreperous urges and narrow loyalties.

That these appealing ideals are complementary rather than contradictory, and are capable of realization together, becomes clear when we observe three important facts: each of them is subject to the same tempting perversions; there is a primary value common to both; and their champions are learning fundamental lessons from each other.

As for the first of these, the most seductive perversion on both sides appears in the ease with which adherents of an ideology confuse progress toward their proclaimed ideal with the preservation of their comfortable and privileged position in the social order already achieved. In the West this takes the form of assuming that freedom for oneself and one's friends is all the freedom needed and at present feasible; other people are not yet ready for it and can properly be treated as instruments for attaining the political and economic ends of those now in power. In the Communist world it takes the form of assuming that maintenance of absolute authority and control in the Communist party *ipso facto* assures progress toward the blessings of the classless society. A related perversion is the unquestioning belief of the leaders on both sides that they are defending a true ideology when they are actually promoting the selfish interests of their own nation. As for the primary value shared by both, is it not a sense of the infinite dignity of man, of the ultimate equality between one man and another, and of the right of every person to the conditions required if he is to fulfill his potentialities and play his part in meeting social needs? In virtue of this common value neither the democratic nor the Communist countries have an imperialist impulse toward the rest of the world, although—because of their mutual fears—each seems to the other to have it in high degree. Actually they are aware that foreign peoples cannot be justifiably, nor even profitably, controlled by external force.

Especially significant is the fact that champions of these two ideals, though hesitant to admit it, are learning from each other. Of course pernicious lessons are being learned as well as good ones: in the West there is the ominous power of those who would adopt the worst features of a totalitarian regime, while in the Communist countries there is the baneful influence of those who want to ape the worst features of a capitalist culture. But this should not obscure the hopeful side of this process. The West is more and more realizing the necessity, if government is to meet its obligations in the modern world, of large-scale social planning and of assuring each citizen an opportunity to fill a constructive economic function. The Communist world is more and more realizing that although according to Marxist doctrine the "dictatorship of the proletariat" is normally established by violent revolution, it is important to organize basic institutions so that the changes called for thereafter can be achieved without revolution. Its leaders are now aware that revisions in policy and even in doctrine are needed from time to time in order to meet changed conditions; in making these revisions they are profiting by the economic and political experience of the West.

An impartial reconciliation of the two ideals is slowly taking form through this process. If the world succeeds in avoiding a nuclear war, it would seem a reasonable faith that this reconciliation will be more rapidly achieved and the policies needed to express it will be more consistently followed. Increasingly will the values common to both sides be mutually recognized, and the special values precious to each freed from the perversions that now weaken them.

For the third clue in spelling out our vision, we can explore more fully what is involved in the maxim that the valid ideal for an individual and for every social group is the same. The ideal for each person might be put into words as follows: It is that he become the medium in which every other person he meets, and hence also himself, can grow toward the richest fulfillment possible. If such a vision is authentic, then it likewise applies to every group of persons. Nothing less is the valid ideal for every nation in relation to other nations, every race in relation to other races, every profession in relation to other professions, every educational or economic system in relation to others, every religion in relation to other religions. In the case of these larger social units, as in the case of an individual, the energy of narrow self-centered demandingness can become the energy of all-encompassing sensitivity and unlimited creation. However far the world may be from the goal thus envisioned—and the distance is surely great—we may have faith that it is moving in this direction.

By the same token, the ideal applies to every philosophy in relation to other philosophies. Just as, to wise insight, the greatest nation is not one that seeks power over others but rather one that inspires all nations to make the most valuable gift they can to man's political experience, just as the greatest economic system has no urge to drive competing economies to the wall but rather so functions that all systems serve the economic needs of men as efficiently as they might, just as the greatest religion does not aggressively strive to win others to its creed but rather encourages in each of them the happiest solution of the ultimate problem of life that its orientation permits—so the great philosophy does not try to destroy its rivals and sit in solitary splendor on the speculative throne but rather knows that its role is best filled when, because of its presence, other philosophies are moved to develop to the utmost whatever constructive possibilities they

harbor. A perceptive philosopher is aware that his ability to explore beyond our present horizon is very limited; his major aim then will be to
evoke, so far as he can, the amplest contribution to man's understanding of
himself and his universe that every other way of philosophizing might
make. His own special contribution will not be lost in pursuing this aim
but will rather achieve its most effective form.

There need be no fear that he will forget his negative task—that of
detecting blunders, inconsistencies, and weaknesses wherever he finds them
—but this is a subordinate task, which can be performed most successfully
when it becomes part of the far more significant positive role.

The creative communication of philosophers with each other and with
other thinkers, which has never been lacking in the past, would be energized to the full in the era we are envisioning. Through that unobstructed
interaction vast ranges beyond our present horizon will be discovered, surveyed, and charted; vast ranges of man's potentiality will be laid bare,
freed, and fulfilled. The philosopher, like the scientist, does his work by
interacting with the environing universe, but the interaction called for in
filling his function is mainly indirect. He communicates with other thinkers, past, present, and future; he enters their experience and opens himself
to the positive possibilities in their ideas. They may be scientists, artists,
theologians, statesmen, each at work in his special sphere; they may be
other philosophers, each proposing his own all-encompassing interpretation. It is largely through such interaction that he reaches into the transcendent region which it is his role to bring within the range of coherent
articulation. By filling this role he so enlightens our experience within the
horizon that petty, cramped, stagnant, and otherwise inadequate ideas of
the universe are progressively replaced by freer, richer, and more fertile
ones. And the world will not allow philosophers to accept any less exciting
function. While it views with amused bewilderment their readiness to escape into neat or airy abstractions, it also looks to them with the hopeful
assurance that they have resources of wise understanding that no one else
can supply.

VI

It would be easy to wish, intrigued by the optimistic vision just elaborated, that we might be born in such an era instead of in our own.

But we know that those who will live a hundred or a thousand years
from now will have their own challenge to meet and their own evils to

conquer; who can tell how severe their ordeal will be? And quite apart from that inescapable truth, do we really want every awesome problem to have been solved before we come on the scene? If the appalling evils that hang over man had all been overcome, his thorny quandaries all resolved, the deep mysteries of existence all laid bare, where would be our opportunity to seek pioneering insight and engage in creative action? The challenge of this century—to faith, to understanding, to courage, to endurance—is our challenge; destiny has called us to meet it. And the fact that our generation enjoys the unprecedented resources that it does—resources both spiritual and material—is because those who came before us were ready to accept the risks of their time and to bear the anguish many of them had to bear. Because of their vision, integrity, and heroism many of the harassing limitations of their day have been overcome. The heritage they have left us is a heritage of great achievement—but, even more, of unwavering dedication to the pilgrimage of man, of hopeful openness of mind and heart, of bold responsiveness to whatever the universe may disclose.

Shall we do less for our successors in the momentous crisis of our time?

Content then to play the part to which we are called in the unfinished drama of man's career, we may realize a truth that upholds, strengthens, and brings inward serenity. Each of us can live, even now, as a member of the universal community. To be committed to it, in active trust, is to be already enfolded by it, sharing whatever may betide of good or of evil with others of every nation, race, or creed who are likewise so committed.

In that dedication and enfoldment one will also be content to acknowledge that no matter how far the boldest vision may penetrate, the mystery that surrounds all existence will remain. Yet no one need fear the vast unknown into which the human race is always advancing. It harbors unlimited possibilities of both tragedy and triumph, but in its wholeness it is not fearful, for it is the mystery of man's infinite self.

If we humbly recognize our limitations, it may be that one further step into the mystery can be taken. What is this infinite self if not the true self of all men, slowly winning its unified fulfillment? And is it, as thus realizing its unity, alone in the universe? It may be that as man is freed from the obstructions of a narrow egotism, finding his identity in the world community, sensitivity is gained at a higher level than that of our present experience—sensitivity to the searching of intelligent beings elsewhere in the cosmic spaces, as they achieve the distinctive unity that their nature and the course of their evolution makes possible. How would sensitivity at this level find expression? What would be its mode of communication?

Man is already living in relation to the whole sidereal universe, however small he is and however immense it may be. What Teilhard de Chardin calls the "noösphere"—brought into being by man's power of expanding awareness—not only covers the earth but, though feebly, the entire astronomical realm. It provides the sensitive medium through which intercommunication is possible with responsive beings anywhere in the celestial vastness. Thinkers today are eagerly exploring this possibility; and they appear to imagine that such intercommunication will necessarily be similar to that now taking place between man and man. But communication of this kind across the solar systems and galaxies seems almost impossible—if for no other reason than the great distances involved and the lengthy span of time that must elapse between one item of conversation and the next.

However, communication at a higher level than that of individual persons may well be possible and may now be going on. Could we enter with assurance the superhuman perspective just suggested, it might appear that the entire career of man on this planet is the life of a cell in some larger organic whole, giving its unique bit—however long or short his career proves to be—toward the fulfillment of that whole. The intercommunication we are trying to glimpse may be between such larger wholes. If entities do take form at that higher level, they must live in a vaster time-span as well as in a vaster and very different spatial structure than we are familiar with, and their intercommunication could plausibly overcome the difficulties that would be insuperable to individual persons with their narrow tempo of experience. Surely the infinite spiritual universe is not limited to the brief time-span of events on the surface of our little earth. By realizing oneness with all our human fellows in their aspiration toward fuller life, we may achieve the capacity to enter this vaster time-span and thus to play our part in the career of that superhuman cell.

Do we catch in this thought an intimation of the immortality open to man? It seems quite improbable that a personality that remains self-centered could exist forever; all that it cares for is narrowly circumscribed by time and space. But it might be a trustworthy intuition that the germ of selfhood in us that does identify with the universal self, and thus finds its fulfillment in the fulfillment of all men, thereby shares the broader temporal span in which that greater reality lives, and through which it wins the promise of unlimited growth. The ancient sages have spoken of a perspective in which a thousand years are but as a day; and we know that the universe has plenty of time.

Notes

CHAPTER II

1. Alfred North Whitehead, *Adventures of Ideas* (New York: The Macmillan Company, 1933), p. 284.
2. F. P. Jevons, *Introduction to the History of Religion* (London: Methuen & Co., Ltd., 1896), p. 16.
3. In Professor A. T. Poffenberger's Foreword to *Modern Learning Theory*, William K. Estes and others (Appleton-Century-Crofts, Inc., 1954).

CHAPTER III

1. Ludwig Wittgenstein, *Tractatus Logico-Philosophicus* (London: Kegan Paul, Trench, Trubner & Co., 1922), pp. 79, 189.
2. Wittgenstein, *Philosophical Investigations* (New York: The Macmillan Company, 1953), I, 339.
3. John L. Austin, "A Plea for Excuses," in *Philosophical Papers,* ed. by J. O. Urmson and G. J. Warnock (London: Oxford Univ. Press, 1961), Ch. 6. See p. 130.
4. Stuart Hampshire, "Identification and Existence," in *Contemporary British Philosophy,* Third Series, ed. by H. D. Lewis (New York: The Macmillan Company, 1956), p. 192.

5. Paul W. Kurtz, "Has Mr. Flew Abandoned the Logic of Ordinary Use?" *Philosophical Studies* (October–December, 1958), p. 77.
6. Henri Bergson, *The Two Sources of Morality and Religion*, tr. by R. Ashley Audra (New York: Doubleday & Co., Inc., 1956), p. 228. (Anchor Book)

CHAPTER IV

1. Sören Kierkegaard, *Concluding Unscientific Postscript*, tr. by David Swenson (Princeton, N.J.: Princeton Univ. Press, 1944), p. 279.
2. Kierkegaard, *Philosophical Fragments*, tr. by David Swenson (Princeton, N.J.: Princeton Univ. Press, 1936), p. xvii of Introduction by Swenson.
3. David Swenson, *Something About Kierkegaard* (Minneapolis, Minn.: Augsburg Publishing House, 1941), pp. 69 f.
4. Carl R. Rogers, "A Therapist's View of the Good Life," *The Humanist*, Vol. XVII, No. 5 (September–October, 1957). See especially p. 295.
5. F. C. Copleston, "Existentialism," *Philosophy*, Vol. XXIII (January, 1948), pp. 20 ff., especially p. 37.
6. Harold J. Blackham, *Six Existentialist Thinkers* (London: Routledge & Kegan Paul, Ltd., 1952), p. 152.
7. George Boas, *Journal of Philosophy*, Vol. LIII (November 8, 1956), p. 749.
8. Jean-Paul Sartre, *Being and Nothingness*, tr. by Hazel E. Barnes (New York: Philosophical Library, Inc., 1956), p. 429.
9. Blackham, *op. cit.*, pp. 79 f.
10. Quoted in Howard Fast, *The Passion of Sacco and Vanzetti* (New York: Blue Heron Press, Inc., 1953, p. 195. For the larger significance of the tragedy of these two men, see pp. 102 ff.
11. Rufus M. Jones, *The Story of George Fox* (New York: The Macmillan Company, 1919), p. 17.
12. Heinrich E. Brunner, *Faith, Hope and Love* (Philadelphia: Westminister Press, 1956), p. 78.
13. Quoted on p. 3 of a paper by Arthur E. Morgan, *Should Quakers Receive the Good Samaritan into Their Membership?* read before the Shrewsbury and Plainfield Friends Meeting on March 27, 1954.
14. Quoted in E. L. Allen, *Existentialism from Within* (London: Routledge and Kegan Paul, 1953), p. 116.

CHAPTER V

1. Francis H. Bradley, *Appearance and Reality* (London, 1899), pp. 518 f. In justice to Bradley, it should be remembered that later in the same chapter a more modest note appears.
2. Friedrich Waismann, "Are There Alternative Logics?" *Proceedings of the Aristotelian Society*, N. S., Vol. 46 (1946), pp. 103 f.
3. *The Philosophy of Nietzsche* (New York: Random House, no date), p. 482. (Modern Library)
4. Group for the Advancement of Psychiatry, "Psychiatric Aspects of the Prevention of Nuclear War," Report No. 57 (September, 1964), p. 259.
5. Whitehead, *Adventures of Ideas, op. cit.*, pp. 198 f. See also the passage on p. 5, which reads: "In considering the history of ideas, I maintain that the notion of mere knowledge is a high abstraction which we should dismiss from our minds. Knowledge is always accompanied with accessories of emotion and purpose." Many other Western thinkers have come to recognize the various

relativities that we have detected and the decisive role among them of interested valuation. One such thinker is Max Scheler, who says: "Every mode of intellectual apprehension of the nature of an object presupposes the presence of an emotional valuation of that object." (*Die Wissensformen und die Gesellschaft,* Leipzig, 1926, p. 122.)

6. C. A. Ellwood, *Methods in Sociology* (Durham, N.C.: Duke Univ. Press, 1933), p. 29.

7. G. J. Warnock, *English Philosophy Since 1900* (London: Oxford Univ. Press, 1958), p. 171.

CHAPTER VI

1. Lewis S. Feuer, "The Sociology of Philosophic Ideas," *The Pacific Sociological Review,* Vol. I, No. 2 (Fall, 1958), pp. 79 f. Feuer calls these forces "sociological mechanisms."

2. Gilbert Ryle, *The Concept of Mind* (London: Hutchinson & Co., 1949), p. 9.

3. Quoted in Nelson N. Foote, *The Professionalization of Labor in Detroit,* dissertation, Cornell University, 1956, p. 73.

4. Quoted in Morris R. Cohen, *The Meaning of Human History* (La Salle, Ill.: The Open Court Publishing Co., 1947), p. 175.

5. *Ibid.,* p. 80.

6. J. P. Corbett, "Innovation and Philosophy," *Mind,* Vol. LXVIII (July, 1959), p. 293.

7. *Ibid.,* pp. 303–304.

CHAPTER VII

1. Norman R. Campbell, *What is Science?* (New York: Dover Publications, Inc., 1952), p. 27.

2. Howard Becker, in a mimeographed paper entitled "The Sociologist and the Supreme Values of our Times," p. 16.

3. Martin Buber, *Between Man and Man,* tr. by R. G. Smith (London: Routledge & Kegan Paul, Ltd., 1947), p. 31.

4. Eugene Rabinowitch, *The Dawn of a New Age* (Chicago: Univ. of Chicago Press, 1963), p. 293.

CHAPTER VIII

1. Plato, *The Republic,* tr. by W. H. D. Rouse (New York: The New American Library, 1956), I, 348, p. 147. (Mentor Book)

2. Charles S. Peirce, *Collected Papers,* Vol. V, ed. by Charles Hartshorne and Paul Weiss (Cambridge, Mass.: Harvard Univ. Press, 1934), p. 268.

3. Bertrand Russell, *Scientific Method in Philosophy* (Chicago and London: Oxford Univ. Press, 1915), p. 3.

4. Harald Höffding, *The Philosophy of Religion,* tr. by B. E. Meyer (New York: The Macmillan Company, 1906), p. 301.

5. Chauncey D. Leake, "Religio Scientiae," *The Scientific Monthly,* Vol. LII (February, 1941), p. 170.

6. Peter Bertocci, *The Human Venture in Sex, Love and Marriage* (New York: Association Press, 1949), p. 125. I take it that "being honest" here is equivalent to "telling the truth."

CHAPTER IX

1. Bertrand Russell, *The Problems of Philosophy* (London: Oxford Univ. Press, 1946), p. 161. (Galaxy Books)
2. Smiley Blanton, *Love or Perish* (New York: Simon & Schuster, Inc., 1956), p. 14.
3. *Ibid.*, pp. 108 f.
4. Rudolph Steiner, *Knowledge of the Higher Worlds and its Attainment,* tr. by G. Metaxas (New York: Anthroposophic Press, 1961), p. 124.
5. Erich Fromm, *The Art of Loving* (New York: Harper & Brothers, 1956), pp. 29 ff.
6. Howard Thurman, *Mysticism and the Experience of Love,* Pendle Hill Pamphlet 115 (Wallingford, Pa., 1961), p. 18.
7. Henry Sigerist, *A History of Medicine,* Vol. I, *Primitive and Archaic Medicine* (New York: Oxford Univ. Press, 1951), p. 31.

Chapter X

1. S. K. Saksena. See the paper he presented to the third East-West Philosophers' Conference in 1959. *Philosophy and Culture, East and West,* ed. by Charles A. Moore (Honolulu: Univ. of Hawaii Press, 1962), p. 63.
2. In *This is My Philosophy,* ed. by Whit Burnett (New York: Harper & Brothers, 1957), pp. 345 f.
3. George Boas, *The Limits of Reason* (New York: Harper and Row, Publishers, 1961), p. 62.
4. From a lecture by Swami Nisreyasananda at the Ramakrishna Institute of Culture at Calcutta on May 21, 1955.

Chapter XI

1. Quoted in Senator Frank Church's article in *The New York Times* Magazine Section, Feb. 14, 1965.
2. Professor C. E. Merriam, on the occasion of his retirement from the University of Chicago.
3. Teilhard de Chardin, *The Phenomenon of Man,* tr. by Bernard Wall (New York: Harper & Brothers, 1959), pp. 279 f.

Index of Names

Mohammed, 196, 289
Montesquieu, Baron de, 4
Moore, G. E., 56

Newton, Sir Isaac, 165
Niebuhr, Reinhold, 81
Nietszche, Friedrich, 65, 117

Peirce, Charles S., 197
Plato, 2, 5, 13, 146, 162, 169, 182, 244
Poffenberger, A. T., 17
Pratt, J. B., 139
Pythagoras, 162

Rabinowitch, Eugene, 189
Radhakrishnan, Sarvepalli, 265
Ramakrishna, Sri, 267
Rogers, Carl, 65
Rousseau, J. J., 4
Russell, Bertrand, 27, 40, 41, 107, 197, 224, 239
Ryle, Gilbert, 144

Sacco, Nicola, 83
Saksena, S. K., 260
Saltmarsh, John, 201
Sartre, Jean Paul, 59, 66, 68, 71, 74, 75, 76, 77, 78, 79, 80, 81, 82, 83, 85, 86

Schelling, F. W. J. von, 144
Second Isaiah, 84
Sigerist, Henry, 231
Socrates, 65, 84, 196, 304
Spinoza, Baruch (or Benedict), 13, 127, 261
Stalin, Josef, 302
Steiner, Rudolf, 225
Strawson, P. F., 38, 39, 54

Thrasymachus, 196
Tillich, Paul, 81
Toulmin, Stephen, 38
Tyndall, John, 19

Vanzetti, Bartolomeo, 83
Vincent of Lerins, 196

Waismann, Friedrich, 108
Warnock, G. J., 126
Watson, J. B., 139
Whitehead, A. N., 17, 121, 239
Whitman, Walt, 10
Wittgenstein, Ludwig, 28, 29, 33, 34, 45, 48, 49, 104, 107

Zoroaster, 289

Index of Subjects

Value, in relation to ethics, 148, 244

in relation to love, 228 f.

in relation to motivations and presuppositions, 132, 140, 142, 181 f., 207 ff., 212 ff., 223, 234 f.

Vertical expansion of awareness, 145 f., 149 f.

Vision, philosophic, 231, 233, 242 f., 248 f., 257, 283, 289, 305 ff., 308, 311 f., 313

War, historical development of, 282

World community, ideal of, 253 f., 279, 283, 290, 292, 296, 305 ff., 314